MICHAEL SENIOR

(formerly Assistant Geography Teacher at Jamaica College,
Jamaica, Head of Geography at Mfantsipim School,
Ghana; Head of Geography at Highway Secondary School,
Kenya)

Tropical Lands

Longman

LONGMAN GROUP LTD

Associated companies, branches and representatives throughout the world

First published 1979

ISBN 0 582 60353 6

Printed in Hong Kong by
Wing Tai Cheung Printing Co Ltd

Acknowledgements

The Publishers are grateful to the following for permission to reproduce photographs:

Afrique Photo for page 262; Australian News and Information Bureau for pages 25, 26, 149 (Neil Murray); Barnaby's Picture Library for pages 264 (J. Faber), 295 (M. J. Roberts); Bruce Coleman Ltd for page 106 (Christine Osborne); Commonwealth Institute for pages 115, 198 and 210; East African Office for page 139; Ghana Information Services for pages 178, 179, 219 and 304; Guyana High Commission for pages 203, 214, 231 and 284; Jamaica Tourist Board for pages 233, 255, 258, 259, 301 and 306; Kenya Information Services for pages 27 and 119; Malaysian High Commission for pages 24, 112, 205 and 231; Malaya House Information Department for page 230; Malaysian Information Service for pages 129, 161 and 206; Ministry of Home Affairs, Salisbury for page 233 (M. W. Mills); M. W. Senior for pages 28, 102, 103, 104, 105, 148, 155, 159, 166, 172, 181, 229, 263, 279, 280, 281, 283, 292 and 299; Tanzania Public Relations Department for page 145; Uganda Department of Information for page 37.

Contents

CHAPTER ONE

Climate

A: General

As is to be expected in an area of such a size, there are considerable variations of climate within the tropics. Fig. 1.1 illustrates the temperature and rainfall regimes of six stations within the tropics. Examine these carefully, and notice the differences which occur.

Temperature

Within the tropics sea level temperatures are high throughout the year. Mean annual temperatures at sea level are usually well above 20°C, although somewhat lower temperatures are experienced in those coastal areas which are influenced by cool ocean currents (see Walvis Bay).

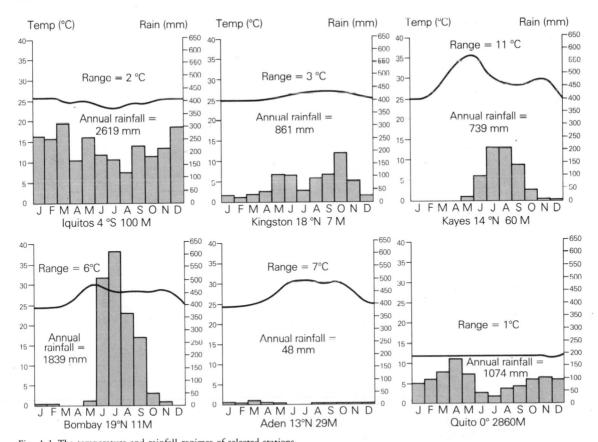

Fig. 1.1 The temperature and rainfall regimes of selected stations

The variations in temperature which occur within the tropics are largely the result of differences in latitude, altitude, distance from the sea, ocean currents and amount of cloud cover. Of these factors, altitude is by far the most important, temperature decreasing upwards at an average rate of about 1°C per 150 metres. Compare the temperatures of Nairobi and La Paz, with those of stations in similar latitudes, but at lower altitudes (Table 1).

Seasonal variations

The mean annual range of temperature is relatively small throughout the tropics. It does, however, tend to become larger, both with increasing distance from the equator, and with increasing distance from the sea.

Close to the equator, mean sea level temperatures of 27°C–30°C are experienced during the hottest months of the year, and 24°C–27°C during the coolest. The annual range of temperature is very small, usually less than 5°C and often less than 3°C (see Singapore and Zanzibar).

Even near the tropics, the annual range of temperature remains fairly small in coastal areas, as a result of the moderating influence of the sea (see Havana and Rio de Janeiro). In the interior of large land masses, however, temperatures tend to become more extreme. In these areas mean monthly temperatures of well over 30°C are experienced during the hottest part of the year, while during the coolest part they may fall below 20°C, with annual ranges sometimes exceeding 10°C (see Timbuktu and Cloncurry).

In some cases the highest mean monthly temperatures occur shortly after the passage of the overhead sun. In areas where the rainfall is markedly seasonal, however, the temperature often falls with the onset of the rains, and may even rise again slightly at the end of them (see Fig. 1.1, Bombay).

Daily variations

Within the tropics diurnal ranges of temperature are often larger than annual ranges. The size of the diurnal range is greatly influenced by the amount of cloud cover. Clear skies favour rapid heating during the day, and also a rapid loss of heat at night, and hence usually result in large diurnal ranges. Abundant cloud tends to prevent both rapid heating during the day, and also rapid cooling at night, and so results in small diurnal ranges.

Areas near to the equator usually have abundant cloud cover, and so generally experience small diurnal ranges. In these areas daily maxima are rarely much above 32°C, while daily minima do not usually fall much below 20°C. Diurnal ranges are usually in the order of 5°C–12°C. Places which are further from the equator, but which are near to the sea, also tend to experience small diurnal ranges.

The largest diurnal ranges are experienced in arid areas, where there is generally little cloud. In these areas, very high daily maxima occur during the hottest part of the year, often well over 40°C, and sometimes over 50°C. At night however, temperatures usually fall rapidly, and diurnal ranges of 15°C–30°C are common.

In areas which have a highly seasonal pattern of rainfall distribution, much larger diurnal ranges are

Table 1 Mean monthly temperatures (°C) for selected stations

Station	Lat.	Alt. (M)	J	F	M	A	M	J	J	A	S	O	N	D	Year	Range
Singapore	1N	3	27	27	27	28	28	27	27	27	27	27	27	27	27	1
Zanzibar	6S	17	28	28	28	27	26	26	25	25	26	26	27	28	27	3
Havana	23N	24	22	22	23	24	26	27	28	28	27	26	24	23	25	6
Rio de Janeiro	23S	61	26	26	25	23	22	21	20	21	21	22	23	24	23	6
Timbuktu	17N	250	22	23	28	33	35	34	32	31	32	32	27	22	29	13
Cloncurry	20S	212	31	29	28	26	22	18	16	19	22	28	29	31	25	15
Walvis Bay	23S	3	18	19	19	18	17	16	15	14	14	16	16	18	17	5
Nairobi	1S	1 675	18	18	19	18	17	16	15	16	17	19	18	17	17	4
La Paz	17S	3 688	11	11	11	9	8	7	8	8	9	10	12	11	9	5

experienced in the dry season than during the rainy season, when there is generally more cloud.

Precipitation

Annual amount

Fig. 1.2 shows that within the tropics there are considerable differences in the amount of rainfall received. Examine this map carefully, and notice which areas receive heavy rainfall, and which areas are very dry.

Fig. 1.2 does not, however, reveal the full extent of the differences in rainfall amount which occur within the tropics. For example, Debundscha on the western side of Mt. Cameroon has a mean annual rainfall of about 10 000 millimetres (mm), and is one of the wettest places in the world; while Iquique in the Atacama Desert is one of the driest, with an average of less than 25 mm per annum. Furthermore, a map of this scale cannot hope to show the sizeable variations in rainfall amount which may occur within a relatively short distance, and which are brought about by differences in relief.

Broadly speaking, heavy precipitation tends to occur in:

1 areas immediately around the equator, where high temperatures throughout the year favour the rising of air;
2 areas close to the sea, where the prevailing winds blow on-shore throughout the year, or for a large part of the year.

This is particularly the case where high mountain barriers such as the Western Ghats of India or the Blue Mountains of Jamaica lie across the path of the prevailing winds, forcing them to rise. In such areas there is usually a marked contrast in the amount of rainfall received by the windward and leeward slopes of the mountains. The eastern end of the island of Jamaica provides a good example of the influence of relief upon rainfall distribution (see Fig. 1.3). Here the Trade Winds are forced to rise over the Blue Mountains, and within a distance of less than 50 kilometres (km) the rainfall varies from under 800 mm to more than 5 000 mm per annum.

On the other hand precipitation tends to be light in:
1 areas which lie under the influence of subsiding air masses;

Fig. 1.3 The influence of relief on the rainfall of the eastern end of the island of Jamaica

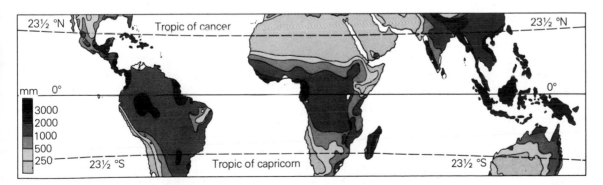

Fig. 1.2 The tropical lands – mean annual rainfall

2 areas which are situated a considerable distance from the sea;

3 areas which are situated on the leeward side of high mountain ranges (rain shadow areas);

4 areas which experience off-shore winds for much of the year.

Cool ocean currents such as the Canary, Humboldt (Peruvian) and Benguela also have the effect of increasing the aridity of the adjacent coastal areas, by cooling the air passing over them, and so reducing its capacity to hold moisture. The upwelling of cool water off the coasts of eastern Ghana, Togo, and Benin (formerly Dahomey) has also been suggested as one of the possible causes of the unusually light precipitation which occurs along that part of the West African coast.

Seasonal distribution

An examination of Fig. 1.1, and of the statistics given in Table 2, will reveal that in addition to the differences in the total amount of precipitation received, there are also considerable variations in the pattern of its seasonal distribution.

Areas close to the equator generally receive rainfall throughout the year, with no prolonged dry period (see Iquitos and Singapore). In some equatorial areas, however, a double maxima of rainfall is experienced, with two particularly wet periods separated by two rather drier periods. The wet periods usually follow, with a lag of a month or two, the passage of the overhead sun (see Axim).

Further from the equator, islands and the eastern sides of land masses which are influenced by winds from the sea throughout the year, also receive a fairly evenly distributed rainfall (see Kingston, Havana and Rio de Janeiro).

On the other hand, in those areas where there is a marked seasonal reversal of the wind system, with winds from the sea for part of the year, and winds from the land for the rest of the year, the pattern of rainfall distribution is highly seasonal. In such areas the year is divided into a wet season and a dry season (see Bombay, Calcutta and Darwin).

Similarly, those areas which for part of the year come under the influence of the equatorial low pressure system, but which for the rest of the year are dominated by the sub-tropical high pressure system and dry trade winds, also have a highly seasonal regime (see Kano and Kayes).

In extremely arid areas precipitation tends to be highly erratic, and the annual cycle is indistinct.

Reliability

Mean monthly and annual statistics disguise the fact that rainfall is variable from year to year, not only in amount, but also in its seasonal distribution. For example, between 1923 and 1947 Nairobi in Kenya received an average of about 860 mm of rain per annum, but the wettest of those years had some 1 550 mm and the driest only 480 mm. Between 1901 and 1918 the annual rainfall of Banjul (formerly Bathurst) in Gambia varied from about 600 mm in the driest year, to more than 1 650 mm in the wettest. During the same period rainfall in the month of October varied from 5 mm to 231 mm, and in the month of May from nil to 48 mm.

Table 2 Mean monthly rainfall (mm) for selected stations

Station	Lat.	Alt. (M)	J	F	M	A	M	J	J	A	S	O	N	D	Year
Singapore	1N	3	251	168	188	193	170	173	173	201	173	206	251	269	2 416
Axim	5N	23	58	61	122	142	404	495	168	58	84	188	196	99	2 075
Havana	23N	24	76	38	43	43	130	142	109	109	127	180	81	61	1 139
Rio de Janeiro	23S	62	127	114	135	107	81	56	43	46	66	84	104	140	1 103
Calcutta	23N	6	10	25	36	56	142	302	323	340	254	124	15	5	1 632
Darwin	12S	30	404	328	257	104	18	3	3	3	13	56	122	262	1 573
Kano	12N	472	0	0	3	8	69	114	203	315	130	13	0	0	855
Lima	12S	120	3	3	3	3	5	5	8	8	8	3	3	3	55

Broadly speaking rainfall is most reliable in areas where it is heaviest, and is most variable in arid areas. The average rainfall for Onslow in Western Australia is only about 230 mm per annum, and yet in 1900, some 280 mm fell during the month of April alone, and a further 250 mm fell in May. In the following year, however, only 12 mm of rain fell during April and May.

Intensity

In general the rainfall tends to be much more torrential in nature in tropical areas, than in the higher latitudes. Particularly high rainfall intensities often occur during the passage of tropical storms. For example, Baguio in the Philippine Islands has recorded about 1 160 mm within 24 hours, and Silver Hill in Jamaica almost 3 000 mm within 5 days.

Climatic types

Although it is convenient to classify climates into broad types, such a classification is necessarily difficult to make. The chief difficulty lies in the fact that climatic conditions usually change gradually, with one type merging into another. As a result there are no real boundaries between climatic types, but broad transition zones instead. Furthermore, considerable variations in climate may occur within a relatively short distance, as a result of purely local factors. The pattern of rainfall distribution is often complicated by relief, and temperatures may be considerably modified by altitude.

Fig. 1.4 represents an attempt to classify the climates which occur within the tropics, and Fig. 1.1 illustrates the temperature and rainfall regimes of stations which are typical of each type. Five main types of climate are shown as occurring in lowland areas. They are:

1 Equatorial (Iquitos);
2 Tropical Marine (Kingston);
3 Tropical Continental (Kayes);
4 Tropical Monsoon (Bombay);
5 Hot Desert (Aden).

Areas where the climate is greatly modified by altitude are shown separately (Quito).

Equatorial

The equatorial type of climate occurs as a belt extending around the world, within about 5°–10° of the equator. The continuity of this belt is, however, interrupted in several places by mountains, such as the Andes of South America and the highlands of East Africa.

The characteristic features of the equatorial climate are:

1 Temperatures are high and even throughout the year, with mean monthly temperatures at sea level never being very far from 27°C. The annual range is very small, never much more than 3°C, and quite often less. The daily range is somewhat larger, usually about 5°C–12°C.
2 Relative humidity is high throughout the year.
3 There is a great deal of cloud.
4 Winds are generally very light.
5 The rainfall is usually abundant, and is well distributed throughout the year. In some areas a double maxima of rainfall is experienced.

Fig. 1.4 The tropical lands – broad climatic divisions

In some coastal areas near to the equator, a marked monsoonal effect is experienced. This is particularly the case in Indonesia, which lies astride the equator, between the two monsoon centres of northern Australia and southern Asia. During the period from December to March the air-flow is from the high pressure area over Asia, towards the low pressure area over northern Australia. At this time of year the islands of Java and Sumatra experience winds from the west or north-west. From May to September, on the other hand, the air-flow is from northern Australia towards the low pressure area over Asia, and Java and Sumatra experience winds from the east or south-east. Indonesia is one of the wettest parts of the world, experiencing both the convection rainfall of the equatorial latitudes, and also heavy relief rainfall deposited by the alternating monsoon winds in their passage over these mountainous islands (see Table 3).

Tropical marine

The tropical marine type of climate occurs on islands and on the east coasts of land masses, roughly between latitude 10° and the tropics. These areas come under the influence of the trade winds, which usually blow on-shore throughout the year. The characteristic features of the tropical marine type of climate are:

1 Temperatures are high and even throughout the year, although the annual range tends to be slightly larger than in the equatorial type (3°C–6°C).

Table 3

Station	Lat.	Alt. (M)		J	F	M	A	M	J	J	A	S	O	N	D	Year
Pontianak (Indonesia)	0	3	°C	26	26	26	26	27	27	27	26	26	26	26	26	26
			mm	274	201	249	274	272	221	160	226	213	376	399	335	3 200
Akassa (Nigeria)	4N	6	°C	26	26	27	27	26	25	24	24	24	25	26	26	26
			mm	66	165	254	218	432	472	257	236	490	627	269	165	3 651
Manaus (Brazil)	3S	44	°C	27	27	27	27	27	27	27	28	28	28	28	27	27
			mm	234	229	244	216	178	91	56	36	51	104	140	196	1 775
Colombo (Sri Lanka)	7N	7	°C	27	27	28	28	28	28	27	27	27	27	27	27	27
			mm	94	89	114	244	165	81	66	84	74	213	244	142	1 610

Table 4

Station	Lat.	Alt. (M)		J	F	M	A	M	J	J	A	S	O	N	D	Year
Honolulu (Hawaii)	21N	12	°C	22	22	22	23	24	25	26	26	26	25	24	22	24
			mm	94	109	97	58	48	28	33	38	38	48	107	104	802
Tamatave (Madagascar)	18S	5	°C	26	27	26	25	23	21	20	21	22	23	25	26	24
			mm	381	363	452	305	249	366	335	216	180	135	99	244	3 325
Port of Spain (Trinidad & Tobago)	11N	40	°C	24	24	24	26	26	26	26	26	26	26	25	25	25
			mm	66	41	46	48	86	201	218	239	191	168	183	119	1 606
Salvador (Brazil)	13S	47	°C	27	27	27	27	25	24	23	23	24	25	26	26	26
			mm	66	135	155	284	274	239	183	122	84	102	114	142	1 900

2 Rainfall is usually moderate or heavy, although differences in relief often bring about considerable variations in rainfall amount. The rainfall is usually fairly evenly distributed throughout the year.
3 Violent tropical storms occur from time to time. These are known as hurricanes in the West Indies, and as typhoons in tropical Asia.
4 Although temperatures are uniformly high, the climate tends to be somewhat more invigorating than the equatorial type. This is partly because of the freshening influence of the trade winds, and partly because the relative humidity tends to be rather lower.

Tropical continental
The tropical continental type of climate occurs mainly in those areas which are situated between the equatorial and the hot desert types. For part of the year those areas lie under the influence of the dry trade winds, but for the rest of the year they are invaded by the belt of convectional rains. Consequently there is an alternation of wet and dry seasons. The characteristic features of the tropical continental climate are:

1 Temperatures are high throughout the year, although both annual and diurnal ranges tend to be larger than in the equatorial type.
2 The rainfall is highly seasonal in its distribution. The bulk of the rain falls during the 'summer' months, and the rest of the year is very dry. With increasing distance from the equator, the rainfall

decreases in amount, and the dry season becomes longer and more severe.
3 Both the relative humidity and the amount of cloud cover vary with the season, being generally high during the rains, and much lower during the dry season.

Tropical monsoon
The climate of much of tropical Asia and of tropical Australia is dominated by seasonal winds, known as monsoons. These winds result from the different rates of heating and cooling of land and water. During the 'summer', the land masses heat up more rapidly than the surrounding seas. Consequently low pressures develop over the land, into which are drawn moisture-bearing winds from the sea. During 'winter', however, the land cools down more rapidly than the sea, resulting in the development of high pressure over the land, from which the winds blow outwards.

This alternation of winds from the land with winds from the sea results in a highly seasonal pattern of rainfall distribution. The bulk of the rain falls during the 'summer' months, and there is a marked dry period during 'winter'. For example, about 95 per cent of Bombay's rainfall occurs in the four months from June to September.

The amount of rainfall received varies considerably, being greatly influenced by relief and by distance from the sea. Thus Akyab in Burma, which lies in the path of the moisture-laden south-west monsoon receives well over 5 000 mm per annum,

Table 5

Station	Lat.	Alt. (M)		J	F	M	A	M	J	J	A	S	O	N	D	Year
Cuiaba (Brazil)	16S	165	°C	27	27	27	27	26	24	24	26	28	28	28	27	29
			mm	249	211	211	102	53	7	5	28	51	114	150	206	1 387
Kayes (Mali)	14N	60	°C	25	27	32	34	36	33	29	28	28	29	28	25	20
			mm	0	0	0	0	15	99	211	211	142	48	8	5	739
Mangoche (Malawi)	15S	475	°C	26	25	26	25	23	21	20	22	24	27	28	26	24
			mm	216	178	102	74	8	3	0	3	5	53	48	163	853
Catalao (Brazil)	18S	830	°C	23	23	23	23	21	19	20	21	23	23	23	23	22
			mm	300	259	224	97	28	8	13	8	58	155	211	378	1 739

Table 6

Station	Lat.	Alt. (M)		J	F	M	A	M	J	J	A	S	O	N	D	Year
Akyab (Burma)	20N	6	°C	21	23	26	28	29	28	27	27	28	28	26	22	26
			mm	3	5	13	51	348	1 255	1 364	1 080	625	295	127	15	5 181
Mandalay (Burma)	22N	76	°C	21	24	28	32	32	31	31	30	29	28	24	22	28
			mm	3	3	5	28	147	140	135	117	145	119	41	10	893
Bombay (India)	19N	11	°C	24	24	27	28	30	29	27	27	27	28	27	25	27
			mm	3	3	0	0	18	505	610	368	269	48	10	0	1 834
Broome (Australia)	18S	19	°C	30	29	29	28	24	22	21	23	25	27	29	30	27
			mm	157	155	97	36	15	25	5	5	3	0	23	94	615

whereas Mandalay in the Irrawady valley is in a marked rain shadow, and receives less than 900 mm.

Temperatures at sea level are high throughout the year, with a small or moderate annual range.

Hot desert

The outstanding feature of the hot desert type of climate is its aridity, but a distinction can be made on the basis of temperature, between coastal deserts and those located in the interior.

Wherever hot deserts reach the west coasts of continents, the climate is very much modified by equator-ward flowing cool ocean currents. One of the effects of these cool currents is to appreciably reduce the summer temperatures of the adjacent coastal areas. Along such coasts mean monthly temperatures are rarely very much above 20°C, even during the hottest part of the year. Both the annual and the diurnal ranges are very much smaller than those experienced in the interior.

The presence of cool ocean currents also serves to increase the aridity of the coastal deserts. On passing over the sea the air is cooled, and its capacity to absorb moisture is therefore reduced. When the winds blow on-shore, however, the air is warmed by contact with the land, and its moisture-holding capacity is increased. In coastal desert areas the rainfall is extremely low, usually averaging less than 125 mm, and sometimes less than 25 mm per annum. The town of Iquique in northern Chile has experienced periods of as long as 14 years without rain. On the other hand, fog and dew are common. Along the coast of Peru a heavy mist known as the garua persists in winter, providing sufficient moisture to support a scanty vegetation.

In the continental interiors temperatures are very much more extreme than on the coast, annual ranges usually exceeding 10°C. Because of the lack of cloud, very high diurnal ranges are often experienced. Maximum daily temperatures in summer are usually

Table 7

Station	Lat.	Alt. (M)		J	F	M	A	M	J	J	A	S	O	N	D	Year
Lima (Peru)	12S	158	°C	23	23	23	21	19	17	16	16	16	17	19	21	19
			mm	0	0	0	0	0	3	5	10	10	10	5	3	46
Iquique (Chile)	20S	9	°C	22	22	21	18	17	17	16	16	17	18	19	21	19
			mm						Practically nil							
Walvis Bay (Namibia)	23S	3	°C	18	19	19	18	17	17	16	16	17	18	19	21	19
			mm						Practically nil							

Table 9

Station	Lat.	Alt. (m)		J	F	M	A	M	J	J	A	S	O	N	D	Year
Khartoum (Sudan)	16N	390	°C	21	23	26	30	33	33	32	31	31	31	27	22	28
			mm	0	0	0	0	3	8	41	56	18	5	0	0	131
Wadi Halfa (Sudan)	22N	128	°C	14	16	21	26	29	31	32	31	29	27	21	16	24
			mm						Practically nil							
Bilma (Niger)	18N	357	°C	17	19	25	28	32	33	33	32	31	27	22	17	26
			mm	0	0	0	0	0	0	3	13	8	0	0	0	24

well over 40°C, and often over 50°C. At night, however, temperatures fall rapidly, and diurnal ranges of 15°C–30°C are common.

Highland areas

Fig. 1.4 shows the main areas within the tropics where the climate is considerably modified by altitude. The most important modification involved is the reduction in temperature. Compare the temperatures (°C) experienced by the three stations in southern Peru (Table 9).

By forcing the ascent of air, mountains bring about an increase in precipitation, at least up to an indefinite level of maximum precipitation. Above this altitude there is a decrease in precipitation, because of the increasing dryness of the air. The distribution of rainfall in highland areas is, however, very much complicated by local relief. Windward facing slopes generally receive abundant precipitation, but marked rain shadows often occur in sheltered valleys.

It is difficult to describe the climate of highland

Table 9

Station	Lat.	Alt. (m)	J	F	M	A	M	J	J	A	S	O	N	D	Year
Mollendo	17S	24	21	22	21	19	18	17	16	15	16	17	19	20	18
Arequipa	17S	2 451	14	14	13	14	14	13	13	14	14	14	14	14	14
El Misti	16S	5 850	−6	−6	−7	−8	−9	−10	−9	−9	−9	−7	−6	−7	−8

Table 10

Station	Lat.	Alt. (m)		J	F	M	A	M	J	J	A	S	O	N	D	Year
Quito (Ecuador)	0	2 850	°C	13	13	13	13	13	13	13	13	13	13	12	13	13
			mm	81	99	122	178	117	38	28	56	66	99	102	91	1 077
La Paz (Bolivia)	17S	3 688	°C	11	11	11	9	8	7	8	9	9	10	12	11	9
			mm	112	112	74	36	13	8	10	15	28	43	48	91	590
Mexico City (Mexico)	19N	2 278	°C	12	14	16	17	18	18	17	17	16	15	14	13	16
			mm	5	8	13	18	48	104	114	109	104	41	13	8	585
Nairobi (Kenya)	1S	1 661	°C	18	18	18	18	17	17	15	15	17	18	18	17	17
			mm	48	91	107	226	142	56	23	28	30	58	135	71	1 015

areas in general terms, as differences in latitude, distance from the sea, aspect and altitude, bring about considerable variations in climatic conditions. Thus, for example, Quito (0°) experiences the extremely even temperatures which are characteristic of the equatorial latitudes, while Mexico City (19°N) has a somewhat larger annual range of temperature. The rainfall of Quito is also much more evenly distributed throughout the year than that of Mexico City, which receives most of its rainfall during the northern summer (Table 10).

B: The climate of West Africa

Causation

Air masses

As in other tropical lowland areas, rainfall is the most important element in the climate of West Africa. The amount and seasonal distribution of rainfall in West Africa is largely determined by fluctuations in the position of two important air masses and their associated wind systems.

The tropical continental air mass originates over the Sahara Desert, and consequently is warm and dusty, with a very low relative humidity. Associated with the tropical continental air mass are easterly or north-easterly winds, which in West Africa are known as the Harmattan, and which have a drying influence on the areas over which they pass.

The tropical maritime air mass originates over the Atlantic Ocean, and consequently is warm and moist. Associated with the tropical maritime air mass are moisture-laden winds, sometimes called the Southwest Monsoon.

Where these two air masses meet is known as the Inter-Tropical Convergence Zone (ITCZ) or Inter-Tropical Front. Because of differences in density, the tropical continental air mass rides over the tropical maritime air mass, which forms a wedge beneath it. The position of the ITCZ is not stationary, but fluctuates slowly throughout the year, following with a lag of a month or two, the apparent movement of the overhead sun.

During the northern summer the ICTZ advances

I.T.C.Z. ———— Inter-Tropical Convergence Zone
mT ⇒ Tropical Maritime Air Mass
cT → Tropical Continental Air Mass

0   500   1000 km

Fig. 1.5b West Africa – air movements in January

northward, and in July is situated at about latitude 20°N (see Fig. 1.5a). The whole of that part of West Africa which lies to the south of the Sahara Desert comes under the influence of the Southwest Monsoon winds in July, and so receives rainfall.

During the northern winter the ITCZ retreats southward, and in January is situated just to the north of the Gulf of Guinea coast (see Fig. 1.5b). As a result, the influence of the Southwest Monsoon winds is restricted to that part of West Africa which lies to the south of about latitude 10°N. The remainder of West Africa in January lies under the drying influence of the Harmattan, and consequently receives very little rainfall at that time of year.

Relief

In West Africa the range of altitude is very much smaller than in East Africa, and consequently the influence of relief upon the climate of West Africa is very much less marked. Only in a few areas, such as the Fouta Djalon, the Guinea Highlands and the Jos Plateau, are temperatures appreciably modified by altitude. Relief does, however, influence the distribution of rainfall, particularly in the south-west, where the Fouta Djalon and the Guinea Highlands lie across the path of the rain-bearing winds.

Ocean currents

The cool, equator-ward flowing Canary Current makes itself felt along the coast of West Africa, as far south as Cape Verde. It is responsible for occasional fogs, and has a cooling effect on the coastal areas of Mauritania and Senegal. An upwelling of cold water off the coast of eastern Ghana, Togo and Benin may be partly responsible for the unusually low rainfall experienced along that section of the West African coast.

Temperature

In West Africa temperatures are high throughout the year, with mean annual temperatures at sea level everywhere exceeding 20°C. The temperature differences which occur in West Africa are largely the result of differences in altitude, distance from the sea and cloud cover. Ocean currents also have some influence on the temperatures of coastal areas.

Seasonal variations

The most even temperatures are experienced in the coastal areas of West Africa. Along the Gulf of Guinea coast, and also in the south-western coastal area, mean monthly temperatures are never far from 27°C. Mean monthly temperatures of 27°C–30°C occur during the hottest part of the year, and 24°C–27°C during the coolest part. The annual range of temperature is small, usually not much more than 3°C.

To the north of Cape Verde, the cool waters of the Canary Current have the effect of lowering temperatures in coastal areas. The annual range of temperature is also somewhat larger along that part of the coast, because of increasing distance from the equator.

Going inland from the Gulf of Guinea the seasonal variation in temperature becomes more marked. During the hottest part of the year the interior of West Africa experiences higher temperatures than the coastal areas. The highest temperatures usually occur just before the onset of the rainy season. At that time of year mean monthly temperatures in the interior are usually well over 30°C, and in some areas are over 33°C. During the coolest part of the year, however, mean monthly temperatures in the interior are usually below 27°C, and in some areas below 24°C.

Daily variations

In West Africa diurnal ranges of temperature are often larger than annual ranges. The smallest diurnal ranges occur in the coastal areas. This is partly because of the moderating influence of the sea, and partly because these areas tend to be more cloudy than the interior. Going inland there is a considerable increase in the size of the diurnal range (compare Warri, Bida, Kano and Agades in Table 11).

In the coastal areas mean daily maxima are rarely much above 33°C, and mean daily minima do not usually fall much below 20°C (except to the north of Cape Verde). Mean diurnal ranges along the coast are usually in the order of 5°C–12°C.

In the interior the largest diurnal ranges occur during the dry season, when there is least cloud. During the dry season mean daily maxima are often well above 33°C, and in some areas above 40°C. At the same time of year mean daily minima are often below 20°C, and in some areas below 15°C. Mean diurnal ranges of well over 10°C are commonly experienced. During the rainy season, however, because of the increased amount of cloud cover, there tends to be a drop in the daily maxima and a rise in the daily minima, with a corresponding decrease in the size of the diurnal range.

Precipitation

Annual amount

Fig. 1.6 shows that broadly speaking in West Africa

Table 11 Mean daily temperatures (°C) for selected stations

Station	Lat.	Alt. (m)		J	F	M	A	M	J	J	A	S	O	N	D	Year
Warri (Nigeria)	6N	6	Max	31	33	33	33	31	30	28	28	29	30	32	31	31
			Min.	22	22	23	23	23	22	22	23	22	22	22	22	23
			Range	11	9	10	10	8	8	6	5	7	8	10	9	8
Bida (Nigeria)	9N	184	Max.	34	36	37	37	34	31	30	29	30	32	35	34	33
			Min.	21	23	24	25	23	23	22	22	22	22	22	20	23
			Range	13	13	13	12	11	8	8	7	8	10	13	14	10
Kano (Nigeria)	12N	472	Max.	30	32	35	38	37	35	31	30	31	34	34	31	33
			Min.	13	15	19	22	24	23	22	21	21	20	16	14	19
			Range	17	17	16	16	13	12	9	9	10	14	18	17	14
Agades (Niger)	17N	520	Max.	28	33	38	42	44	44	41	39	41	41	37	32	38
			Min.	10	12	16	20	25	25	23	23	23	20	15	12	19
			Range	18	21	22	22	19	19	18	16	18	21	22	20	19

rainfall is heaviest in the south, and becomes progressively lighter towards the north, as the rain-bearing south-westerly winds get further from their source of moisture.

Along the Gulf of Guinea coast (with the exception of an unusually dry belt in the middle) the rainfall is heavy, in many places averaging more than 1 500 mm per annum. The rainfall is particularly heavy in south-eastern Nigeria, parts of which receive more than 2 500 mm per annum. Very heavy rainfall is also experienced in the south-western coastal area, where the moisture-bearing south-westerly winds are forced to rise by the Fouta Djalon and the Guinea Highlands.

To the east of Cape Three Points, there is an unusually dry belt, which extends along the coast of eastern Ghana into southern Togo and Benin. The existence of this dry belt is difficult to explain

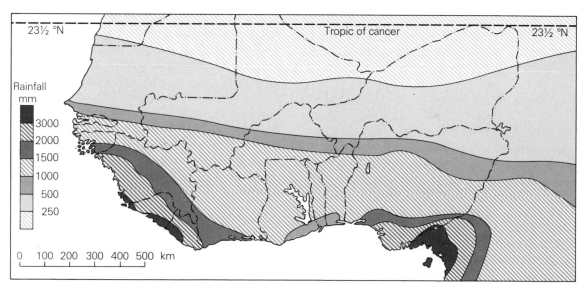

Fig. 1.6 West Africa — mean annual rainfall

Fig. 1.7 West Africa – seasonal distribution of rainfall

satisfactorily. Suggested reasons for its existence include:

1 This section of the coastline trends roughly from south-west to north-east. Because of this, the rain-bearing south-westerly winds tend to blow parallel to the coastline, instead of crossing it and penetrating inland.

2 The upwelling of cold water off this section of the coast causes lower air temperatures, and thus restricts the conditions which are favourable to convection rainfall.

Going inland from the Gulf of Guinea, the rainfall decreases in amount quite rapidly. The 250 mm isohyet is reached about 1 300 km inland from the Guinea coast.

Seasonal distribution

Fig. 1.7 illustrates the seasonal distribution of the rainfall in West Africa. The lands bordering the Gulf of Guinea (with the exception of the extreme eastern area) have rainfall throughout the year, with a well

marked double maxima. The wettest period usually occurs between May and July, with a second somewhat less wet period between September and November. Separating these two wet periods are two somewhat drier periods, a short one in August, and a longer one from December to April. The two wet periods are related to the passage northwards and southwards of the ITCZ. In West Africa the passage of the ITCZ is often marked by 'line squalls'. These are north-east to south-west moving thunderstorms, which are usually accompanied by strong winds and torrential rain.

In the south-western coastal area, although the rainfall is very heavy, it is much more seasonal in its distribution. There is a single maximum during the northern summer, and a marked dry period from December to March. Thus, although Freetown has a mean annual rainfall of 3 510 mm, more than 70 per cent of this total falls in the three months from July to September. South-eastern Nigeria also has a single maximum during the northern summer.

Going inland from the Gulf of Guinea, the two

13

Fig. 1.8 Ghana – seasonal distribution of rainfall

wet periods which are experienced along the coast become progressively closer together, and eventually merge into a single summer maximum. Fig. 1.8 illustrates this transition in Ghana.

14

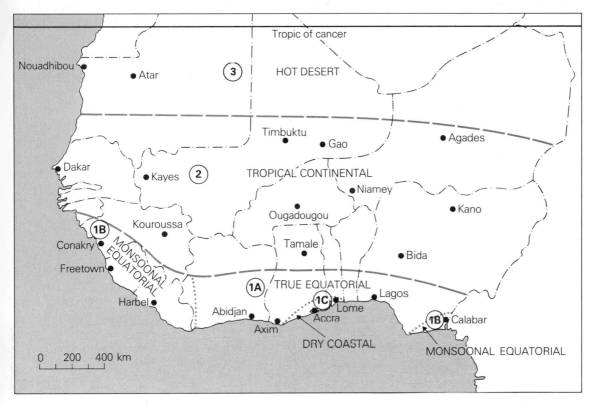

Fig. 1.9 West Africa – broad climatic divisions

Climatic divisions

Fig. 1.9 shows a suggested division of West Africa into broad climatic regions. Three major types of climate occur in West Africa:

1 Equatorial;
2 Tropical Continental;
3 Hot Desert.

Equatorial
That part of West Africa which lies to the south of about latitude 8°N, experiences an equatorial type of climate. In the equatorial region mean annual temperatures are never far from 27°C, and the annual range of temperature is rarely much more than 3°C. On the basis of the total amount and seasonal distribution of the rainfall, the equatorial region of West Africa can be divided into the following sub-regions:

a) true equatorial;
b) monsoon equatorial;

c) dry coastal.

The true equatorial type of climate is experienced along most of the Gulf of Guinea coast, with the exception of the unusually dry belt in the middle, and a small area in the extreme south-east of Nigeria. In that part of West Africa which experiences the true equatorial type of climate, the rainfall is heavy, usually averaging more than 1 500 mm per annum. There is no real dry season, but a well marked double maxima of rainfall occurs (see Table 12).

The monsoonal equatorial type of climate occurs along the south-west coast of West Africa, from Guinea Bissau (formerly Portuguese Guinea) to eastern Liberia. Although this area receives very heavy rainfall, most of it is concentrated in the northern summer, and there is a marked dry season from December to March. A similar monsoonal effect is experienced in the extreme south-east of Nigeria (see Table 13)

The climate of that part of the Gulf of Guinea coast which lies to the east of Cape Three Points, and

Table 12

Station	Lat.	Alt. (m)		J	F	M	A	M	J	J	A	S	O	N	D	Year
Abidjan (Ivory Coast)	5N	20	°C	27	28	28	28	27	26	25	25	26	26	27	27	27
			mm	41	53	99	125	361	495	213	56	71	168	201	79	1 962
Axim (Ghana)	5N	23	°C	26	27	27	27	26	26	25	25	25	26	26	26	26
			mm	58	61	122	142	404	495	168	58	84	188	196	99	2 075
Lagos (Nigeria)	6N	3	°C	27	28	28	28	27	25	25	24	25	26	27	26	26
			mm	25	38	99	140	277	439	277	69	142	201	71	25	1 803

Table 13

Station	Lat.	Alt. (m)		J	F	M	A	M	J	J	A	S	O	N	D	Year
Conakry (Guinea)	10N	5	°C	27	28	28	28	28	27	26	25	26	27	27	28	27
			mm	3	3	10	23	158	559	1 298	1 054	683	373	122	10	4 296
Freetown (Sierra Leone)	9N	11	°C	27	28	28	28	28	27	26	25	26	26	27	27	27
			mm	5	3	15	64	150	315	955	912	650	269	137	41	3 516
Calabar (Nigeria)	5N	52	°C	27	27	28	27	27	27	25	25	26	26	27	27	27
			mm	43	76	152	213	312	406	450	406	427	310	191	43	3 029

which extends through eastern Ghana into Togo and Benin resembles the true equatorial type of climate in almost every respect. The only major difference is that the rainfall is unusually light. Most parts of this dry coastal belt receive an average of less than 1 000 mm of rain per annum, and some parts have less than 750 mm (see Table 14).

Tropical continental
In West Africa the tropical continental climate is experienced between about latitudes 8°N and 18°N.

In this region temperatures tend to be rather more extreme than in the equatorial region. The major difference between the equatorial and the tropical continental types of climate, however, is in the amount and seasonal distribution of the rainfall. The tropical continental region lies under the influence of the moist Southwest Monsoon winds for part of the year, but during the rest of the year comes under the drying influence of the Harmattan. Consequently the rainfall regime is a highly seasonal one. The double maxima of rainfall which is experienced along the

Table 14

Station	Lat.	Alt. (m)		J	F	M	A	M	J	J	A	S	O	N	D	Year
Accra (Ghana)	6N	6	°C	27	27	28	28	27	26	25	25	25	26	27	27	27
			mm	18	38	56	76	127	191	51	15	38	58	36	25	729
Lomé (Togo)	6N	10	°C	26	27	27	27	27	26	24	24	24	25	26	26	26
			mm	15	23	46	117	145	224	71	8	36	61	28	10	784

Table 15

Station	Lat.	Alt. (m)		J	F	M	A	M	J	J	A	S	O	N	D	Year
Tamale (Ghana)	9N	194	°C	27	30	31	30	29	27	26	26	26	27	28	27	28
			mm	3	8	56	81	119	140	140	206	226	94	18	5	1 096
Ouagadougou (Uppper Volta)	12N	302	°C	25	27	31	33	33	30	28	27	27	30	29	26	29
			mm	0	3	15	20	74	125	213	264	142	23	0	0	879
Niamey (Niger)	14N	216	°C	27	27	30	34	34	32	29	28	29	31	28	25	29
			mm	0	0	5	8	33	71	132	188	94	13	0	0	544
Gao (Niger)	16N	267	°C	23	25	29	32	35	35	32	30	32	32	29	24	30
			mm	0	0	3	3	8	31	74	91	25	3	0	0	238

Table 16

Station	Lat.	Alt. (m)		J	F	M	A	M	J	J	A	S	O	N	D	Year
Atar (Mauritania)	22N	231	°C	21	23	25	29	32	35	34	34	34	31	25	21	29
			mm	3	0	0	0	0	3	8	31	28	3	3	0	79
Nouadhibou (Mauritania)	21N	7	°C	19	20	21	21	22	23	22	25	27	24	23	20	22
			mm	3	0	0	0	0	0	0	0	8	13	3	10	37

Gulf of Guinea coast is replaced by a single maximum in the northern summer, and there is a marked dry season in the northern winter. Going northwards towards the edge of the Sahara Desert, the rainfall becomes progressively smaller in amount, and the dry season becomes longer and more severe. (see Table 15).

Hot desert

The hot desert climate is experienced in West Africa to the north of about latitude 18°N. In this region the rainfall is very light, everywhere averaging less than 250 mm per annum. It is also highly irregular in its occurrence. In the interior temperatures are more extreme than in any other part of West Africa, with particularly large diurnal ranges being experienced (see Atar in Table 16). Along the coast, however, the Canary Current exerts a moderating effect of temperatures (see Nouadhibou).

C: Climate and man

Temperature

In tropical lowland areas temperatures are high enough throughout the year for plant growth. Consequently, in such areas human activities are much more influenced by the amount and seasonal distribution of the rainfall, than by differences in temperature.

In tropical highland areas, however, the reduction of temperature with altitude profoundly influences the pattern of settlement and land use. In those parts of the tropics where a wide range of altitude occurs, a great variety of different crops can be grown. In East Africa, for example, where the altitude ranges from sea level to more than 5 800 m above sea level, both tropical and temperate crops can be successfully grown. Along the coast of East Africa, coconuts and cashew nuts are widely cultivated, at heights of roughly 1 500 to 2 000 m above sea level, temperature conditions are suitable for the cultivation of arabica coffee and tea; while at heights of from 2 000 to 2 700 m, wheat and potatoes grow well.

In Central America and the northern parts of the Andes, the relationship between altitude and land use is also a very close one. In those areas four major altitudinal zones are commonly recognised, although no sharp line separates one zone from another. Furthermore, the exact height of the upper limit of each zone varies somewhat, because of the differences in latitude which are involved. Fig. 1.10 shows the altitudinal zones which occur in the northern part of the Andes, and a brief description of each is given below:

1 Between sea level and about 1 000 m is the *tierra caliente* or hot zone. In this zone mean annual temperatures are usually over 24°C, and typically tropical crops such as cocoa, sugar cane, bananas and coconuts are grown.

2 Between about 1 000 and 2 000 m is the *tierra templada* or temperate country, where mean annual temperatures of 18°C–24°C are experienced. Coffee is the main crop grown in this zone.

3 Between about 2 000 and 3 000 m is the *tierra fria* or cold country. In this zone mean annual temperatures of 13°C–18°C are experienced, and crops such as maize, wheat and potatoes are grown.

4 Above 3 000 m and extending to the snow line, is the zone of alpine meadows. In the northern parts of the Andes these are known as *paramos*. This zone experiences mean annual temperatures of 0°C–13°C and is largely devoted to the rearing of livestock.

The variation of temperature with altitude has also profoundly influenced the pattern of European settlement within the tropics. The European settler has generally found the cooler conditions of the tropical highlands to be more agreeable than the heat of the tropical lowlands.

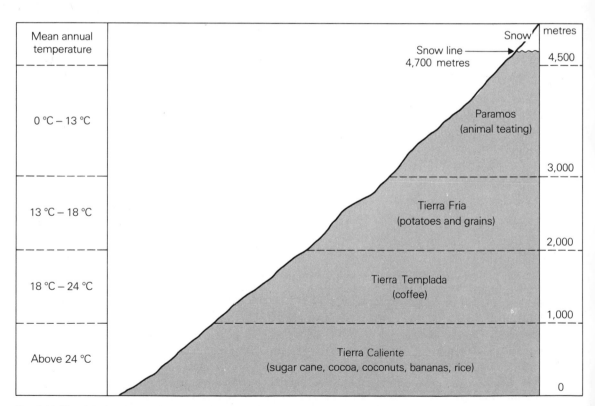

Fig. 1.10 The altitudinal zones of the northern Andes

18

Precipitation

Within the tropics, at least in lowland situations, rainfall is the most vital element in the climate. It exerts considerable influence not only over the natural vegetation, but also over man's activities. From the human standpoint, the seasonal distribution of the rainfall, its reliability and its intensity are just as important as its total amount.

Rainfall is of particular importance to the cultivator. In the lowland tropics, the amount and seasonal distribution of the rainfall to a large extent determines the type of crops which can be grown in a particular area. Perennial tree crops such as cocoa, oil palm and rubber, for example, require abundant moisture throughout the year, and so their cultivation is limited to those parts of the tropics where the rainfall is both heavy in amount, and fairly evenly distributed. In the parts of the tropics which experience a long dry season, only crops which have a short growing period can be successfully cultivated. In areas of low rainfall, however, the fact that the rain is concentrated into a short wet season is often an advantage, for if it were spread over the whole year, it would be inadequate for the growth of any kind of crop. On the other hand, in areas where very heavy rainfall is concentrated into a short wet season, much of the rainwater is useless to the farmer.

The reliability and intensity of the rainfall are also of great importance to the cultivator. Variations in the amount and time of its occurrence may cause considerable reductions in crop yields, or even result in total crop failure. In India, for example, the late onset or partial failure of the monsoon rains, have in the past been a frequent cause of famine. In the late 1960s and early 1970s, the occurrence of a series of unusually dry years in the Sahelian zone of West Africa, caused great hardship to both the cultivators and the pastoralists of that area. Particularly badly affected by the Sahelian drought were the countries of Mauritania, Senegal, Mali, Upper Volta, Niger and neighbouring Chad. In Senegal, for example, it has been estimated that drought conditions caused the loss of about half the 1972–3 groundnut crop.

In areas where the rainfall occurs mainly in the form of torrential downpours, its effectiveness is greatly reduced. Under such conditions the soil is often unable to absorb all the rain water, much of which runs off down the slope, and so never becomes available to the farmer. Furthermore, torrential rain greatly increases the likelihood of soil erosion.

Rainfall is of no less importance to the pastoralist. The pattern of life of the nomadic herders of tropical Africa is governed by their need to find water and pasture for their livestock, and hence their movements are intimately related to the seasonal distribution of rainfall. The rainfall tends to be highly unreliable in the areas occupied by the nomadic pastoralists, and this sometimes has disastrous consequences for them. In the recent Sahelian drought, for example, it has been estimated that 90 per cent of cattle died in some areas of Mauritania, and about 60 per cent died in that country as a whole. Thousands of Mauritanian nomads who had lost their herds, migrated to the towns. During the severe drought of 1959–61, the Masai of East Africa lost many of their cattle, and they also suffered severely in the heavy rains and floods which followed the drought. Rainfall variability is also a problem to the ranchers of tropical Australia and South America, who frequently experience heavy losses of livestock, as a result of both droughts and floods.

The amount and seasonal distribution of the rainfall is also of considerable importance in the development of water power resources. The production of hydroelectricity is favoured by a heavy and evenly distributed rainfall. In areas where the rainfall is highly seasonal in nature, and where as a consequence the level of water in the rivers fluctuates considerably, artificial lakes have to be created in order to store water for use in dry periods. This usually necessitates the building of large and expensive dams.

Means of transport in tropical areas are also considerably affected by rainfall. In many areas the torrential nature of the rainfall makes the building and maintenance of roads and railways difficult and expensive. In several parts of the tropical lands the seasonal nature of the rainfall limits the use of rivers for transport.

Exercises

1 'Within the tropics, rainfall is the most vital element in the climate.' Discuss this statement.

2 'The seasonal distribution of the rainfall, its reliability and its intensity, are just as important as its
total amount.' Discuss this statement in relation
to the tropical lands.

3 Describe the important ways in which the climate
of tropical areas is modified by altitude. With
reference to specific examples, discuss how these
modifications influence land use and settlement
patterns.

4 With reference to specific examples, discuss the
influence of ocean currents upon the climate of
coastal areas within the tropics.

5 Outline the distribution and seasonal nature of the
rainfall in West Africa. Discuss the ways in which
differences in the amount and seasonal distribution
of the rainfall influence human activities in West
Africa.

6 With the aid of sketch maps, describe and attempt
to account for the distribution and seasonal nature
of the rainfall in your own country.

Suggested reading

General works on climatology include:

HOWARD J. CRITCHFIELD: *General Climatology*
AUSTIN A. MILLER: *Climatology*

Detailed information about the climate of particular
tropical areas can be found in the following:

JOHN I. CLARKE, Ed.: *An Advanced Geography of
Africa* – Chapter 3
E. H. G. DOBBY: *Monsoon Asia* – Chapter 3
E. H. G. DOBBY: *Southeast Asia* – Chapter 2
R. J. HARRISON-CHURCH: *Africa and the Islands* –
Chapter 2
R. J. HARRISON-CHURCH: *West Africa* – Chapter 3
H. R. JARRETT: *Africa* – Chapter 2
D. C. MONEY: *South America* – Chapter 2
OOI JIN-BIE: *Peninsular Malaysia* – Chapter 2
J. M. PRITCHARD: *Africa. A Study Geography for
Advanced Students* – Chapter 1
K. W. ROBINSON: *Australia, New Zealand and South-
west Pacific* – Chapter 3
O. H. K. SPATE AND A. T. A. LEARMOUTH: *India and
Pakistan* – Chapter 2
M. F. THOMAS AND G. W. WHITTINGTON: *Environ-
ment and Land Use in Africa* – Chapter 4

Natural vegetation

A: General

Factors influencing the distribution of vegetation

The type of plant life which develops naturally in a particular physical environment, and which is best suited to that environment, is commonly known as the natural vegetation. The distribution of natural vegetation over the earth's surface is influenced by four main groups of factors:

1 climatic factors (particularly temperature, humid ity, precipitation, light intensity and wind);
2 edaphic factors (those related to the soil);
3 geomorphic factors (those related to land forms);
4 biotic factors (those related to living organisms).

Of these groups of factors, climate is by far the most important. In tropical lowlands, temperatures are continuously favourable to plant growth, and so in such areas it is rainfall which plays the dominant role in determining the natural vegetation. Broadly speaking, in areas where rainfall is heavy and well-distributed throughout the year, the natural vegetation is likely to be forest; in areas where rainfall is moderate or light, and is highly seasonal in its distribution, savanna vegetation is commonly found; while in areas where rainfall is deficient, there is likely to be semi-desert scrub or desert vegetation.

Within the tropics, as in other parts of the world, man has modified the original vegetation cover to such an extent that very little, if any, true natural vegetation now remains. Furthermore, it is often difficult to deduce what the vegetation would have been, had man not interfered. In some parts of the tropical world man has completely removed the original vegetation, replacing it with cultivated vegetation, buildings, roads, etc. In other areas wild plant life still exists, in the sense that it has not been planted or tended by man. In many cases, however, such vegetation can only be described as semi-natural, for man has influenced it to some extent, either directly by cutting and burning, or indirectly through the grazing habits of his animals.

Vegetation types within the tropics

Fig. 2.1 represents an attempt to show in a very generalised way, the distribution of natural vegetation within the tropics. More detailed maps can be found in your atlas. You will probably find that different maps may not always agree with each other, as to the exact pattern of distribution of natural vegetation. This is partly because the natural vegetation of many parts of the world is imperfectly known, but mainly because different classifications have been used in making the maps.

The natural vegetation map attempts to show what the vegetation would have been, if man had not interfered. Unfortunately, such maps do not usually give any indication of the extent to which the original vegetation has in fact been modified by man. Although on natural vegetation maps, sharp divisions are usually shown between one type of vegetation and another, it would be wrong to infer that such abrupt boundaries do in fact exist. As in the case of climate, one type of natural vegetation usually merges into another, through a broad zone of transition.

Tropical rain forest

Tropical rain forest (sometimes known as equatorial

Fig. 2.1 The tropical lands – natural vegetation (greatly simplified)

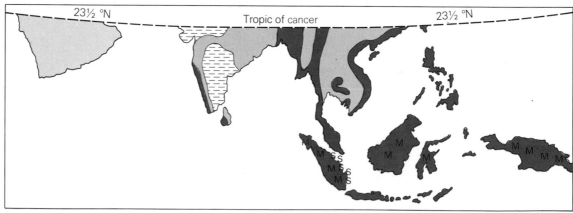

forest or selva) occurs in tropical lowlands which have an abundant and well-distributed rainfall. There are three distinct formations of tropical rain forest. These are usually referred to as the American, the African, and the Indo-Malaysian formations. The American formation has its most extensive development in the Amazon Basin, but also occurs in the wetter lowlands of Central America, Colombia and eastern Brazil, as well as in the wetter parts of some of the larger West Indian islands. The African formation covers much of the Zaire Basin, and extends along the coast of West Africa as far west as Sierra Leone. It also occurs along the east coast of the island of Madagascar. The Indo-Malaysian formation covers most of the Malay Peninsula, the Indonesian archipelago and the Philippine islands. It also occurs in the wetter

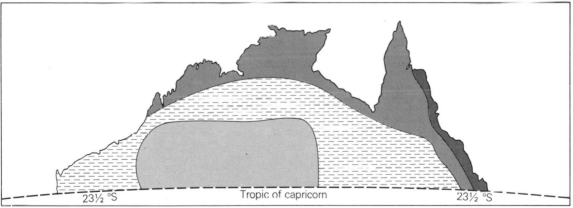

lowlands of Burma, Thailand, the Khmer Republic (Cambodia) and Vietnam, in south-western Sri Lanka (formerly Ceylon), and in the Western Ghats of India. The Indo-Malaysian formation also extends along parts of the east coast of Queensland in Australia.

In those areas, the combination of high temperatures and abundant precipitation throughout the year results in a very luxuriant type of vegetation. Many thousands of different species of plant are found in the tropical rain forest. In the Malay Peninsula, for example, there are estimated to be about 2 500 species of tall tree. Some of the trees of the tropical rain forest, such as mahogany, rosewood, and greenheart, are highly valued for their timber. The individuals of a particular tree species are usually

Tropical rain forest in the Malay Peninsula. Note the straight, smooth trunk and the buttress roots of the large tree in the fore ground; and also the lianas.

widely scattered, and this is one of the factors which makes the commercial extraction of timber from the tropical rain forest difficult.

In the tropical rain forest, the crowns of the trees tend to form two or three distinct layers. The tallest trees grow upwards towards the light, and often attain a height of well over 30 metres. These trees have straight, smooth-barked trunks, and few branches before the crown. Many of the trees develop 'plank buttresses' from the lowest few metres of the trunk. At one time it was thought that trees evolved these buttresses as a means of support, but this now seems doubtful, as it has been found that trees with buttresses are as prone to uprooting in strong winds, as are trees of a similar height which do not have buttresses.

The vast majority of the trees of the tropical rain forest are evergreen, shedding their old leaves and growing new ones simultaneously and continuously. A few species are deciduous, but because of the lack of any well marked seasonal rhythm in the climate, they shed their leaves at irregular intervals.

In addition to trees, there are many climbing plants in the tropical rain forest. Particularly numerous are the lianes. These are woody climbers, which twine from tree to tree, sometimes attaining lengths of more than 100 metres. There are also many epiphytes (plants which grow on others without actually feeding on them), including numerous varieties of ferns and orchids.

Tropical swamp forest

A common feature of many tropical coastal areas is mangrove forest. The name mangrove is applied collectively to a number of different trees, all of which have certain physical characteristics in common, notably their ability to survive in unstable, submerged mud. They have complicated root systems, which serve to anchor the plant in the mud, and which also act as aerating organs.

Mangrove forest develops on mud flats which are exposed at low tide, but which are otherwise normally covered by salt or brackish water. Particularly favourable conditions for the development of mangrove forest are found in creeks and river estuaries, where tidewaters cause the deposition of river sediment. Mangrove forests occur widely along the coast of West Africa. They also occur along the East African coast, particularly around the mouth of the Rufiji river. Mangrove forests are widespread in Southeast Asia, forming an almost continuous fringe along the west coast of the Malay Peninsula, and along the east coast of Sumatra. On the landward side, mangrove swamp forest is usually replaced by fresh-water swamp forest.

Tropical seasonal forest

In areas where rainfall is fairly heavy, but where there is a well marked dry season, tropical evergreen rain forest is usually replaced by tropical seasonal forest. This type of vegetation occurs along the margins of the tropical rain forest in Africa, and in Central America and South America (these areas are not shown in Fig. 2.1). It is most widespread, however, in tropical Asia, where it is known as monsoon forest.

The vegetation of the tropical seasonal forest is similar in many ways to that of the tropical rain forest, but it is less luxuriant and more open. Many of the trees of the tropical seasonal forest are decidu-

Mangrove swamp along the north-eastern coast of Australia

ous, shedding their leaves during the dry season. Although lianas and epiphytes are usually present, they are much less numerous than in the tropical rain forest. In the monsoon forests of tropical Asia, important timber trees include pyinkado and teak.

Savanna

Savanna vegetation is widespread in those parts of the tropics which are subject to a marked seasonal drought. It covers large areas in tropical Africa, both to the north and south of the tropical rain forest, and also on the drier plateaux of East Africa. In South America it occurs in the lowlands drained by the Orinoco river, on the Guiana Highlands, and on the Brazilian Highlands. In Venezuela the savanna areas are commonly known as the *llanos*, while in Brazil they are known as the *campos*. Savanna vegetation is also found in the drier parts of the Deccan Plateau in India, while in Australia it extends to the north and east of the central desert.

The term savanna has been used to refer to a wide range of plant communities, from unbroken treeless grasslands, to woodlands in which trees and shrubs form an almost continuous cover. In the wetter areas, savanna vegetation usually consists of clumps of trees, interspersed with tall grasses. The trees are much shorter than those of the tropical rain forest, and many of them are deciduous. The grasses in these areas are never less than 1½ metres in height, and in the case of elephant grass may reach 5 metres. As the rainfall decreases in amount, and the dry season becomes longer and more severe, the savanna vegetation becomes progressively poorer. In the driest savanna areas there are scattered thorny bushes instead of trees, and the grasses are short and do not form a continuous cover. Unlike the tropical rain forest, the appearance of the savanna varies considerably with the season. During the rains the general appearance is one of greenness, but during the dry season the trees shed their leaves and the grasses turn brown and die off.

Considerable doubt has been expressed as to whether or not savanna is the true natural vegetation of the areas which it now occupies. Many authorities

Savanna vegetation in the Kimberley District of Western Australia. Note the baobab tree in the foreground. At what time of the year was the photograph taken?

feel that the present savannas are largely the result of man's repeated cutting and burning of what at one time was probably some type of seasonal forest. Certainly in the African savannas, fires are very widespread during the dry season. Some of these fires are started accidently, but others are deliberately set. Hunters sometimes burn the bush, to drive out wild animals. Fires are also started by cultivators to clear the land for growing crops, and by pastoralists to burn off the old grass and thus stimulate the growth of new shoots for their livestock to feed on.

Repeated burning tends to favour the growth of perennial grasses which have underground stems, at the expense of woody plants. After burning occurs, these grasses rapidly produce new shoots. Most woody plants, on the other hand, are severely damaged by fire. It is noticeable that many of the trees of the savanna do in fact have an unusually thick bark. It is thought that this bark helps to protect them

against the worst effects of fire. Experiments in the Zamfara forest reserve, south of Sokoto in Nigeria, have shown that where an area of savanna is protected from fire, there is a very considerable increase in the number of woody plants.

In some areas it may well be that the existence of savanna vegetation is due to local soil conditions, rather than to the effects of burning. In the Orinoco Delta in Venezuela, for example, the soil is water-logged for most if not all of the year, and it is felt that this prohibits the growth of forest trees.

Thorn woodland

In some parts of the tropics where there is a very prolonged and severe dry season, thorn woodland occurs. This type of vegetation is dominated by low thorny bushes, which sometimes form an almost impenetrable jungle. Some succulents (plants which store water in their tissues), such as various species of cacti, are also usually found in thorn woodland. All the plants of this vegetation type are markedly xerophytic (adapted to withstand drought). The trees vary in height from 3 to 10 metres, and most of them are thorny. During the long dry season the landscape appears almost lifeless, but when the rains begin the vegetation bursts into intensive life.

Thorn woodland is widespread along the northern coastlands of Venezuela and Colombia, and also occurs in dry lowland areas in Central America and some of the West Indian islands, particularly in the interior of Hispaniola. It also covers a vast area in north-eastern Brazil, where it is known as *caatinga*.

Semi-desert scrub and desert

On its dry side thorn woodland gives way to semi-desert scrub. In this type of vegetation the plants are more widely spaced than in thorn woodland. Succulent plants are more numerous, although thorny bushes are also common.

Tropical deserts occur under still drier conditions, and so the vegetation is even more sparse. Tropical deserts are, however, rarely completely without vege-tation, except in areas of drifting sand or bare rock. Desert plants are adapted in various ways to withstand extremely dry conditions. Many of them have long roots which reach down to subterranean water. Others are densely tufted or compacted, or have hairs or spines instead of leaves.

In these very dry environments most plant life exists in a virtually dormant condition for much of the time, but after the occasional heavy shower of rain it bursts into growth. At such times annual plants spring up, usually completing their life cycle within a very few weeks, before the soil completely dries out again.

The vegetation of tropical mountains

Although the distribution of natural vegetation in tropical lowlands is influenced mainly by rainfall, in tropical highland areas the reduction of temperature with altitude has a marked effect upon plant life. In nearly all places where high mountains rise from lowlands clothed in tropical rain forest, a similar succession of altitudinal vegetation zones can be distinguished. Tropical rain forest is replaced

Semi-desert vegetation in Northern Kenya.

upwards by montane forest, which in turn gives way to alpine vegetation. Finally, if the mountain is sufficiently high, the zone of perennial snow is reached.

With increasing altitude, the trees of the tropical rain forest become shorter, and branch closer to the ground. Eventually, at heights of about 1 500–2 000 metres above sea level, the tropical rain forest merges into montane forest. In montane forest the trees are only about 9–12 metres in height, and their trunks and branches are often very twisted. In areas where mist prevails, the trunks and branches of the trees are usually covered with epiphytic mosses and lichens. The term mossy forest is sometimes applied to this type of montane forest. At higher altitudes still, the trees become even shorter and more twisted, and the term elfin woodland is sometimes applied. This marks the end of the montane forest, and the beginning of the treeless alpine zone. Within the tropics the tree line (the upper limit of tree growth) is usually reached at heights of between 2 500 and 3 500 metres. Many types of plant communities occur in the alpine zone. Sometimes elfin woodland gives way to a community of shrubs, but in other areas there is open grassland. Within the tropics the

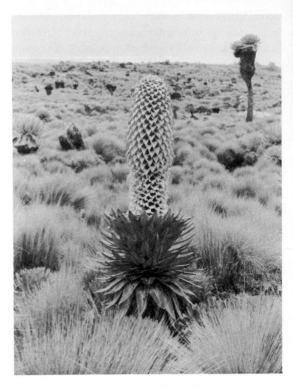

Alpine vegetation on the slopes of Mount Kenya, at an altitude of about 3 600 metres. Note the tussock grasses, and the giant lobelia (foreground) and groundsel (right background).

permanent snow line (the height above which there is snow throughout the year) is usually reached at heights of between 4 500 and 5 500 metres.

Not all tropical mountains rise from lowlands clothed in rain forest. Some rise from arid or semi-arid plains and plateaux, and so their lower slopes only support desert vegetation or scrub. At heights of several hundred metres above sea level, however, increased precipitation may permit the growth of forest. It is only on the western side of the Andes, from northern Peru to northern Chile, that there are high tropical mountains which have desert or semi-desert vegetation throughout their entire height.

Most of the East African mountains rise from plateaux covered with thorn woodland or acacia savanna. On these mountains montane forest generally replaces savanna vegetation at a height of about 1 800 metres. At heights of 2 400–2 600 metres, trees are often replaced by a zone of mountain bamboo, which extends up to a height of about 3 000 metres. Above this altitude is the treeless alpine zone. The lower part of the alpine zone in East Africa

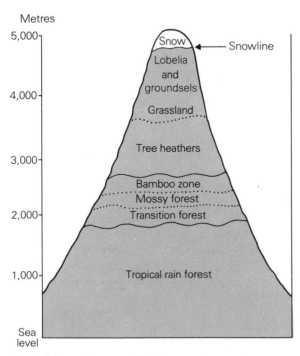

Fig. 2.2 Vegetation zones of Mt. Ruwenzori

is often dominated by tree heathers, which on Mt. Kilimanjaro attain heights of up to 9–12 metres. At altitudes of above 3 500 metres giant groundsels and lobelias are common, and tussock grasses also occur. The upper limit of plant growth in East Africa is reached at about 4 500 metres.

B: The vegetation of West Africa

In West Africa the relationship between rainfall and natural vegetation is a particularly close one (compare Fig. 2.3 with Fig. 1.6). Plant life in West Africa is influenced not only by the total amount of rainfall received, but also by the length and severity of the dry season. As has already been noted in Chapter 1, the rainfall is heaviest and most evenly distributed in the southern part of the region, becoming progressively lighter in amount and more seasonal in distribution towards the north.

Man has profoundly modified the original vegetation cover in West Africa. For many centuries traditional forms of agriculture have involved widespread cutting and burning, and the present vegetation pattern of West Africa is to a considerable extent the result of man's activities.

Forest

A broad belt of forest, averaging some 150–300 km in width, extends along the coast of West Africa from Sierra Leone eastwards. There is, however, a break in this belt, corresponding with the dry coastal strip to the east of Cape Three Points.

Mangrove forest occurs along many parts of the West African coast, but is particularly extensive in the Niger Delta and along the south-west coast. In parts of Gambia, Guinea Bissau, Guinea and Sierra Leone, areas of mangrove swamp have been reclaimed for the cultivation of rice. Fresh-water swamp forest occurs in part of the Niger Delta, and also along fresh-water lagoons and rivers. Useful trees of the fresh-water swamp forests of West Africa include the raphia palm and the screw-pine (pandanus). The leaf stalks of the raphia palm provide piassava fibre, which is used in the making of stiff brooms. The best quality of piassava fibre comes from the swamps of the Bonthe district of Sierra Leone. The leaves of the screw-pine are used for the making of mats and baskets.

Tropical rain forest occurs in those parts of West Africa which have a mean annual rainfall of at least 1 000 mm, and not more than three months in the year with less than 25 mm of rain. During comparatively recent times the extent of the high forest in

Fig. 2.3 West Africa – vegetation (simplified)

Desert
Sahel savanna
Sudan savanna
Guinea savanna
Derived savanna
Rain forest
Mangrove swamp
Montane vegetation

0 100 200 300 400 500 km

Gulf of Guinea

23½ °N   Tropic of cancer   23½ °N

West Africa has been considerably reduced, as a result of the increasing demand for agricultural land, and, during the present century, for commercial timber. The most widely practised form of agriculture in the forest zone of West Africa is that known as bush fallowing. Bush fallowing involves the clearing of patches of forest by cutting and burning, and the growing of crops on the cleared land for a short number of years. When the fertility of the soil begins to decline, the clearing is abandoned, and wild plant life quickly grows back over it. After a few years have elapsed, the abandoned clearing is covered with almost impenetrable vegetation. Very often, at this stage the land is cleared and cultivated again. In many parts of the forest zone, particularly in Sierra Leone, the present vegetation consists mainly of various stages of bush fallow. If the land is not recleared for cultivation, the forest may eventually be able to re-establish itself. This type of forest is known as secondary forest, to distinguish it from the original vegetation. Much of the forest which still remains in West Africa is of a secondary nature.

Savanna

The present boundary between forest and savanna is an unusually abrupt one in West Africa. It is not, however, a natural boundary, but is the result of persistent cutting and burning by man. On the northern edges of the present high forest, areas of derived savanna occur. These areas were formerly forested, but the original forest trees have been destroyed by man, and savanna species have replaced them. Experiments have shown that where areas of derived savanna are protected from cutting and burning, forest vegetation gradually re-establishes itself. In recent years the forest-savanna boundary in West Africa has tended to move southwards.

Between the northern edge of the forest and the southern edge of the Sahara Desert, three main types of savanna vegetation are commonly distinguished. These are:

a) Guinea savanna;
b) Sudan savanna;
c) Sahel savanna.

The Guinea savanna is the most southerly of the three savanna zones. It is a relatively moist type of savanna, occurring in areas which have a mean annual rainfall of more than 900 mm, and a dry season of at least four months. The vegetation of the Guinea savanna zone consists of tall grasses and clumps of trees. The grasses average $1\frac{1}{2}$–3 metres in height. The trees are mainly deciduous, and have an average height of 6–15 metres. They lose their leaves for only a short period in the year. Useful trees of the Guinea savanna zone include the shea-butter tree and the dawa dawa.

The Sudan savanna replaces the Guinea savanna to the north. It occurs in areas which have a mean annual rainfall of about 600–900 mm, and a dry season of about seven months. Grasses are shorter than in the Guinea savanna, averaging only $1–1\frac{1}{2}$ metres in height. Trees almost always occur singly rather than in clumps, and include such species as the baobab and the doum palm.

The Sahel savanna is the most northerly of the savanna zones. It occurs in areas which have a mean annual rainfall of about 250–600 mm, and a dry season of at least eight months. The vegetation of the Sahel savanna consists mainly of small thorny bushes, with several species of acacia being common. Grasses are usually less than 1 metre in height, and do not form a continuous cover.

Although the main areas of savanna lie to the north of the high forest, savanna vegetation also occurs in the dry coastal belt to the east of Cape Three Points. The original vegetation of this area was probably an open type of forest, but this has been degraded by repeated cutting and burning. The vegetation now consists of dense scrub in the wetter areas, and grassland, with patches of scrub in the drier areas.

Semi-desert scrub and desert

To the north of the Sahel savanna lies the Sahara desert, which has a mean annual rainfall of less than 250 mm. In the more southerly part of this region many of the acacias and other trees and shrubs of the Sahel savanna still occur, although they are usually widely scattered. Grasses also occur in isolated tufts.

Montane vegetation

Very few parts of West Africa are sufficiently high for the reduction of temperature with altitude to have any marked effect upon the natural vegetation. It is only on Mount Cameroon that a distinct altitudinal zonation of vegetation is found.

Exercises

1 Describe and discuss the distribution of savanna vegetation.
2 With the aid of a map, describe and attempt to account for the distribution of natural vegetation in West Africa.
3 Discuss the relationship between climate and natural vegetation within the tropics.
4 Examine the effect of altitude upon climate and natural vegetation within the tropics.

Suggested reading

General works on vegetation include:

S. R. EYRE. *Vegetation and Soils* – Chapters XIV, XV, XVI, XVII, XVIII and XX
D. RILEY and A. YOUNG: *World Vegetation* – Chapters 4, 6 and 7

More detailed information on the vegetation of West Africa can be obtained from:

R. J. HARRISON CHURCH: *West Africa* – Chapter 4
BRIAN HOPKINS: *Forest and Savanna* – Chapters 2, 3, 4 and 5
G. W. LAWSON: *Plant Life in West Africa* – Chapters 2, 3, 4 and 5

CHAPTER THREE

Soils

Within the tropics, as in other parts of the world, soils are of great importance to man. Compared with the total volume of the earth, the soil forms but a thin layer at the surface, a few centimetres to several metres in thickness. Yet it is this thin layer of soil which produces the bulk of man's food supply. The few centimetres of productive topsoil upon which agriculture depends have required hundreds of years for their development, but if they are misused they can be destroyed within the space of a few years.

Soil formation

Soil is the product of two processes:

1 the decomposition of rock;
2 the decay of plant and animal life.

The processes of physical and chemical weathering are responsible for breaking down the bedrock into fragments. These rock fragments provide the original material from which residual soils are formed (soils may also be formed from transported materials).

The purely mineral matter of the residual or transported materials is first colonised by plants such as mosses and lichens. By the partial decay of these organisms, humus begins to accumulate. Ferns and grasses are now able to take root, and later shrubs and trees can find a footing. The plant rootlets work downwards, burrowing animals bring up inorganic matter, and the growing mass becomes porous and sponge-like, so that it can retain water and permit the passage of air. The weathering processes continue to play their part, and eventually a mature soil, a complex mixture of mineral and organic products is formed.

Soils vary considerably in their nature. The principal factors upon which soil type depends are:

1 climate;
2 vegetation and other biological activity;
3 parent material;
4 topography;
5 time.

Climate

Climate is possibly the most important of the factors which influence soil formation. Climate affects the soil type both directly through its weathering effects, and also indirectly as a result of its influence upon vegetation.

In the lowland tropics temperatures are high throughout the year, and as a result the intensity of weathering is very much greater than that experienced in higher latitudes. It has been estimated that in tropical regions the effectiveness of weathering is almost ten times that of polar regions, and more than three times that of temperate regions. Furthermore, in the tropical regions weathering has not been interrupted by changes of climate, such as the glacial periods which have been experienced in the higher latitudes. As a result, deeper weathering is characteristic of tropical regions. In the arid parts of the tropical world, the lack of protective plant cover and the large diurnal ranges result in physical weathering being of particular importance. In the humid parts of the tropical world, on the other hand, chemical weathering is of very much greater significance.

In those areas which experience heavy rainfall for most of the year, there is a net downward movement of water in the soil. The water dissolves the soluble minerals and soluble humus in the soil, and carries both downwards. This process is known as 'leaching'. Left near the surface of strongly leached soils are the sesquioxides of aluminium and iron, which are most resistant to leaching. In areas which have a prolonged dry season, evaporation exceeds precipitation for a large part of the year, and so water tends to move upwards by capillary action. The water evaporates, leaving behind in the soil those salts which were dissolved in it.

Vegetation and other biological activity

Both plants and animals influence soil development. Dead plants provide the humus content of the soil. The humus content provides nitrogen and other elements such as phosphorous, calcium and potassium, which are broken down from decaying plant tissues by bacteria, and so made available in a form which plants can absorb through their roots. Humus also has the beneficial effect of improving the texture of the soil. The amount of plant material which is returned to the soil, obviously depends to a large degree upon the type of vegetation cover which exists. The topsoils of forest areas generally have a far higher humus content than do those of savanna areas.

The influence of animals on the soil is largely mechanical. Earthworms are of particular importance as they change the texture and chemical composition of the soil as it passes through their digestive systems. Ants and burrowing animals also disturb and rearrange the soil. In most parts of the tropical world, man plays an important role in modifying the soil by his agricultural practices.

Parent material

It might be thought that the parent material would largely determine the type of resulting soil, but on a world basis this is not generally the case. For example, the type of soil which develops upon granite in one area is not necessarily the same as the type of soil which develops upon granite in another area. Also, the same type of soil may develop upon very different types of rock. The influence of the parent material is, however, very marked in the case of young soils which have not had time to develop, and also in areas of limestone rock.

Topography

The steepness of slope may influence soils. Generally speaking, on steep slopes erosion by run-off is more rapid than on gentle slopes, and consequently steep slopes tend to have thinner soils. Drainage also influences soil type. The type of soil which develops on well-drained sites usually shows marked differences from soils which develop under water-logged conditions.

Time

A soil is considered to be mature when it has been acted upon by all the soil-forming processes for a considerable period of time, and has developed a profile which remains essentially the same with the passage of time. Soils which are evolving from recently deposited alluvium are considered to be young. In young soils the characteristic horizons are very poorly developed. The length of time which is needed for a soil to mature varies from a few hundred years to several thousand years.

The soil profile

The soil profile is a section through the soil, from the surface to the underlying rock. In a mature soil, the profile usually consists of a series of successive layers, which are known as horizons. The A and the B horizons represent the true soil, while the C horizon is the sub-soil or weathered parent body. The D horizon consists of unweathered bed rock. Different soil profiles are found under different conditions, and soils are recognised and classified on the basis of the parts of the profile which are present.

Tropical soils

Although during the last two or three decades the soil scientist has greatly increased his understanding of tropical soils, much less is generally known about the soils of the tropical world than about those of the temperate latitudes. Many attempts have been made to classify the world's soils into major soil groups. There is still, however, a great deal of controversy about soil classification. Fig. 3.1 is an attempt to show the distribution of the major soil types which occur within the tropics. Some of the more important tropical soils are briefly discussed below.

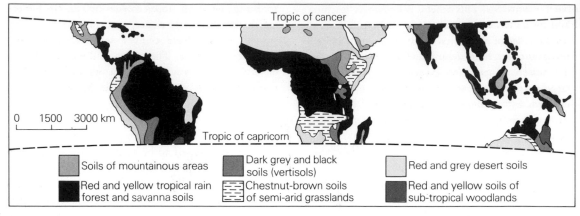

Fig. 3.1 The tropical lands – distribution of soils (greatly simplified)

Desert soils

Grey or red desert soils are found in the extremely arid parts of the tropical world. Because of the lack of moisture in desert areas, soil forming processes operate only slowly, and the parent rock exerts considerable influence upon soil type. Because of the sparsity of the plant cover, desert soils lack any significant organic content. Concentrations of soluble salts often occur at or just below the surface.

Desert soils generally lack the basic requirements for agriculture, namely moisture and nutrient content. Applications of water and fertilisers are necessary, before these soils are suitable for crop cultivation.

Chestnut-brown soils

On the desert margins the rainfall becomes somewhat heavier and more reliable, so that grass growth may occur. The soil now has a source of humus, and it is this humus content which gives the soil its brown colour. When irrigated, these soils are more agriculturally productive than are the desert soils.

Tropical black soils

Many of the most valuable soils in the tropical world are dark grey or black in colour, and are known collectively as tropical black earths or vertisols. Tropical black earths are generally found in areas where there is a marked dry season, and where the vegetation consists of some form of savanna grassland. They have generally developed over base-rich rocks, either calcareous rocks or rocks rich in ferromagnesian minerals.

Tropical black earths cover extensive areas of the Deccan Plateau in India, where they are known as regur. They are also found in parts of the interior of Queensland in Australia. In tropical Africa they occur in Sudan, and in parts of East Africa and Rhodesia. In East Africa they are commonly known as black cotton soils. In West Africa there are important areas of tropical black earths on the Accra plains, and also to the south of Lake Chad.

During the wet season tropical black earths become sticky, and are difficult to work. During the dry season they become extremely hard and crack. Material from the upper horizons may fall down the cracks, so that the soil horizons become mixed. Tropical black earths generally have a high calcium content.

Red and yellow tropical soils

Soils of a reddish or yellowish colour occur very widely in the more humid parts of the tropical world. These soils have been affected by a process known as laterisation. The formation of lateritic soils is complex. Where temperatures are high and there is an abundance of moisture in the soil, silica is leached downwards and accumulates in the lower layers of the soil. The sesquioxides of iron and aluminium, on the other hand, remain behind in the surface layers of the soil. If the sesquioxide-rich horizon remains covered by several feet of soil, it remains relatively soft. Where, however, it is exposed at the surface, a hardening process may set in, leading ultimately to the formation of laterite. This is a hard crust, which will support virtually no vegetation. Where it

34

occurs, laterite is often dug out and used as a building material.

A very large part of West Africa is covered by tropical red soils. A distinction is now made between the *ferrallitic* soils of West Africa, and the *ferruginous* soils. The ferrallitic soils are mainly associated with the tropical rain forest. These soils are very deeply weathered. They contain a considerable proportion of free iron oxide, as well as hydrated alumina. In the past it was commonly thought that the soils associated with tropical rain forest must be very rich, because of the luxuriance of the vegetation which they are able to support. It has been found, however, that once the forest is cleared for cultivation, these soils quickly lose their fertility. The ferruginous soils are mainly associated with savanna vegetation. They are not as deeply weathered as the ferrallitic soils, nor do they contain free aluminium.

Soil erosion

Soil erosion is the removal of the soil by wind or by running water. In moving across the surface of the land, wind and water exert an abrasive force, picking up particles of soil and carrying them away. In a natural undisturbed environment the dense cover of vegetation reduces erosion to a pace so slow, that new soil is generally formed from the underlying parent material, as rapidly as the finished product is removed. Under these conditions, the removal of the soil is known as normal erosion.

When, however, the land is for some reason stripped of its protective cover of vegetation, and the soil is exposed to the full force of the elements, erosion is likely to become extremely rapid, and soil which has taken centuries to develop may be largely removed within the space of a very few years. Under these conditions, the removal of the soil is better referred to as accelerated soil erosion.

There are two main forms of accelerated soil erosion:

1 that which results from the action of running water;
2 that which is caused by wind.

In many parts of the tropical world the rainfall tends to be torrential in nature, and erosion by running water is widespread. Erosion by wind, on the other hand, is generally less common.

Water erosion
Accelerated soil erosion by running water may take the form of either sheet erosion or gully erosion. At first the principal loss is by sheet erosion. This occurs when water runs off all or most of the ground surface, carrying with it a very thin film of topsoil from a wide area of land. The effects of sheet erosion are gradual rather than sudden, and are generally not noticed as easily as those of gully erosion.

Gully erosion generally occurs on steeper slopes, and tends to be a more localised and spectacular form of erosion. It results from run-off water becoming channelled into well-defined depressions, which are rapidly deepened to form gullies. Gully erosion is generally most serious in areas where the rainfall is heavy, and where steep slopes occur.

Wind erosion
Erosion by wind is of particular importance in arid areas, and also in areas which experience a very marked dry season. Where the plant cover has been removed, and the dry soil is exposed to strong winds, the lighter particles of the soil may be picked up and carried away.

The causes of soil erosion
Man is largely responsible for the removal of the soil's protective cover of vegetation, and accelerated soil erosion is to a large extent the result of his misuse of the land.

One of the most common causes of soil erosion is the cultivation of steeply sloping land, without the use of adequate measures to check the rapid run-off of surface water. In several of the West Indian islands such as Haiti and Jamaica, the pressure of population on limited land resources has led peasant farmers to clear the forest from steeply sloping hillsides, and to attempt to grow crops on them. Heavy rainfall on the exposed slopes often results in much of the valuable topsoil being washed down into the valleys below.

In many parts of the tropical world poor agricultural practices have led to soil erosion. In parts of tropical Africa where bush fallowing is practised, the rapid growth of population in recent times has necessitated a drastic reduction in the length of the fallow period. This has often led to a deterioration in the texture of the soil, making it more susceptible to both sheet and gully erosion. In some areas monoculture (the practice of growing the same kind of crop on a piece of land year after year) has resulted in the impoverishment of the soil, thus making it more susceptible to erosion. Certain types of crop offer better protection against erosion than do others. Crops which are grown in rows, such as cotton and tobacco, generally offer very little protection against erosion, as the soil between the rows is exposed, especially when the plants are young. In the past it was common practice to weed between the rows of trees on plantations of crops such as rubber and oil palm, but it is now generally felt that it is better to maintain a protective cover of low crops. On rubber plantations in Malaysia, for example, special cover crops are now often planted between the rows of trees.

In some of the grassland areas of the tropical world, 'over-stocking' is an important cause of erosion. In the grassland areas of tropical Africa, for example, pastoral peoples often try to keep more livestock than the available pasture can adequately support. In their efforts to obtain food, the animals nibble the grass right down to its roots, thus exposing the topsoil and making it readily available for removal by wind and water. The widespread practice of burning off the old grass at the end of the dry season, also creates conditions which favour erosion. The widespread erosion which occurs in the central highlands of Madagascar, for example, can largely be attributed to the destruction of the natural forests by deliberate burning, and the subsequent overgrazing of the grasslands which have replaced them.

A notable example of the effect of soil erosion is to be found in the Yallahs valley, in the Blue Mountain area of Jamaica. At the time of the creation of the Yallahs Valley Land Authority (YVLA) in 1951, the catchment area of the Yallahs river was largely ruined by soil erosion brought about by over a century of misuse by man, in his efforts to make a living in a difficult physical environment. The terrain in this part of Jamaica comprises deep valleys and very steep hillsides, and the area is subject to torrential rains in May–June and again in September–October. The greater part of the catchment area was once covered with forest, and although soil and rock-slides occurred even before man started to farm the area, they were on a relatively small scale and only followed exceptionally heavy rains or severe earthquake tremors.

The upper part of the Yallahs valley remained almost entirely under forest until the end of the eighteenth century, when the hillsides began to be cleared for the planting of coffee. The coffee planter liked clean cultivation without any weeds or quick-growing crops to compete with the coffee bushes, and on steep slopes this inevitably led to sheet erosion. When the price of coffee dropped, the coffee estates fell into ruin, but after the abolition of slavery in the early part of the nineteenth century, many freed slaves used the hillsides for the cultivation of food crops. These small farmers used fire to clear the land, and also burned patches of the remaining forest to obtain charcoal. Erosion became progressively more severe. The effects of erosion in the higher part of the valley became felt in the lower part of the valley in the form of frequent floods, as the rainwater ran straight off the bare slopes into the rivers. By the middle of the present century the whole of the Yallahs valley had become a distressed area, in which the population grew progressively poorer.

In 1951 the government of Jamaica established the YVLA, and gave it the task of rehabilitating the area. The steepest slopes have been withdrawn from cultivation, and planted with quick-growing trees such as Caribbean Pine, Mahoe, and Eucalyptus. The burning of the land has been prohibited, and on the gentler slopes farmers have been encouraged to use better agricultural practices. In the lower part of the valley the river banks have been protected by the building of bunds.

The effects of soil erosion

The effects of soil erosion are very widespread. The most obvious of these effects is the reduction of crop yields in the eroded areas. The surrounding areas, although not themselves eroded, may also suffer a reduction in productivity, as a result of eroded material being deposited over them. It is usually the coarser and less fertile particles of soil which are deposited on the surrounding areas, while the finer and more fertile particles are transported longer

Soil conservation in the Kigezi District of Uganda. Notice that the cultivated strips follow the contours, and are separated by grass bunds to check surface run-off.

distances.

Soil erosion may also result in a deterioration of water supplies. The soil generally retains part of the rainwater which falls on it, only gradually releasing it to the streams and rivers, and thus helping to regulate the flow of water throughout the year. In areas from which much of the topsoil has been removed, an unusually high proportion of the rainwater runs directly off the valley sides into the streams and rivers. As a result, the rivers which originate in badly eroded areas tend to flood immediately following periods of heavy rain, but during periods of dry weather their flow is abnormally reduced. These marked fluctuations in river level have important repercussions for such people as the hydroelectric engineer, who would prefer a fairly even flow of water throughout the year. Marked fluctuations in water level also limit the usefulness of rivers as a means of transport.

Severe soil erosion may also be responsible for the rapid silting up of reservoirs and harbours. The water storage capacity of reservoirs may be considerably reduced as a result of the deposition of large quantities of silt, brought down by streams and rivers originating in badly eroded areas. The depth of water in harbours which are located at the mouth of rivers may also be greatly reduced by the deposition of silt. In both cases, costly dredging operations may become necessary to remove the silt.

Soil conservation

In the case of soil erosion, prevention is very much easier than cure. Once an area has become badly eroded, the rehabilitation of the land tends to be a long and difficult process. Soil conservation is basically a matter of using the land as it should be used. Important methods of checking soil erosion include afforestation, terracing, contour ploughing, strip-cropping, planned crop rotation, and controlled grazing.

37

Very steeply sloping hillsides should not be brought under cultivation, but if possible they should be kept under forest. Forest provides the most complete protection against soil erosion of any type of vegetation. It is particularly important that eroded water catchment areas should be re-afforested. In some parts of the tropical world, great care is now taken to maintain forest reserves on steep watershed areas. Protection forests are maintained, for example, in many of the more mountainous areas of East Africa. In some of the more mountainous islands of the West Indies also, re-afforestation programmes have been undertaken to protect watershed areas.

Where population pressure makes it necessary to cultivate steep hillsides, the land should be protected by terracing. Terracing checks the flow of water down the slope, and has been used as an anti-erosion measure in several parts of the tropical world for hundreds of years. Where sloping land has not been terraced, it should be ploughed or ridged along the contour, and not up and down the slope. By ploughing along the contour each individual furrow acts as a check to run-off. The use of terracing is very important in some of the more mountainous parts of Southeast Asia, and was also important in the past in the Andean region of Peru. Terracing and contour ploughing are also used as anti-erosion measures in several parts of tropical Africa, including in the mountainous and densely populated territories of Rwanda and Burundi, in the Kigezi District of Southwestern Uganda, in parts of the highland areas of Kenya, and in parts of the island of Madagascar.

Some agricultural crops, especially those which are generally grown in rows, offer practically no protection against soil erosion. Where these kinds of crops are cultivated they should be grown in strips, and should be flanked by strips of other crops such as grass which give good protection against erosion. A suitable rotation of crops should be employed, in order to keep the soil in good condition. Where wind erosion is likely to be a problem, rows of trees should be planted at intervals to act as wind-breaks.

In areas where pastoralism is practised, the numbers of animals should be carefully regulated, in order to avoid overgrazing. Unfortunately the control of livestock numbers is not always easy, as many pastoral peoples are unwilling to dispose of their surplus animals.

Exercises

1 With reference to tropical areas, discuss the main causes and effects of soil erosion.
2 Describe the various measures which can be taken to conserve the soil.

Suggested reading

PETER M. AHN: *West African Soils*

PIERRE GOUROU: *The Tropical World* – Chapter 3

B. W. HODDER: *Economic Development in the Tropics* – pp. 35–43

R. P. MOSS: *The Soil Resources of Tropical Africa*

A. M. O'CONNOR: *An Economic Geography of East Africa* – pp. 236–9

J. M. PRITCHARD: *Africa – A Study Geography for Advanced Students* – Chapter 1

M. F. THOMAS and G. W. WHITTINGTON, Ed.: *Environment and Land Use in Africa* – Chapter 7

C. C. WEBSTER and P. N. WILSON: *Agriculture in the Tropics* – Chapter 5

H. P. WHITE and M. B. GLEAVE: *An Economic Geography of West Africa* – pp. 20–26

CHAPTER FOUR

Population distribution and racial composition

A: General

In studying the population of a country or region, the geographer is particularly concerned with its distribution, composition, growth and movement. He must also examine and attempt to explain the relationship between differences in population on the one hand, and variations in the nature of places on the other.

Types of data

The two main types of population data which are available to the geographer are:

1 national censuses;
2 vital statistics.

The census

The object of the modern population census is to count every person within a given area. During the process of enumeration, not only is the absolute size of the population measured, but a wide variety of information is also gathered about its important characteristics. This information usually includes:

a) physical characteristics, e.g. age, sex and race;
b) social characteristics, e.g. marital status, religion, language, education and housing;
c) economic characteristics, e.g. occupation.

From the census it should therefore be possible to obtain a fairly comprehensive picture of the state of the population at the time at which the census was taken. Unfortunately, both the frequency with which censuses are taken, and the type and accuracy of the information collected, vary considerably from one country to another. Broadly speaking, it is for the less developed countries that the census material is most scanty and least reliable. In the early 1970s some countries such as Ethiopia, the Somali Republic, Laos and South Vietnam had still never undertaken an official census, while considerable inaccuracies are thought to exist in the census material of others. It is thought, for example, that the 1963 census grossly overstated the population of Nigeria. The 1963 Nigerian census showed a total population of more than 55 million, whereas the United Nations Population Division estimated the country's population to be only in the region of 46 million.

Among the difficulties which the governments of the less developed countries experience in census-taking are the high costs involved, the lack of skilled enumerators, and the widespread illiteracy of the population.

Vital statistics

Because census-taking is laborious and expensive, most countries only take a census at infrequent intervals, usually not more than once every 10 years. It is, however, possible to obtain a fairly reliable estimate of the population in non-census years, by making use of vital statistics. The size of the population at any given time can be estimated by adding the number of births and immigrants to, and subtracting the number of deaths and emigrants from, the population enumerated at the last census. This, of course, is providing that continuous and accurate records of births, deaths and migrants have been kept.

Once again, it is in the less developed countries of the world that the registration of births and deaths is usually least complete. For example, virtually nowhere in tropical Africa does a nation-wide system of registration exist. Accurate data on migration is also extremely difficult to obtain, especially where, as in West Africa, many of the migrants do not pass through official check-points when crossing political boundaries.

The density of population

The density of population is simply the ratio between the size of an area of land, and the number of people living there. It is usually expressed as the average number of persons per square kilometre (sq km). In order to find the average density of population of a country, simply divide the total population by the total area. For example, Ghana has a total area of 238 537 sq km and at the 1970 census had a population of 8 559 313. The average density of population at that time was therefore 8 559 313 ÷ 238 537 = approximately 35,9 per sq km.

Fig. 4.1 shows that within the tropics the distribution of population is highly uneven. The most densely populated countries, such as Barbados, Hong Kong and Singapore, support mean densities of well over 500 persons per sq km, while the most sparsely populated ones, such as Niger, Mauritania and Surinam, have well under 5 per sq km. Furthermore, the distribution of population within individual countries is often highly uneven. In Guyana, for example, nearly all the population is concentrated in a narrow coastal strip less than 15 km in width, extending between the Essequibo and the Courantyne rivers. In parts of this coastal strip, rural population densities exceed 400 per sq km, although Guyana as a whole has an average density of less than 4 per sq km.

B: Factors influencing the distribution of population within the tropics

Why are some parts of the tropical world so densely populated, while others have so few inhabitants? There is no simple answer to this question, as a wide variety of factors, both physical and non-physical, influence the distribution of man over the earth's surface. Broadly speaking, man is attracted to those areas where natural and other conditions are most favourable to him making a living, and if possible he avoids those areas where conditions are difficult.

Physical factors

The most important physical factors which influence the distribution of population are:

1 relief;
2 climate;
3 drainage and soils;
4 mineral deposits.

Relief
If you compare Fig. 4.1 with a relief map, you will find that some mountainous areas support high densities of population, while others are virtually uninhabited. Some mountainous areas do in fact seem to attract settlement, while others discourage it.

Fig. 4.1 The tropical lands – distribution of population

Steep slopes are difficult to cultivate, and as a result, steeply sloping areas tend to be more sparsely populated than areas where the slopes are more gentle. In the West Indies, for example, there is often a close relationship between relief and the distribution of population. The island of Barbados, which has a high proportion of gently sloping and easily cultivable land, had an average density of 568 per sq km in 1975. On the other hand, Dominica, which is one of the most mountainous and rugged of the West Indian islands, had an average density of only 75.

It should be noted, however, that although steep slopes are unfavourable to settlement, they do not necessarily prevent it. Man can create flat land in mountainous areas by terracing the hillsides. Terracing has been practised from time immemorial in some of the more mountainous parts of Southeast Asia. It was also practised in the past by the Incas, in the central parts of the Andes Mountains in South America.

As well as exerting a direct influence upon the distribution of population, relief may also influence it indirectly, through climate. In some parts of the tropical world, the reduction of temperature with altitude imposes an upper limit on the cultivation of crops. The height at which cultivation ceases, varies. In Peru, for example, grain crops can be grown at heights of 3 000–4 000 metres, while potatoes can be grown up to about 4 250 metres. Above the upper limit of cultivation, the population tends to be sparse, as agricultural activities are limited to the rearing of livestock.

Below the upper limit of cultivation, however, upland areas within the tropics often attract settlement. In such areas, temperatures are pleasantly cooler than in the surrounding lowlands, and the rainfall is often more abundant and more reliable. Furthermore, highland areas within the tropics are often healthier than the lowlands. On the mainland of Central America, the hot coastal lowlands are for the most part fairly sparsely populated, much of the population being concentrated in inter-mont basins in the highlands. Similarly in the Andean states of tropical South America, the population is densest in the Sierra (the highland area), while the coastal lowlands and the lowlands of the Amazon Basin are generally much more sparsely peopled. In Bolivia,

for example, about three-quarters of the total population lives at heights of more than 3 000 metres. It is interesting to note that with the exception of Lima, the capital cities of all the inter-tropical Andean states are situated at a considerable altitude, ranging from about 1 000 metres in the case of Caracas, to about 3 600 metres in the case of La Paz.

Climate

Now compare Fig. 4.1 with Fig. 1.2, which shows the distribution of rainfall within the tropics. This comparison will reveal that most of the arid parts of the tropical world are extremely sparsely populated. Over large parts of the Sahara, Namib, Kalahari, Arabian and Australian deserts, the average density of population is less than 1 per sq km. Man needs water, not only for himself and for his animals to drink, but also for the cultivation of crops. Consequently, he finds it difficult to make a living in arid areas. In West Africa, for example, permanent cultivation without the use of irrigation, is largely confined to areas which have a mean annual rainfall of at least 300 mm. In those parts of West Africa which have appreciably less than this amount, agricultural activities are restricted to nomadic pastoralism, and the population is generally sparse.

Although deserts are usually sparsely populated, some pockets of high population density do occur in areas where water is available for irrigation. Widely scattered throughout the Sahara and Arabian deserts, for example, there are cultivated areas which depend for their existence upon water from underground sources. Of more importance than this type of oasis, however, are the ones which occur in the valleys of such rivers as succeed in flowing through the desert. The best known of these valleys is that of the river Nile, only part of whose course lies within the tropics. In northern Sudan, parts of the Nile valley support rural population densities of more than 200 per sq km, although the surrounding desert is only sparsely populated by nomadic pastoralists. In the arid coastal region of Peru, settlement is largely concentrated in the valleys of the rivers which flow down from the Andes Mountains into the Pacific Ocean. There are some forty distinct oases along the coast of Peru.

A comparison of Fig. 4.1 with the rainfall map will also reveal that many of the very wet parts of the tropical world, such as the Amazon Basin, the Zaire Basin, and the islands of Borneo and New Guinea, are also sparsely populated. These hot, wet lands tend to be hostile to man for several reasons. They support dense rain forests which are difficult to clear, and their soils tend to lose their fertility quickly once they are brought under cultivation. Furthermore, the hot, wet lands are generally unhealthy, man in these areas being subject to a wide variety of diseases. In tropical Africa, for example, major human diseases include malaria, yellow fever, sleeping sickness, bilharzia and numerous intestinal disorders.

While it is true that many of the hot, wet lands of the tropical world are sparsely populated, some of those in Asia support unusually high population densities. Notable examples include the islands of Java and Bali, the deltas of the Red river and the Menam river, and the valley and delta of the Ganga (Ganges) river. In the delta of the Red river in North Vietnam, rural population densities exceed 500 per sq km, although the surrounding uplands frequently have less than 10 per sq km. There are also a few pockets of unusually high population density in the hot, wet lands of tropical Africa. In some of the Ibo and Ibibio districts of south-eastern Nigeria, for example, population densities of well over 500 per sq km occur. This is in marked contrast to the Zaire Basin, large parts of which have less than 5 per sq km.

Drainage and soils

The population pattern may also be influenced by the drainage, and by the nature of the soil. Badly drained areas are of limited use for agriculture, and are generally sparsely peopled. In the East Coast swamp of Sumatra, for example, there are large areas which have less than 10 inhabitants per sq km. A large part of the Niger Delta in Nigeria is covered with mangrove swamp, or fresh-water swamp forest, and is also sparsely peopled. In areas where man has reclaimed swamp land, however, very high population densities are sometimes found.

Broadly speaking, the more fertile a soil is, the more food it is capable of producing, and hence the greater the number of people it can support. Some of the highest densities of rural population within the tropics are associated with rich alluvial soils, such as those of the valley of the Ganga river; others are

associated with fertile soils derived from volcanic material, such as those which occur over a large part of the island of Java, and in the highlands of Rwanda and Burundi. There are, however, some notable exceptions to this correlation between soil fertility and high population density. In southeastern Nigeria, for example, some very high population densities occur in areas of infertile sandy soils.

Mineral deposits

The presence of useful minerals may also exert an influence upon the distribution of population. The development of mining has been responsible for the growth of several important concentrations of population in tropical Africa, notably those of the Zambian Copperbelt, and Shaba Province (formerly Katanga Province) of Zaïre. Before the development of copper mining, the Zambian Copperbelt was very thinly populated. It has been estimated that in 1931 there were less than 20 thousand Africans living in the area, compared with some 300 thousand in 1961. In the Malay Peninsula the presence of large and easily accessible deposits of tin ore along the western flanks of the Main Range, was originally responsible for attracting large numbers of people to that area.

In some cases mineral deposits have attracted man to areas which would otherwise have been unsuitable for human habitation. Some mining settlements are located at very high altitude. In Peru, for example, the important mining centre of Cerro de Pasco is situated at a height of about 4 500 metres. Other mining settlements, such as the copper mining centre of Chuquicamata in northern Chile, have developed in very arid areas.

Non-physical factors

Although physical factors play a very important role in attracting or discouraging settlement, the distribution of population over the earth's surface cannot be fully understood by reference to the physical environment alone, as man himself has greatly helped to change its pattern. Man has succeeded in increasing the habitability of some areas through the control of disease. In countries such as Sri Lanka and Mauritius, for example, vigorous campaigns against malaria have brought about a sharp decline in the death rate, thus enabling the population to grow much more rapidly than it would otherwise have done. Man has also reduced the habitability of other areas. This is particularly the case where poor agricultural practices have brought about severe soil erosion. Some areas have also been rendered uninhabitable because of flooding. The building of the Akosombo Dam across the Volta river in Ghana, for example, resulted in the formation of Lake Volta, with a surface area of almost 8 500 sq km. Because of the formation of Lake Volta, 78 thousand people had to be evacuated, and re-settled elsewhere.

The importance of history

In many parts of the tropical world, the present population pattern cannot be fully understood unless reference is made to the past. In some areas population densities are lower than they would otherwise have been, because of the effects of wars in the past. The compulsory transfers of population which in some instances have followed wars, have served to increase the population of some areas, while reducing that of others. The relatively low population densities which occur today in several parts of tropical Africa, can be at least partly attributed to the depopulation caused by slave raiding in the past.

In the past, people were sometimes attracted to remote mountainous areas by the fact that such areas provided more easily defendable settlement sites than did the surrounding lowlands. For this reason, weak people often sought refuge from the attacks of their stronger neighbours in rugged hill country. In tropical Africa there are numerous examples of hill settlements which owe their origin to the need for defence, including those of the Nuba Mountains in the Sudan, the Bandiagara escarpment in Mali, and the Mandara Massif in Cameroon.

The development of agricultural settlements in the Nuba Mountains of central Sudan began when mounted Arab nomads invaded the grasslands of the basin of the Upper Nile during the sixteenth century. Some of the indigenous Negroid peoples of these grasslands intermixed with the Arab invaders, and adopted their language and religion. Others, however, sought refuge in the more inaccessible parts of the Nuba Mountains, and were able to preserve their native culture. By necessity, the people of the Nuba Mountains developed a fairly intensive system of agriculture, using such techniques as terracing, crop rotation and manuring, in order to maintain the fertility of the soil. During the present century, with the establishment of more peaceful conditions, the people of the Nuba Mountains have started to move down from their hill villages, and to settle in the surrounding plains. This down hill movement of population in response to the establishment of more peaceful conditions, has also been very evident in several other parts of tropical Africa.

Economic development

In rural areas, the density of population which can be supported depends not only upon the nature of the physical environment itself, but also upon the way in which man uses the land. The more intensively the land is used, the more food it can be made to produce, and the greater the number of people it can support. In some parts of the tropical world primitive communities still depend for their livelihood upon the gathering of wild products. Where food gathering is the dominant way of life, population densities of less than 1 per sq km are commonly found. Although nomadic pastoralism represents a significant advance over gathering as a food producing system, in pastoral areas population densities are usually under 5 per sq km. In areas where primitive forms of cultivation are practised, substantially higher population densities can be supported. The highest densities of rural population found within the tropics, are usually associated with the cultivation of swamp rice. In those parts of tropical Asia where abundant irrigation water is available, the land is usually kept continuously under cultivation, and two or even three crops are produced each year. Under such favourable circumstances, rural population densities of well over 400 per sq km are not uncommon.

The population pattern may also be influenced by the development of manufacturing industry. A good example of how the establishment of industry may attract population is provided by the islands of the Dutch West Indies. In the island of Bonaire, low rainfall restricts agriculture, and as a result the density of population is fairly low (29 per sq km in 1974); and yet very high population densities occur in the neighbouring islands of Aruba (320) and Curacao (349), where physical conditions are very

43

similar to those in Bonaire. The high densities which occur in Aruba and Curacao can largely be attributed to the establishment in those islands of oil refineries, which process petroleum imported from Venezuela. The employment opportunities which were created as a result of the establishment of the refineries, attracted large numbers of immigrants from other West Indian islands, and brought about rapid population growth.

Population and resources

Although some parts of the tropical world support high population densities, while others are sparsely peopled, it would not necessarily be correct to assume that the former areas have too many inhabitants and the latter too few. The density of population which a country or area can support at a given standard of living, obviously depends to a considerable extent upon the natural resources which it possesses. Thus, a country or area with fertile soils, a favourable climate, and rich mineral deposits, is capable of supporting a higher density of population than one which is less fortunate in these respects.

In theory, every country has an optimum population. This is the size of population which is considered to be the most desirable for the full utilisation of its natural resources, and which produces the highest standard of living. Countries or areas where the population is too small for the full utilisation of the natural resources, or where a higher population could be supported without any fall in living standards, are said to be underpopulated. On the other hand, if a country or area has a higher population than its natural resources can reasonably support, then it is said to be overpopulated. Overpopulation implies that there are too many people for economic efficiency. It also implies that if the population had not grown so large, a higher standard of living would have been possible.

In several parts of the tropical world, overpopulation has become a serious problem. It is particularly severe in some of the West Indian islands such as Barbados, and also in parts of South Asia and Southeast Asia. Although the economy of Barbados still depends to quite a considerable extent upon agriculture, the island supports an average population density of well over 500 per sq km. Virtually all the cultivable land in Barbados is already under cultivation, and the island's mineral resources are negligible. The problem of unemployment is very severe in Barbados, about 13 per cent of the island's population being unemployed in 1970. If it had not been for the fact that during the last hundred years, many thousands of Barbadians have left their homeland to seek a living elsewhere, the island's population problem would have been even more severe than is at present the case. Although in the past emigration has played an important role in helping to relieve population pressure in several parts of the tropical world, it seems likely that it will be of much less importance in the future, as few countries are now willing to accept the surplus population of others.

It should be noted that the terms overpopulation and underpopulation are relative. For example, an average density of 50 per sq km might constitute severe overpopulation in a country or area which has limited natural resources, and yet another country or area with the same density but richer resources, might be underpopulated. Furthermore, the number of people a country or area can support at a given standard of living, depends not only upon the natural resources which it possesses, but also upon the extent to which man has developed those resources. It is therefore not constant, but is capable of expansion. Many tropical countries could make fuller use of their natural resources than they are at present doing, thus enabling them to support a larger population, or to provide a better standard of living for the existing population.

C: The distribution of population in selected areas

West Africa

There is no simple explanation for the distribution of population in West Africa; a wide variety of factors, both physical and non-physical, having influenced its present pattern. Because so many West Africans depend upon agriculture for their livelihood, the

Fig. 4.2 West Africa – distribution of population

population pattern is related in a broad way to the physical environment, and in particular to the amount and seasonal distribution of the rainfall. There are, however, numerous variations in population density which cannot be related to differences in the physical environment, and whose explanation must be sought in history. In particular, the existence of pockets of low population density in areas where physical conditions are highly favourable to settlement, can often be attributed to the depopulation caused by tribal warfare and slave raiding in the past.

Broadly speaking, it is possible to distinguish two main east–west zones of relatively high population density in West Africa; a northern or Sudanic zone, and a southern or Guinean zone. Neither zone is continuous, however, each consisting of several nuclei of high population density, separated from each other by more sparsely peopled areas. Many of the densely populated nuclei correspond with the most favoured portions of the areas occupied by distinct communities, such as those of the Hausa and the Mossi in the north, and the Igbo and the Yoruba in the south. The more sparsely peopled areas in these zones, on the other hand, often correspond with the frontiers between communities, it being common practice in the past to leave a 'no-man's land' of thinly populated forest or bush between neighbouring tribes.

The Guinean zone

The more densely populated of the two zones is that which extends along the coast, from Sierra Leone to eastern Nigeria, and which corresponds roughly with the zone of high forest. Within this southern zone, population densities tend to be much lower in the west than in the east, large parts of Liberia and the southwestern Ivory Coast in particular being relatively thinly populated. Much of the southern zone has population densities of between 20 and 75 per sq km, although appreciably higher densities do occur in some areas. Large parts of Igboland and the cocoa growing areas of Yorubaland, for example, support population densities of over 150 per sq km. A number of factors help to account for the relatively high population densities which occur over much of the southern zone:

1 In most parts of the zone the rainfall is abundant and fairly well distributed over the year, thus making possible the cultivation of heavy-yielding root crops such as yams, and also the double-cropping of quick-growing plants such as maize and vegetables.

45

2 The rainfall conditions are also highly favourable for the cultivation of such important export crops as cocoa, coffee, oil palm and rubber.

3 The occurrence of several important mineral deposits and their exploitation during recent times, has attracted migrants from other parts of West Africa, and has resulted in the development of several minor concentrations of population.

4 The existence in early times of strong states such as those of Ashanti, Abomey, Porto Novo, Yorubaland and Benin, created politically stable conditions which favoured economic development and population growth.

5 During the modern period a longer and closer contact with the outside world has stimulated the production of crops and minerals for export, thus helping to make this zone attractive to settlement.

The Sudanic zone

The other relatively densely populated zone extends across the Sudan savanna, from the coastlands of Senegal and Gambia to northern Nigeria. Over a large part of this northern zone, population densities are generally between 10 and 20 per sq km. Appreciably higher densities do occur in some areas, however, particularly around Kano, Katsina and Sokoto in northern Nigeria, around Ouagadougou in Upper Volta, in the north-east of Ghana, and in the groundnut growing areas of Senegal and Gambia. On the intensively farmed lands around Kano, for example, rural population densities exceed 150 per sq km. As in the Guinean zone, a number of factors help to account for the relatively high population densities which occur over much of the Sudanic zone:

1 Although the Sudanic zone has a relatively short rainy season, climatic conditions are highly favourable for the cultivation of such subsistence crops as millet, sorghum and groundnuts, and also for such export crops as cotton and groundnuts.

2 In some parts of the Sudanic zone the water table is unusually shallow, which means that water can easily be obtained by digging wells.

3 Some relatively good soils are available, such as the easily worked drift soils of the Kano area.

4 The fact that cattle rearing is possible in the Sudanic zone, means that some animal manure is available for the soil.

5 The creation during the eighth to sixteenth centuries of a series of extensive and powerful states provided stable conditions, favouring economic development and population growth. Notable examples of such states included the Mossi kingdom, and the Hausa states of Kano, Katsina and Zaria.

The Middle Belt

It is also possible to distinguish two less densely populated zones in West Africa. In between the Sudanic and the Guinean zones, and corresponding roughly with the Guinea savanna, is the sparsely peopled Middle Belt. Over large parts of this zone, population densities of less than 10 per sq km are found.

Physically, the Middle Belt seems to have many of the handicaps of both the Guinean and the Sudanic zones, and few of the advantages of either. The rainy season is generally too short to permit double cropping, and also for the cultivation of most perennial tree crops. At the same time, the prevalence of the tsetse fly discourages cattle rearing.

In spite of these handicaps, however, there are some pockets of relatively high population density within the Middle Belt, notable examples being the area occupied by the Tiv people of Nigeria, and the area around Bouake in the central part of the Ivory Coast. It seems therefore, that the basic explanation for the existence of low population densities over much of the Middle Belt must be sought in history. This part of West Africa suffered very severely from slave raiding in the past, with raiders coming both from the north and from the south. A notable example of an area which has been depopulated in the past is the western part of Kwara State in Nigeria, which was raided by the Fulani during the nineteenth century, and large parts of which today have less than 5 inhabitants per sq km.

It has been suggested that the partial depopulation of the Middle Belt by slave raiding, would cause farm land to be abandoned and to revert to bush. This in turn would result in an increase in the prevalence of the tsetse fly, thus making the area less attractive to settlement. Observations in Nigeria seem to confirm the view that a certain minimum human population is required to control the tsetse fly and to make habitation possible.

The Sahelian zone

To the north of the Sudanic zone is the sparsely populated Sahel. In the Sahelian zone, population densities are generally well below 10 per sq km. The main factor limiting settlement in this zone is the low and unreliable rainfall, which restricts the cultivation of crops. Within the Sahelian zone, notable exceptions of relatively high population density are associated with the valley of the Senegal river, and with the middle course and inland delta of the Niger, where water is available for irrigation.

East Africa

Because so many of the people of East Africa depend upon agriculture for their livelihood, the population tends to be heavily concentrated on the better lands, while there are vast areas of low agricultural potential which are very sparsely populated. Of particular importance in influencing the population pattern in East Africa, is the amount and reliability of the rainfall. The highest rural population densities mainly correspond with the areas which receive a mean annual rainfall of at least 750 mm, as it is in these areas that intensive arable farming is possible.

Fig. 4.3 East Africa – distribution of population

Other physical factors which influence the population pattern in East Africa include the distribution of

Table 17 Population numbers and densities in West Africa, 1975

Country	Area (thousand sq km)	Estimated population (in thousands)	Density (per sq km)
Benin	113	3 112	28
Gambia	11	524	46
Ghana	239	9 866	41
Guinea	246	4 416	18
Guinea Bissau	36	525	15
Ivory Coast	322	4 885	15
Liberia	111	1 708	15
Mali	1 240	5 697	5
Mauritania	1 031	1 318	1
Niger	1 267	4 600	4
Nigeria	924	62 925	68
Senegal	196	4 136	21
Sierra Leone	72	2 750	38
Togo	56	2 222	40
Upper Volta	274	6 032	22

47

tsetse fly, the nature of the soil, and the reduction of temperature with altitude.

Broadly speaking, there are three major concentrations of population in East Africa:

1 On the lands bordering Lake Victoria, which for the most part have an abundant and fairly reliable rainfall. Climatic conditions around the lake are suitable for the cultivation of a wide variety of subsistence crops, and also for such export crops as robusta coffee and cotton.
2 In the highland areas, at heights of up to about 2 500 metres. These areas generally have an abundant rainfall, and temperature conditions there favour the cultivation of such labour intensive export crops as arabica coffee, tea and pyrethrum. The highland areas also have a lower incidence of several tropical diseases and tsetse fly, than do the surrounding lowlands. In the highland areas, some rich volcanic soils occur, particularly on the slopes of Mounts Kenya, Kilimanjaro, Meru and Elgon.
3 In a narrow strip along the coast, and on the islands of Zanzibar and Pemba. The coastal area, except for the extreme northern section in Kenya, is also favoured by having adequate rainfall. Climatic conditions along the coast are suitable for the cultivation of sisal, coconuts and cashew nuts, while on the islands of Zanzibar and Pemba the rainfall is adequate for the cultivation of cloves. The coastal area also contains East Africa's main commercial gateways, of particular importance being the ports of Mombasa and Dar-es-Salaam. In recent years, the development of the tourist industry has created additional employment opportunities in the coastal area.

The most sparsely populated parts of East Africa mainly correspond with the areas of low and unreliable rainfall. Large parts of northern Kenya have a mean annual rainfall of less than 500 mm, and are sparsely populated by such pastoral peoples as the Turkana, Boran, Samburu and Somali. Also thinly peopled are large parts of the low eastern plateau region in both Kenya and Tanzania, which have a low and unreliable rainfall. Much of this low eastern plateau region is inhabited by the pastoral Masai, while large areas have been set aside as game reserves. Also sparsely populated are the higher parts of Mounts Kenya, Kilimanjaro, Meru, Elgon, Ruwen-

zori, and the Aberdare Range. In East Africa there is generally very little cultivation above about 2 500 metres.

Kenya

In 1975 Kenya had a mean density of population of 23 per sq km, but this average figure disguises very wide variations. Only about one sixth of Kenya has favourable precipitation, and this portion supports about 88 per cent of the total population. At the other extreme, about 76 per cent of the area has only 8 per cent of the population. The highest population densities are found around the shores of Lake Victoria. Both Nyanza Province and Western Province support mean densities of more than 150 per sq km, while in the Kisii Highlands and in the southern part of the Kakamega District rural densities of over 400 per sq km occur. A second well developed cluster of population is found in the highlands to the east of the Rift Valley, extending northwards from the capital city of Nairobi, over the lower slopes of the Aberdare Range and Mount Kenya. Large parts of this highland area support densities of more than 100 per sq km, while in parts of the Kiambu, Muranga and Nyeri Districts there are rural population densities of over 400 per sq km. A third but less important concentration of population extends along the coast of Kenya, from Malindi southwards to the Tanzanian border.

Tanzania

Tanzania, with a mean density of only 16 per sq km in 1975, is the least densely populated of the East African states. As in Kenya, however, the population pattern in Tanzania is a highly uneven one. The islands of Zanzibar and Pemba are much more densely peopled than the mainland of Tanganyika, with a mean density of 171 per sq km. In both islands, precipitation is high and fairly reliable, averaging about 1 500 mm per annum in Zanzibar and over 1 750 mm in Pemba. Climatic conditions are highly favourable for the cultivation of coconuts and cloves. In Zanzibar, the bulk of the population lives on the western side of the island, which has the most favourable soils.

On the mainland of Tanganyika, the mean density of population was only 15 in 1975, but marked concentrations of people occur in some areas. Around the shores of Lake Victoria, densities exceed 40 per sq km over a large area. Along the coast there are concentrations of population in the Tanga area, around Dar-es-Salaam, and in the south around Lindi and Mtwara. Other concentrations of population are associated with the highland areas. In the area around Moshi and Arusha, particularly high densities occur on the lower slopes of Mounts Kilimanjaro and Meru. Parts of the Usumbara Mountains are also densely peopled. To the south of Morogoro, the Uluguru Mountains have densities exceeding 150 per sq km. The highland area to the north of Lake Malawi is also relatively densely populated.

Uganda

Uganda is by far the most densely populated of the East African states, having a mean density of 49 per sq km in 1975. Furthermore, the population is much more evenly distributed than in either Kenya or Tanzania. This greater evenness in the population pattern reflects the fact that only a small part of Uganda has a mean annual rainfall of less than 750 mm. Buganda Region is the most densely populated of the four regions, with a mean density of 52 per sq km, while Northern Region is the most sparsely populated, with 32 per sq km.

The highest rural population densities in Uganda are found around the shores of Lake Victoria, on the lower slopes of Mount Elgon, in the highlands of Kigezi District, and in parts of West Nile District. The lands bordering Lake Victoria have abundant rainfall and some fertile loam soils, and in the area between Kampala and Jinja there are rural population densities of over 200 per sq km. In the Bugisu District of the Eastern Region, where the rainfall is abundant and where there are good volcanic soils on the lower slopes of Mount Elgon, the mean density

exceeds 150 per sq km. In Kigezi District in the extreme south-west of Uganda, the rainfall is abundant and the soils are generally fertile, and this hilly area supports densities of over 100 per sq km, by means of intensive farming involving the terracing of unusually steep slopes.

The most sparsely populated part of Uganda is Karamoja District in the extreme north-east, with an average of about 10 per sq km. This area is a continuation of the dry zone of northern Kenya, and is inhabited by the pastoral Karamojong.

Indonesia

In 1971 Indonesia had a total population of 119 million, and ranked fifth in the world in terms of population size, after China, India, the USSR and the USA. The mean density of population in 1971 was 59 per sq km. This average figure, however, is not very meaningful, as there are wide variations in density, not only between the different islands, but also between different parts of the same island. Although Java and the adjoining island of Madura comprise only 7 per cent of the land area of Indonesia, they support about 66 per cent of the total population. At the other end of the scale, West Irian (the Indonesian portion of the island of New Guinea) has 22 per cent of the land area and less than 1 per cent of the population, and Kalimantan (the Indonesian portion of Borneo) supports 4 per cent of the population on 28 per cent of the land area.

Java

Java and the adjoining island of Madura, with a mean density of 565 per sq km in 1971, constitute one of the most densely peopled parts of the world. The

Table 18 Population numbers and densities in East Africa, 1975

Country	Area (thousand sq km)	Estimated population (in thousands)	Density (per sq km)
Kenya	583	13 399	23
Tanzania	945	15 312	16
a) Tanganyika	943	14 734	15
b) Zanzibar Pemba	2	421	171
Uganda	236	11 549	49

Table 19 The population of Indonesia, 1971

Island or island group	Area (thousand sq km)	Population (in thousands)	Density (per sq km)
Java and Madura	135	76 103	565
Sumatra	541	20 813	38
Kalimantan	551	5 152	9
Sulawesi	228	8 535	37
Bali	5	2 120	424
Musa Tengarra	67	4 559	68
Moluccas	75	995	13
West Irian	422	955	2
Total	2 024	119 232	59

reasons for this exceptionally high density are complicated, with no single reason being significant on its own. Physical conditions are generally highly favourable to settlement. Most parts of Java have high temperatures throughout the year and an abundant rainfall; there are extensive lowlands which are suitable for the cultivation of rice; and large parts of the island are covered with highly fertile soils derived from volcanic materials. The narrowness of Java, and the absence of any marked relief barrier, result in its being much more easily penetrable than some of the other Indonesian islands such as Sumatra, Borneo and New Guinea. Furthermore, under Dutch rule Java enjoyed a very long period of political stability, and long association with western methods has led to a remarkable intensity of both subsistence and cash cropping.

Not all parts of Java are equally densely peopled. The highest rural population densities show a close correlation with soils which have been derived from neutral or basic volcanic materials, while the more acidic soils tend to be more sparsely peopled. Very high rural population densities, in some places well over 1 000 per sq km, are found in the south central plains, in the northern plains between Semarang and Tjirebon, around Djakarta, and in the Bantas river valley to the south of Surabaja. The rugged mountain country of the south-eastern corner of Java, and the limestone ridges of the east, are relatively thinly populated, with mean densities of less than 150 per sq km.

Bali and Lombok

In spite of having rugged interior highlands and a dry western section, the island of Bali supports a mean density of well over 400 per sq km. Much of Bali receives abundant rainfall, and has very fertile soils. Most of the population of Bali is located in the southern section of the island, on an alluvial plain whose fertility is constantly being replenished by water-borne volcanic ash. In parts of this plain, rural population densities exceed 750 per sq km. The Balinese have improved upon nature, by the construction of a complex system of irrigated terraces. The Balinese irrigation system has been in existence for hundreds of years. The neighbouring island of Lombok is also very densely populated, although the proportion of land under cultivation is lower than in Bali. The islands to the east of Lombok are generally much more sparsely peopled.

Sumatra

Although Sumatra is four times the size of Java, it has only about one-quarter the number of inhabitants. In 1971 Sumatra had a mean density of 38 per sq km. The highest densities occur around Medan in North Sumatra. In this area plantation agriculture is well developed, and rural population densities exceed 150 per sq km. Densities of more than 75 per sq km occur in the Padang Highlands, in the north coast lowlands of Artjeh, and in the upland area between Medan and Lake Toba. The broad coastal plain on the eastern side of Sumatra, on the other hand, is largely covered with dense rain forest or swamp, and supports densities of less than 10 per sq km.

The other islands

Sulawesi (the Celebes) had an average density of 37 per sq km in 1971. Most of the island is very sparsely peopled, however, the bulk of the population living in the Makassar District in the south, and in the Menado District in the north-east. The Makassar District has fertile volcanic soils permitting intensive agriculture, and has densities of over 100 per sq km. Kalimantan supports an average of only 9 inhabitants per sq km. Large parts of Kalimantan are virtually uninhabited, most of the population being concentrated near to the coast in the west and the southeast West Irian has an average of 2 inhabitants per sq km. The distribution of population is very uneven, however, large areas being virtually uninhabited. The main concentrations of population in West Irian are found on the islands in Geelvink Bay, and in some of the valleys in the central highlands.

Central America

Central America is on the whole fairly thinly peopled. The population pattern is, however, a highly uneven one. Most of the people of Central America live in the valleys and on the slopes of the chain of volcanic mountains which run roughly parallel to the Pacific coast. In this highland region, the soils are generally very productive, and climatic conditions are highly suited to the cultivation of the region's chief cash crop, coffee. The least densely populated part of Central America, on the other hand, is the

lowland area bordering the Caribbean Sea. The Caribbean lowlands are for the most part densely forested, and tend to be less healthy than the highlands.

Guatemala has the largest population of any country in Central America, and the second highest mean density. Only the southern third of Guatemala is densely populated. In the basins of the highlands bordering the Pacific coast, rural population densities of over 100 per sq km are often found. The lowest densities, on the other hand, occur in the northern part of Guatemala, where the vast forest-covered lowland known as Petén supports an average of less than one inhabitant per sq km. The relative emptiness of Petén dates from the abandonment of the area by the highly civilised Mayan Indians more than a thousand years ago.

Although El Salvador is the smallest of the states of Central America, it is by far the most densely peopled, supporting an average of 190 inhabitants per sq km in 1975. The backbone of El Salvador, is the volcanic highland area which continues southward from Guatemala. Within this highland area there are numerous small basins. The soil in these basins is highly fertile, and is intensively cultivated. The pressure of population on land resources has, however, led to much soil erosion. In the last few decades large numbers of Salvadorans have crossed into the much more sparsely populated neighbouring country of Honduras, where many of them have squatted on unoccupied government lands. It is estimated that in 1969 there were some 300 000 Salvadorans living in Honduras. As the number of Salvadoran immigrants grew larger, their presence became increasingly resented by the Hondurans, and

Table 20 Population numbers and densities in Central America, 1975

Country	Area (thousand sq km)	Estimated population (in thousands)	Density (per sq km)
Belize	23	140	6
Costa Rica	51	1 968	39
El Salvador	21	4 007	190
Guatemala	109	5 540	51
Honduras	112	3 037	27
Nicaragua	130	2 155	17
Panama	76	1 668	22

this resentment was one of the major causes of the brief war which broke out between Honduras and El Salvador in 1969.

Honduras, although almost six times the size of El Salvador, has a much smaller population. Most of the people of Honduras live in the southern and central uplands, particularly around Comayagua and the capital city of Tegucigalpa. The Caribbean lowlands in the past were generally sparsely peopled. During the present century, however, the development of American-owned banana plantations along the Caribbean coast has led to a remarkable growth of population in this area.

Belize (formerly British Honduras) is by far the most sparsely populated of the states of Central America, with a mean density of 6 per sq km. The bulk of the population of Belize is concentrated in a number of settlements along the coast. The interior of the country is for the most part densely forested, and is very little developed. The chief port and former capital, Belize City, contains about one-third of the country's total population.

In contrast to most of the Central American states, the bulk of the population of Nicaragua is concentrated in the lowlands. The most densely populated part of Nicaragua is that section of the Nicaraguan Lowland which lies between the Pacific coast and the shores of Lakes Managua and Nicaragua. In parts of the Nicaraguan Lowland densities exceed 60 per sq km, while around Masaya rural population densities of over 150 per sq km occur. The lowlands bordering the Caribbean Sea are generally very sparsely inhabited.

In Costa Rica, well over half of the total population is concentrated in the Meseta Central. The basin in which the capital city San José is situated, contains some of the most densely populated rural areas in Central America, supporting densities of between 100 and 600 per sq km. In the Meseta Central, soils and climatic conditions are ideal for the cultivation of coffee. The lowlands of the Caribbean and Pacific coasts are much more thinly populated than the highlands.

The bulk of the inhabitants of Panama live in the lands bordering the Panama Canal, particularly in the city of Panama on the Pacific side of the isthmus, and in Colon on the Caribbean side. Many of the rest occupy the Pacific lowlands to the west of the canal.

The Caribbean coast of Panama is generally sparsely populated, as is the province of Darien to the east of the canal.

D: Racial composition

Anthropologists generally agree that all living men belong to a single physical species, Homo sapiens. Considerable physical differences do exist, however, particularly in body size, skin colour, texture of hair, and shape of nose and mouth. The term race is used to imply groups of mankind which have well developed physical differences from other groups.

Although anthropologists frequently disagree about the exact classification of mankind, three great human stocks are commonly distinguished:

1 The *Caucasoid* – this group includes not only the white Europeans and people of European descent in other parts of the world, but also the Arab peoples and most of the inhabitants of the Indian sub-continent.
2 The *Mongoloid* – this group is found mainly in central and east Asia, but the American Indians are also usually considered to belong to it.
3 The *Negroid* – this group is largely confined to that part of Africa which lies to the south of the Sahara Desert, but groups of Negroes are also found in several other parts of the world, largely as a result of the slave trade.

Tropical America

Before the time of Christopher Colombus, tropical America was occupied entirely by various groups of American Indians. These groups differed tremendously in the level of development which they had achieved. Since the time of Colombus, large numbers of people from Europe, Africa and Asia have settled in tropical America, with the result that the present population is composed of several racial elements. The relative importance of each of these elements varies considerably from one country to another, as does the extent to which they have inter-mixed.

The West Indies

The early inhabitants of the West Indian islands, the Arawak Indians and Carib Indians, have contributed little to the present population of the West Indies. Except possibly in the island of Aruba, any trace of Arawak blood in the present West Indian population must be very slight indeed. A few people claiming Carib descent are still to be found in some of the islands such as St. Vincent and Dominica, although it is probable that very few are of pure blood.

Numerically the most important elements in the present population of the West Indies are people of African and European origin, with people of Asiatic origin forming small but important minorities in several territories. The relative importance of each of these racial stocks varies considerably from one territory to another, as does the extent to which inter-mixing has taken place.

The largest numbers of people of pure European origin are to be found in the Spanish-speaking territories, particularly in Cuba and in Puerto Rico. Of the English-speaking territories, only in the Cayman Islands do Europeans form a sizeable element in the popultion. In most of the other West Indian territories, the people are predominantly of African origin. In the Dominican Republic there is a predominance of Mulattoes (people of mixed African and European origin). Mulattoes also form a sizeable element in the population of several other territories.

Table 21 The population of selected West Indian territories, by racial origin

Territory	Percentage of total population			
	European	African	Asiatic	Mixed
Bahamas	15	85	—	—
Barbados	5	89	—	6
Cayman Is.	33	17	—	50
Cuba	73	12	1	14
Dominican Republic	15	15	—	70
Haiti	5	95	—	—
Jamaica	1	77	2	20
Puerto Rico	73	4	—	23
Trinidad and Tobago	2	43	38	17

Small groups of Asiatics are found in many West Indian territories. Numerically the most important of the Asiatics are the so-called East Indians, who are the descendants of indentured workers from the Indian sub-continent. East Indians are of particular importance in Trinidad and Tobago, where they form almost two-fifths of the total population. Small groups of Chinese, Lebanese and Syrians are found in many of the West Indian territories. Table 21 gives a rough impression of the racial composition of the West Indian islands.

The multi-racial nature of the population of the West Indies can be seen very clearly in Jamaica, whose national motto is 'Out of Many, One People' (see Table 22).

Table 22 The population of Jamaica, by racial origin, 1960

Race	Percentage of total population
African	76,8
European	0,8
East Indian	1,7
Chinese	0,6
Syrian	0,1
Afro-European	14,6
Afro-East Indian	1,7
Afro-Chinese	0,6
Others	3,1
All races	100,0

The mainland of Central America

On the mainland of Central America, the most important elements in the population are the descendants of the indigenous Indians, and of later arrivals from Europe. In only a few parts of the mainland of Central America are people of African or Asiatic descent numerous.

Guatemala is the only country of Central America where pure-blooded Indians predominate, although there is also a large Indian element in the population of Mexico. In most of the other states, a great deal of racial inter-mixture has taken place over the last few centuries, and Mestizos (people of mixed American Indian and European descent) form the largest element in the population.

53

Table 23 The population of selected countries in Central America, by racial origin

Country	Percentage of total population				
	American Indian	Mestizo	European	African & Mulatto	Asiatic
Costa Rica	1	17	80	2	—
El Salvador	11	78	11	—	—
Guatemala	60	35	5	—	—
Mexico	30	60	10	—	—
Nicaragua	5	69	17	9	—
Panama	10	65	11	13	1

The only country in which people of pure European origin predominate is Costa Rica, although there are sizeable European elements in several of the others. Almost all of the Europeans are of Spanish origin.

In Belize the population is predominantly of African descent. There are also sizeable numbers of people of African descent in Panama, and along the Caribbean coasts of Costa Rica, Honduras and Nicaragua. African slaves were brought to the Caribbean coastal region of Central America by English smugglers and woodcutters as early as the seventeenth century. Many of the people of African origin in Central America, however, are the descendants of English-speaking West Indians, who went there during the early part of the twentieth century, to work on the banana plantations and in the construction of the Panama Canal.

Tropical South America

In tropical South America the highest proportion of pure-blooded American Indians is found in the Andean states of Bolivia, Ecuador and Peru. Mestizos are also numerous in these states, and form the largest single element in the population of Colombia, Paraguay and Venezuela.

The highest proportion of people of pure European descent is found in Brazil. Many Brazilians are the descendants of Portuguese settlers. People of Italian, Spanish and German descent are also numerous in Brazil, particularly in the south and south-east of the country. European emigration to Brazil was particularly heavy during the second half of the nineteenth century and the early part of the twentieth century, when there was a great demand for labour in the coffee growing areas.

People of African descent are particularly numerous in the north-eastern coastal zone of Brazil, and in the Guianas (French Guiana, Guyana and Surinam). They are also fairly numerous in some of the coastal lowlands of Colombia, Ecuador and Venezuela. They are the descendants of slaves shipped from Africa to

Table 24 The population of selected South American countries, by racial origin

Country	Percentage of total population				
	American Indian	Mestizo	European	African & Mulatto	Asiatic
Bolivia	53	32	15	—	—
Brazil	2	11	51	36	—
Colombia	7	68	20	5	—
Ecuador	60	22	15	3	—
Paraguay	3	97	—	—	—
Peru	46	38	15	—	1
Surinam	3	—	1	42	54
Venezuela	3	67	20	10	—

work on the plantations. Slavery was abolished in Guyana in 1834, but continued until 1888 in Brazil.

Asiatics form a very important element in the population of both Surinam and Guyana. In Surinam, East Indians constituted 37 per cent of the total population in 1971. These are the descendants of indentured workers brought from India to work on the plantations, in the period following the emancipation of the African slaves. A further 16 per cent of Surinam's population is Indonesian. Like the East Indians, the Indonesians (mainly from the island of Java) were brought to Surinam as indentured workers. The Chinese form about 2 per cent of Surinam's population.

In Guyana, East Indians constituted half of the total population in 1970. Many of the East Indians in Guyana are still plantation workers, while others have become independent farmers. Relations between the East Indians and the other racial groups in Guyana have not always been harmonious.

Table 25 The population of Guyana, by racial origin, 1970

Race	Number	Percentage of total population
East Indian	365 515	50,7
African	222 665	30,8
Mixed	82 240	11,4
American Indian	32 013	4,4
Portuguese	9 522	1,3
Chinese	4 581	0,7
European	3 992	0,6
Others	570	0,1
All races	721 098	100,0

Tropical Pacific

The three main racial stocks in the islands of the tropical Pacific are the *Melanesians*, *Micronesians* and *Polynesians*. Opinions differ as to when these peoples came to the islands of the tropical Pacific, and also where they came from. To the three major stocks, European and Asiatic elements have been added in more recent times.

The various racial groups inhabiting the islands of the tropical Pacific have frequently intermixed to a considerable extent. This is particularly the case in the Hawaiian Islands, which are often referred to as 'the melting pot of the Pacific'. The first population census of Hawaii in 1832 showed a total population of about 130 thousand, of whom very few were non-Hawaiians. The Hawaiians are of Polynesian stock, and are believed to have arrived in the Hawaiian Islands some time after 400 AD.

In the time since the first census, the population of the Hawaiian islands has grown considerably, but the proportion of Hawaiians in the population has greatly declined. Today the number of pure-blooded Hawaiians is very small. After about the middle of the nineteenth century, the shortage of labour for Hawaii's sugar cane and pineapple plantations made it necessary to recruit workers from other parts of the world. Some of these plantation workers were of Portuguese origin, while others came from Spain, Norway and Germany. The transport of European workers proved very expensive, however, and so the largest number of people were recruited from Asia, particularly from Japan, China and the Philippines. Relations between the various racial groups in Hawaii are very harmonious, and a great deal of inter-marriage has taken place. Table 26 shows the population of Hawaii by racial origin in 1950. Since the census of 1950, racial data has not been recorded in Hawaii, as the great amount of racial admixture which has taken place has made it impracticable to do so.

Table 26 The population of Hawaii, by racial origin, 1950

Race	Number	Percentage of total population
Hawaiian	86 091	17,2
Caucasian	114 793	23,0
Chinese	32 376	6,5
Filipino	61 071	12,2
Japanese	184 611	36,9
Others	20 852	4,2
Total	499 794	100,0

People of Asiatic origin are also very numerous in Fiji. About half the inhabitants of Fiji are descendants of immigrants from the Indian sub-continent. In the other islands of the tropical Pacific, Asiatics are generally much less numerous than in Hawaii or Fiji, although most islands have at least a handful of Chinese traders.

People of European origin are most numerous in Hawaii, where they form about a quarter of the total population. Europeans also form about one-third of the population of New Caledonia.

Tropical Asia

The majority of the inhabitants of tropical Asia belong to one or other of two main racial stocks, the *Caucasoid* and the *Mongoloid*. The dividing line between these two stocks roughly follows the border between India and Burma, the Caucasoids being found to the west and the Mongoloids to the east of it. Within these two main stocks, however, wide differences occur, particularly in language and religion.

West Malaysia

Past migrations have resulted in the formation of plural societies (societies composed of several distinct racial, cultural, religious or linguistic groups) in several parts of tropical Asia. In West Malaysia, for example, the population is composed of three main racial elements, the Malays, Chinese and Indians. Each of these groups has its own cultural, linguistic and religious background, and there has been very little inter-marriage. Relations between the different groups have, however, on the whole been fairly harmonious.

The present population pattern in West Malaysia has arisen as a result of the large-scale immigration of people from China and India, which mainly took place between the establishment of British rule in the Malay Peninsula and the outbreak of the Second World War. It was the discovery of rich deposits of tin ore in the Malay Peninsula, which led to the rapid influx of Chinese during the latter part of the nineteenth and the early part of the twentieth centuries. The influx of people from the Indian sub-continent, on the other hand, was closely linked

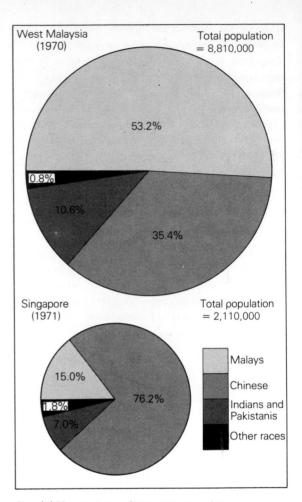

Fig. 4.4 The population of West Malaysia and Singapore by racial origin

with agricultural development, and in particular with the growth of the rubber industry during the twentieth century.

Table 27 The population of West Malaysia, by racial origin, 1970

Racial origin	Number (thousands)	Percentage of total population
Malays	4 686	53,2
Chinese	3 122	35,4
Indians, Pakistanis, etc.	933	10,6
Others	69	0,8
All races	8 810	100,0

Singapore

The population of Singapore is composed of the same three main racial groups as that of West Malaysia, although in Singapore the Chinese far outnumber the Malays. This predominance of Chinese was an important reason for the separation of Singapore from the Federation of Malaysia in 1965.

Table 28 The population of Singapore, by racial origin, 1971

Racial origin	Number (thousands)	Percentage of total population
Chinese	1 607	76,2
Malays	317	15,0
Indians and Pakistanis	147	7,0
Others	39	1,8
All races	2 110	100,0

Sri Lanka

Sri Lanka (formerly Ceylon) is another example of a plural society. The Sinhalese form the largest element in the population of Sri Lanka. They are Buddhist by religion, and came from the north to conquer the island during the sixth century BC. The northern part of the island, however, is mainly inhabited by the Tamils, who came over in the past from Indian mainland, and who are Hindu by religion. A distinction is usually made between the Sri Lanka Tamils who are the descendants of early invaders, and the Indian Tamils who came at a much later date to work on plantations. Although the Sri Lanka and Indian Tamils have a basic common language and a common Hindu culture, in the past there has been relatively little contact between the two communities. Other smaller elements in the population are the Moors and the Burghers. The Moors are of Arab descent, and are Moslem by religion. Their forbears came to the island several centuries ago at a time when the Arabs dominated trade in the Indian Ocean. The Moors mainly live in coastal communities. The Burghers are mainly the descendants of mixed marriages between the early Dutch and Portuguese settlers, and the Asian peoples of the island.

Although the Sinhalese and the Tamils live side by side in Sri Lanka, the two communities have always been kept apart by differences in religion, language and social customs. Although the Sri Lanka Tamils are regarded as citizens of Sri Lanka, prior to 1964 most Indian Tamils were not. The status of the Indian Tamils has in fact been the subject of much contention between the government of Sri Lanka and that of India. In 1964, however, an agreement was reached whereby India recognised 525 000 Indian Tamils as Indian citizens and agreed to their eventual repatriation, while Sri Lanka granted citizenship to 300 000 others. A further 150 000 Indian Tamils were not covered by the 1964 agreement.

Unfortunately, relations between the Sinhalese and the Tamils have not always been harmonious. In 1957 a bill was passed through parliament making Sinhalese the official language of the island. This legislation was bitterly resented by the Tamils, and in 1958 there were communal riots in the capital Colombo, and in many other towns and villages. In 1966 Tamil was made an alternative official language for the Northern and Eastern Provinces.

Table 29 The population of Sri Lanka, by racial origin, 1971

Race	Number (thousands)	Percentage of total population
Sinhalese	9 147	72,0
Sri Lanka Tamils	1 416	11,1
Indian Tamils	1 195	9,4
Moors	824	6,5
Others	129	1,0
All races	12 711	100,0

Tropical Africa

The people of tropical Africa may conveniently be divided into the following groups:

1 Pygmy Negrillos;
2 Bushmen and Hottentots;
3 Semites;
4 Hamites;

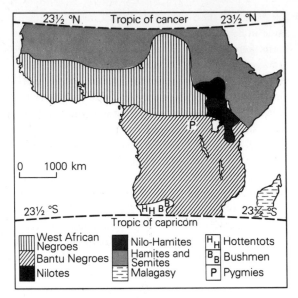

Fig. 4.5 The peoples of tropical Africa (simplified)

Map legend:
West African Negroes | Nilo-Hamites | H H Hottentots
Bantu Negroes | Hamites and Semites | B B Bushmen
Nilotes | Malagasy | P Pygmies

5 West African Negroes;
6 Bantu Negroes;
7 Nilotes and Nilo-Hamites;
8 Malayans;
9 People of recent overseas origin.

The Pygmy Negrillos

The Pygmies are among the oldest of the African peoples. They are now mainly found in the densest parts of the tropical rain forest, but it is believed that in the past they were much more widely distributed. The Pygmies are noted for their small stature, adult males averaging well under 1,5 metres in height.

The Pygmies are food-gatherers, living by hunting wild animals and collecting wild plant life. They live in small scattered groups, spread over a vast area of equatorial Africa from Cameroon in the west, to the Zaïre–Uganda border in the east. They are thought to now number only about 150 000. The Mbuti Pygmies, who are estimated to number some 40 000, live in the Ituri Forest in north-eastern Zaïre. They live in hunting bands of from about three to 30 families. Each band may occupy several hundred sq km of territory.

The Mbuti Pygmies live in beehive shaped huts, made of a framework of sticks covered with leaves. After they have stayed about a month in one locality, all the fruits of the forest have been gathered, and the game has either been killed off or scared away to a greater distance than is comfortable for daily hunting. When this happens, the camp is moved to another part of the forest. Because of the heat the Pygmies need very little in the way of clothes. Their clothing usually consists of a tiny strip of cloth, worn around the loins. This cloth is made by pounding the bark of various vines.

Some groups of Mbuti Pygmies hunt with bows and arrows, but other groups mainly use nets. Each family of net hunters owns a net, which is usually between 30 and 100 metres in length and about 1 metre in height. When hunting, the men of the band join several nets together to form a semi-circle. The women then beat the undergrowth with sticks, to frighten the small game in the area towards the nets. The men wait by the nets, and use spears to kill any animals which become entangled in them

The women gather a wide range of fruits, berries, roots, mushrooms and nuts. The men collect wild honey, by climbing the trees and filling the hives with smoke to drive out the bees. In addition to the plant life which they themselves collect in the forest, the Mbuti Pygmies obtain plantains and cassava from neighbouring tribes of Negroes. In return they supply the Negroes with game meat.

The Bushmen

The Bushmen are another old African people, but they live in a very different physical environment from the Pygmies. It is believed that at one time their ancestors occupied large parts of central and eastern Africa, but now they are only found in the Kalahari Desert and its borderlands.

Like the Pygmies, the Bushmen are small in stature, adult males rarely being much more than 1,5 metres in height. It is estimated that only about 55 000 Bushmen still survive, and not all of those continue to practise their traditional food-gathering way of life.

Game is fairly scarce in the dry environment in which the Bushmen live, and the collecting of plant life probably contributes more to their daily food supply than does hunting. The women gather a wide range of fruits, nuts, roots, tubers and leafy vegetables. The men mainly hunt with bows and arrows. They tip their arrows with poisons, which they obtain from various plants and animals. Although these arrows can bring down small game almost immediately, large animals when wounded have often to be followed on foot for considerable distances, before they finally fall down exhausted. Important game are the various large antelope of the region. Other foods eaten by the Bushmen include lizards, snakes and termites.

As well as having to obtain food, the Bushmen have the problem of finding water, for in the Kalahari Desert permanent waterholes are few and far between. The Bushmen know that water can be obtained from certain melons, roots and trees. Ostrich eggshells are used for the storage of water. The shelters of the Bushmen are very simple, consisting of a framework of branches covered with grass.

The Hottentots

The Hottentots are believed to be the result of the admixture of Bushmen with early invading Hamitic peoples. They are somewhat taller than the Bushmen, but otherwise resemble them in appearance. In the past they were distributed over the whole of that part of south-western Africa which lies to the south of the Cunene river.

Traditionally the Hottentots were nomadic pastoralists, rearing cattle and sheep. Their encampments consisted of beehive shaped huts, which were surrounded by a thorn fence. Milk formed a very important part of their diet. The Hottentots were the first of the peoples of southern Africa to come into contact with European settlers, and have to a large extent been absorbed by admixture with Europeans and Asians who came to live in the Cape area.

The Semites

The Semites and the Hamites are both of Caucasoid stock. The Semites are known locally as Arabs. In tropical Africa, the Semitic peoples are mainly found in the semi-arid and arid areas in the north. They are essentially nomadic pastoralists, although some are sedentary cultivators in the oases. The Baggara Arabs live in the grassland areas of Sudan, and are mainly nomadic cattle rearers, although they also plant some crops during the rainy season. The Arab influence is also marked along the coast of East Africa and on the islands of Zanzibar and Pemba, where Arab traders have been active for several centuries.

The Hamites

The Hamites are believed to have entered Africa from south-western Asia, and are divided into two main groups, the Northern Hamites and the Eastern Hamites. The Northern Hamites include such peoples as the Tuareg and the Fulani. The Tuareg occupy an extensive area in the central Sahara, extending almost as far south as Timbuktu. The northern group of Tuareg are estimated to number only about 8 000, and live in the Ahaggar mountains and the mountains of Tassili-n-Ajjer. They live in true desert conditions, and rear camels, goats and sheep. The southern Tuareg number about 235 000, and live mainly in steppe and dry savanna country, where they are cattle rearers. The Fulani (also known as Peuhls) probably number about 6 million, and have been established in the Sudan savanna zone of West Africa for the last five or six centuries. More recently they have moved southward into the highlands of the Fouta Djalon and the northern part of Cameroon. Traditionally the Fulani are a nomadic cattle rearing people, although some have become sedentary or semi-sedentary cultivators.

South of the Tropic of Cancer, the Eastern Hamites are mainly represented by the peoples of the Eastern Horn. The Somalis are essentially Hamitic in origin, and are mainly nomadic pastoralists. The people of Ethiopia are probably the result of admixture between Hamites, Semites and Negroes, and are mainly cultivators.

The West African Negroes

South of the Sahara Desert, the peoples of tropical Africa are predominantly Negroid. The purest type of Negro is found in West Africa. The West African Negroes are divided into a vast number of tribes, and are predominantly cultivators. In the past they were grouped into kingdoms, some of which were of great extent and considerable influence.

The Bantu Negroes

The Bantu are a broad language group of central and southern Africa. They are found to the south of a line running roughly from the coast of Cameroon, to the coast of Kenya in the vicinity of Malindi. They are sometimes divided into three groups; a western, an eastern and a southern group. The Western Bantu mainly occupy the forests of the Zaïre Basin, and are predominantly cultivators. Most of the Southern and Eastern Bantu peoples combine cultivation with the rearing of cattle, except where the presence of tsetse fly makes this impossible. Among the Eastern Bantu, Negroid features are not as marked as in the other groups, possibly as a result of admixture with Hamitic peoples in the past. The Eastern Bantu include such tribes as the Baganda of Uganda, and the Kikuyu and the Akamba of Kenya.

The Nilotes and Nilo-Hamites

The Nilotes and Nilo-Hamites are the result of the mixing of Negroid and Hamitic blood. The Nilotes tend to be tall, slender and dark, and live mainly in the basin of the Upper Nile. Some of the best known of the Nilotic tribes are the Dinka and Nuer of Sudan, the Acholi of Uganda, and the Luo of Kenya. The Dinka and Nuer are mainly cattle herders, although they plant some crops during the rainy season, and also practise some fishing. The Luo and Acholi are mainly cultivators.

The Nilo-Hamites are limited to East Africa. As their name suggests, they have a larger proportion of Hamitic blood than do the true Nilotes. Most of the Nilo-Hamites are nomadic pastoralists, although a few tribes such as the Nandi of Kenya are mainly cultivators. The best known of the Nilo-Hamitic tribes are the Masai, the Turkana, and the Karama-jong.

The Malayans

The origin of the peoples of the island of Madagascar is uncertain. The language and culture of Madagascar are principally Malayan, and it seems probable that the early inhabitants of the island came across the Indian Ocean from the East Indies. In the coastal areas, however, there is a marked Negroid influence, and it is probable that Bantu Negroes from the East African mainland came to these areas in the past, using the islands of the Comoro Archipelago as stepping stones.

Peoples of recent overseas origin

In recent years people of non-African origin have settled in some parts of tropical Africa. Europeans have settled particularly in those parts of East Africa and Central Africa where the temperature is considerably modified by altitude. People from the Indian sub-continent are particularly numerous in East Africa, and also in the islands of Mauritius, Réunion and Madagascar. The number of Lebanese and Syrians in tropical Africa is much smaller, but they do play an important role as traders in several West African countries.

Exercises

1 a) Explain what is meant by the term 'density of population'.
  b) Describe and attempt to account for the differences in population density which occur within your own country.
2 Illustrating your answer with examples from the tropical lands, discuss the major factors which influence the distribution of population.
3 'The present distribution of population cannot be fully understood by reference to the physical environment alone.' Discuss this statement in relation to any major area within the tropics.
4 a) With the aid of sketch maps, locate one extensive area of sparse population and one extensive area of dense population in the tropical lands.
  b) Attempt to account for the differences in population density between the two areas.
5 With the aid of sketch maps, describe and attempt to account for the distribution of population in either West Africa or East Africa.
6 a) Explain what is meant by the term 'overpopulation'.
  b) With reference to any major area within the tropics, discuss the causes of overpopulation, and suggest how the problem of overpopulation might be overcome.
7 a) What are 'plural societies', and where within the tropics do they occur?
  b) Explain how such societies have come into existence, and discuss the problems associated with them.

Suggested reading

See Chapter 7.

CHAPTER FIVE

Population growth

One of the most important events of recent times has been the rapid growth of world population. It has been estimated that in 1820 the total world population amounted to about 1 000 million. By 1930 it had increased to 2 000 million, and only 30 years later to 3 000 million. It is expected to reach 4 000 million by the late 1970s.

Between 1965 and 1974 world population increased at the average rate of 2,0 per cent per annum. There were, however, wide variations in the rate of increase, between one part of the world and another. It was highest on the mainland of Middle America (3,2 per cent per annum), and lowest in Northern Europe (0,4).

A: The causes of change in population size

Basically, any change in the size of the population of a country or area is determined by three factors. These are:

1 births;
2 deaths;
3 migration.

Of these factors, the first two are usually far more important than the third.

In all parts of the world today, the number of births in a year considerably exceeds the number of deaths. The difference between the number of births and the number of deaths is known as the natural increase. Table 30 shows that in 1965, 69 800 births were registered in Jamaica. During the same year only 14 300 deaths were registered, and so the natural increase was 69 800 − 14 300 = 55 500. What was the natural increase during each of the other years shown in Table 30?

The fact that in 1965 births exceeded deaths by 55 500 does not necessarily mean, however, that the total population of Jamaica increased by that amount during the year. The remaining factor, that of migration, still has to be considered (see Chapter 6). Table 30 shows that in 1965 the number of people emigrating from Jamaica, exceeded the number of immigrants by 6 500. The net increase of population during the year therefore was 55 500 (the natural increase) − 6 500 (the net emigration) = 49 000. The total population of Jamaica at the end of 1965 was 1 762 000 (the total population at the start of the year) + 69 800 (the total number of births) − 14 300 (the total number of deaths) − 6 500 (the net

Table 30 The growth of Jamaica's population, 1965–8

Year	Total pop. at start of year	Total births	Total deaths	Natural increase	Net emigration	Net increase	Total pop. at end of year
1965	1 762 000	69 800	14 300	55 500	6 500	49 000	1 811 000
1966	1 811 000	71 400	14 300	?	8 900	?	1 859 200
1967	1 859 200	67 400	13 300	?	20 000	?	1 893 300
1968	1 893 300	65 400	14 600	?	20 000	?	?

emigration) = 1 811 000. What was the net increase of population in each of the other years shown in the table, and what was the total population of Jamaica at the end of 1968?

Birth, death and natural increase rates

So far we have only considered the total number of births and deaths, and no attempt has been made to relate them to the size of the total population. The most commonly used measure of fertility is the crude birth rate. This is simply the annual number of births, per 1 000 of the total population. It is calculated by dividing the number of births in a given year by the total population (usually the population at mid-year is used for this purpose), and multiplying the result by 1 000. The table below shows that in 1960 (at mid-year) the total population of Jamaica was 1 629 000, and that 68 413 births were registered during the year. The crude birth rate therefore was 68 413 ÷ 1 629 000 × 1 000 = approximately 42,0 per 1 000. What was the crude birth rate in each of the other years shown in Table 31?

The corresponding measure of mortality is the crude death rate, i.e. the annual number of deaths per 1 000 of the total population. This is calculated by dividing the number of deaths in a given year by the total population, and multiplying the result by 1 000. Table 31 shows that in 1960, 14 321 deaths were registered in Jamaica. The crude death rate therefore was 14 321 ÷ 1 629 000 × 1 000 = approximately 8,8 per 1 000. What was the crude death rate in each of the other years shown in the table?

The difference between the crude birth rate and the crude death rate is known as the rate of natural increase. In 1960 Jamaica had a crude birth rate of 42,0 per 1 000, and a crude death rate of only 8,8 per 1 000. The rate of natural increase during that year therefore was 42,0 − 8,8 = 33,2 per 1 000. What was the rate of natural increase in each of the other years shown in the table?

Although in many ways crude birth and death rates are convenient measures of the natural increase of population, they can also be misleading, as they fail to take into account the age and sex composition of the population. For example, countries which have a high proportion of their population in the older age groups, can be expected to have a higher death rate than countries which have a high proportion of their population in the younger age groups. Thus, although many West Indian territories now have a lower death rate than countries in Europe, it would be wrong to infer from this that the people of the West Indies enjoy better health and living standards. An examination of Fig. 5.1 will show that Jamaica has a much more youthful population than England and Wales.

The age structure of the population can also influence the birth rate. For example, in areas where large numbers of young adults leave home in search of work, the birth rate may be unusually low. Sex composition is also important, and low birth rates may result from the fact that the numbers of one sex far exceed the numbers of the other sex.

It should be noted that in bringing about changes in population size, the absolute levels of birth rates and death rates are of less importance than the ratio between them. Thus, for example, a country with a birth rate of 40 per 1 000 and a death rate of 25 per 1 000 will have a smaller rate of natural increase (15

Table 31 Crude birth, death and natural increase rates (per 1 000) for Jamaica, 1960–4

Year	Population at mid-year	Total births	Birth rate	Total deaths	Death rate	Rate of natural increase
1960	1 629 000	68 413	42,0	14 321	8,8	33,2
1961	1 646 000	66 128	?	14 193	?	?
1962	1 661 000	64 913	?	14 167	?	?
1963	1 698 000	66 189	?	15 159	?	?
1964	1 742 000	68 359	?	13 267	?	?

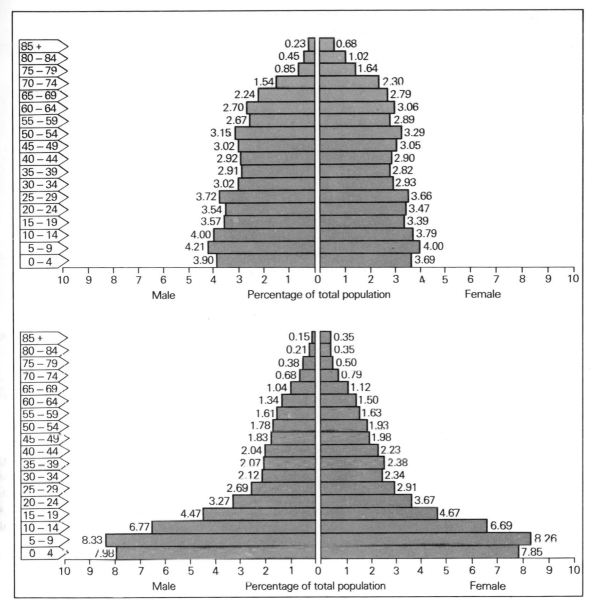

Fig. 5.1a The population of England and Wales, 1973 – age and sex structure
Fig. 5.1b The population of Jamaica, 1970 – age and sex structure

per 1 000), than a country with a birth rate of 30 per 1 000 and a death rate of 5 per 1 000 (25 per 1 000).

Declining mortality

The principal cause of the present world population explosion is the fact that in most parts of the world the death rate has declined very considerably in recent years, while the birth rate has fallen at a much slower rate. In the past, world population growth was very slow, as the number of births only slightly exceeded the number of deaths. Frequent famines, and epidemics of such diseases as cholera, plague and influenza kept the death rate very high. With improvements in medical knowledge, agriculture,

63

and living standards, the mortality rate began to fall. The decline was first experienced in Western Europe, where the mean death rate fell from about 30 per 1 000 at the beginning of the nineteenth century to about 11 per 1 000 in 1970. This decline has since gradually spread to most other parts of the world. Although in many parts of the world the birth rate has also declined, it has generally done so much more slowly, and the average birth rate for the world as a whole, is now more than twice as great as the average death rate.

B: Population growth in the tropical lands

Although it is often difficult to obtain accurate statistics, it seems that in most parts of the tropical world the annual rate of population growth is now well above the world average. Although in the past migration played an important role in the population growth of some tropical areas, the present growth can largely be attributed to the high rate of natural increase.

Mortality

Generally speaking, the decline in the death rate began much later in the tropical lands, than in most other parts of the world. Death rates of considerably above the world average are still experienced in many tropical countries, particularly those in Africa. The continued existence of high death rates can largely be attributed to poor living standards, and to inadequate medical facilities which are often unable to bring under control such diseases as malaria, yellow fever and a wide variety of intestinal disorders. Particularly noteworthy is the high infant mortality rate (the number of deaths of infants under one year of age, per 1 000 live births), which for many countries in tropical Africa is over 100 per 1 000, and in some possibly exceeds 200. In most European countries, on the other hand, infant mortality rates are less than 30 per 1 000.

Experience has shown, however, that with the control of disease, the provision of better hospital facilities, etc., a very rapid reduction in the death rate can be achieved. In Sri Lanka, for example, the death rate was reduced from 22 per 1 000 in 1945 to 8 in 1965, largely as a result of the eradication of malaria by DDT spraying. In recent years there has also been a sharp decline in the death rate in many

Table 32 Crude birth and death rates, and rates of population increase for selected areas, 1965–75

Area	Birth rate (per 1 000)	Death rate (per 1 000)	Annual rate of pop. increase (per cent)
World	32	13	1,9
Europe	16	10	0,6
Western Africa	49	24	2,5
Eastern Africa	48	21	2,7
Middle Africa	45	23	2,3
Tropical S. America	39	10	2,9
Middle America	43	9	3,2
Caribbean	35	9	1,9
Middle S. Asia	42	19	2,4
Southeast Asia	43	15	2,7
Melanesia	42	18	2,4
Polynesia and Micronesia	33	6	2,6

West Indian territories. That of Barbados, for example, fell from more than 30 per 1 000 in 1920 to less than 8 in 1970.

Fertility

In most tropical countries birth rates are much higher than the world average. A number of factors seem to contribute to this high fertility, although their relative importance varies from one area to another:

1 In most parts of the tropical world it is customary to marry at an early age. In India, for example, about 80 per cent of girls are married by the time they are eighteen. Early marriage increases the number of children that a married woman can bear.

2 In many parts of the tropical world it is traditional to have large families. In the past a large proportion of the children born usually died before reaching maturity, and so it was essential to have a large number of offspring to ensure that at least some survived. Furthermore, in traditional agricultural societies, where much of the work is done by hand, a large family provides a useful source of cheap labour.

3 In some tropical areas, particularly in Latin America and Africa, the male gains pride and prestige if he is able to prove his virility by begetting a large number of children.

4 In most parts of the tropical world family planning is not, or until very recently, has not been practised. Attitudes towards family planning vary considerably. Some religions, notably the Roman Catholic and the Islamic religions, have in the past strongly opposed artificial limitation of family size.

The problem of rapid population growth

In many of the developing countries of the tropical world, rapid population growth has become a serious problem, greatly hampering the efforts which are being made to improve the standard of living of the existing population. Rapid population growth means that each year the land has to be made to produce more food, in order to feed the additional mouths;

more money has to be spent on education and on health services, simply to maintain existing standards; and more employment has to be created.

The governments of many tropical countries are now acutely aware of the problems brought about by rapid population growth, and some are attempting to slow down the rate of growth, by active family planning campaigns designed to bring about a reduction in the birth rate. In a few countries there is already some evidence to suggest that these campaigns are beginning to have an effect. It seems likely, however, that in the immediate future the birth rate of most tropical countries will decline more slowly than the death rate, and that for some time to come the population of the tropical world will increase at an even faster rate than is at present the case.

Tropical America

The population of tropical America is growing at a faster rate than that of any other major part of the world. For the area as a whole birth rates remain very high, but death rates are now substantially lower than in most other tropical areas.

In many of the predominantly Roman Catholic countries of tropical South America and mainland Central America, birth rates still exceed 40 per 1 000, and as yet show little sign of declining. In most countries, however, death rates are now less than 20 per 1 000, and in some less than 10. The countries with the highest death rates are those such as Bolivia, which have a large American Indian element in the population.

In the West Indies the rate of population growth is somewhat slower than in either tropical South America or mainland Central America. This is largely because of the lower birth rates. In most West Indian territories the death rate is now below 10 per 1 000, although 50 years ago it was more than twice this figure. The very low death rate reflects both the improved health conditions now enjoyed, and also the youthful composition of the West Indian population. A notable exception is Haiti, which is economically and socially by far the most backward of the West Indian territories. In Haiti housing is poor, malnutrition is widespread, and medical services are extremely limited.

Although birth rates in the West Indies are still fairly high, with the exception of Haiti and the Dominican Republic they are lower than in most other parts of the tropical world. Because of the high population densities already existing in most territories, the need to curb population growth is widely recognised. The governments of many territories are now actively encouraging family planning, and some success has already been achieved in reducing the birth rate. That of Barbados, for example, fell from 32,4 per 1 000 in 1957 to 22,1 in 1972. Since the end of the Second World War, the high rate of natural increase in many West Indian territories has been partly offset by emigration.

The island of Puerto Rico provides a good example of the rapid growth of population which has taken place in the West Indies during the present century. The population of the island grew from less than 1 million in 1899 to more than 3 million in 1974. This growth has occurred in spite of massive emigration to the United States during recent decades. As a result of improved public health measures, Puerto Rico's infant mortality rate fell from 113 per 1 000 in 1940 to 24 in 1973, while the average expectancy of life at birth (the number of years a person can expect to live) increased from 38 years in 1910 to 70 years in 1973. In the past the Roman Catholic Church in Puerto Rico strongly opposed attempts at family planning, and up until 1939 it was a felony to even offer information on birth control. With an average population density of 341 per sq km in 1974, Puerto Rico's population problem is an acute one; and the administration is now actively encouraging family planning.

Tropical Africa

Although tropical Africa probably has the highest birth rates of any major part of the world, high mortality rates have until recently resulted in a somewhat slower rate of population growth than is experienced in most other parts of the tropical world.

In most tropical African countries birth rates are still well over 40 per 1 000, and in some exceed 50. So far, they show little sign of declining. Death rates, although they have declined in recent years, are still in most countries well over 20 per 1 000. Infant mortality rates are particularly high. The greatest child-killers in tropical Africa are malaria, gastro-

Table 34 Crude birth, death and natural increase rates (per 1 000) for selected countries

Country	Period	Birth rate	Death rate	Rate of natural increase
Central America				
Belize	1972	39,0	5,3	33,7
Costa Rica	1973	28,3	5,1	23,2
El Salvador	1973	40,3	8,3	32,0
Guatemala	1973	43,4	15,4	28,0
Honduras	1970–75	49,3	14,6	34,7
Mexico	1970–75	42,0	8,6	33,4
Nicaragua	1970–75	48,3	13,9	34,4
Tropical South America				
Bolivia	1970–75	44,0	19,1	24,9
Brazil	1970–75	37,1	8,8	28,3
Colombia	1970–75	40,6	8,8	31,8
Ecuador	1970–75	41,8	9,5	32,3
Peru	1970–75	41,0	11,9	29,1
Venezuela	1970–75	36,1	7,1	29,0
West Indies				
Bahamas	1973	22,4	5,7	16,7
Barbados	1972	22,1	8,5	13,6
Cuba	1973	25,4	5,8	19,6
Dominican Republic	1965–70	48,5	14,7	33,8
Guadeloupe	1973	28,0	7,3	20,7
Haiti	1965–70	43,9	19,7	24,2
Jamaica	1974	30,4	7,1	23,3
Puerto Rico	1973	23,3	6,5	16,8
St. Vincent	1973	34,4	10,0	24,4
Trinidad & Tobago	1973	26,5	6,7	19,8

enteritis, measles, meningitis and pneumonia. The average expectancy of life at birth is less than 50 years in most countries, and less than 40 in some. This compares with an average life expectancy of more than 60 years in many West Indian territories, and about 70 years in most European countries.

In marked contrast to the mainland of tropical Africa, the Indian Ocean islands of Mauritius, Réunion and the Seychelles now all have low death rates. In Mauritius the sharp decline in the death rate did not begin until the late 1940s. The virtual elimination of malaria in 1947 removed what had been one of the most important causes of death in the island, and the death rate fell from 23,8 per 1 000 in 1948 to 7,3 in 1974.

Table 34 Crude birth, death and natural increase rates (per 1 000) for selected countries in 1970–75

Country	Birth rate	Death rate	Rate of natural increase
Benin	49,9	23,0	26,9
Cameroon	40,4	22,0	18,4
CAR	43,4	22,5	20,9
Ethiopia	49,4	25,8	23,6
Gambia	43,3	24,1	19,2
Ghana	48,8	21,9	26,9
Guinea	46,6	22,9	23,7
Guinea Bissau	40,1	25,1	15,0
Ivory Coast	45,6	20,6	25,0
Kenya	48,7	16,0	32,7
Mali	50,1	25,9	24,2
Mauritania	44,8	24,9	19,9
Mauritius	25,1	8,1	17,0
Mozambique	43,1	20,1	23,0
Niger	52,2	25,5	26,7
Nigeria	49,3	22,7	26,6
Senegal	47,6	23,9	23,7
Sierra Leone	44,7	20,7	24,0
Sudan	47,8	17,5	30,3
Togo	50,6	23,3	27,3
Uganda	45,2	15,9	29,3
Upper Volta	48,5	25,8	22,7
Zaïre	45,2	20,5	24,7
Zambia	51,5	20,3	31,2

Tropical Asia

Table 35 shows that in recent years the population of most countries of tropical Asia has greatly increased.

In a few cases part of this population growth can be attributed to immigration. For example, after the end of the Second World War the population of Hong Kong and Macao was swollen by a flood of refugees from Mainland China. The population of

Table 35 The growth of population in selected countries, 1955–75 (millions)

Country	1955	1960	1965	1970	1974	1975
Burma	20,4	22,4	24,7	27,6	30,1	31,2
Hong Kong	2,5	3,1	3,7	4,1	4,2	4,4
India	386,6	429,0	486,7	550,4	586,1	598,1
Indonesia (exl. W. Irian)	83,9	93,5	104,9	121,2	127,6	136,0
Khmer Rep.	4,7	5,4	6,1	6,7	7,9	8,1
Philippines	23,6	27,4	32,4	38,5	41,5	42,5
Singapore	1,3	1,6	1,9	2,1	2,2	2,3
Sri Lanka	8,7	9,4	11,2	12,5	13,7	14,0
Thailand	22,8	26,4	30,7	35,8	41,0	42,0

Hong Kong increased from little over 1 million in 1941 to more than 4 million in 1970. The greatest influx of refugees into Hong Kong occurred in 1949 at the beginning of the communist regime in China, and again in 1961–2 when southern China experienced a severe shortage of food. Between 1945 and 1964 the increase of Hong Kong's population by immigration amounted to almost 2 million.

In most countries, however, the rapid growth of population has largely been the result of a high rate of natural increase. In most parts of tropical Asia birth rates remain very high, and, with a few notable exceptions, have as yet shown little sign of declining. In many countries the crude birth rate is still in excess of 30 per 1 000, and in some is over 40.

Notable exceptions are Hong Kong and Singapore, both of which have succeeded in drastically reducing their birth rate. In Singapore the birth rate fell from 45 per 1 000 in 1950 to 20 in 1974 as a result of family planning campaigns. In 1966 the government of Singapore assumed full responsibility for family planning, and established the Singapore Family Planning and Population Board. A massive educational programme designed to show the people of Singapore the importance of family planning was undertaken in 1966–7, using such media as radio, television and newspaper publicity. In spite of the efforts of the Board, it is estimated that Singapore's population will double within the next 20 years.

In 1974 Hong Kong's 1 045 sq km supported a population of 4 249 000, with an average density of 4 066 per sq km. The rapid growth of population has resulted in severe shortages of both building land and fresh water. To overcome the problem of land shortage, a large proportion of Hong Kong's population has been housed in multi-storey flats. To overcome the problem of water shortage, during the 1960s the government purchased water from Mainland China, and in 1975 opened a desalination plant to produce fresh water from sea water. The Family Planning Association of Hong Kong was established as early as 1951. In 1951 there were only two family planning clinics in Hong Kong, but by 1964 there were 52. The efforts of the Association appear to have been effective, as the birth rate fell from 34 per 1 000 in 1951 to 19 in 1974.

In most of the countries of tropical Asia the death rate has fallen very considerably during the last few decades. In countries such as Brunei, Hong Kong, Singapore and Sri Lanka, death rates are now appreciably lower than those experienced in Europe. In countries such as Burma, India, the Khmer Republic and Laos, however, death rates can still be appreciably reduced, and thus there is the possibility that even higher rates of natural increase will occur in future.

Probably nowhere in the world is the problem of population growth more serious than in India. The population of India increased from 345 million in 1947 to 586 million in 1974. The growth of India's population since the achievement of independence has largely been the result of a sharp decline in the death rate, brought about by vastly improved medical conditions. The death rate fell from 27 per 1 000 in 1955 to 17 in 1970. During the same period the average expectancy of life at birth rose from 32 to 52 years. The number of hospital beds in India increased from 113 000 in 1950–1 to 256 000 in 1968–9, and the number of registered doctors increased from 56 000 to 103 000. A national programme of protected water supply and sanitation has benefited many areas, and killing diseases such as malaria, cholera, smallpox and tuberculosis have largely been brought under control.

During the early 1970s India's population grew at a rate of 2,1 per cent per annum. Each year some 12 million people were added to the country's population. Because of the magnitude of the problem, the government of India launched what is probably the world's largest and most widespread family planning campaign, the aim of which is to reduce the birth rate from nearly 40 per 1 000 to 25 in the next decade. A network of family planning clinics has

been set up throughout India, where contraceptive devices are supplied free of charge. By 1971 India had nearly 37 000 such centres, an increase of 80 per cent in four years. By the end of 1972, $12\frac{1}{2}$ million sterilisations had been performed. Extensive use has been made of television, radio and the press to spread the message of family planning. The amount of money allocated by the government of India for the implementation of its birth control policies was increased from $1\frac{1}{2}$ million rupees during the First Five Year Plan (1951–6), to 3 150 million rupees during the Fourth Five Year Plan (1969–74).

Table 36 Crude birth, death and natural increase rates (per 1 000) for selected countries

Country	Period	Birth rate	Death rate	Rate of natural increase
Brunei	1973	34,7	4,8	29,9
Burma	1970–75	39,5	15,8	23,7
Hong Kong	1974	19,3	5,2	14,1
India	1973	34,6	15,5	19,1
Indonesia	1970–75	42,9	16,9	26,0
Khmer Rep.	1970–75	46,7	19,0	27,7
Laos	1970–75	44,6	22,8	21,8
Malaysia (West)	1972	33,3	6,9	26,4
Philippines	1965–70	44,7	12,0	32,7
Singapore	1974	19,9	5,3	14,6
Sri Lanka	1972	29,5	7,7	21,8
Thailand	1970–75	43,4	10,8	32,6
Vietnam (South)	1965–70	37,5	16,1	21,4

Exercises

1 a) Discuss briefly the factors which are responsible for changes in population size.

   b) With reference to actual examples, attempt to explain why the rate of population growth is higher in some tropical countries than in others.

2 a) Explain briefly why the population of the tropical lands has grown so rapidly in recent years.

b) What major problems have resulted from this population explosion?

c) Outline the measures being taken by any one tropical country to control population growth.

3 a) With reference to either tropical Africa or tropical Asia, write a detailed account of the changes in population size which have taken place during the last few decades.

b) Attempt to explain how these changes have been brought about.

4 a) Discuss briefly the changes in population size which have taken place in your own country in recent decades.

b) What have been the causes and the consequences of these changes?

Suggested Reading

See Chapter 7.

CHAPTER SIX

Population movements

The term migration is applied to the movement of people, and those who are involved are known as migrants. Population movements have gone on for thousands of years, and have profoundly influenced the distribution of man over the earth's surface.

Some population movements have been of a purely voluntary nature, but in other cases the migrants have been compelled to move. Among the most noteworthy compulsory movements are those associated with the slave trade, and with the exchange of population as a result of wars. It has been estimated that the African slave trade involved the removal of some 20 million Africans to the New World, and a further 10–15 million to the East. An example of the compulsory movement of population as a result of war, is that which took place between India and Pakistan in 1947, involving the transfer of some 17 million people.

In discussing population movements, it is possible to distinguish two main types:

1 Permanent migrations, which involve people leaving their homes without the intention of returning.
2 Migrations of a temporary nature, which involve people leaving their homes for a relatively short period of time.

A: Migrations of a permanent nature

Migrations of a permanent nature can be further divided into:

1 external migrations, which involve the crossing of international boundaries;

2 internal migrations, which take place entirely within a country.

External migrations

In the case of external migrations, the movement out of a country is known as emigration, and the people who leave are known as emigrants. The movement into a country is known as immigration, and the people who enter are known as immigrants. The person who changes his place of abode from one country to another, does in fact both emigrate and immigrate. He leaves his old home as an emigrant, and enters his new one as an immigrant.

Why do people emigrate? The basic cause of most voluntary external population movements are the migrant's dissatisfaction with the conditions existing in his own country, and the belief that he will find better conditions elsewhere. Most commonly, international migrations result from the existence of differences in economic opportunity between one country and another.

External migrations have profoundly modified the present population pattern in many parts of the tropical world, and a few of the more noteworthy examples are discussed below.

Population movements in the West Indies
In the time between their discovery by Columbus in 1492, and the early part of the nineteenth century, the West Indian islands experienced a net inward movement of population. During this period, large numbers of people migrated to the West Indies from the continents of Europe, Africa and Asia.

Over the centuries there has been a considerable influx of Europeans into the West Indies. The early European settlers in the British West Indian islands established small farms, on which they grew crops such as maize, cassava and vegetables for subsistence, and tobacco, ginger, cotton and indigo for export. During the seventeenth century, however, when sugar cane became the most profitable crop in the West Indies, many small farmers found themselves unable to compete with the new class of large plantation owners which came into existence at this time. Many thousands of small farmers sold their lands to the plantation owners, and left the West Indies, going mainly to the mainland of North America. As a result the number of Europeans in some islands declined. During the nineteenth and early twentieth centuries, however, a considerable amount of European settlement took place in the Spanish-speaking territories of the West Indies, particularly in Cuba. More than 700 000 settlers from Spain have entered Cuba since 1902.

Within a century of the arrival of Columbus the early inhabitants of the West Indian islands, the Arawak and the Carib Indians, had virtually been exterminated, as a result of the introduction of European diseases and the harsh treatment meted out to them by the early European settlers. When the cultivation of sugar cane became important during the seventeenth century, the European plantation owners found themselves faced with a severe shortage of agricultural labour, and to remedy this situation vast numbers of slaves were shipped from Africa to the West Indies. Most of these came from the lands bordering the Gulf of Guinea in West Africa. At the time of their emancipation in 1834, there were about 700 000 African slaves living in the British West Indian islands alone, outnumbering the European inhabitants by about seven to one.

During the nineteenth century, the abolition of the slave trade and later of slavery, resulted in there once again being a severe shortage of labour on West Indian sugar plantations. Attempts were therefore made to obtain agricultural workers from other parts of the world, mainly under the indentured labour system. This involved the recruitment of workers for a specific number of years, at the end of which time they were free to return to their homeland if they so desired. Many of the indentured workers did in fact remain in the West Indies, after their period of indenture was completed. The bulk of the indentured workers were from southern India. Some 134 000 Indians went to Trinidad alone, in the period up to 1917, when the recruitment of indentured workers was discontinued. Smaller numbers of Chinese were also recruited under the indentured worker system. During the early part of the twentieth century there was also a small influx of Lebanese and Syrians into many of the West Indian islands. These came of their own accord, and most of them entered the retail trade.

Although the present population of the West Indies has thus resulted from successive waves of immigration, since the latter part of the nineteenth century several territories have in fact experienced a net outward movement of population. In some cases the movement has been from one West Indian territory to another, while in other cases it has been to areas outside of the West Indies.

The movement of population between one West Indian territory and another has generally resulted from the existence of differences in the level of economic development. Movement has been from the more crowded or less developed territories, to the less crowded or more developed ones. As early as 1860 there was a movement of people from the densely populated island of Barbados, to the more thinly populated ones of Antigua, Grenada, St. Lucia, St. Vincent, Trinidad and the Virgin Islands. As a result, the population of Barbados actually declined from 183 000 in 1891 to 156 000 in 1921. The establishment of oil refineries in the Dutch West Indian islands of Curacao (in 1916) and Aruba (in 1925) created considerable opportunities for employment, and attracted workers from many of the neighbouring islands. Thus, although the population of Curacao trebled between 1925 and 1957, and that of Aruba increased sixfold, the less-developed Dutch territories of Bonaire, St. Maarten, Saba and St. Eustatius all experienced a decline in numbers.

Emigration to areas outside of the West Indies has also been considerable in the last hundred years. During the latter part of the nineteenth century and the early part of the twentieth century, large numbers of West Indians emigrated to the mainland of Central America, particularly to Costa Rica, Honduras and Panama. They found work on the sugar cane and banana plantations, or in the construction of the Panama Canal.

The exodus from the West Indies has, however, been heaviest since the end of the Second World War, with large numbers of West Indians emigrating to Europe and to the mainland of North America, in search of better living standards. Much of the recent emigration from the English-speaking territories has been to the United Kingdom. Between 1956 and 1965, for example, the net emigration of Jamaicans to the United Kingdom amounted to about 150 000. This was roughly equivalent to one tenth of the island's total population. Since 1965, however, the number of West Indians emigrating to the United Kingdom has fallen sharply, as a result of the introduction of restrictions on immigration by the British Government.

Since the Second World War, there has also been a veritable flood of emigrants from Puerto Rico to the United States. During the 1950s some 50 000 emigrants per year left Puerto Rico, and by 1970 there were about 1 million people of Puerto Rican origin living in the United States, mainly in New York City. Today, more than one out of every four Puerto Ricans lives away from his native land.

The migrations of Chinese and Indians

The population patterns of several parts of the tropical world have been considerably modified, as a result of the migration of people from China and from the Indian sub-continent. Chinese migration to Southeast Asia can be traced back to very early times, but the modern movement can be said to have begun with the flow of migrants to Singapore during the 1820s. After about 1870 the scale of Chinese emigration increased, as millions of Chinese left their overcrowded homeland and moved southwards. As a result, there are now considerable concentrations of people of Chinese origin in many of the countries of Southeast Asia.

The Chinese have also migrated in smaller numbers to other parts of the tropical world, notably to the West Indies, where they form small but economically important minorities in several of the teritories. There are also small communities of Chinese in tropical South America, notably in Guyana, Surinam and Peru. The Chinese also form an important element in the population of several of the

Table 37 People of Chinese origin in Southeast Asia in 1968

Country	Estimated number of Chinese (in thousands)	Percentage of total population
Thailand	3 800	11,6
Malaysia	3 674	36,0
a) West Malaysia	3 256	37,0
b) East Malaysia	418	28,0
Indonesia	3 200	2,9
Vietnam (South)	1 550	8,9
Singapore	1 450	75,5
Khmer Rep.	450	7,5
Philippines	400	1,1
Burma	370	1,5
Vietnam (North)	142	0,7
Laos	33	1,2
Brunei	29	26,0

islands of the tropical Pacific. In several parts of the tropical world, the Chinese occupy an important position in the retail trade.

There has also been considerable emigration from the Indian sub-continent, particularly to the lands bordering the Indian Ocean. Migration to Sri Lanka began as early as the eleventh to thirteenth centuries, with the invasion of the island by the Tamils from southern India. The descendants of these early invaders, who are known as the Sri Lanka Tamils, are mainly peasant farmers, and in 1971 they formed 11,1 per cent of the island's total population. At a much later date, the development of rubber and tea plantations in Sri Lanka led to the immigration of large numbers of agricultural labourers from the Indian mainland, and these Indian Tamils formed a further 9,4 per cent of the island's population in 1971.

It has been estimated that between 1834 and 1934 a total of about 30 million people emigrated from the Indian sub-continent. Many of these emigrants went as indentured workers to the plantations of the West Indies, Guyana, Malaya, Fiji, Mauritius, Réunion and South Africa. Towards the end of the nineteenth century large numbers of Indians emigrated to Burma, where they either found employment as labourers or became rice farmers. In 1956 there were about 800 000 Indians living in Burma, but since that time many of them have left the country. In the period after 1895 large numbers of Indians went to East Africa, to help in the construction of the railways. Since the end of the Second World War, considerable numbers of people from the Indian sub-continent have emigrated to Britain. Table 38, although by no means a complete list, gives a rough indication of the number of people from the Indian sub-continent, who are living outside of their homeland.

Table 38 People from the Indian sub-continent living overseas

Country	Year	Estimated number (in thousands)	Percentage of total population
Sri Lanka	1971	2 611	21
W. Malaysia	1970	933	11
South Africa	1970	620	3
Mauritius	1971	575	69
Trinidad & Tobago	1970	380	37
Guyana	1970	377	51
Burma	1970	300	1
Fiji	1971	272	51
England & Wales	1966	224	1
Surinam	1971	142	37
Singapore	1973	154	7
Kenya	1969	139	1
Uganda	1968	94	1
Tanzania	1967	75	1
Madagascar	1971	41	1
Jamaica	1960	28	2

In the West Indies and Guyana, immigrants from the sub-continent of India and their descendants are commonly known as East Indians, to distinguish them from people of American Indian origin. In this part of the tropical world, the East Indians have tended to remain largely in agriculture. In Guyana, for example, many East Indians still work on sugar plantations, while others have become rice farmers. In East Africa, on the other hand, a great many 'Asians' (this is the name commonly applied in East Africa to immigrants from the Indian sub-continent and their descendants) are now engaged in the retail trade. Although the Asians have undoubtedly contributed a great deal to the economic development of East Africa, their domination of the retail trade, and their unwillingness to integrate with the local Africans, has resulted in their presence becoming resented by the latter. At the time when the East African territories achieved their independence from Britain, many Asians opted to retain their British citizenship, rather than to become citizens of Kenya, Tanzania or Uganda. These non-citizen Asians now feel that their position in East Africa is not very secure, and in recent years many of them have emigrated. In Kenya, for example, the number of Asians fell from 177 000 in 1962 to 139 000 in 1969. In 1972 all the non-citizen Asians in Uganda, were ordered to leave the country at very short notice. Many of the Ugandan Asians emigrated to Britain after their expulsion.

European settlement in tropical Africa
Throughout the colonial period, a considerable number of Europeans went to live in tropical Africa. Many of these were government officials or missionaries, while others were employed by the mining companies or were in commerce. The majority went for relatively short periods of time, and had no intention of making a permanent home in Africa. In only a few parts of tropical Africa has there been any permanent European settlement on a large scale. Such settlement has, for the most part, been confined to the cooler, healthier upland areas.

In the past European settlement has been of considerable importance in East Africa, particularly in Kenya and Tanzania. European settlers were introduced into Kenya following the building of the Kenya–Uganda Railway in 1897–1901. The policy of white settlement in Kenya was officially adopted in 1901, and large areas of the best agricultural land in the Kenya Highlands was reserved for European farmers. In 1959 the land alienated to non-Africans in the so-called 'White Highlands' amounted to more than 5 per cent of the total area of Kenya. Since 1961 schemes for land re-distribution have taken place in Kenya, and many Africans have been settled on lands formerly held by European farmers. Since that time, European emigration from Kenya has exceeded immigration, and the number of Europeans in the country fell from 66 000 in 1961 to 41 000 in 1969.

In Tanzania, German settlers were encouraged in the Usambara Highlands after the arrival of the railway at Moshi in 1911. European settlement was, however, much less concentrated than in Kenya. The main areas of European farms and plantations were on the slopes of Mt. Kilimanjaro and Mt. Meru, in parts of the Southern Highlands, and in the sisal growing areas. In 1967 there were some 17 000 Europeans in Tanzania. European settlement has never been encouraged in Uganda.

European settlement in Zimbabwe began in about 1890, when a small group of settlers organised by Cecil Rhodes reached the site of modern Salisbury. In 1969 there were some 228 000 Europeans in Zimbabwe, forming roughly $4\frac{1}{2}$ per cent of the total population. Most of the European settlement has taken place on the High Veld, at altitudes of over 1 200 metres. The Europeans found conditions on the High Veld highly favourable for agriculture, and quickly came to occupy large areas of the best land. In 1969, 36 per cent of the land in Zimbabwe was reserved for use by Europeans, although in fact almost four-fifths of the European population lived in the urban areas. By contrast, only 44 per cent of the land was reserved for use by the Africans, who formed 95 per cent of the population.

The influence of the European settler is far less marked in Zambia than in Zimbabwe. In 1969 there were some 67 000 Europeans in Zambia, forming about $1\frac{1}{2}$ per cent of the total population. Most of the Europeans living in Zambia are employed by mining companies on the Copperbelt, and unlike the Europeans in Zimbabwe, do not regard Africa as their permanent home. Only 3 per cent of the land in Zambia was assigned to European farmers. In Malawi, Europeans numbered only 7 000 in 1966. The chief areas of European settlement in Malawi are in the Shire Highlands.

In the past there was a considerable amount of European settlement in the former Portuguese territories of Angola and Mozambique. In the early 1970s there were more than 300 000 Europeans living in Angola forming 6 per cent of the total population. The high plateau areas of Angola are climatically well suited to European settlement, and until recently were regarded by the Portuguese Government as a convenient outlet for Portugal's surplus rural population. Many of the Portuguese settlers arrived after 1953, under government-sponsored schemes. The 1953 Development Plan encouraged the settlement of Portuguese farmers in the central and southern parts of the Angola plateau. Among the most noteworthy of these settlements were those at Cela on the plateau to the north of Huambo (formally Nova Lisboa), and at Matala in the valley of the Cunene river. The farms on these schemes were very much smaller than the typical European farm in Zimbabwe or Kenya, and the Portuguese settlers were discouraged from employing African workers. When Angola achieved its independence from Portugal in 1975, most of the European settlers left the country.

Because Mozambique has only limited areas of highland it is much less well suited to European settlement than is Angola. Although there were some 150 000 Europeans in Mozambique in 1971, they were heavily concentrated in the coastal towns of Maputo and Beira, and European land settlement schemes have not generally been very successful. Most of the Europeans left Mozambique, when it gained its independence from Portugal in 1975.

Very little permanent European settlement has taken place in West Africa. Climatically West Africa is much less suitable for European settlement than East Africa, because of the smaller proportion of highland. In the former British territories of West Africa, Europeans were never allowed to own land, and the number of Europeans in these countries has always been small. The number of Europeans living in the former French territories, however, is considerably larger. The greatest concentrations of Europeans are found in the Ivory Coast and Senegal. In the Ivory Coast European planters produce most of the bananas, many of the pineapples, and some of the coffee and cocoa which are exported. As well as working in government administration and in industry, the Europeans in the former French territories own or manage hotels, restaurants, bars and shops.

The future of the European in tropical Africa now seems highly uncertain. In many parts of East and Central Africa the alienation of large areas of the best agricultural land to small groups of European settlers has been bitterly resented by the local Africans. In Kenya this resentment was the root cause of the Mau Mau rebellion of 1952–6. Since Kenya achieved independence, the Government has bought out many European farmers, and redistributed their land among the local Africans.

The existence of sizeable numbers of European settlers in Central Africa has caused certain political problems. For example, the Federation of Rhodesia and Nyasaland which was formed in 1953 was broken up in 1963, largely as a result of the fear held by African leaders in Zambia (formerly Northern Rhodesia) and Malawi (formerly Nyasaland) that the Federation would be dominated by the white settler element in Zimbabwe (formerly Southern Rhodesia). The later unwillingness of the European settler government in Zimbabwe to see political control of that country pass into the hands of the African majority led to its Unilateral Declaration of Independence from Britain in 1965.

Although the existence of European minorities has been responsible for the creation of political problems, very often the white settler has made a significant contribution to the economic development of the area in which he has settled. In both Zimbabwe and Kenya, for example, European farmers have played a large part in the development of modern commercial agriculture. The presence of sizeable European populations has also probably helped to stimulate the growth of manufacturing industry in those countries.

Internal migrations

In the case of migrations which take place entirely within a country, the movement of people out of an area is known as out-migration, while the movement of people into an area is known as in-migration. Two main types of internal migrations can be recognised:

1 those involving movement from one rural area to another rural area;
2 those involving movement from a rural area to an urban area (these are fully discussed in Chapter 7).

Migration in rural areas

Permanent movements of populations from one rural area to another, are often associated with the development of new agricultural land. The need to develop new land may be the result of a decline in soil fertility, as occurs in areas where shifting agriculture is practised. More commonly, however, it is associated with the growth of population, the existing agricultural land being incapable of supporting the additional numbers.

In the past the opening up of new land for agriculture was usually undertaken by an individual settler or group of settlers. An increasing amount of such development, however, is now taking place in the form of government-sponsored settlement schemes.

During the present century, land settlement has been undertaken in several parts of tropical Asia, notably in Indonesia, Malaysia and Sri Lanka. In Indonesia, for example, attempts have been made to alleviate Java's population problem by resettling farmers from the densely populated central and eastern parts of that island in the less crowded 'outer territories'.

Java and the adjoining small islands of Madura, Bali and Lombok together form only 7 per cent of the total land area of Indonesia, but have 66 per cent of the population. Already more than 40 per cent of their rural inhabitants are landless farmers. The rapid growth of population in Java has greatly increased the proportion of young people, and there is an urgent need to create employment for them. It is estimated that in the period 1974–9 at least 3,5 million new jobs will have to be created in Java, of which 2,7 million will have to be for people aged between 19 and 24. By contrast, in Sumatra, Kalimantan, Sulawesi and West Irian, economic development is hampered by the sparseness of the population. An ideal solution would therefore seem to be to transfer some of the surplus population from Java and the adjacent small islands, to hitherto unoccupied lands in the outer territories.

There have in fact already been a few attempts at population resettlement in Indonesia. As early as 1905 the Dutch authorities undertook a pioneer settlement of Javanese farmers and their families in South Sumatra. Between 1936 and 1940, the number of Javanese settlers in the outer territories increased from 68 000 to 206 000. The resettlement programme was interrupted by the outbreak of the

Second World War, but was revived after the war ended. Between 1950 and 1954 the Indonesian Government sponsored the movement of some 90 000 people from Java to the outer territories.

Until 1972, Java was the only source of migrants to the outer territories, but the Transmigration Law No. 3 of that year also included Madura, Bali and Lombok. The Five Year Development Plan (1975–9) fixed a target of 250 000 families to be resettled in the outer territories, of which 11 000 were to be moved in 1974–5. It proved difficult, however, to find enough people willing to undertake the hardships of pioneer life, and in that year only 5 700 families were actually resettled.

In Malaysia also, the growth of population in recent years has caused considerable pressure on existing agricultural land. To meet this problem the Federal Land Development Authority (FELDA) was set up in 1956. FELDA has already established a number of successful agricultural settlements. Many of FELDA's settlements are based on the production of rubber, but in some of the more recent schemes oil palm is the main cash crop. Each settler in FELDA's schemes is given a small house lot, two to three hectares of land for the cultivation of rubber or other cash crops, about one hectare for orchards and one hectare for rice. Most of FELDA's schemes have been fairly small, usually in the order of 2 000 hectares in size. A very much larger FELDA scheme is that of the Jengka Triangle in the state of Pehang involving the resettlement of some 40 000 hectares of land formerly covered by rain forest.

In Sri Lanka, there has been a considerable amount of settlement in the dry zone during recent decades. The lowland dry zone comprises about two-thirds of Sri Lanka by area, but at present only contains one-fifth of the island's population. In the past the lowland dry zone was irrigated by an extensive system of tanks and was the most densely populated part of the island. During the eleventh to thirteenth centuries, however, Sri Lanka was invaded by the Tamils from southern India. During the centuries of political disintegration which followed these invasions, many of the irrigation tanks fell into disrepair, malaria became prevalent, and the dry zone became partly depopulated. Since the end of the Second World War, however, malaria has been eradicated by DDT spraying, and numerous irrigation projects have

been undertaken in the dry zone, the most important being that in the valley of the Gal Oya river. The habitability of the dry zone has thus been considerably increased, and in recent years the government has been encouraging people from the more densely populated parts of the island to settle there. Between 1945 and 1955 about 100 000 people moved into the dry zone from other parts of Sri Lanka.

In tropical South America also, new lands have been, and are in process of being developed. During the present century, for example, the Peruvian Government has been paying special attention to the development of the potentially fertile but remote and at present sparsely populated valleys of the montana (the forested region to the east of the Andes). As a result of road building programmes, a significant amount of settlement has already taken place in the montana, particularly along the road from Cerro de Pasco to Tingo Maria and thence to Pucallpa. It is hoped that the development of new agricultural settlements in the montana will make it possible to increase national food production, and also help to relieve overpopulation in the Sierra. There are a number of similar new agricultural settlements in the montana region of Bolivia.

In the drier parts of tropical Africa, some recent population movements have been associated with the development of irrigation. For example, the Gezira Scheme of Sudan, and the Inland Niger Delta Scheme in Mali have attracted settlers from the surrounding areas. In other cases rural resettlement has become possible as a result of the improvement in health conditions. This is particularly the case in areas which have been cleared of tsetse fly. In the Anchau Corridor to the south of Kano in Nigeria, some 1 800 sq km have been cleared of tsetse fly. The Anchau Settlement Scheme, which was started in 1937, involved the removal of people from several districts which were badly infested with tsetse fly, and the building of 16 new villages and the model town of Takalafiya. Some 4 300 people were resettled under this scheme.

Of a somewhat different nature are those population movements involving the resettlement of people from areas which have been flooded as a result of dam construction. In Ghana, for example, alternative settlement had to be found for 78 000 people who formerly lived in the areas now beneath Lake Volta.

Large numbers of people had also to be resettled, as a result of the formation of the Kainji lake in Nigeria. The construction of the Aswan High Dam in Egypt, necessitated the evacuation and resettlement of a large number of people who formerly lived in that part of the Nile valley which is now flooded by Lake Nasser.

B: Migrations of a temporary nature

As well as permanent migrations, there are other population movements of a more temporary nature, which involve people leaving their homes for a relatively short period of time, and later returning to them. These movements may take place entirely within a country, or they may involve the crossing of international boundaries. They may involve absences of just a few days, or of several years. Temporary migrations can be divided into two broad categories, according to their purpose:

1 migrations for leisure;
2 migrations for work.

Migrations for leisure

Migrations for the purpose of leisure are fully discussed in Chapter 17, but a brief mention might be made here of pilgrimages. These are journeys to sacred places, which are undertaken as an act of religious devotion. The most noteworthy are the Moslem pilgrimages to Mecca, and the pilgrimages associated with the Hindu religion. According to Islamic belief, the pilgrimage to Mecca should be made at least once in the lifetime of every Moslem. Thus, every year large numbers of pilgrims converge upon the holy city, from places as far apart as West Africa and Southeast Asia.

Migrations for work

The main types of migrations for purposes of work are:

1 those associated with nomadic pastoralism (discussed in Chapter 10);
2 those in response to seasonal variations in the demand for agricultural labour;
3 those involving other types of work.

In many types of agriculture the demand for labour fluctuates considerably throughout the year, being generally heaviest at planting time and harvest. Population movements associated with seasonal employment in agriculture are common in many tropical areas. The movement is generally from the less developed areas where subsistence agriculture predominates, to the more highly developed ones where the emphasis is on the production of cash crops. Many of the seasonal migrants make arrangements for employment individually, while others are employed under special recruitment schemes.

The seasonal migration of agricultural workers probably attains its greatest importance in tropical Africa, but it is also important in many other parts of the tropical world. The seasonal demand for agricultural labour on the farms of the United States, for example, has in the past attracted great numbers of migrant workers from Mexico. West Indian workers are also recruited for the United States, particularly to help with the citrus and sugar cane harvests in Florida. In South America there is a seasonal movement of Indians from the highland areas of Peru, to pick cotton in the coastal oases. In the north-east of Brazil, migrant workers are recruited from the interior to harvest cocoa on the coastal plantations.

Outside of agriculture, the main sources of employment for migrant workers are mines and factories. In tropical Africa in particular, a great deal of labour migration is associated with mining.

Migrant labour movements in tropical Africa

Migration was widespread in tropical Africa long before the colonial era. In the past African population movements were particularly associated with tribal warfare and slave trading, pilgrimages and nomadic pastoralism. The colonial era saw the gradual disappearance of tribal warfare and slave trading, but it also saw the development of new forms of population movements, particularly those associated with the

Chief areas of attraction.

→ Approximate direction of
   main movements of population

1 Groundnut growing areas of
  Senegal and Gambia

2 Abidjan and coffee and cocoa growing
  areas of the Ivory coast

3 Towns of southern Ghana and cocoa
  growing and mining areas

4 Lagos and cocoa growing area
  of south-western Nigeria

5 Kano and groundnut growing area
  of northern Nigeria

6 Tin fields of Jos Plateau

7 Port Harcourt and the oilfields

8 Plantation areas of Cameroon

9 Plantation areas of Fernando Poo

10 Kinshasa and Brazzaville areas

11 Khartoum and Gezira

12 Coffee and cotton growing areas to north
   and west of Lake Victoria

13 Nairobi and cash crop growing areas of
   highlands of Kenya

14 Mombasa

15 Tanga

16 Dar-es-Salaam

17 Mining areas of Shaba Province of Zaire

18 Copper belt of Zambia

19 Mining and industrial areas of Zimbabwe

20 Mining and industrial areas of the Province of
   Transvaal in the Republic of South Africa

Fig. 6.1 Population movements in tropical Africa

temporary migration of labour, and with the process of urbanisation.

It has been estimated that at least 5 million people every year are involved in labour migration in Africa, south of the Sahara. The greatest demand for migrant labour is in the areas of export crop production, in mines and factories, and at commercial centres and seaports.

West Africa

In West Africa, the most important form of temporary migration is that involving the seasonal movement of agricultural workers. The main axis of migration is from north to south, with migrants originating in Mali, Niger, Upper Volta, and the northern parts of Ghana and Nigeria, and seeking work in the economically more advanced areas further south. The areas most in need of migrant labour are the coffee and cocoa producing areas of the Ivory Coast, and the cocoa producing areas of Ghana and Nigeria. The distances involved are considerable, often several hundred kilometres. In the past the migrants travelled on foot, but now many of them use modern forms of transport. The migrants are usually men between the ages of about 16 and 35 years.

In addition to the north to south movement, there is also an east to west one, from the poorer areas of Mali, Guinea Bissau and Guinea, to the groundnut growing areas of Senegal and Gambia. The migrant workers are known as 'navetanes' in Senegal, and as 'strange farmers' in Gambia. In return for helping with the cultivation of the local farmers' groundnuts, the migrant workers are often allocated a piece of land to cultivate for themselves. In the past, this westward movement probably involved as many as 75 000 people annually, but in recent years it has declined very considerably in importance.

Other West African migrant workers find employment in the iron ore mines of Liberia and Sierra Leone, in the gold mines of Ghana, and in major towns such as Dakar, Abidjan, Takoradi, Kumasi, Accra, Ibadan and Lagos. During the 1950s large numbers of Africans from neighbouring countries, particularly from Liberia and Guinea, flocked into Sierra Leone to engage in the surface digging for diamonds. Some of these illegal immigrants were later expelled by the Sierra Leonean authorities.

East and Central Africa

There is also a considerable amount of labour migration in East Africa and in Central Africa, associated both with agriculture and with mining. The migrants are usually 'target workers', who leave home with the intention of saving a specific amount of money, and return home when they have succeeded in doing so.

The main sources of migrant labour in East Africa and Central Africa are Mozambique, Malaŵi, Rwanda and Burundi. The most important sources of employment for migrant workers are the mines of the Rand of South Africa and the Zambian Copperbelt, the farms and industrial establishments of Zimbabwe, the coffee growing areas of Uganda, and the sisal growing areas of Tanzania.

Large numbers of migrant workers from the densely populated countries of Rwanda and Burundi find employment in the coffee growing areas of Uganda. In Tanzania the most important source of employment for migrant workers is the sisal industry. In the past there was a considerable seasonal movement of workers from the mainland of Tanganyika, to help with the clove harvest on the islands of Zanzibar and Pemba, but in recent years the trend has been towards a greater dependence upon local workers.

Large numbers of migrant workers from Botswana, Malaŵi and Mozambique find employment in the Republic of South Africa. In 1974 there were an estimated 130 000 Malaŵians in South Africa. Prior to the breakup of the Federation of Rhodesia and Nyasaland in 1963, large numbers of Malaŵians found employment in Zimbabwe (then Southern Rhodesia). The economy of Malaŵi is heavily dependant upon the earnings of her migrant workers. These earnings usually rank third, after exports of tobacco and tea, as a source of foreign exchange. Almost half a million migrants leave Mozambique each year, mainly to seek work in the Republic of South Africa.

Other parts of tropical Africa

On the islands of Fernando Pó, São Tomé and Príncipe, there is a considerable shortage of agricultural labour, and workers are recruited from Angola, the Cape Verde Islands, Mozambique and Nigeria, to work on the coffee and cocoa plantations. In the

Sudan, there is a considerable movement of migrant workers to the Gezira, during the cotton picking season.

C: The consequences of migration

Migration has many important consequences, both for the areas which the migrants leave, and also for the areas which receive them. Although some of these consequences are beneficial, migration can also create problems.

The source areas

1 One of the most obvious consequences of permanent migration is the reduction of numbers in the areas which the migrants leave. In some cases migration may result in an actual decline in the total population of the source area. More commonly, however, it simply slows down the rate of population growth. This reduction in the rate of population growth is often very welcome. For example, had it not been for the relief provided by emigration, the problem of unemployment in many of the overcrowded islands of the West Indies, would have been even more severe than is at present the case.

2 Migration also affects the age and sex structure of the population of the source areas. Very often the migrants are predominantly young adults, and as a result there tends to be an unusually high proportion of older people in the areas which they leave. In some cases the migrants are predominantly of one sex, thus causing an imbalance in the sex structure of the population. These changes in age and sex structure often lead to a reduction in the birth rate, thus slowing down the rate of population growth still further.

3 Many migrants remit money to relatives back at home. These remittances play an important role in the economic life of several West Indian territories, by helping to offset the unfavourable balance of visible trade. For example, in 1965 migrants' remittances to Barbados were equivalent to about 16 per cent of the total value of the island's domestic exports for that year. The corresponding figures for Grenada and St. Vincent were 20 per cent and 24 per cent respectively. The earnings of migrant workers are also important to the economies of several tropical African countries, particularly to Botswana, Malaŵi, Mozambique and Upper Volta.

4 At the same time the absence of large numbers of able-bodied men for part of the year, may also have an adverse effect on the economy of their homeland. This is particularly the case in some parts of tropical Africa, where many of the men are away at planting time or harvest, when their labour is most needed at home.

The receiving areas

1 Another important consequence of permanent migration is the increase in the population of the receiving area. While migration is responsible for slowing down the rate of population growth in the source areas, it also increases the rate of growth in the receiving areas.

2 The influx of migrants often alters the age and sex structure of the population. In areas which attract migrants, there is often an unusually high proportion of young adults in the population. Very often also, men far outnumber women. In the fast growing city of Calcutta in India, for example, about two-thirds of the population is male. Changes of this sort not only influence the birth rate, but may also have important social consequences, such as an increase in the incidence of prostitution.

3 The drift of population from rural areas into the towns often causes serious social problems (see Chapter 7).

4 One very important consequence of external migration is the bringing together of peoples of different race, language and religion. Although in some cases the immigrants have been successfully integrated into the society of their new homeland, in several parts of the tropical world the development of plural societies has created serious problems.

5 Migrants may be responsible for the spread of disease. For example, in many parts of tropical Africa the movements of pilgrims, nomadic pasturalists and migrant workers make the control of malaria difficult.

Exercises

1 With special reference to the West Indies, show how past migrations have influenced present population patterns.
2 a) Write a brief account of European settlement in tropical Africa.
   b) Attempt to explain why Europeans have settled in some parts of tropical Africa rather than in others.
   c) What have been the main consequences of European settlement?
3 Illustrating your answer with examples from the tropical lands, discuss the major causes and consequences of large-scale permanent movements of population.
4 a) Write a brief account of labour migration in tropical Africa.
   b) Attempt to explain why labour migration takes place, and assess its consequences for both source and receiving areas.
5 Write a brief account of some of the main land resettlement schemes which have taken place in the tropical world during the last few decades.

Suggested reading

See Chapter 7.

CHAPTER SEVEN

Urbanisation

A: General

In recent years by far the most important form of internal migration has been that involving the movement of people from the countryside into the towns. It has been estimated that at the start of the nineteenth century only 2,4 per cent of the world's population lived in towns of more than 20 000 inhabitants, and only 1,7 per cent lived in towns of more than 100 000. By 1960, however, 27,1 per cent of the world's population lived in towns of more than 20 000 inhabitants, and 19,9 per cent lived in towns of more than 100 000. The process whereby an increasing proportion of the total population becomes concentrated in towns, is known as *urbanisation*.

A number of different criteria may be used in defining an area as urban. These include population size, population density and function, as well as legal, administrative, social and economic criteria. The most widely used criterion is that of population size, and in most countries a population cluster with well-defined boundaries and having more than a certain number of inhabitants is classified as an urban centre. The distinction between rural and urban population is not, however, an easy one to make, as there is no clear-cut division between country and town, but rather a continuum of population clusters ranging in size from the smallest to the largest. Furthermore, the threshold between rural and urban population varies from country to country. In Kenya, for example, centres with more than 2 000 inhabitants are classified as towns, while in Ghana the cut-off point between rural and urban is taken as 5 000, and in Malaysia as 10 000 inhabitants. The United Nations classifies urban centres as those having more than 20 000 inhabitants.

The ratio of urban to rural population varies considerably from one part of the world to another. In most parts of the tropical world only a relatively small proportion of the total population lives in towns. In recent years, however, the rate of population growth has generally been far higher in towns than in the rural areas. For example, in the period from 1914 to 1950, the urban population of Venezuela increased by 79 per cent, while the rural population showed a slight decline. In Brazil, the rural population increased by 18 per cent between 1940 and 1950, but the urban population increased by 49 per cent.

Causes of urbanisation

Although the rapid growth of urban population in recent years can be partly attributed to a high rate of natural increase, in most tropical countries it has to a large extent been the result of a drift of people away from the countryside into the towns. In Brazil, for example, only 29 per cent of the population growth of the eight largest towns between 1940 and 1950 was due to natural increase, while 71 per cent was the result of migratory movement.

What has caused this drift of population into the towns? One of the major attractions of the towns is that they offer, or at least to many people they appear to offer, better opportunities for employment than are to be found in the rural areas. In some countries such as India, the high rate of natural increase has in recent years resulted in severe overpopulation in many rural areas, and in the creation of a large landless class. In other countries there has been an actual decline in the amount of employment available in the rural areas, as a result of the increased mechanisation of agriculture. In Puerto Rico, for example, 214 000 people (35,9 per cent of total employment) were engaged in agriculture in 1950, but by 1965 only 122 000 (17,7 per cent) were thus engaged.

While employment opportunities in rural areas have often failed to keep pace with population growth, in some tropical countries the number of jobs available in the towns has increased considerably during the last few decades. This is particularly so in those countries which have embarked upon ambitious industrialisation programmes. In such countries, the bulk of the new industrial establishments have in most cases been located in and immediately around the main towns.

People from rural areas are also attracted to towns by the superior amenities which they usually offer. Most large towns in the tropical world can now offer electricity and piped water supplies, and also modern sanitation. These amenities, on the other hand, are still not widely available in the rural areas. The towns also generally offer better medical and educational facilities than do the rural areas, as well as more opportunities for entertainment. The last aspect in particular attracts many young people to the towns.

The consequences

In many parts of the tropical world, the drift of large numbers of people from the rural areas into the towns has caused serious social problems. In many tropical towns the provision of housing, sanitation, electricity, piped water and other amenities, has failed to keep pace with the rapid growth of population. Very often immigrants from the rural areas have found it extremely difficult to obtain shelter as legitimate home-owners or tenants, and in desperation have 'squatted' on whatever unoccupied land they have been able to find. In recent years 'shanty towns' have sprung up on the outskirts of many tropical cities. These slum settlements are known by different names in various parts of the world. In India they are commonly known as 'bustees', in Peru as 'barriadas', in Venezuela as 'ranchos', in Brazil as 'favelas' and in French-speaking Africa as 'bidonvilles'. In 1950 Rio de Janeiro had 58 favelas, with a total of 165 000 inhabitants. By 1970, however, the number of favelas in Rio had increased to 165, containing 565 000 inhabitants.

In the crowded shanty towns the migrants construct flimsy shelters from whatever cheap building materials are available to them, including metal sheeting, packing cases and matting. In many shanty towns there is no piped water supply, no adequate sanitation, no electricity supply and no proper roads. Very often the migrants from rural areas discover that employment is more difficult to obtain than they had anticipated, and in many tropical towns unemployment has become a serious problem. In 1965, for example, it was estimated that about one-third of the labouring force of Lagos was out of work. Considering the unsatisfactory living conditions which prevail in shanty towns, it is not surprising that disease and crime proliferate, and are difficult to bring under control.

Naturally, municipal authorities generally disapprove of the setting up of shanty towns on the outskirts of their cities. In some cases squatters have been forcibly evicted from their homes by the authorities, and their dwellings pulled down. As the authorities are rarely able to provide any alternative accommodation, however, the evicted squatters usually quickly rebuild their shacks in some other part of the city.

In some countries, such as Tanzania, attempts have been made to stem the flow of migrants from the rural areas into the towns. In a few cases, unemployed migrants in the towns have been rounded up by the authorities, and returned to the countryside. Such measures seem unlikely to be successful in the long-term, unless much more is done to develop the rural areas, making them better places in which to live.

B: Urbanisation in tropical America

In recent decades there has been a rapid growth of urban population in many parts of tropical America.

In several South American countries more than half the total population is now classified as urban. In a few countries, such as Venezuela, immigration from Europe has played a significant role in urban growth during the present century. In most countries, however, the bulk of urban growth can be attributed to a high rate of natural increase, and to the influx of migrants from rural areas. As in other parts of the tropical world, the rapid growth of urban population has created serious social problems. In particular a great many South American cities are today marred by the existence of squalid shanty towns on their outskirts.

Among the South American cities which have grown particularly rapidly in recent decades are Lima and Caracas. The population of the Peruvian capital of Lima grew from 100 000 in 1850 to 250 000 in 1910, and to 650 000 in 1940. In 1972 the population of Greater Lima amounted to 3 158 000, representing 23 per cent of Peru's total population. A great deal of Lima's recent growth can be attributed to the large-scale influx of migrants from the mountainous and poverty-stricken interior of Peru. The Venezuelan capital of Caracas had a population of only 200 000 in 1939. By 1953 it had grown to 500 000, and reached 2 million by 1970 when it accounted for

18 per cent of Venezuela's total population. In the 10 years following World War Two some 1 million migrants arrived in Venezuela, and many of these settled in Caracas.

Urban growth has also been rapid in parts of Central America, particularly in Mexico. During the present century there has been a considerable movement of people from the rural areas of Mexico into the towns, and by the mid-1970s 62 per cent of Mexico's population was urban. Mexico has 39 towns with more than 100 000 inhabitants, of which three are millionaire cities. Many of the migrants from the rural areas have settled in the capital Mexico City, the population of which has increased tremendously during the present century. In 1900 the Federal District had 541 000 inhabitants, representing 4 per cent of Mexico's total population. By 1975, however, its population had grown to 8 299 000, representing 14 per cent of the total population.

The drift of population from the rural areas into the towns has also been very marked in recent decades in several of the West Indian territories. Fig. 7.1 shows that between 1950 and 1960 considerable changes took place in the distribution of population in the island of Puerto Rico. During this period the population of the island increased by 6,3 per cent, in

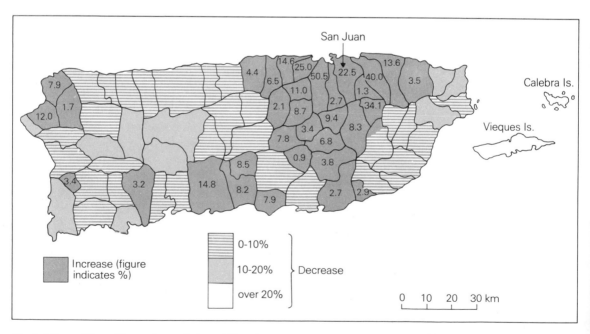

Fig. 7.1 Puerto Rico – Changes in population, 1950–1960

84

spite of large-scale emigration to the mainland of North America. A number of municipalities, however, showed a decline in numbers, amounting to as much as 35,4 per cent in one case. On the other hand, the population of several municipalities expanded at a far faster rate than the national average. This was particularly so in the case of the capital San Juan, and the municipalities immediately around San Juan. It is in these municipalities that much of the recent industrial development has taken place, and where consequently many new job opportunities have been created.

Table 39 shows the level of urbanisation in selected countries in the early 1970s.

The cities of Brazil

In 1974, 59 per cent of Brazil's population was urban. There were 77 centres of more than 100 000 inhabitants. Of these five were millionaire cities, and a further three each had more than half a million inhabitants.

Although in the past immigration from Europe contributed considerably to the growth of Brazil's urban population, in recent decades the very high rate of urban growth can mainly be attributed to natural increase and to internal migration. In particular there has been a large influx of migrants from the dry, poverty-stricken interior of north-eastern Brazil into the main urban centres.

Table 40 shows the growth of Brazil's five largest cities during the present century.

Virtually all the larger cities of Brazil are situated either on or near the coast, and the vast interior of the country has few towns of any size. Notable exceptions are the important river port of Manaus (389 000), and the new capital Brasilia.

With a population of over 7 million, São Paulo is Brazil's largest and fastest growing city. It is situated

Table 39 Urban population in tropical America

Country	Year	Urban pop. as % of total pop.	No. of large towns	
			Over 100 thousand	Over 1 million
South America				
Brazil	1974	59	77	5
Colombia	1974	64	24	3
Ecuador	1974	41	2	0
Peru	1974	55	10	1
Venezuela	1970	76	12	1
Central America				
Costa Rica	1973	41	1	0
El Salvador	1973	39	1	0
Guatemala	1973	34	1	0
Honduras	1974	31	2	0
Mexico	1974	62	39	3
Panama	1974	50	1	0
West Indies				
Antigua	1970	34	0	0
Cuba	1971	61	6	1
Dominican Rep.	1972	42	2	0
Haiti	1971	19	1	0
Jamaica	1970	37	1	0
Puerto Rico	1973	58	3	0

Table 40 Population of Brazil's largest cities (thousands), 1960–75

City	1900	1940	1960	1970	1975	1975 as % of 1900
São Paulo	240	1 139	3 872	5 187	7 199	3 000
Rio de Janeiro	692	1 782	4 370	4 252	4 858	702
Belo Horizonte	13	211	684	1 107	1 557	11 977
Recife	113	353	974	1 046	1 250	1 106
Salvador	206	294	639	998	1 237	600

at an altitude of 750 metres, and is 65 km from the coast. Although São Paulo was founded as early as 1554, it remained a very small town until a century ago. With the opening up of São Paulo State and the development of the Brazilian coffee industry, however, the town began to expand rapidly. From less than 25 000 inhabitants in 1872, São Paulo reached 250 000 by 1901 and 1 million by 1933. Several factors have favoured the development of São Paulo as a major urban centre:

1 because of the altitude at which it is situated, its climate is much healthier and more invigorating than that of the coastal towns;
2 it is the centre of a rich agricultural region;
3 abundant hydro-electric power is available nearby, and this has favoured the development of manufacturing industry;
4 it has excellent communications, particularly with the port of Santos.

São Paulo is an extremely modern city, with many sky-scraper buildings. It is Brazil's most important manufacturing centre having a wide variety of industry including textiles and clothing, the assembly of motor vehicles, the processing of foodstuffs, and the manufacture of petrochemicals, machinery and electrical equipment, leather, and paper products. There are two airports near São Paulo, which handle both domestic and international flights.

Rio de Janeiro is Brazil's second largest city, and was the federal capital from 1763 to 1960. The city is strung out for some 10 km along the western shores of Guanabara Bay, and is wedged in between the sea and the mountains. Further expansion of the city will be difficult because of the lack of flat land, and already some land is being reclaimed from the sea for building purposes. Guanabara Bay provides a

magnificent natural harbour, and Rio has developed as Brazil's main port. It is also an important manufacturing centre, its industries including food processing and the manufacture of metallurgical products, textiles, chemicals, paper products and tobacco products. There are shipyards both in Rio, and across the bay in the suburb of Niteroi. Rio has two airports, one on the mainland and the other on a small island in Guanabara Bay. There are several fine beaches nearby, and Rio is an important holiday resort.

The rapidly growing city of Belo Horizonte is the capital of the state of Minas Gerais. Belo Horizonte was Brazil's first planned town, being built to replace the old state capital of Ouro Preto in 1896. Belo Horizonte expanded from 56 000 inhabitants in 1920 to 353 000 in 1950, and to 1½ million in 1975. Belo Horizonte is the centre of an important mining and agricultural area. Its industries include the manufacture of textiles and iron and steel products, and diamond cutting.

Several large cities are located along the northeastern coast of Brazil, of particular importance being Recife, Salvador, Fortaleza and Belem. Recife (also known as Pernambuco) is an important port, with a rich agricultural hinterland which produces sugar and cotton. Its industries include cotton textiles, sugar refining, the extraction of vegetable oils and cement manufacture. Salvador (Bahia) was the capital of Brazil between 1549 and 1763. It is an important port, and the largest market centre in Brazil for cocoa and tobacco. Salvador has developed as an important manufacturing centre, its industries including the making of cigarettes and cigars, cotton textiles, chemicals, cement and the refining of sugar. Nearby at Mataripe is a petroleum refinery. Fortaleza (Ceara) with a population of 1 110 000, is the capital of the

Fig. 7.2 Brasilia

state of Ceara. It is a centre for coastal trade and fishing, and its industries include cotton textiles and the extraction of vegetable oil. Belem (Para) with a population of 772 000 is situated near the mouth of the Amazon river, some 150 km from the open sea. It is a port handling the products of the Amazon Basin, its exports including rubber, cocoa, timber and Brazil nuts.

The federal capital of Brazil is Brasilia. In 1970 the city had a population of 272 000. As early as 1823, just after Brazil achieved its independence from Portugal, it was suggested that a new capital should be established on the Planalto Central, near the geographical centre of the country. It was hoped that the establishment of such a city would act as a magnet to draw people away from the coastal areas, thus helping to open up the interior of Brazil. The idea of a capital located in the interior was embodied in the constitution of 1891, but it was not until 1956 that the site for the new federal capital was finally selected.

Brasilia is located in the west central state of Goias at an altitude of 900 metres, and is 885 km north of São Paulo, 930 km west of Rio de Janeiro and 1 030 km south-west of Salvador. As soon as the site for the new capital was selected in 1956, the

87

Companhia Urbanizadora da Nova Capitas do Brazil was set up to finance, construct and move the capital, which was inaugurated in 1960. Highways were extended to Brasilia from the north and south-east, and in 1968 a 240 km long railway extension was completed from Pires do Rio. The city is also served by a large number of internal air services.

The plan of Brasilia represents a bird in flight. A residential axis runs roughly north to south, while a monumental axis runs east to west. At the west end of the monumental axis are the municipal buildings, while at the east end are the legislative, executive and judicial buildings. The city is bordered on the eastern side by an artificial lake, the Lago de Brasilia. Around the lake shores are areas reserved for private homes, hotels, restaurants, clubs and foreign embassies.

One thing which the planners have sought to prevent is the development of shanty towns of the type which are found around most large Brazilian cities. The government undertook a programme to provide houses for the low income groups, and so far it has been possible to prevent the development of slum areas within the city itself. The government housing programme, however, has not been able to keep pace with the influx of people from rural areas, and a shanty town has grown up some 8 km to the south-west of Brasilia.

C: Urbanisation in tropical Africa

At present in most tropical African countries less than one quarter of the total population lives in towns, compared with more than three-quarters in most of the highly industrialised countries of the temperate lands. Although most of the inhabitants of tropical Africa still live in rural areas, in many countries there has been a rapid growth of urban population during the last few decades. In fact, although accurate data is often lacking, it seems likely that at present the rate of urban growth is higher in tropical Africa than in any other major part of the world.

The growth of towns

Although many of the large towns of tropical Africa have grown up since the arrival of the Europeans, towns existed in tropical Africa for several centuries before this. The small town of Aksum in Ethiopia, for example, is thought to date back to the first century AD. During the seventh century the town of Gao in Mali grew up as a Saharan trade terminal and a centre of the Songhai Empire, while in the eighth century a number of towns were established by the Arabs along the coast of the Indian Ocean, including Mombasa in Kenya and Mogadishu in Somalia. In the tenth and eleventh centuries a number of other towns appeared in West Africa, including Kano, Katsina and Zaria in northern Nigeria, and such Yoruba towns as Ife and Ilorin in south-western Nigeria.

During the sixteenth and seventeenth centuries there was another development of town-building in West Africa, as capitals emerged in many African kingdoms and tribal groups. Some of these capitals have since declined in importance, but others remain significant towns today, including Abomey and Porto Novo in Benin, Kumasi in Ghana, Segou and Sikasso in Mali, Bobo-Dioulasso and Ouagadougou in Upper Volta and Zinder in Niger. The sixteenth century also saw the establishment by the Europeans of a number of settlements in West Africa. Most of these were situated on the coast and were centered around forts used as bases for trading and slaving. They included Rugisque in Senegal; Sekondi, Cape Coast and Accra in Ghana; Ouidah in Benin; and Lagos and Calabar in Nigeria. During the eighteenth century there was very little new town formation, although a notable town founded in this period was Freetown in Sierra Leone, which was established in 1787 as a settlement for freed slaves.

The main period of urban growth in tropical Africa, however, did not occur until the late nineteenth and early twentieth centuries, and in particular until after the European partition of Africa. During this period a great many towns were founded by the Europeans. These included many of the present capitals, such as Dar-es-Salaam (1862), Kinshasa (1881), Bamako (1883), Brazzaville (1883), Salisbury (1890), Kampala (1890), Bangui (1899) and Abidjan (1903). During this period, although new towns were founded, both African and European-established towns grew only slowly in size. Before the First World War, the vast majority of towns in tropical Africa had less than 20 000, and many had less than 10 000 inhabitants. For example, in 1911 Kumasi had a population of 19 000, while in 1910 Bamako had 7 000, Conakry 6 000 and Cotonou 2 000 inhabitants. Notably larger, however, were some of the Yoruba towns of south-western Nigeria, with Ibadan having a population of 200 000 in 1900.

In the period between the two world wars there was a steady growth of urban population, and by the outbreak of the Second World War a number of towns including Dakar, Lagos, Addis Ababa and Tananarive had over 100 000 inhabitants. A number of towns were founded during the inter-war period, including Niamey in Niger and the new mining centres of the Zambian Copperbelt and the Shaba Province of Zaïre.

Since the end of the Second World War the pace of urbanisation has quickened markedly, and in most tropical African countries is still continuing to do so. Only a few towns have been founded since 1945. These include Nouakchott in Mauritania, Tema in Ghana and a number of small mining centres. The population of many of the existing towns, however, has expanded rapidly. For example, the population of Abidjan grew from a quarter of a million in 1963 to half a million in 1969.

As in most other parts of the tropical world, this rapid growth of urban population can be attributed to two main processes:

1 a high rate of natural increase, which has mainly come about as a result of the lowering of the urban death rate due to better sanitation, improved medical facilities, etc.;
2 the influx of people from rural areas into the towns.

Although the relative importance of these two processes varies from country to country, in most cases the role played by in-migration has been far greater than that of natural increase. In the period between 1963 and 1969, for example, Abidjan's population grew at an annual rate of 12 per cent. Of this, only 2,5 per cent was accounted for by natural increase, while 9,5 per cent resulted from in-migration.

Urban functions

Towns tend to be placed into categories according to their size, status or main function. It is not always easy to identify a town's main function, however, as many towns are in fact multi-functional. For example, as well as being the administrative capital of Ghana, Accra also has an important commercial function, and is a growing industrial centre.

1 *Commercial centres* – these include seaport towns, river and lake port towns, and those commercial towns which have grown up at inland cross roads. Many of the largest towns in tropical Africa are seaports. With the exceptions of Congo, Zaïre, Kenya, Ethiopia and Sudan, all the coastal countries have their largest town on the coast, although some such as Accra in Ghana are no longer important ports. River and lake ports also owe their existence to break of bulk functions, as goods are transferred between land and water-borne forms of transport. Notable river ports include Brazzaville, Bangui and Kinshasa on the Zaïre river, Bamako and Niamey on the Niger and Khartoum on the Nile. Lake ports are of significance in East Africa and Central Africa, of particular importance being Kisumu and Mwanza on Lake Victoria. Commercial centres have also grown up at the nodes of land routes. Examples include such towns as Kumasi, which is the focus of nearly all the major north–south trading routes in Ghana. In the sub-Saharan zone of West Africa a number of towns developed in the Middle Ages as the terminii of trans-Saharan caravan routes.

2 *Mining towns* – a number of towns have grown up largely as a result of the development of mining during the present century. The largest of these towns are to be found in the Zambian Copperbelt, and in the neighbouring Shaba Province of Zaïre. Other mining centres include the coal mining centre of Enugu and the tin mining centre of Jos in Nigeria, the gold mining centres of Obuasi and Tarkwa in Ghana, the coal mining centre of Wankie in Zimbabwe, and the zinc and lead mining centre of Kabwe in Zambia.

3 *Agricultural towns* – these are on the whole very few in number, although they are frequent in south-western Nigeria, where in some of the Yoruba

towns almost half the working population is still engaged in agriculture.

4 *Industrial towns* – although many of the larger African towns now have some manufacturing establishments, in only a few towns is the industrial function dominant. Towns in which manufacturing is the dominant factor include Rufisque in Senegal, Jinja in Uganda and Redcliff in Zimbabwe.

5 *Administrative towns* – towns in which administration is the dominant function are also comparatively rare, as most administrative centres also have an important commercial function. Only a few of the smaller capitals such as Gaberones in Botswana can be described as predominantly administrative centres, although many of the larger towns originally owed their existence to administration.

In the post-independence period many of the capitals of tropical Africa have grown considerably in population, as they have generally been able to offer expanding opportunities for employment. Very few of these capitals occupy a geographically central position within the country. In most of the countries which front on to the sea the capital is located on the coast, although there are a number of notable exceptions such as Khartoum, Addis Ababa, Nairobi and Kinshasa. In the case of the landlocked countries, only the Upper Voltaian capital of Ouagadougou occupies a really central position. The marginal location of the capital has often been found a disadvantage, and in a few cases the capital has been or is about to be transferred. For example, in 1975 the capital of Malaŵi was changed from Zomba to Lilongwe. Zomba was originally chosen as a suitable site as it was situated at the confluence of slave routes, at a time when the British were determined to put an end to the slave trade. Unfortunately, Zomba is not easily accessible from the administrative point of view, whereas Lilongwe is much more centrally positioned. In the past the north of Malaŵi has been much less developed than the south of the country, and it is hoped that by transferring the capital to Lilongwe it will be easier to remedy this situation. In 1976 Nigeria decided to change its Federal Capital from the seaport of Lagos. A new Federal Capital Territory has been established south of the town of Abuja, which is situated in the middle of the country. There are also plans to transfer the capital of Tanzania from the large seaport of Dar-es-Salaam, to the small inland town of Dodoma.

Regional differences

Although the degree of urbanisation in tropical Africa as a whole is low, marked regional differences do in fact occur. Broadly speaking, the most highly urbanised countries are those which are economically the most advanced, while the least urbanised are generally the poorer ones. West Africa, which has had longer contact with the countries of the western world than have other parts of tropical Africa is the most highly urbanised, while East Africa is the least urbanised. Table 41 shows the degree of urbanisation in selected countries in the early 1970s.

Table 41 Urban population in tropical Africa

Country	Year	Urban pop. as % of total pop.	No. of large towns	
			Over 100 thousand	Over 1 million
Benin	1973	13	1	—
Burundi	1970	2	—	—
Chad	1974	14	1	—
Ethiopia	1974	11	2	1
Gambia	1972	14	—	—
Ghana	1974	31	3	—
Kenya	1969	10	2	—
Nigeria	1970	15	26	1
Zimbabwe	1974	19	2	—
Rwanda	1971	3	—	—
Sudan	1974	13	4	—
Tanzania	1973	7	1	—
Togo	1974	15	1	—
Zaïre	1974	26	12	1
Zambia	1973	34	6	—

Towns in West Africa

Within West Africa a distinction can be made between the traditional towns, several of which have histories dating back for many centuries, and the towns which developed during the colonial period. Many of the traditional towns are or were formerly walled, and tend to be much more congested and less well laid out than their colonial counterparts. The colonial towns are often laid out on a grid plan, and some of them, particularly those in French-speaking West Africa, have broad avenues and tree-lined boulevards.

The towns of West Africa are not evenly distributed, but tend to fall into three main groups:

1 the coastal towns;
2 the towns of the forested interior;
3 the towns of the savanna interior.

Several of the towns with more than 100 000 inhabitants are located on the coast. These include the capitals of all the countries which front on to the sea, with the exception of those of Benin (Porto Novo), Guinea Bissau (Bissau) and Gambia (Banjul). The existence of so many large towns on the coast is a reminder of the fact that West Africa was opened up from the coast towards the interior, and also of the fact that the modern political and economic development of the interior has been very recent. The large coastal towns have mainly grown up under European influence, and with the notable exception of Accra, all those with over 100 000 inhabitants are seaports. In addition to their functions as ports, since the Second World War many of the larger coastal towns have emerged as important centres of manufacturing industry. That industries should have developed in seaport towns is not surprising, as many of the new industries are to a large extent based upon imported raw materials.

In the forest zone away from the coast there are three main groups of towns, namely: those of the Yoruba in south-western Nigeria; those of the Igbo in south-eastern Nigeria; and those of the Ashanti in Ghana. Several of the Yoruba towns were already large before the colonial period, and were originally based upon a subsistence economy. In many of these towns a relatively large proportion of the population still farm in the surrounding area. As late as the 1952 census, for example, about two-thirds of the working males in the towns of Ogbomosho, Oshogbo and Iwo were employed in agriculture, and even in Ibadan about one third were thus engaged. Many of the larger towns of south-eastern Nigeria, on the other hand, were founded under European influence. The towns of Ashanti, although in many cases long-established, have mainly become important since the development of cocoa farming during the latter part of the nineteenth century.

Many of the towns of the savanna interior date back for several centuries, some of them owing their origin and early growth to the trans-Saharan trade routes. Several of the older towns of northern Nigeria have become increasingly important in recent times, because of the establishment of rail links with the coast, which has stimulated the development of commercial agriculture. Some of the other towns of the savanna interior are of comparatively recent origin, including Bamako in Mali and Kaduna in Nigeria, both of which were originally established as administrative centres by the Europeans.

By far the largest urban centre in Nigeria is Lagos, at present the Federal capital. Lagos is also the country's main commercial and industrial centre, and its leading general port. In 1971 the city of Lagos had a population of 901 000, but the Lagos Metropolitan District which consists of Lagos and a number of suburban towns such as Shomolu, Mushin, Ikeja and Ajegunle contained a total of 1 477 000 inhabitants. Lagos originally grew up on a group of small islands in Lagos Lagoon, but has since spread on to the mainland. Although Lagos owes much of its recent growth and development to European influence, it was probably founded early in the seventeenth century by a Yoruba sub-group, who chose the island site because it was relatively easy to defend. Lagos is situated near the only permanent break through the sandspit which separates the lagoon from the open sea. Its early development as a trading centre was hampered by the shallowness of the water at the entrance to the lagoon, which prevented large ships from entering. Work began on the building of a railway inland from Lagos in 1895, and this event marked a turning point in its history. In 1914 the narrow channel was dredged to allow ocean-going ships to enter the lagoon, and in 1926 the Apapa wharves on the mainland were inaugurated. The population of Lagos which was only 33 000 in 1891, grew to about 250 000 in 1950. In addition to its importance as a port, Lagos has become Nigeria's major manufacturing centre. Many of the industries are located on industrial estates. The largest of these is situated to the north-west of the Apapa wharves, and there are others at Ijora, Ebute Metta, Yaba and Ikeja.

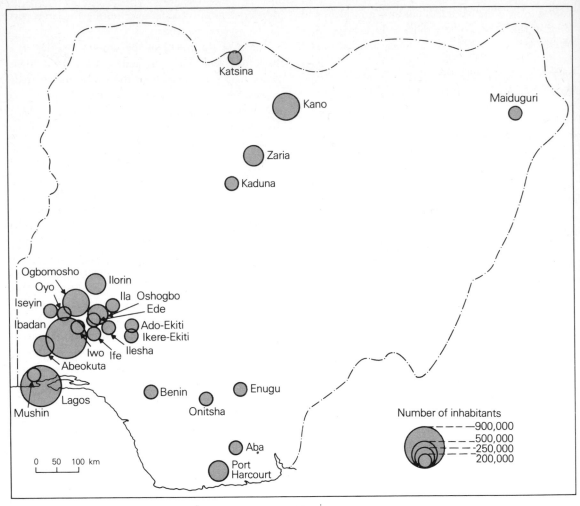

Fig. 7.3 Nigeria – Distribution of towns of more than 100 000 inhabitants

The second largest town in Nigeria is Ibadan (758 000), which is situated some 140 km to the north-east of Lagos in the heart of the cocoa growing belt. Ibadan is the largest indigenous town in tropical Africa. It has the remains of an old city wall, and an unplanned street layout which causes traffic congestion. Many of its inhabitants are still engaged in farming or in craft industry. Ibadan is the capital of Oyo State, and is an important commercial and education centre. A number of modern factory industries have also been developed.

In south-eastern Nigeria the largest towns are Port Harcourt (217 000), Onitsha (197 000), Enugu (167 000) and Aba (158 000). Port Harcourt is situated on the Bonny river some 65 km from the sea,

and was founded as a coal port in 1912. It is the eastern terminus of the Nigerian railway system, and the country's second most important general port. The recent rapid growth of Port Harcourt has largely been due to the development of the oil industry. It has a number of modern industries, of particular importance being oil refining. Enugu owes its origin to the existence of coal along the Udi escarpment, and its early growth to the building of the railway which links it to Port Harcourt. It has a number of modern industries including the manufacture of steel and asbestos cement. Aba is also a European creation. Its location on the railway resulted in its early growth as a commercial centre, and in more recent times it has developed a number of modern industries such as brewing. Onitsha at the confluence of the Anambra and Niger rivers is an important river port, and also the focus of many roads.

The largest urban centre in northern Nigeria is Kano (357 000), which is a very ancient town dating back to at least the tenth century AD. Kano is situated in the heart of Nigeria's main groundnut growing area, and is an important commercial centre. It is also an important focus of routes. It is the southern focus of the Ghadames-Air caravan route across the Sahara; it is linked by road and rail with the ports of Lagos and Port Harcourt; and it has an international airport. It is the capital of Kano State. Kano has a number of long-established craft industries such as leather working and dyeing, as well as several modern factory industries.

Other sizeable towns in the northern part of Nigeria are Kaduna (181 000), Zaria (201 000), Maiduguri (169 000) and Sokoto. Katsina, Sokoto and Zaria are fairly old towns, although the latter in particular has recently developed a number of modern factory industries. Unlike most of the larger towns of northern Nigeria, Kaduna is a relatively new town, only having been established in 1913 when it was chosen as the site for the administrative centre of the northern provinces. During the last two decades Kaduna has become an important centre of the modern textile industry. Other relatively recently established towns include Jos (1903) and Maiduguri (1907). Jos was selected as administrative centre for Plateau Province and owes much of its development to the growth of the tin mining industry. Maiduguri is the centre of a groundnut and cotton growing and cattle rearing area, and its importance has been enhanced by the construction in 1962–4 of a railway extension from the main line near Jos.

In 1974 31 per cent of Ghana's population was classified as urban. By far the largest town in Ghana is Accra, whose population grew from 38 000 in 1921 to 564 000 in 1970. Accra originally started as three separate fishing villages, and its early development was due to the activities of European traders who built forts and castles there. Numerous African traders came from the interior to trade with the Europeans, and by the early part of the nineteenth century Accra was one of the most important commercial centres along the West African coast. In 1877 the British transferred the country's capital from Cape Coast to Accra. At one time Accra was an important surf port, but since the opening of the deep-water harbour at Tema in the early 1960s, this function has disappeared. In recent decades many light industries have been established in Accra. Some 30 km to the east of Accra, and linked to it by road and rail, is the modern town of Tema. In 1970 the Accra–Tema Metropolitan Area had a population of 738 000. Until 1962 Tema was only a fishing village, but since that time it has grown into a modern town. It is now Ghana's leading port, and has also become an important manufacturing centre. Its industries are largely based upon imported raw materials, and include petroleum refining, the smelting of aluminium, and the manufacture of textiles, steel and cement.

The second largest town in Ghana is Kumasi (260 000 in the city proper, and 345 000 in the conurbation), which is the capital of Ashanti Region. Kumasi is about 300 years old, and is situated in the heart of the cocoa growing belt. It is an important commercial centre. It is also an important route centre, being the northern terminus of the Ghanaian railway system, and the focus of several main roads linking southern Ghana with the north of the country. Kumasi has an airport, with regular flights to several other Ghanaian towns. A number of modern industries have developed in recent decades.

Sekondi-Takoradi (161 000) originally consisted of two separate towns, of which Sekondi was the larger. Sekondi is the capital of the Western Region and in the past was an important port. Takoradi did not really develop until the 1920s. Since the opening there of Ghana's first deep-water port in 1928, however, Takoradi has grown rapidly. In addition to its function as a port, Takoradi has a number of modern industries. The only other significant town on the coast is Cape Coast (52 000), which until 1877 was the country's capital. In the past it was an important surf port. Today Cape Coast is mainly an administrative, commercial and educational centre.

Most of the towns to the north of Kumasi are extremely small. The largest of the northern Ghanaian towns is Tamale (84 000), the capital of Northern Region. Tamale is mainly an administrative centre, and its development began in 1907 when it was chosen by the British to be the administrative headquarters for the whole of northern Ghana.

The largest towns in French-speaking West Africa are Abidjan in the Ivory Coast and Dakar in Senegal. Abidjan was founded in 1903, and is situated on the northern shore of the Ebrie Lagoon. It was made capital of the country in 1934. Abidjan's development has been particularly rapid since the opening of the Vridi Canal in 1950, which gave ocean-going ships access to the sheltered Ebrie Lagoon, thus permitting Abidjan to develop as an important port. Abidjan's population grew from 48 000 in 1948 to 500 000 in 1969. Abidjan is the terminus of the Abidjan–Niger railway, which runs inland to Ouagadougou in Upper Volta. This railway carries a great deal of Upper Volta's overseas trade. Abidjan has a substantial European population, and also has attracted large numbers of migrants from all over the Ivory Coast, as well as from neighbouring countries such as Upper Volta and Mali. In recent decades Abidjan has developed as an important manufacturing centre.

Senegal is the most highly urbanised of the West African countries. By far the largest town is Dakar, with a population of 436 000 (693 000 in Greater Dakar). Dakar is situated on the south-eastern side of the Cape Verde promontory, which gives it natural protection from both west and north. It is by far the most important of the Senegalese ports, and is also an important manufacturing centre. Dakar was selected as capital of French West Africa in 1904, but has lost some of its original importance as its hinterland has been adversely affected by the dissolution of the French West African federation in 1959. Like Abidjan, Dakar has a sizeable European population.

The towns of Kenya

Only a small proportion of East Africa's population at present live in towns. Although Kenya is the most highly urbanised of the three East African countries, in the early 1970s about nine-tenths of Kenya's population still lived in rural areas. In the last two or three decades, however, some of the towns of Kenya have grown considerably in population, largely as a result of the influx of migrants from rural areas. The population of Nairobi, for example, rose from 119 000 in 1948 to 267 000 in 1962, and to 509 000 (for a larger municipal area) in 1969.

Although the population of Kenya's towns is now predominantly African in racial origin, many still contain sizeable Asian communities, while some of the larger ones also have a considerable number of European inhabitants. This is in marked contrast to West Africa, where the towns contain few Asians, and with the notable exception of Abidjan and Dakar, very few Europeans. The coastal towns of Kenya such as Mombasa, Malindi and Lamu also have sizeable Arab communities. Table 42 shows the population of Kenya's six largest towns by main racial group.

Table 42 Population of towns by race, 1969

Town	% of total population			
	African	Asian	European	Arab
Nairobi	82,7	13,2	3,8	0,2
Mombasa	75,7	15,8	2,0	6,4
Nakuru	89,5	8,6	1,5	0,4
Kisumu	77,0	20,2	1,8	0,8
Thika	90,1	8,2	1,2	0,5
Eldoret	85,3	12,9	1,4	0,4

As Table 43 shows, the bulk of Kenya's urban population lives in two large towns, namely Nairobi and Mombasa. In 1969 Nairobi's population was more than twice that of Mombasa, and almost 11 times that of the country's third largest town.

Table 43 Population of major towns (thousands), 1962 and 1969

Town	1962	1969
Nairobi	267	509
Mombasa	180	247
Nakuru	38	47
Kisumu	23	32
Thika	14	18
Eldoret	20	18
Nanyuki	11	12
Kitale	9	12
Malindi	6	11
Kericho	8	10
Nyeri	8	10

Number of inhabitants

— — — — 500,000
— — — 250,000
— — — 50,000
— — 20,000

0   100   200 km

Fig. 7.4 East Africa – Distribution of towns of more than 20 000 inhabitants in late 1960s

By far the largest town in Kenya, and indeed in the whole of East Africa, is Nairobi. Not only is Nairobi the capital of Kenya, but it is also the country's leading commercial and industrial centre. Nairobi was chosen in 1899 as a suitable site for railway yards, on the railway line which was being built from the coast at Mombasa to Uganda. Situated on the Athi Plains, Nairobi occupies the last considerable area of flat land, before the hills bordering the Rift Valley are reached. In 1899 the headquarters of the railway were moved from Mombasa to Nairobi, and in the same year the government administration was transferred to Nairobi from Machakos.

Nairobi is situated at an altitude of about 1 700 metres, and has an invigorating and healthy climate, highly suitable for the European settler. Today

Nairobi has a large number of light manufacturing industries, many of which are located in a specially designed industrial area in the south-east of the city. Nairobi is also the main centre of the Kenya tourist industry. Most of the overseas visitors to Kenya arrive at Embakasi Airport, which is situated just to the east of the city. To the south of the city is Wilson Airport, which is used by light aircraft. Nairobi has several large hotels, and is rapidly becoming an important international conference centre. The Nairobi National Park, with its great abundance of wild life, is situated only a few kilometres from the city centre.

Whereas Nairobi owes its origin and development to the Europeans, Mombasa was founded by the Arabs, and dates back to the eighth century AD Today Mombasa is an important commercial, industrial and tourist centre. It is the most important seaport in the whole of East Africa, and is the coastal terminus of the Uganda railway which runs inland through Nairobi to Kampala and Kasese in Uganda. This railway carries much of the overseas trade of both Kenya and Uganda. Mombasa also has an airport, which is served by Kenya Airways internal flights. In recent decades a number of modern manufacturing industries have been developed in Mombasa, of particular importance being petroleum refining and the manufacture of cement. Mombasa is an important tourist centre. There are several hotels in the town itself, and many others are situated near the beaches both to the north and south of the town. and south of the town.

All the other towns of Kenya are extremely small, and in 1969 none of them had reached a population of 50 000. Most of the inland towns such as Nakuru, Thika, Eldoret, Nanyuki, Kitale, Kericho and Nyeri serve large agricultural areas as centres for selling and collection. Kisumu, which is situated on Lake Victoria, is an important lake port and rail ferry terminal. In recent decades some of these small towns have developed a number of manufacturing industries. The small coastal town of Malindi is primarily a tourist centre, with several beach hotels.

The towns of Zambia

Zambia is more highly urbanised than most other tropical African countries, largely as a result of the development of the copper mining industry. In 1973 34 per cent of Zambia's population was classified as urban. In that year Zambia had six towns of more than 100 000 inhabitants, and a further two with between 50 000 and 100 000. All the towns of more than 50 000 inhabitants are located in the Copperbelt, with the exception of Lusaka, Kabwe and Livingstone. All the Zambian towns are modern European creations.

Table 44 Main towns of Zambia (thousands), 1974

Lusaka	415
Kitwe (including Kalulushi)	314
Ndola	222
Chingola (including Chililabombwe)	202
Mufulira	136
Luanshya	119
Kabwe	95
Livingstone	58

Lusaka is the capital of Zambia. Its population grew from 121 000 in 1963 to 238 000 in 1969, and to 415 000 in 1974. Lusaka is situated at an altitude of just over 1 200 metres, and is on the railway line roughly half way between Livingstone and the Copperbelt. It came into being in 1905, as a siding on the single track line which was being extended northward to Broken Hill (now Kabwe). The site of Lusaka at first seemed very unfavourable, as during the dry winters water was difficult to obtain, while during the wet summers the streets were often flooded. In spite of these disadvantages, the capital of the country was moved from Livingstone to Lusaka in 1930. Lusaka is an important route centre. As well as being on the railway, it is the focus of road routes from neighbouring countries, and has an international airport. Lusaka is also an important commercial and educational centre, and has a number of light industries.

The largest concentration of urban population is in the Copperbelt. The two most important Copperbelt towns are Ndola and Kitwe. Until the re-opening of the Bwana Mkubwa mine in 1970, Ndola was not a mining settlement. It is the gateway to the Copperbelt, being situated on the main railway line, and also having an international airport. Ndola is also an important manufacturing centre. As well as having an electrolytic copper refinery, Ndola's industries include the manufacture of cement, furniture, soap, clothing, footwear, vehicle ryres and the refining of sugar. A petroleum refinery was opened at Ndola in 1973, using crude oil brought by pipeline from the Tanzanian port of Dar-es-Salaam. Kitwe is an important mining centre, and also rivals Ndola as an industrial centre. The other Copperbelt towns are largely mining centres.

The only other sizeable towns in Zambia are Kabwe and Livingstone. The mining industry and the railway form the basis of Kabwe's prosperity. The lead and zinc mine at Kabwe was opened in 1902. Kabwe is also an administrative and commercial centre, and has a number of industries. In 1970 the Zambian Railways opened new workshops at Kabwe. Livingstone was established in 1905, and is situated on the Zambezi river just above the Victoria Falls. After the Second World War the tourist industry based on the falls was of some importance, but because of differences with neighbouring Zimbabwe, the number of tourists visiting Livingstone has declined. Livingstone is on the railway, and has an international airport. A number of light industries have been established there.

D: Urbanisation in tropical Asia

With a few notable exceptions such as Brunei, Hong Kong, Macao and Singapore, most of the countries of tropical Asia are still not very highly urbanised. In recent decades, however, in many parts of the region there has been a considerable drift of people away from the rural areas, and this, coupled with a high rate of natural increase, has resulted in the population of many towns expanding rapidly. The Indonesian capital of Djakarta, for example, grew from 533 000 inhabitants in 1930, to 4 576 000 in 1971, while in Thailand the capital Bangkok grew from 782 000 in 1947 to 2 228 000 in 1970. Table 45 shows the degree of urbanisation in selected countries in the early 1970s.

Fig. 7.5 Indonesia – Distribution of towns of more than 100 000 inhabitants in 1971

Table 45 Urban population in Tropical Asia

Country	Year	Urban pop. as % of total pop.	No. of large towns	
			Over 100 thousand	Over 1 million
Brunei	1971	64	—	—
India	1974	21	148	9
Indonesia	1974	18	27	3
Laos	1973	15	1	—
Malaysia (West)	1970	29	5	—
Philippines	1970	32	20	1
Sri Lanka	1971	22	3	—
Thailand	1970	13	2	1
Vietnam (South)	1973	30	11	1

The towns of West Malaysia

In 1970 29 per cent of West Malaysia's population was classified as urban, and there were 49 centres with more than 10 000 inhabitants. Although the degree of urbanisation is thus low compared with western countries, the 1970 figures do represent a significant increase on the early part of the century. In 1911 less than 11 per cent of West Malaysia's population was urban, and there were only eight urban centres.

The majority of West Malaysia's urban centres are located in the western belt of high population density, and most of them originated during the colonial period when they grew up either as ports or as inland commercial centres serving rubber growing and tin mining areas. A characteristic feature of the towns of West Malaysia is their multi-racial nature. In the early days of urban growth the vast majority of town-dwellers were non-Malays. As recently as the 1947 census only 7,3 per cent of the Malays lived in towns, compared with 31,1 per cent of the Chinese, 25,8 per cent of the Indians and 46,2 per cent of the other races.

In the first half of the twentieth century urban growth in West Malaysia was relatively slow, but in the period following the Second World War the rate of urbanisation increased rapidly. That this should be so was partly the result of improved medical facilities which permitted a much higher rate of natural increase, and partly the result of the migration of people from rural areas. The major cause of im-migration was rather different from that found elsewhere in the tropical world, being related to the communist uprising of 1948–60. During this period the towns were safer places in which to live than the rural areas, and government resettlement schemes brought much of the suburban population within the town boundaries. In the post-war period the size of the Malay element in the urban population has increased, and it seems likely that it will continue to do so in the future, as present government policy is to encourage Malays to play a greater role in the commercial and industrial life of Malaysia.

As in other tropical countries, urbanisation has brought its problems. In particular, the expansion of employment opportunities has tended to lag behind urban population growth. The result has been that in many urban centres unemployment and under-employment have become a problem. In 1970, for example, unemployment was as high as 10 per cent in the towns, compared with just over 5 per cent in the rural areas. Many of the migrants from the rural areas have been obliged to take low-status jobs, such as petty trading, food hawking, domestic service and trishaw pedalling. Urbanisation has also brought with it the problems of overcrowding, and the growth of shanty towns.

In 1970 five towns had a population of more than 100 000, and these together accounted for almost half of West Malaysia's urban population.

By far the largest town in West Malaysia is Kuala Lumpur, the capital. Kuala Lumpur is situated in the

Table 46 Population of main towns (thousands), 1970

	Town proper	Urban conurbation
Kuala Lumpur	452	707
Georgetown (Penang)	270	332
Ipoh	248	257
Johore Bahru	136	145
Klang	114	

central part of the Malay Peninsula, at the confluence of the Klang and Gombak rivers. The town dates back to the middle of the nineteenth century, when the tin deposits in the area began to be worked by Chinese miners and a trading centre was established there. In 1880 Kuala Lumpur was brought under British administration. In 1895 the town was selected as capital of the newly founded Federated Malay States, thus adding an administrative function to the existing commercial one. A major factor in the development of Kuala Lumpur has been its central position on the western side of the peninsula. In the late nineteenth and early twentieth century it was the natural transport focus and service centre for the tin mining and rubber growing industries. Today it is linked by road or rail with Ipoh and Georgetown in the north, with Klang and Port Swettenham in the west, with Khota Bharu and Kuala Trengganu in the east, and with Johore Bahru and Singapore in the south. It also has an international airport. Today Kuala Lumpur is the most important industrial centre in Malaysia. Many new industries have been established in the satellite town of Petaling Jaya, which is situated some 8 km away. A few kilometres down the Klang river from Kuala Lumpur is the town of Klang. At one time Klang was an important river port, but only small steamers could reach its jetties, and so in the early part of the twentieth century it was replaced by Port Swettenham as the main port of Kuala Lumpur.

The towns of India
In 1971, of the 547 million people constituting the population of India, less than one-fifth lived in urban areas. During the present century, however, there

has been a slow but steady drift of people away from the rural areas into the towns.

Table 47 Urban population (percentage of total), 1921–71

1921	1931	1941	1951	1961	1971
11,2	12,0	13,9	17,3	18,0	19,9

In 1971 there were 914 towns in India with more than 20 000 inhabitants. Of these, 148 had a population of more than 100 000, and nine were millionaire cities. In India large towns tend to be more evenly spread than is the case in most other tropical countries. Although several of the millionaire cities such as Calcutta, Bombay and Madras are located on the coast and are major seaports, others such as Delhi, Hyderabad and Bangalore are in the interior.

Table 48 Population of millionaire cities (thousands), 1971

Calcutta	7 031
Bombay	5 971
Delhi	3 647
Madras	3 170
Hyderabad	1 796
Ahmadabad	1 742
Bangalore	1 654
Kanpur	1 275
Poona	1 135

Calcutta is the largest city in India. In 1971 the city proper had just over 3 million inhabitants, but Greater Calcutta (the city plus the suburbs and dependent towns) contained over 7 million people. The population of Greater Calcutta has grown very rapidly in the last few decades. At the time of the partition of India and Pakistan in 1947, Greater Calcutta had less than 3 million inhabitants. Immediately after the partition the rapid growth of Calcutta was largely due to the influx of Hindu refugees from East Pakistan (now Bangladesh), but more recently the main cause of its growth has been the influx of people from the rural areas of India. The 1961 census revealed that less than half of the people living in Greater Calcutta had been born there. The main reason why Calcutta has attracted so many migrants is the fact that it is the only sizeable city for hundreds of kilometres, and so it draws upon an area which contains about a quarter of the country's population. A very large number of migrants are young, married men, many of whom leave their wives behind in the villages. As a result there is a preponderance of males in the population of Greater Calcutta. The rapid growth of Greater Calcutta has been responsible for the creation of serious social problems. In particular Calcutta is faced with a severe shortage of accommodation. Large numbers of people live in highly crowded conditions in slum settlements known as 'bustees', while probably half a million people are completely homeless and live entirely upon the streets.

Calcutta itself is built on the left bank of the Hoogly river. It was founded in 1692 as a British trading port. It is some 190 km from the sea on a river which is difficult to navigate, and which tends to silt up. Opposite Calcutta, and joined to it by the Hoogly Bridge, is the important industrial town of Howrah. Upstream from Calcutta and Howrah on both banks of the river, a continuous built-up area known as Hooghlyside extends northwards for some 40 km. Calcutta is one of India's most important ports, and has become a great industrial centre. The major industries of Calcutta and Hooghlyside are jute manufacturing, engineering, cotton textiles, and paper making.

Exercises

1 In many parts of the tropical world there has in recent decades been a considerable movement of people from the rural areas into the towns.
   a) What have been the major causes of this movement towards the towns?
   b) Describe the important consequences of this movement.
2 Describe and attempt to explain the distribution of towns with more than 100 000 inhabitants in tropical Africa.
3 Illustrating your answer with examples from the tropical world, show how the location of mineral deposits have influenced the growth of towns.

4 a) How far is it true to say that nearly all the large towns in tropical Africa are seaports?
   b) Name one large tropical African town which is not a seaport, and give a brief account of its establishment and growth.

Suggested reading

K. M. BARBOUR AND R. M. PROTHERO, Ed.: *Essays in African Population*

J. BEAUJEAU-GARNIER: *Geography of Population* — Chapters 3 and 4

J. C. CALDWELL AND C. OKONJO, Ed.: *The Population of Tropical Africa*

C. CLARK: *Population Growth and Land Use*

JOHN I. CLARKE: *Population Geography*

JOHN I. CLARKE: *Population Geography and the Developing Countries*

JOHN I. CLARKE, Ed.: *An Advanced Geography of Africa* — Chapters 7–9

SONIA COLE: *Races of Man*

PIERRE GOUROU: *The Tropical World* — Chapters 9 and 10

WILLIAM A. HANCE: *Population, Migration and Urbanization in Africa*

R. J. HARRISON CHURCH: *West Africa* — Chapter 10

A. L. MABOGUNJE: *Urbanization in Nigeria*

A. M. O'CONNOR: *The Geography of Tropical African Development* — Chapter 8

S. H. O NDE: *Land and Population Movements in Kenya* — Chapters 7 and 8

R. M. PROTHERO: *Migrants and Malaria* — Chapter 3

C. G. SELIGMAN: *Races of Africa*

G. T. TREWARTHA: *A Geography of Population: World Patterns*

G. T. TREWARTHA: *The Less-Developed Realm: a geography of its population*

H. P. WHITE AND M. B. GLEAVE: *An Economic Geography of West Africa* — Chapters 3 and 10

Useful sources of population statistics include:

United Nations — *Statistical Yearbook*
United Nations — *Demographic Yearbook*
The Statesman's Yearbook
Whitaker's Almanack
The Geographical Digest

CHAPTER EIGHT

Agriculture: the growing of crops

In its broad sense the term 'agriculture' includes both the growing of crops and the rearing of livestock. Agriculture plays an outstanding role in the economic life of nearly all the countries which lie wholly or mainly within the tropics. In many tropical countries appreciably more than half of the economically active population is still engaged in agriculture. In most of the highly industrialised countries of Western Europe and North America, on the other hand, appreciably less than one-fifth is engaged in this way. Agricultural products form a very important part of the export trade of the vast majority of tropical countries.

The main types of agriculture

Within the tropics there are striking regional differences in agricultural practices and in types of agricultural enterprises, and for this reason it is extremely difficult to generalise about tropical agriculture. The size of agricultural holding, for example, ranges from less than one hectare in the case of the smallest peasant farms, to many thousands of hectares in the case of the largest plantations and ranches. The agricultural techniques employed also vary, from being extremely primitive, to being highly scientific and efficient. There are also marked variations in the purposes for which crops are grown and livestock are reared. In some cases production is entirely for the subsistence of the farmer and his family, while in other cases the emphasis is on the production for sale.

Some of the more important types of agriculture which are found within the tropics are discussed in this chapter, and in Chapter 10. They include:

1 Primitive subsistence agriculture: a) shifting cultivation; b) rotational bush fallowing.
2 Intensive subsistence agriculture: a) wet rice cultivation; b) intensive dry farming.
3 Plantation agriculture.
4 Nomadic herding.
5 Livestock ranching.

Primitive subsistence agriculture

Large areas of land within the tropics are still devoted to primitive forms of cultivation. Although several divisions of primitive subsistence agriculture can be recognised, certain features are characteristic of nearly all of them:

1 Much of what is produced is consumed by the farmer and his family, and there is generally very little surplus for sale.
2 The farms are small, rarely having more than a few hectares of land under cultivation at any give time.
3 The farms are often fragmented, each consisting of several scattered plots.
4 The methods of cultivation are generally simple. Very little use is made of manures or fertilisers, and crop yields per unit area are often low. Much of the work on the farm is still done by hand, using only simple tools.

Shifting cultivation

The most primitive form of cultivation practised within the tropics, is that which is commonly known as shifting cultivation. Shifting cultivation is prac-

Table 49 The percentage of the economically active population engaged in agriculture, 1970

Tropical Africa					
Benin	52	Kenya	80	Sierra Leone	73
Burundi	86	Liberia	74	Sudan	80
Cameroon	82	Malaŵi	88	Tanzania	86
C.A.R.	87	Mali	91	Togo	75
Ethiopia	85	Niger	91	Uganda	86
Ghana	55	Nigeria	67	Upper Volta	89
Guinea	84	Zimbabwe	63	Zaïre	78
Ivory Coast	81	Senegal	76	Zambia	69
Tropical America					
Bolivia	58	Dominican Rep.	61	Honduras	67
Brazil	44	El Salvador	57	Jamaica	27
Colombia	45	Guatemala	63	Mexico	47
Cuba	33	Haiti	77	Peru	46
Tropical Asia					
Burma	64	Khmer Rep.	76	Philippines	70
India	68	Laos	78	Sri Lanka	52
Indonesia	70	Malaysia	57	Thailand	77
Non-tropical countries					
Belgium	5	France	14	New Zealand	12
Canada	8	Japan	21	U.K.	3
Denmark	12	Netherlands	11	U.S.A.	4

Shifting cultivation: an area of dense bush cleared by cutting and burning tised by many different peoples under a variety of natural conditions, and a large number of local names are used to describe this form of primitive subsistence agriculture. True shifting cultivation is only found in areas where population is very sparse, and is mainly practised by very primitive communities. Some of these communities, such as the Boro of the Amazon Basin, combine shifting cultivation with the food-gathering way of life.

Shifting cultivation is probably most widely practised in tropical Africa, but it is also found in parts of tropical America, Asia and the Pacific. Although the exact details vary from one area to another, certain essential features are found wherever this form of cultivation is practised. The shifting cultivator clears the wild vegetation from a plot of land, and plants his crops in this clearing. In most areas where shifting cultivation is practised, little or no animal manure is available, and as a result the soil tends to lose its fertility quickly once it is brought under cultivation. After a few harvests have been taken from the plot, the crop-yields begin to decline. When this happens the shifting cultivator abandons his existing plot, and makes a new clearing elsewhere. The settlements of the shifting cultivators are generally of a temporary nature, and when all the surrounding land has been exhausted, the whole settlement is usually moved to a new site some distance away. Wild vegetation quickly grows back over the abandoned plots, helping to re-stock the soil with organic matter and nitrogen. After many years have elapsed, the shifting cultivator may return to an area which he has previously cropped. By this time, however, all traces of former cultivation have usually disappeared.

Exactly how the shifting cultivator clears the land depends to some extent upon the kind of wild vegetation growing there, but cutting and burning are almost always involved, and for this reason shifting cultivation is sometimes referred to as 'slash and burn' agriculture. When a patch of forest is to be cleared, the largest trees are usually left standing, as are any useful food producing trees. The smaller trees are felled with axes or cutlasses. No attempt is made to remove the stumps of the felled trees, and so the fields of the shifting cultivator present a very untidy appearance. The trunks and branches of the felled trees are burned during a spell of dry weather. One

important effect of burning, is that the ash from the fires temporarily enriches the soil.

The shifting cultivator plants his crops at the start of the rains. In most cases very little preparatory cultivation of the soil is undertaken. In some areas the seeds are simply dropped into holes which the cultivator makes with a planting stick. In other areas, particularly in parts of tropical Africa, the soil is loosely worked with a hoe before planting takes place. The kind of crops which are grown varies from one part of the tropical world to another. In Papua New Guinea, for example, the main food crops are sweet potatoes, taros (cocoyams) and yams. In those parts of the lowland forest zone of Central America where shifting cultivation is still practised, the outstanding food crops are maize, beans and squash.

Very often several different kinds of crops are grown together on the same piece of land. This

Shifting cultivation: planting a newly cleared field in the forest zone of West Africa. Note the large size of felled tree, and the thin layer of ash resulting from the burning of cleared vegetation.

practice is known as *mixed cropping*, and appears to have several advantages:

1 As different crops make different demands upon the soil, a higher density of plants per unit area is possible under this system, thus enabling the farmer to obtain the maximum amount of food from the land which he has under cultivation.
2 The mixture of plants of different heights provide a good cover for the soil, thus helping to protect it from erosion.
3 It provides a form of insurance policy for the farmer, as at least some of the crops are likely to yield a fair harvest, even if others fail on account of unfavourable weather conditions or because of the ravages of pests or diseases.

The practice of shifting cultivation has often been condemned, and in some tropical countries is now illegal. Although burning initially helps to increase the fertility of the soil by the addition of ash, it also destroys vast quantities of organic matter which would be better used as timber, firewood or compost. In many parts of the tropical world, shifting cultivators have been responsible for the destruction or degradation of vast areas of natural forest. In Thailand, for example, some 3 million hectares of land,

Using a hoe to prepare a field for planting millet in Northern Ghana

representing about 70 per cent of the country's evergreen forests, have been denuded by hill tribes of shifting cultivators.

Shifting cultivation, however, is not entirely without merit. It is not an unsuitable method of cultivation in areas where population is very sparse, and where soils are poor. Shifting cultivation, for example, provides an effective way of dealing with the severe weed problem which faces many tropical farmers. Burning not only destroys the weeds, but also checks the growth of weed seeds for some time. It is also claimed that shifting cultivation requires less labour to produce a given amount of food, than do permanent forms of cultivation.

Rotational bush fallowing

The major limitation of true shifting cultivation, lies in the fact that this form of agriculture can only support a very sparse population. When the density of population rises above a certain level, the system of true shifting cultivation tends to break down. It is usually replaced by a somewhat more advanced form of primitive subsistence agriculture, known as rotational bush fallowing. The rotational bush fallowing system has replaced true shifting cultivation in many parts of tropical Africa. This is particularly the case in West Africa, where the average density of population is somewhat higher than in most other parts of tropical Africa. In West Africa, true shifting cultivation is virtually unknown in areas where population density exceeds 10 per sq km.

The distinction between true shifting cultivation and rotational bush fallowing is not a clear-cut one, the two practices in fact merging into each other. Both rely upon a period of vegetative fallow in order to maintain soil fertility, and in both cases use is generally made of fire in the clearing of land. In areas where rotational bush fallowing is practised, however, settlements are usually permanent. Each village has its own land, which is cultivated according to a fixed rotation. Unlike in the case of true shifting cultivation, the land is never allowed to revert fully to forest or woodland, and fields often have permanent or near permanent boundaries. The length of time for which the bush fallower cultivates a particular field varies from as little as one year to as long as 10 years, but two to five years is probably most common. After this, the land is allowed to lie fallow

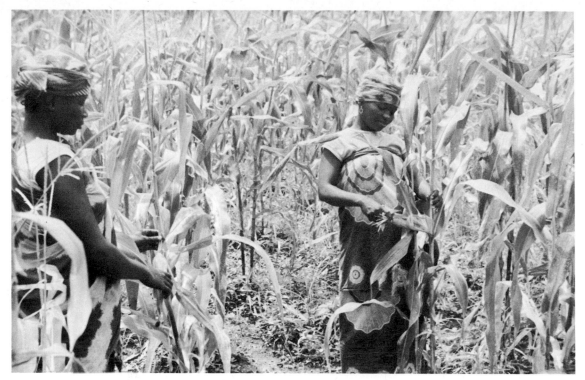

Harvesting maize near Cape Coast, Ghana. Maize is a very important subsistence crop in many parts of the tropical world.

for a number of years, while the other fields are cultivated in their turn. The length of the fallow period varies considerably, depending mainly upon the demand for land. This in turn depends largely upon the density of population in the area concerned. In the sparsely peopled parts of Ghana, for example, the fallow period may be as long as 15 years; but in more densely populated areas it may be as short as three years. A reasonably long period of fallow restores the nitrogen and humus contents of the soil to near their original level and leaves the soil in excellent physical condition.

In some areas where rotational bush fallowing has been the traditional agricultural system in the past, the rapid growth of population and the introduction of cash crops, have in recent times resulted in severe pressure upon the available land resources. Once the population reaches a point at which the land can no longer be given an adequately long resting period, soil exhaustion and soil erosion are likely to occur. Under these circumstances, a change-over to some form of permanent-field cultivation becomes necessary.

Permanent-field cultivation

In order to keep the land continuously under cultivation it is generally necessary to introduce such techniques as manuring and crop rotation. In some highland areas within the tropics, a form of primitive subsistence agriculture has been developed in which the growing of crops is combined with the rearing of livestock. In the tierra fria or cold zone of the tropical Andean highlands, for example, Indian peoples cultivate such crops as wheat, barley and potatoes, and also rear cattle, sheep, llamas and alpacas.

Intensive subsistence cultivation

In many of the densely populated parts of tropical Asia, the farmers use much more intensive methods of cultivation than those so far discussed. In most cases however, there is still a great deal of emphasis on production for subsistence.

Wet rice cultivation

In many of the wetter lowland areas of tropical Asia,

Wet rice cultivation

the dominant agricultural system is that which involves the permanent-field cultivation of wet rice. Rice is one of the world's two most important food crops, the other being wheat. In tropical Asia rice is primarily grown as a subsistence crop, although it is also an important source of cash income in some areas, and forms a major export item from such countries as Burma and Thailand. There are a vast number of different varieties of rice, each of which has been adapted over a long period of time to suit diverse conditions of soil and climate. These varieties may, however, be divided into two main classes:

1 'upland' or 'hill' or 'dry' rice, which is grown without irrigation, and which is of relatively minor importance;
2 'swamp' or 'lowland' or 'wet' rice, which is grown in flooded fields.

For its successful cultivation wet rice requires:

1 a mean temperature of at least 20°C during its growing period. The maturation period of rice is relatively short, ranging from three to eight months according to variety and to the favourability of the natural conditions, and consequently its cultivation extends to areas which lie well outside the tropics;
2 an abundant supply of moisture throughout its growing period;
3 medium to heavy soils, with an impervious subsoil to retain the water;
4 level land.

In areas where rice is cultivated by hand, as is generally the case in tropical Asia, an abundant supply of cheap labour is needed.

In the wet rice growing areas of tropical Asia farms are generally small, usually less than 5 hectares and often less than 2 hectares in size. The floodable land on these farms is divided up into small, flat fields, which in Southeast Asia are known as 'sawahs'. The sawahs are separated from each other by low banks of earth, which serve to hold on the land the water which is needed for cultivation. The construction and maintenance of sawahs is a laborious task. The most favourable conditions for their construction are usually found in alluvial lowlands, where the land is already reasonably flat, and where river water is available either through natural flooding, or by means of easily constructed irrigation channels.

In some areas of very high population density, such as in parts of Sri Lanka, Indonesia and the Philippines, the shortage of natural lowland has made it necessary to undertake the terracing of steeply sloping hillsides. In these areas, the terraced fields are usually very narrow, often not more than a few metres in width. Water supplies for the terraced fields are obtained from springs, from diverted rivers or from rainfall. The water is usually led down from one level of terraces to the next, by means of bamboo pipes inserted in the embankments. In the southern part of the Indonesian island of Bali, the terraces are irrigated by means of an intricate network of small canals. Many of these canals are lined with concrete, and the flow of water is controlled by small sluice-gates.

In wet rice cultivation, water control is of greatest importance. The methods by which water is supplied to the fields vary. In some areas, such as the Irrawady Delta of Burma, the heavy summer rainfall is simply impounded on the fields. In other areas, reliance is placed on the seasonal flooding of rivers. The regimes of most rivers, however, are not sufficiently reliable to guarantee a good crop of rice every year. If the floods come too early the rice seedlings may not be sufficiently advanced to withstand flooding without damage. If, on the other hand, they come too late, the rice may have already received a severe check to its growth. Unusually late floods may interfere with the ripening and harvesting of the crop. In order to ensure adequate water control, some form of artificial irrigation system is therefore used in most wet rice growing areas.

Although there are many local variations in the way in which wet rice is grown, in nearly all cases the techniques involved are simple, with a great deal of the work being done by hand. The farmer's first task is to ensure that the earthen banks are in a good state of repair, so that the fields can be adequately flooded. In some parts of tropical Asia the seed is broadcast directly on to the fields, but more commonly it is first sown in special nurseries and later transplanted. The soil in the nursery beds is worked into a fine mud, using water from rivers, wells, small storage reservoirs or from early rains.

While the seedlings are growing in the nurseries, the fields themselves are prepared. The land is generally first flooded with water to a depth of several centimetres. In some parts of tropical Asia the soil is worked with the hoe, but in others oxen or water buffaloes are used to pull wooden ploughs or harrows through the flooded fields. When the seedlings are about six weeks old, they are dug up from the nurseries, and planted out in neat rows in the fields. Transplanting involves a great deal of work, but in most of the rice growing areas labour is both abundant and cheap, while there is generally an acute shortage of good land. Transplanting ensures that the rice plants are spaced the optimum distance apart, thus enabling the farmer to obtain the maximum amount of food from the limited area of land which is available to him.

After transplanting, the level of the water in the field must be carefully regulated, as the upper part of the rice plant should not be submerged. As the rice approaches maturity, the fields are generally allowed to dry out. Harvesting is done by hand. In some areas rice is cut with a sickle, but in Southeast Asia a small semi-circular knife is commonly used. By using this knife it is possible to cut each stalk of rice separately, and so wastage is negligible.

Threshing (the separation of the grain from the stalk) is often carried out shortly after the crop has been harvested. Various methods are employed. In some areas the grain is shaken loose by beating the heads of the plants against a wooden frame. Another method is to lay the rice on a threshing floor, and beat it with flails. A third method is to lay the rice on a threshing floor, and drive oxen or water buffaloes round and round on it. The tramping of the animals' hooves loosens the grain from the stalks. Winnowing (the separation of the grain from the chaff) is usually done by tossing the threshed rice in the air, thus allowing the wind to blow the lighter chaff to one side.

In most parts of tropical Asia, only one crop of rice is taken per year. For the rest of the year the fields are generally left fallow, and may be grazed over by domestic livestock if any are kept. In areas where the density of population is very high, and where there is a plentiful supply of water, a second crop of rice may be taken from the land in the same year. More common than double-cropping with rice, however, is the practice of following the main rice crop with another annual crop such as vegetables.

In addition to his flooded rice fields, the Asian farmer often has a plot of unirrigated, higher land around his dwelling place. On this plot he usually grows a mixture of annual and perennial crops. A great variety of annual crops may be grown, including vegetables, root crops, spices and tobacco. Most of the plot, however, is usually devoted to the cultivation of tree crops. These commonly include coconuts, bananas, and various other fruit trees. In parts of Malaysia and Indonesia many peasant farmers may grow some rubber on these plots, to provide themselves with a source of cash income.

In many parts of tropical Asia, wet rice has been grown continuously on the same land for centuries. In spite of the fact that very little manure or fertiliser is applied to the land, in most cases there has been no serious decline in soil fertility. Exactly why this should be so is not fully understood, but the conditions under which wet rice is grown are clearly very different from those experienced in the dry land cultivation of annual crops, and in general they are much more conducive to the maintenance of soil fertility because:

1 the level, embanked fields provide very good protection against soil erosion;
2 there is an inflow of soil and plant nutrients with the irrigation water;
3 crop remains and weeds are ploughed into the land, and these provide a regular addition of organic matter to the soil;
4 there is some evidence to suggest that significant amounts of nitrogen are fixed in water-logged rice fields, probably by the algae which grow on the soil, or which float on the surface of the irrigation water.

Although wet rice cultivation is laborious, this type of agriculture is capable of producing a large amount of food per unit area, and in many parts of tropical Asia it does support exceptionally high rural population densities. Oriental methods of rice cultivation have not as yet been widely adopted in other parts of the tropical world, although the cultivation of wet rice is now increasing in several parts of the African and American tropics.

In tropical Africa, the cultivation of wet rice is of particular importance in the island of Madagascar. Rice cultivation supports high rural population densities among the Merina and Betsileo peoples of the central highland area of Madagascar. These peoples are skilled in the arts of terracing and water control. In spite of the large domestic consumption of rice, Madagascar is able to export considerable quantities. In West Africa, wet rice is now widely grown on lands reclaimed from mangrove swamps in the coastal areas of Sierra Leone, Guinea, Guinea Bissau, Gambia and the Casamance region of Senegal. It is also grown on 'fadamas' (riverain floodlands) in parts of the savanna zone of West Africa. In East Africa, rice growing is important around the Rufiji river in Tanzania. In Kenya, rice production comes mainly from the Mwea-Tebere Irrigation Scheme to the east of Mount Kenya.

Wet rice has for a long time been an important crop in Guyana and Surinam, in the northern coastal area of South America. In both countries rice is grown on coastal plains which have been protected from the sea by the construction of dykes. Rice was introduced into Guyana from the southern USA during the eighteenth century, but at first was only grown on a small scale. When Chinese and Indian indentured workers were introduced into the Guianas during the nineteenth century, they took with them their knowledge of rice growing, and gradually the cultivation of rice became of more importance. Most of the rice farms in Guyana are between one and five hectares in size, although there are also a number of large farmers who cultivate as much as 200 hectares. The Guyanese rice farmers now make considerable use of machinery, both for the preparation of the land and for harvesting. About half the rice produced in Guyana is exported, mainly to the territories of the West Indies.

In recent years, several experimental rice growing schemes have been established in various parts of tropical Australia. On these schemes, modern machinery is used in the preparation of the land, and in planting and harvesting. In the 1950s Territory Rice Limited, a company with both American and Australian capital, undertook to develop some 200 000 hectares for rice growing at Humpty Doo

Table 50 The leading producers of rice, 1975 (thousand tonnes)

World total: 348 374					
Leading tropical producers				Other producers	
India	74 186	Brazil	7 538	China	116 267
Indonesia	22 570	Philippines	6 217	Bangladesh	19 143
Thailand	15 300	Malaysia (W)	2 013	Japan	17 097
Vietnam	12 000	Madagascar	1 844	Korea (S)	6 485
Burma	9 221	Colombia	1 614	USA	5 805

between the East Alligator and the Adelaide rivers in the Northern Territory. Initially this scheme encountered several difficulties. One of the major problems was the fact that the river water which was being used for irrigation contained too much salt. Rice-eating birds, particularly wild geese, were responsible for heavy losses of grain at Humpty Doo. Another rice-growing scheme was also established during the 1950s at Liveringa, in the extreme north of Western Australia. This scheme obtains its irrigation water from the Fitzroy river.

Intensive dry farming

In the drier parts of tropical Asia, and in particular over a large part of India, the dominant agricultural system is intensive dry-field agriculture. In intensive dry-field agriculture no single crop is dominant, as is the case in wet rice cultivation. In the wetter areas dry rice and maize are generally important cereal crops, while in the drier areas these tend to be replaced by wheat, or by one of several varieties of millet or sorghum. Other food crops which are commonly grown include groundnuts, sesame, and gram (chick peas). A very common cash crop over much of peninsular India is cotton.

As in wet rice cultivation, it is possible in intensive dry farming for two crops to be taken in a year from the same piece of land, a quick-growing crop being cultivated during the monsoon rains, followed by a drought-resistant crop planted when the rains are over. In India the crops which are planted at the start of the monsoon rains and harvested when the rains are over are known as 'kharif' crops, while the crops which are planted at the end of the rains and harvested in spring are known as 'rabi' crops.

Plantation agriculture

Unlike the various types of peasant farming already discussed, plantation agriculture is not indigenous to the tropical world, but has been introduced by Europeans in comparatively recent times. The first tropical plantations were established in Brazil and the West Indies, as early as the sixteenth and seventeenth centuries. At the end of the eighteenth century the distribution of plantations was still largely confined to the Americas, but the early part of the nineteenth century saw the development of the plantation system in tropical Asia, and by the end of that century plantations were also being started in parts of Africa and the Pacific.

A plantation or estate is a large farm on which the cultivation of a limited number of cash crops is carried out, usually by scientific and efficient methods. The characteristic features of plantation agriculture are:

1 The holdings themselves are large.
2 Large numbers of workers are employed. In the past, plantations were often established in areas of relatively sparse population. Where sufficient labour was not available locally, workers had to be recruited from other areas. The development of plantation agriculture has thus often been the cause of substantial population movements, and in some areas has been responsible for the development of plural societies.
3 A great deal of capital is usually involved. Many plantations have their own factories for the preliminary processing and preparation of their crops, and some have their own light railway systems for the transport of the harvested crop from the fields

109

to the factory. Many plantations are owned by outside interests. In Central America, for example, many banana plantations are owned by North American fruit companies; while in East Africa many tea plantations are owned by British companies.

4 Plantations usually specialise in the production of a single crop. This practice is known as *monoculture*. In a few cases, however, two or more different crops are grown on the same plantation. The crops grown on plantations are mainly intended for export.

The crops which are most commonly grown on plantations are bananas, coffee, rubber, sisal, sugar cane and tea. Other crops which are sometimes grown on plantations include cocoa, coconuts, cotton, oil palm, pineapple, spices and tobacco. None of these crops, however, is grown exclusively on plantations; peasant farmers are now also very important producers of all of them.

In Brazil, for example, cocoa is mainly grown on plantations, but in West Africa it is almost entirely a peasant farmer's crop. In Malaysia rubber is grown both on plantations and on peasant farms. Similarly, in East Africa coffee and tea are grown on both these types of holding.

Plantations make a significant contribution to agricultural production in several parts of the tropical world. In tropical America, plantations are of particular importance in several of the West Indian islands. Here sugar cane is the main plantation crop, but some bananas, cocoa, coconuts, coffee, citrus, sisal and spices are also grown in this way. In parts of Central America bananas and coffee are important plantation crops, and there are also some cocoa, coconut, cotton, sisal and sugar cane plantations. In Brazil cocoa, coffee and sugar cane plantations are important.

In tropical Asia, plantations are of particular importance in Sri Lanka, Malaysia, Indonesia and the Philippines. In Sri Lanka tea, rubber and coconuts are important plantation crops; while in Malaysia rubber is by far the most important crop, although there are also plantations of coconuts, oil palm, pineapples and tea. In Indonesia there are plantations of coffee, rubber, tea and tobacco; while in the Philippines sugar cane is the most important plantation crop, with some coconuts and tobacco also being grown in this way. In the Kerala region of India there are rubber and tea plantations.

Plantation agriculture is of importance in several parts of the tropical Pacific. In Hawaii, pineapples and sugar cane are the main plantation crops. There are coconut plantations in several territories, particularly in the coastal areas of Papua New Guinea, and in Fiji, the New Hebrides, and the British Solomon Islands. In Papua New Guinea there are rubber plantations owned by Australian companies.

In tropical Africa, plantation agriculture is of considerable importance in parts of East Africa and Central Africa. Plantations produce most of East Africa's sisal and sugar cane, much of its tea, and some of its coffee, wattle and coconuts. In Zimbabwe there are plantations of tea, citrus fruits, and sugar cane. The main tea growing area in Zimbabwe is near Umtali in the eastern highlands. The Mazoe Citrus Estate occupies over 20 000 hectares of land to the north of Salisbury, while in recent years the cultivation of sugar cane has become important on irrigated land on the Triangle and the Hippo Valley estates in the south-eastern lowveld. In Malaŵi there are tea plantations in the Cholo and Mlanje districts. In Zaïre plantations are mainly concerned with the cultivation of coffee, oil palm and rubber. In Mozambique there are extensive coconut plantations, particularly around Quelimane. One of these plantations is believed to be the largest coconut plantation in the world, covering 20 000 hectares, and having some 4 million palms.

In West Africa, plantation agriculture is of much less importance than in either East Africa or Central Africa. Plantation agriculture is best developed in Liberia, where there are several large rubber plantations, mainly owned by North American companies. There are also rubber plantations in Nigeria, while in the Ivory Coast there are both European owned and African owned banana and coffee plantations. There are state-owned plantations in Guinea, and in southern Ghana the State Farms Corporation has plantations of oil palm, rubber and sugar cane.

The relative merits of plantation agriculture and peasant farming have often been the subject of discussion. In favour of the plantation system it can be argued that:

1 The methods of cultivation employed on plantations are generally more scientific and efficient than those used by peasant farmers. Much greater use is made on plantations of fertilisers, herbicides, and pesticides, with the result that crop yields per unit area are often appreciably higher than on peasant farms.

2 The plantation has a considerable advantage in the production of such crops as oil palm, sisal, and sugar cane, which require a great deal of processing before they are ready to be sold. Because of the large scale nature of their operations, plantations are able to use modern factory methods in processing their crops. By using modern machinery they are able to achieve higher extraction rates in the case of such crops as oil palm and sugar cane, than can the peasant farmer using simple hand methods. In West Africa, for example, the peasant farmer using traditional methods is only able to extract 55–60 per cent of the total oil content from his oil palm fruit, whereas modern factory methods make it possible to extract 90–95 per cent. Efficient methods of processing also yield a more uniform and better quality product, which is likely to command a higher price on the world market. In some areas the problem of processing the peasant farmers' crops has been overcome by the establishment of co-operative factories. In other areas the peasant farmers send their crops to the factories of neighbouring plantations for processing.

3 Because of the size of the enterprise, the plantation is able to take advantage of the specialisation of labour. The peasant farmer, on the other hand, often has to perform all the various farm tasks himself.

The main disadvantages of the plantation system seem to be:

1 Concentration on the production of a single crop makes the plantation extremely vulnerable to fluctuations in world market prices. During the late 1960s, for example, competition from synthetic fibres brought about a sharp decline in the world market price of sisal, and as a result many of the smaller sisal estates in East Africa went out of production. The peasant farmer, on the other hand, usually grows a number of different crops on his holding, at least some of which are for his own subsistence. Consequently, a reduction in the price of a single crop is not likely to affect him quite so severely.

2 The fact that on plantations a single crop is grown over a large area increases the risk of the spread of disease. During the 1920s and 1930s, for example, the spread of Panama Disease in the Caribbean coastal lowlands of Central America was so serious that the United Fruit Company had to abandon its vast banana plantations in that area. Disease is not likely to spread so quickly on peasant farms, where very often a mixture of different crops are grown.

3 Many tropical plantations are owned by foreign companies or individuals. Most of the profits from such plantations leave the country. To prevent this happening, in some countries foreign owned plantations have been nationalised in recent years. A notable example is Indonesia, where all Dutch owned estates were nationalised without compensation in 1958. In 1964, the British owned estates in Indonesia were also nationalised.

Exercises

1 a) Explain what is meant by:
      (i) shifting cultivation;
      (ii) rotational bush fallowing.
  b) Discuss the merits and limitations of these forms of land use.

2 a) Describe the characteristic features of plantation agriculture.
  b) In what parts of the tropical world do plantations make an important contribution to the agricultural economy?

3 Discuss the relative merits of plantation agriculture and peasant farming.

4 a) Write a brief account of wet rice cultivation in tropical Asia.
  b) In what other parts of the tropical world is wet rice cultivation now of importance?
  c) What would be the possible benefits of introducing wet rice cultivation into other tropical areas?

Suggested reading. See Chapter 11.

CHAPTER NINE

Agriculture: important export crops

A vast number of different crops are grown for export in tropical countries, only a few of the most important being discussed here. Some crops, such as oil palm and rubber, are grown only within the tropics; but the cultivation of others such as cotton, sugar cane and tea, extends to areas which lie well outside the tropics. In tropical countries many different types of agricultural holdings are involved in the production of crops for export, from vast plantations to tiny peasant farms.

Rubber

The chief source of natural rubber is the *Hevea brasiliensis*, a tree native to the rain forests of the Amazon Basin. Until the latter part of the nineteenth century, the demand for rubber was small, and most of the world's production came from trees growing wild in the forests of the Amazon. The invention of the pneumatic tyre and the automobile, however, resulted in a tremendous increase in demand. During the early part of the twentieth century rubber commanded a very high price on the world market, and the rubber industry of the Amazon enjoyed boom conditions.

The prosperity of the Amazon Basin did not last for long, however, because of competition from newly established plantations in Asia. In 1876 rubber seeds were taken from the Amazon Basin, and propagated in the hot houses of the Royal Botanical Gardens at Kew, near London. From Kew Gardens seedlings were taken to Malaya, where physical conditions were found to be ideal. Within a short space of time large plantations were established in several parts of tropical Asia. These plantations were

Tapping a rubber tree on a Malaysian plantation. Note the cup for collecting the latex.

able to produce rubber in larger quantities and of a higher quality, than could be obtained from the scattered trees of the Amazon Basin. During the twentieth century rubber plantations were also established in parts of Africa and the Pacific.

The rubber tree thrives best in hot, wet lowlands. For its successful cultivation it requires:

1 high temperatures throughout the year, with a mean annual temperature of at least 21°C;

2 a heavy rainfall of at least 1 900 mm per annum. This should be fairly evenly distributed throughout the year;
3 although the rubber tree will thrive on a variety of soil types, good drainage is essential.

The Amazon Basin is today only a very minor producer of rubber. The bulk of the world's natural rubber now comes from tropical Asia, with Malaysia and Indonesia being the outstanding producers. In the past rubber was entirely a plantation crop in Asia, but an increasing amount of the region's rubber is now being produced on peasant small-holdings. In Indonesia, for example, small-holders accounted for about 70 per cent of the total production in 1970, with 30 per cent coming from estates.

Outside of Asia, the main natural rubber producing countries are in tropical Africa, with Liberia, Nigeria and Zaire being of particular importance. Rubber planting in Liberia began in 1910, but the real development of the Liberian rubber industry started in 1926, when the American owned Firestone Plantations Company obtained a 99 year lease for a vast area of land, and began planting trees. In every year from 1934, when the first trees on Firestone's plantations began to produce latex, to 1951 when the Bomi Hills iron ore mine came into production, rubber accounted for more than half the total value of Liberia's exports. Since 1951 the relative importance of rubber to the Liberian economy has declined, because of the development of iron ore mining. In 1973, however, rubber still accounted for 13 per cent of Liberia's export earnings. In 1972 Firestone had more than 37 000 hectares under rubber in Liberia, of which 24 000 were in production, the remainder being immature trees. Firestone has a very large plantation near Harbel a few kilometres inland from

Monrovia, and a smaller one on the Cavalla River near the Ivory Coast border. There are five other foreign-owned companies with rubber plantations in Liberia. In recent years a large number of independent growers have begun to plant rubber. In 1972 these independent growers accounted for 26 per cent of Liberia's rubber production. In future the relative importance of these growers is likely to increase as in 1972 they owned more than half of the country's rubber acreage, although much of this consisted of immature trees.

The Malaysian rubber industry

In 1975 Malaysia accounted for 45 per cent of the world's natural rubber. The first consignment of rubber seedlings reached the Malay Peninsula in 1876, but until the end of the nineteenth century rubber was only grown on an experimental basis. During the twentieth century, however, the area under rubber expanded rapidly, and rubber now accounts for about two-fifths of the total cropped area in Malaysia. In 1973 rubber accounted for 34 per cent of Malaysia's export earnings.

In the early days of the industry, rubber was entirely grown on estates, but during the twentieth century peasant small-holdings have come to play an increasingly important role. At present about three-fifths of the land which is under rubber in Malaysia is on small-holdings. Yields tend to be higher on estates, however, and although they have a smaller area under rubber than have the peasant farmers, estates still account for slightly more than half the country's rubber production.

In Malaysia any individual holding of more than 40 hectares is considered to be an estate. Most Malaysian rubber estates are, however, appreciably

Table 51 The production of natural rubber, 1975 (thousand tonnes)

World total: 3 495					
Leading producers					
Malaysia	1 478	Liberia	83	Brazil	19
Indonesia	825	Nigeria	45	Cameroon	16
Thailand	349	Philippines	35	Ivory Coast	15
Sri Lanka	149	Zaïre	25	Khmer Rep.	10
India	136	Vietnam	20	Burma	10

Fig. 9.1 West Malaysia — main rubber growing areas

Legend:
- —·—· International boundary
- — — State boundary
- Main areas of rubber production

0   100   200
km

Of the small-holdings which grow rubber, about half are owned by Malays, two-fifths by Chinese, and the remainder by Indians and others. These small-holdings present a very different appearance to that of the estates. Most of them are very small, the majority being less than five hectares in size. Unlike the estates, rubber is not the only crop grown on most peasant farms Very often the rubber trees are not grown in pure stands, but are interplanted with fruit, coconut and other trees.

The rubber tree takes from five to seven years before it is ready for tapping. Tapping consists of making a slanting cut in the bark, using a special knife. A cup is placed below the cut, to collect the latex. The yield of latex per tree varies considerably. The estates usually plant high yielding rubber, but many small-holders still plant unselected seedlings which give a much lower yield. When latex is being prepared for export, it is first coagulated by adding a small quantity of acetic or formic acid. The small-holder then passes the coagulum through rollers, and dries the sheet rubber in the sun or by smoking. On estates the coagulum is treated in one of several different ways. It may be passed through rollers and then dried in a smoking shed, in which case the final product is ribbed smoked sheet; or it may be passed through a crêping machine and air-dried for ten to fifteen days, in which case crêpe rubber is produced. Some estates prepare concentrated latex for export.

Although rubber is an important crop in East Malaysia (Sabah and Sarawak), more than nine-tenths of the country's production of rubber comes from West Malaysia. From the climatic standpoint, rubber trees can be grown in most parts of the Malay Peninsula, up to an altitude of about 300 metres. The main rubber growing area, however, is along the western littoral of the Peninsula, from Kedah in the north to Johore in the south. This rubber growing zone varies in width from 8 to 60 km, and covers the coastal plain and the lower foothills of the Main Range.

A number of factors seems to have favoured the development of the rubber industry in this part of Malaysia

1 Physical conditions are highly suitable for the growth of the hevea tree. Mean monthly temperatures are generally between 25°C and 28°C, and

larger than this, some of them extending to several thousand hectares. The largest estates are generally owned by European companies or individuals, but many of the medium-sized ones are Chinese-owned, while the smallest are often owned by Indians. Malays own only a very small percentage of the total estate area. Unlike the peasant small-holdings, the rubber estates depend upon hired labour. About half the labour force employed on the estates is Indian, one-third Chinese, and the remainder Malay. The estates usually present a picture of orderliness, with trees planted in neat rows, and the undergrowth kept down by constant cutting. Each estate is served by a network of roads or paths, which radiate out from the processing factory. On the estates a division of labour is usually practised. One group of workers is employed in tapping the trees and collecting the latex; another is engaged in the preparation and processing of the latex; while a third group packs the sheets of rubber.

the mean annual rainfall is for the most part between 1 800 and 3 000 mm, with no month receiving less than 75 mm. The soils, although not highly fertile, are generally well drained.

2 The rubber growing areas are highly accessible. At the time when the rubber industry was being developed, there was already a skeleton network of roads and railways in the area, which had been laid out to serve the tin mining industry of the western foothills. The proximity of the deep-water harbours of Penang and Port Swettenham has made the export of rubber easy.

3 The land which was suitable for rubber was practically uninhabited, as conditions in these areas did not suit the cultivation of wet rice.

4 A cheap and plentiful labour supply was available from southern India.

Cocoa

The cacao tree (the form 'cacao' is usually used for the tree, and 'cocoa' for the product) is native to the rain forests of Central America. It has, however, been introduced into many other parts of the hot, wet tropics. For its successful cultivation the cacao tree requires:

1 high temperatures throughout the year, with a mean annual temperature of at least 21°C;

2 a mean annual rainfall of at least 1 150 mm, which should be fairly evenly distributed throughout the year;

3 shelter from strong winds;

4 shade from strong sunlight. When an area of forest is being cleared for the planting of cacao, some of the forest trees are left standing for this purpose. In some areas special shade trees are planted. Young cacao trees are often grown in the shade of bananas or plantains.

Up until the end of the nineteenth century, tropical America produced the bulk of the world's cocoa. Cocoa is still an important crop in several parts of tropical America, particularly in north-

Cocoa harvest in Ghana. Notice the women splitting the pods and scooping out the beans.

Table 52 The production of cocoa beans, 1975 (thousand tonnes)

World total: 1 566					
Leading producers					
Ghana	396	Cameroon	102	Dominican Rep.	33
Brazil	290	Ecuador	74	Colombia	26
Nigeria	220	Mexico	37	Venezuela	19
Ivory Coast	205	Papua New Guinea	36	Togo	17

eastern Brazil. In Brazil cocoa is mainly grown in sheltered valleys on the coastlands from Salvador southwards as far as Vitoria. The bulk of Brazil's production of cocoa comes from large plantations. Other important cocoa producers on the mainland include Ecuador, Colombia, Mexico and Venezuela. Cocoa is also an important export item from several of the territories of the West Indies, particularly the Dominican Republic, Trinidad and Tobago, and Grenada.

Although the cacao tree was not introduced to the West African mainland until the latter part of the nineteenth century, the forest zone of West Africa is now responsible for more than half the world's annual production of cocoa. The outstanding West African producers and exporters of cocoa are Ghana, Nigeria and the Ivory Coast. The bulk of West Africa's production comes from small peasant farms. Other important African producers include Cameroon, Equatorial Guinea, and São Tomé and Principe. Cocoa also forms an important export from some of the territories of the tropical Pacific, particularly Papua New Guinea.

Cocoa in Ghana

The cacao tree was introduced into Ghana from the

Fig. 9.2 West Africa – main areas of export crop production (cocoa, cotton, rubber, bananas, ginger)

116

island of Fernando Poo in about 1879. Its cultivation spread rapidly, and Ghana now usually accounts for more than one-quarter of the world's annual production of cocoa beans.

Although the cacao tree is grown in most parts of the forest zone of Ghana, the main producing area is in a broad belt extending roughly from Koforidua in the south-east, to Sunyani in the north-west. The cacao tree requires a rainfall which is well distributed throughout the year, and the northern limit of cocoa production in Ghana is related to the length of the dry season, rather than to the total amount of rainfall. Extremely heavy rainfall tends to favour the spread of fungoid diseases, and because of this, the extreme south-western part of the forest zone is not very suitable for the production of cocoa. In the past the Eastern Region produced the bulk of Ghana's cocoa, but owing to the high incidence of swollen shoot disease in that area, the main centre of production has in recent years tended to move north-westwards into Ashanti and Brong Ahafo Regions.

The production of cocoa in Ghana is entirely in the hands of African farmers, most of whom have less than two hectares under this crop. In some cases, the whole of a farmer's cocoa may be in one block, but more commonly it is divided into several separate blocks. Some Ghanaian farmers have larger cocoa farms, in which case they often employ caretakers to look after parts of their farms. These caretakers usually receive a share of the crop as payment for their work. Most cocoa farmers grow some food crops for their own use. Very often cacao seedlings are planted among cocoyams, plantains or other food crops. These shelter the young trees from the sun, and also provide the farmer with food and a source of cash income, while he is waiting for his cacao trees to mature.

The cacao tree begins bearing when it is between three and five years old. In Ghana there are two harvests each year. The main crop is harvested between September and January, with a smaller crop between April and August. The Ghanaian farmer uses a cutlass to harvest the lower pods, and a knife on the end of a long pole for the higher ones. The pods are gathered into piles on the ground. They are carefully split open, and the beans and sticky pulp surrounding them are scooped out. The pulp is removed by fermentation. The beans are placed on the ground, and covered with plaintain leaves to retain the heat which is produced by the fermentation process. Fermentation usually takes about six days. Every second day the beans must be mixed, to ensure uniform fermentation. The fermented beans are then placed on mats on raised platforms, and allowed to dry in the sun. The period of drying usually takes between one and two weeks, depending on the weather. While the beans are drying, they are turned at frequent intervals, so as to expose all of them to the sun. When thoroughly dry, they are put into sacks and taken to the buying stations. Before the beans are sold they are graded according to quality by government graders.

In the past, the purchase of cocoa from the farmer and its re-sale on the world market, was undertaken by private companies such as Cadbury and Fry, and the United Africa Company. Today, however, the whole crop is handled by the State Cocoa Marketing Board. This board purchases cocoa beans through its licensed agents. The board fixes the price which is to be paid to the farmer. Usually the price received by the farmer is lower than the world market price. Part of the money saved by the board is used to support an increase in the local price of cocoa, during years when the world market price is unusually low.

The cocoa farmer has to cope with a number of pests and diseases. The most serious problem facing the cocoa industry in Ghana has been the outbreak of swollen shoot disease, which was first recognised in 1936. Swollen shoot is a virus disease, which is spread by an insect known as the mealy bug. No cure has as yet been found for this disease. The only effective method of controlling the spread of swollen shoot is to cut down and destroy the infected trees. The government has sponsored a cutting out scheme, and millions of trees have been cut down. This has led to a marked decline in cocoa production in those parts of Ghana which have been most affected by the disease. Black pod is a fungoid disease, which causes the pods to turn black, and destroys the beans inside. The best way to check black pod is to harvest the pods as they ripen, and to remove from the tree any pods which show signs of disease. The capsid insect also causes a great deal of damage to the cacao tree in Ghana. Fortunately the capsid insect can be controlled by spraying the trees with an insecticide called Gammalin 20.

Coffee

Several species of coffee bush are cultivated, but only two, *Arabica* and *Robusta*, are of much commercial importance. The Arabica bush produces the best quality coffee, and is the more widely grown. It is believed to be native to the highlands of Ethiopia, but has been cultivated in Arabia since about the sixth century AD. Nearly all the coffee grown in tropical America is Arabica. Robusta coffee is native to the forests of western tropical Africa. Although it does not command as high a price on the world market as Arabica coffee, Robusta gives a higher yield per unit area, is more resistant to disease, and is able to thrive under hotter conditions.

Coffee is now cultivated in a great many tropical countries, and forms an important export item from quite a number of them. For its successful cultivation the coffee bush requires:

1 temperatures of from warm to very hot. Arabica prefers constant temperatures of 16°C–21°C, and within the tropics is mainly grown in highland areas at altitudes of 600 to 2 600 metres. Robusta thrives best in areas where temperatures are con-

stant at about 24°C, and consequently is usually grown at lower altitudes. The coffee bush is highly susceptible to damage by frost.

2 moderately heavy rainfall of 1 250 to 2 000 mm per annum. This should be fairly evenly distributed throughout the year, but there should be a relatively dry period during the picking season.

3 deep well drained soil. Coffee is often grown on hill slopes.

4 shelter from strong winds.

The coffee bush first begins to blossom in its third or fourth year. The flowers are replaced by dark green berries which turn red on ripening. The ripe berries, known as cherries, each contain two seeds or beans. The cherries are picked by hand. There are two different methods of processing, the wet method and the dry method. Where the wet method is used, the cherries are picked from the bush when they are ripe, and are fed with water into a pulping machine, which separates the beans from the skins. The beans are then put into fermenting tanks, to get rid of the sticky mucilage which still adheres to them. Finally the beans are dried in the sun. Where the dry method of processing is used, the cherries are either left on

Fig. 9.3 West Africa – main areas of export crop production (coffee, goundnuts, oil palm, piassava fibre, kola nuts)

Harvesting coffee in the highlands of Kenya. Note the baskets for carrying the berries.

the bush until they are dry, or are picked when they are ripe and are sun-dried with the beans still inside the fruit. To remove the dry husk, the cherries are either pounded in a mortar, or hulled by machine. The wet method of processing produces the best quality coffee. The dry method, although simpler and requiring less expensive machinery, is gradually falling into disuse.

A very large part of the world's coffee production comes from tropical America, with Brazil being by far the most important producer and exporter. The second largest producer is Colombia. Other important producers on the mainland include Mexico, El Salvador, Ecuador, Guatemala, Costa Rica and Peru. Coffee is an important export crop in several of the territories of the West Indies, particularly in the Dominican Republic, Haiti and Puerto Rico.

During the twentieth century, several African countries have become important producers and exporters of coffee. Coffee is the most important of the East African export crops. It is the leading export of both Uganda and Kenya, and rivals cotton as the leading export of Tanzania. Both Arabica and Robusta coffee are grown in East Africa, with Robusta accounting for about two-thirds of the total area. Some coffee is grown on plantations, especially in Kenya, but the bulk of East Africa's production comes from small peasant farms, most of which have less than one hectare under coffee. The most important areas for Robusta coffee are around the northern and western sides of Lake Victoria, at a height of about 1 250 metres. Arabica coffee, on the other hand, is mainly grown in the central highland areas of Kenya, and on the lower slopes of Mount Elgon, Mount Meru and Mount Kilimanjaro.

The only major coffee producing country in West Africa is the Ivory Coast, where coffee is very widely grown in the forest zone. It is mainly Robusta, and the Ivory Coast is now the world's largest producer of this variety. A small amount of coffee is grown on plantations, but the bulk of the production comes from small peasant farms. Coffee is now the Ivory Coast's leading export, accounting for about one-quarter of its export earnings in 1973. The development of coffee growing in the Ivory Coast has been greatly stimulated by the existence of a guaranteed market in France. Other important African producers are Angola and Ethiopia.

During the twentieth century, the world market price of coffee has been subject to violent fluctuations. In many years the amount produced has far exceeded world demand, with the result that coffee producing countries have had difficulty in selling their crop at a favourable price. Since the end of the Second World War, attempts have been made to regulate the production of coffee by international agreement. By 1962, an International Coffee Agreement had been signed by 54 governments. Of these signatories, 32 were coffee exporting countries, accounting in 1961 for about 95 per cent of the world's coffee exports. The remaining 22 signatories were coffee importing countries, which between them accounted for almost 95 per cent of the world's coffee imports. Under the terms of the International Coffee Agreement, each of the participating coffee producing countries were allocated an export quota.

The Brazilian coffee industry

For a long time world coffee productions and trade have been dominated by Brazil. Coffee was introduced into north-eastern Brazil in about 1727. Its cultivation spread southwards, and the first large plantations were established in the state of Rio de Janeiro in about 1774. Throughout the history of the Brazilian coffee industry, there has been a tendency for the main centre of production to continually shift. As the older coffee lands became exhausted, the coffee growers moved into new areas, as they found

that costs of production were lower in regions of virgin soil. The older coffee growing areas were abandoned, much of the land reverting to poor pasture. In the early days of the coffee industry in south-eastern Brazil, the main growing area was in the valley of the Paraiba river, but today very little coffee is grown there. During the latter part of the nineteenth century, coffee production spread across the state of São Paulo and into Minas Gerais. During the 1920s, a great deal of coffee planting took place in the northern part of the state of Paraná. Between 1970 and 1974 the state of São Paulo accounted for 39 per cent of Brazil's coffee production, Paraná also for 39 per cent, Minas Gerais for 15 per cent and Espirito Santo for 5 per cent.

Brazil's export trade in coffee began in 1800, when 13 bags were shipped. The relative importance of coffee to the economy expanded rapidly during the nineteenth century. By 1821 coffee accounted for 16 per cent of Brazil's export earnings, by 1852 for 50, and by 1889 for 67 per cent. At the end of the nineteenth century Brazil accounted for three-quarters of the total world production of coffee. During the twentieth century Brazil's relative importance as a coffee producer has declined, although in 1974 one-third of the world's coffee still came from Brazil. In 1974 coffee accounted for almost one-quarter of Brazil's export earnings.

Large areas in south-eastern Brazil are highly suitable for the cultivation of Arabica coffee, and Brazil is capable of producing the whole of the world's requirements of this commodity. The main coffee areas are on the Brazilian plateau, at altitudes of below 900 metres. The gently rolling surface of

Table 53 The production of coffee, 1975 (thousand tonnes)

World total: 4 410 Leading producers					
Brazil	1 228	Indonesia	162	Angola	68
Colombia	540	Guatemala	129	Kenya	66
Ivory Coast	258	India	93	Venezuela	65
Mexico	214	Madagascar	88	Zaïre	64
Uganda	213	Cameroon	87	Philippines	62
El Salvador	193	Costa Rica	79	Peru	59
Ethiopia	174	Ecuador	76	Tanzania	55

Fig. 9.4 East Africa – main areas of export crop production

the plateau makes for good drainage, and there are extensive areas of iron-rich 'terra roxa' soil which is particularly suitable for the cultivation of coffee. The coffee bushes are grown almost exclusively on ridges and slopes. The valley bottoms are generally avoided because, as cold air drains downwards, they tend to

be subject to frost during the winter months. In the coffee growing areas the rainfall is generally between 1 000 and 2 000 mm per annum, with a summer maximum and a relatively dry period during harvest.

Much of Brazil's coffee is grown on large estates called *fazendas*. During the latter part of the

121

nineteenth century, the rapid expansion of the coffee industry was largely made possible by the arrival of south-eastern Brazil of large numbers of immigrants from Europe. Many of these new arrivals went to the *fazendas* as *colonos* (tenants). The landowner would draw up a contract with a *colono*, obliging the latter to clear an area of virgin land and to plant it with coffee. The *colono* was provided with work animals and tools, and was permitted to grow food crops such as maize, beans and cassava for his own subsistence. When the coffee bushes came into bearing, the *colono* had to hand the land back to the landowner, and to move elsewhere. Under this system, the area under coffee expanded rapidly, and at very little expense to the landowner. In more recent times, there has been a tendency for some of the larger *fazendas* to become sub-divided between the former tenants.

Brazil is remarkably free from coffee diseases and pests. In the state of Paraná, however, frost in winter is a serious problem. In 1962–3 frosts killed 70–80 per cent of the bushes in northern Paraná. The most serious problem facing the Brazilian coffee industry, however, is that of over-production. This danger had already become apparent by the end of the nineteenth century, and in 1902 further plantings of coffee were prohibited. Surplus coffee was bought by the government, and stored for release in years when the harvest was small. During the 1920s, however, there was a renewal of planting, and large stocks of surplus coffee built up. During the period 1930 to 1943, some 80 million bags of coffee had to be destroyed. The present policy in Brazil, is to reduce drastically the output of coffee. An extensive programme was launched in 1962, to subsidise the uprooting of some 2 000 million bushes, and to replace them with pasture or other crops such as maize, rice, beans and cotton.

Tea

The tea bush is native to the monsoon lands of Asia, but it is now widely cultivated in the sub-tropics, and in highland areas within the tropics. For its successful cultivation tea requires:

1 a long growing period, with temperatures of between 12°C and 30°C. Unlike coffee, however, it is not damaged by occasional frosts.
2 moderate to heavy rainfall of at least 1 000 mm per annum, which should be fairly evenly distributed throughout the year;
3 well-drained soils. For this reason, like coffee, it is often grown on hill slopes.

The young bushes are first grown in nurseries, and the seedlings are planted out into the fields when they are about one year old. Plucking begins when the bushes are about three years old, although full yield is not achieved until about six years. The bushes are usually plucked at five to ten day intervals throughout the year. For the best quality tea, only the two end leaves and the bud are plucked. The leaves are taken to the factory for processing, as soon as possible after plucking.

For the manufacture of ordinary black tea, the leaves are first 'withered' by passing either hot or cold air over them. The withered leaves are passed through a machine which breaks up the leaf cells, and releases the juices. Fermentation then follows, and finally the leaf is dried. After grading, the tea is packed for export into tea-chests, which are usually made of plywood and lined with tin-foil or some similar material. Green tea, which is popular in some parts of Asia, is made when the leaves are treated by steam or by scalding before manufacture, thus preventing fermentation taking place.

Several of the world's largest producers are situated entirely or largely outside the tropics. The bulk of the world's tea is still produced in Asia, with India and Sri Lanka being by far the most important tropical producers. In India the bulk of tea production is concentrated in two widely separated regions, in both of which tea growing is the dominant economic activity. The major tea producing region is in Assam, which lies outside of the tropics. The less important region is in the Nilgiri Hills in the south-west. In the Nilgiri Hills the plantations are generally at heights of over 1 200 metres, in areas with an annual rainfall of from 1 500 to 2 500 mm per annum. In 1972–3 tea accounted for about eight per cent of India's export earnings.

Although Sri Lanka produces far less tea than India, the tea industry is of much greater importance to its economy. In the period 1972–4 tea accounted for 43 per cent of Sri Lanka's export earnings. In Sri Lanka tea is grown mainly in the south central part of the island, at heights of up to 2 100 metres. The teas coming from the higher elevations are generally of

Table 54 The production of tea, 1975 (thousand tonnes)

World total: 1 593 Leading tropical producers				Other producers	
India	490	Malaŵi	26	China	334
Sri Lanka	214	Uganda	18	Japan	103
Indonesia	59	Mozambique	17	USSR	85
Kenya	56	Tanzania	14	Turkey	47
Burma	46	Zaïre	6	Bangladesh	29

better quality than those grown at lower altitudes.

During the twentieth century tea has become an important export crop in several countries in East Africa and Central Africa, particularly in Kenya, Uganda, Malaŵi, Mozambique and Tanzania. In these countries the bulk of the tea production comes from European-owned estates, although increasing numbers of African small-holders are now growing tea as a cash crop.

Tea growing in Kenya

Tea was first planted in Kenya at Limuru in 1903. The Kenya tea industry at first grew very slowly, but after 1925 there was a rapid expansion of tea planting as international tea companies bought up land, particularly in the Kericho area. This expansion was checked by the economic depression of the 1930s and the Second World War. In the post-war period,

▲ K.T.D.A. factories under construction or planned
△ K.T.D.A. factories in operation in mid-1970's
⌒ Roads
▨ Main small-holder tea growing areas   km 0   50   100

Fig. 9.5 Kenya – small-holder tea growing

however, the Kenyan tea industry expanded rapidly, and the area under tea increased from less than 7 000 hectares in 1945 to almost 49 000 in 1972.

In only a small part of Kenya are physical conditions suitable for the cultivation of tea. Most of Kenya's tea is grown at heights of 1 500 to 2 100 metres, in areas which have a well-distributed and reliable rainfall of 1 500 to 1 800 mm per annum. Tea now ranks as Kenya's second most important export crop, accounting for 14 per cent of the country's overseas export earnings in 1974.

Before 1950, tea production in Kenya came entirely from plantations owned by European companies, and these plantations still provide a substantial proportion of the country's tea. The leading tea producer is Brooke Bond Liebig Kenya Limited, which in 1972 owned 15 000 hectares of land in the Kericho, Limuru and Kiambu areas, of which 5 500 were planted with tea. On this land there were 12 tea factories. The other large tea company in Kenya is the African Highlands Produce Company Limited, which has large plantations around Kericho.

Since 1950 there has been a marked development of tea growing on African small-holdings. In 1974–5 the area under tea on African small farms amounted to more than 37 000 hectares. More than 97 000 small farmers grew tea in that year, with an average of 0,38 hectares under the crop. The development of the small-holder tea industry in Kenya is the responsibility of the Kenya Tea Development Authority (KTDA). The KTDA provides advisory services for the small tea grower, and also arranges the collection, processing and marketing of his crop. In 1974–5 the KTDA had 15 tea factories in operation. In those parts of Kenya where physical conditions are suitable, tea seems to be a crop well suited to the needs of the African small farmer. It is a labour intensive crop which produces throughout the year, thus providing him with a regular income.

The Kericho District is the most important tea growing area in Kenya. Around the town of Kericho, most of the land is occupied by tea estates. Situated at almost 2 000 metres, the Kericho area is relatively cool and receives about 1 800 mm of rain per annum. The rolling land surface ensures good drainage. The second most important area is in the Nandi Hills, where again production comes mainly from estates. There are also estates in the Sotik and Limuru areas. Tea growing on African small farms is of particular importance in the Kisii, Murang'a, Meru, Nyeri, Embu, Kirinyaga, Kiambu and Kakamega Districts.

Bananas

Although their original home is believed to have been Southeast Asia, the banana and its close relative the plantain are now grown in many parts of the hot, wet tropics. In many tropical countries, eaten either cooked or raw (in common usage the starchy cooking fruits are known as plantains, while those which can be eaten raw are known as bananas), they form an important item in the diet of the local people. In East Africa, for example, they are the staple food crop over most of southern Uganda, and also of the peoples who live on the slopes of Mount Kilimanjaro and Mount Meru in Tanzania. In some parts of the tropical world bananas have become an important export crop, but relatively few plantains enter world trade.

Bananas grow well in areas which have a hot, wet climate. For their successful cultivation they need:

1 high temperatures throughout the year. Minimum temperatures should not fall much below 16°C.
2 mean annual rainfall of not less than 1 250 mm, which should be fairly evenly distributed throughout the year. In some areas, however, bananas are grown under irrigation.
3 deep friable soils;
4 shelter from strong winds. The banana plant has a soft pithy trunk, and is very easily blown over.

The banana plant is susceptible to a number of diseases, which in the past have caused heavy crop losses. The most important of these are Panama disease and Leaf Spot disease. Panama disease is a fungoid disease, which not only kills the existing plants, but also infects the soil, thus making it impossible to grow bananas again until several years later. So far, no really satisfactory method of controlling Panama disease has been found. In Central America attempts have been made to rid the soil of Panama disease by flood fallowing. This involves flooding the land to a depth of a few centimetres, and leaving it under water for a period of several months. The results produced by flood fallowing have not generally justified the expense involved, however, since it has been found that the disease quickly reappears, once new planting of bananas takes place. Fortunately there are some varieties of banana which are immune to Panama disease. Leaf spot disease, or Sigatoka, is another fungoid disease. Unlike Panama disease, however, Sigatoka can be controlled by spraying the plants with fungicides.

Bananas which are grown for export are cut while still green. Great care has to be taken in handling the fruit, as bananas bruise very easily. In many of the exporting countries bananas are now either wrapped in polythene or packed into boxes, before being shipped in specially refrigerated 'banana boats'. A large part of the bananas entering world trade are sold in Europe and North America. The overseas transport and distribution of bananas is mainly in the hands of large companies, such as the United Fruit Company, the Standard Fruit and Steamship Company, Elders and Fyffes and Geest Industries.

The bulk of the bananas which enter world trade are grown in Central America, tropical South America and the West Indies. The largest exporter is now Ecuador. Banana production in Ecuador has expanded rapidly since the end of the Second World War. The main banana growing areas are the coastal lowlands to the south and to the east of Guayaquil. Most of the commercial production of bananas in Ecuador comes from farms of between 4 and 12 hectares. Other important South American exporters are Colombia and Brazil.

In Central America, the bulk of commercial banana production comes from large plantations owned by North American companies. Both the United Fruit Company and the Standard Fruit and Steamship Company have vast plantations in Central

America. The earliest plantations were established at the beginning of the twentieth century in the Caribbean coastal lowlands of Costa Rica, Guatemala, Honduras and Panama. Climatic conditions in the Caribbean coastal lowlands were found to be ideal for bananas. During the 1920s and 1930s, however, the ravages of Panama disease caused many of the plantations on the Caribbean coast to be abandoned, and new ones were established in the Pacific coastal lowlands. Climatic conditions are generally less favourable for banana cultivation on the Pacific coast, because the long dry season makes irrigation necessary. Furthermore, both Panama disease and Sigatoka have now invaded the Pacific coastal lowlands. Since 1960 many Central American plantations have turned to the cultivation of varieties of banana which are immune to Panama disease, and these are now rapidly supplanting the better known Gros Michel banana. In recent years also, an increasing part of Central America's production of bananas has begun to come from small farmers, who sell their fruit to the large companies.

In the West Indies bananas are an important export crop in several territories, particularly in Jamaica, Martinique, Guadeloupe, Dominica, St. Lucia and St. Vincent. Some bananas are grown on plantations, but in many of the islands production is now mainly in the hands of small farmers.

Bananas also form an important export item from several tropical African countries, and from a few of the territories of the tropical Pacific. The Ivory Coast is the largest exporter of bananas in tropical Africa. In the Ivory Coast bananas for export are mainly grown on European owned plantations, most of which are fairly close to Abidjan. In Guinea the bulk

of the commercial production also comes from plantations, most of which are located in the Kindia district, some 100 km inland from Conakry. In Cameroon bananas are grown on plantations owned by the Cameroon Development Corporation, on privately owned plantations, and also by African small-holders. In the Somali Republic bananas are mainly grown on irrigated plantations in the valley of the Juba river.

The Jamaican banana industry

The banana plant was introduced into Jamaica in the middle of the sixteenth century, but for a long time it was only grown on a small scale for domestic consumption. It was not until the middle of the nineteenth century that American sailing ships calling at ports along the north coast of the island, began to take small quantities of bananas back to the United States. The fruit sold well there, and American companies were soon formed to promote the banana trade, with regular shipments beginning in the 1880s. By 1900 banana exports had become more valuable than sugar exports, and continued to be so, except in a few years up until the outbreak of the Second World War.

The peak year for production was 1937, when nearly 27 million stems of fruit were exported. This was twice as many as were exported from any other single country. Up until 1932, the bulk of Jamaica's banana exports went to the United States. In that year, however, as a result of the signing of the Ottawa Agreement and the adoption of the Empire Preference rates of duty, Jamaican banana producers found themselves in a very favourable position in the

Table 55 The export of bananas, 1975 (thousand tonnes)

World total: 6 641					
Leading tropical exporters					
Ecuador	1 450	Guatemala	260	Somalia	80
Costa Rica	1 077	Martinique	168	Cameroon	74
Philippines	823	Brazil	147	Jamaica	68
Panama	558	Ivory Coast	136	St. Lucia	40
Colombia	486	Nicaragua	135	Surinam	38
Honduras	420	Guadeloupe	108	Angola	35

United Kingdom market. The bulk of Jamaica's bananas now go to the United Kingdom.

During the Second World War, very few bananas could be exported, because of the shortage of shipping. The United Kingdom Government, however, helped to maintain the Jamaican banana industry during this period, by buying all the exportable fruit, even though it could not be shipped. After the Second World War, the Jamaican banana industry never regained its 1937 level. Between the two world wars, Panama disease had become a serious problem to the Jamaican grower, and Leaf Spot disease also made its appearance in the island. Before the Second World War, the Gros Michel was the chief variety grown in Jamaica. Unfortunately the Gros Michel is particularly susceptible to Panama disease, and since 1947 it has largely been replaced in Jamaica by the Lacatan variety, which is immune to this disease.

In Jamaica bananas are mainly grown by small farmers, although estates also account for part of the production. More than 90 per cent of Jamaican growers have less than two hectares under bananas. The bulk of the production comes from the valleys and foothills which lie near to the northern and eastern coasts of the island. These areas are very suitable for bananas, because they receive abundant rainfall. In some of the drier southern parts of the island there are estates which grow bananas under irrigation.

Great care has to be taken in the handling of bananas for export. Of particular importance is the time element. Because bananas are a highly perishable commodity, the interval between cutting the fruit and placing it in refrigerated storage should be as short as possible. The Banana Board, which was set up by the government in 1953, purchases the fruit from the growers at buying stations which are located all over the island, and arranges its shipping and overseas sales. The Banana Board estimates the quantity of fruit which is likely to be ready each month, and requests the shipping companies to make available the required number of ships. The bananas are loaded at the ports of Bowden, Port Antonio, Oracabessa, Montego Bay and Lucea.

Until recently all the bananas exported from Jamaica were shipped on the stalk. The bunches of fruit were wrapped in wadded paper and bagged in diothene before shipment. Today, however, the hands of fruit are cut from the stalk and boxed in ventilated cartons. The boxed fruit is less easily damaged during transport, and commands a higher price than unboxed fruit. Large growers are permitted to operate their own boxing plants, but the Banana Board operates public boxing plants to handle the small farmers' fruit.

The relative importance of the banana industry to the Jamaican economy has declined since the Second World War, particularly since the development of the bauxite industry during the 1950s. In 1974 bananas accounted for less than 2 per cent of Jamaica's export earnings, whereas before the war they were the leading export.

Coconuts

The coconut palm is probably native to tropical Asia, but is now grown in many parts of the hot, wet tropics. For its successful cultivation it requires:

1 high temperatures throughout the year. It thrives best in areas which have a mean annual temperature of about 27°C and a small annual range;

2 a mean annual rainfall of at least 1 250 mm, which should be fairly evenly distributed throughout the year;

3 a well-drained soil. Because it is tolerant to salinity and grows well in sandy soil, the coconut palm is an important crop in many tropical islands, and other tropical coastal areas.

In many parts of the tropical world the coconut palm is mainly grown on peasant farms. The coconut palm provides the peasant farmer with many of the necessities of life. The young nuts contain a liquid known as coconut water, which is a refreshing drink. The dried kernel of the nut, known as copra, is an important source of oil used in cooking. The fibre from the husk, known as coir, is used for stuffing mattresses, and also for making ropes, mats and brooms. The shells can be used as cups or scoops, or can be burned to make charcoal. The flowering stalk of the palm can be tapped. The juice or toddy thus obtained can be used as a source for the preparation of sugar, or can be allowed to ferment and then distilled to produce a powerful alcoholic beverage known as arrack. The trunk of the palm can be used for building purposes, and the leaves to thatch house roofs.

In many areas where it is grown, the coconut palm also provides the peasant farmer with an important source of cash income, mainly through the sale of nuts and copra. In some parts of the tropical world, coconuts are also grown on plantations. The coconut palm usually begins to bear nuts after about six years, although some dwarf varieties may begin bearing after only four years. The maximum yield is usually obtained when the palms are between 10 and 30 years old, and economic bearing continues to ages of 50–100 years. In some areas the ripe nuts are collected from the palms, by men who climb the trunk and cut down the bunches. Usually five or six harvests a year are taken from a palm, with one or two bunches being cut on each occasion. In other areas, however, the nuts are left on the palm until they fall off, and are then collected from the ground.

Where copra is to be made, the nuts first have to be husked. This is usually done by hand, by driving the nuts down onto a sharp spike. After husking, the shell is broken open, and the meat is removed and dried. In some cases the meat is dried before it is removed from the broken shell. In some areas copra is made by drying the meat in the sun. In other areas, however, it is more commonly made in special kilns, through which hot air is passed. In some producing countries, the coconut oil is extracted from the copra locally, and then exported. The residue which is left after the oil has been extracted is known as 'coconut cake' or 'poonac', and is an excellent animal food. Much of the production of many countries, however, is still shipped in the form of copra, and the oil is extracted in the importing countries. As well as being used for cooking purposes, coconut oil is used in the production of margarine, soap and synthetic detergents.

The most important copra producing countries are in Asia. The leading exporter of coconut products is the Philippines, which in 1973 accounted for 70 per cent of the world export trade in copra, and 60 per cent of that in coconut oil. Although some coconuts are grown on plantations, the bulk of the production comes from peasant farms. About 90 per cent of the coconuts gathered go to make copra, one-third by sun-drying and the remainder by smoke-drying. Coconuts are widely grown in the coastal areas of the

Table 56 The production of copra, 1975 (thousand tonnes)

World total: 4 124					
Leading producers					
Philippines	1 890	Mexico	135	Fiji	25
Indonesia	782	Mozambique	65	Vietnam	23
India	350	Thailand	39	W. Samoa	20
Sri Lanka	170	New Hebrides	37	Venezuela	17
Malaysia	164	Br. Solomon Is.	28	Ghana	16
Papua New Guinea	140	Tanzania	27	Fr. Polynesia	14

Table 57 The export of copra, 1975 (thousand tonnes)

World total: 1 085					
Leading exporters					
Philippines	761	Indonesia	30	New Hebrides	22
Papua New Guinea	96	Mozambique	27	W. Samoa	20
Malaysia	31	Br. Solomon Is.	25	Tonga	19

Table 58 The export of coconut oil, 1975 (thousand tonnes)

World total: 1 031			
Leading tropical exporters			
Philippines	614	Papua New Guinea	27
Sri Lanka	50	Singapore	26
Malaysia	40	Fiji	16
Indonesia	27	Fr. Polynesia	11

Philippines, but the most important producing area is in the southern part of the island of Luzon. The island of Mindanao also has a considerable area under coconuts. Small boats collect copra from the various islands, and carry it to Manila and Cebu for export. Manila is the centre of the oil extraction industry. Other important producers and exporters of coconut products in Asia are Malaysia, Indonesia and Sri Lanka.

Coconut products form an important export from several of the islands of the Pacific. They are also an important export from a few territories of the West Indies and from some African countries such as Tanzania and Mozambique. In Tanzania coconuts are particularly important on the islands of Zanzibar and Pemba, where most of the production now comes from small farms. In Mozambique coconuts are an important crop on plantations around Quelimane.

Coconut growing in Melanesia

Coconut products form an important export from several of the territories of Melanesia. Copra is the main exported form from the region as a whole, although most of Fiji's trade is in the form of coconut oil, and Papua New Guinea also exports considerable quantities of oil.

The coconut palm has been widespread in the coastal areas of Melanesia since early times. Coconuts are now grown on both expatriate owned plantations and on Melanesian owned small farms. Large-scale plantings by expatriates began in Fiji in the 1870s and over the next 40 years extended to other parts of coastal Melanesia. After 1920 plantings by expatriates declined, owing to the poor world market price of copra. Since the 1930s, however, planting by

Melanesians has expanded rapidly, and the production of copra from Melanesian farms now generally exceeds that from expatriate plantations.

The size of coconut plantations varies considerably; some of the largest extend to thousands of hectares, but most are much smaller. In northern Fiji, for example, about 40 per cent of the estates are less than 20 hectares in size. A high proportion of plantation palms are old, and are approaching the end of their useful life. The standard practice in Melanesia is to allow the nuts to fall from the trees, and to collect them from the ground. Some copra is made by sun-drying, but on plantations it is more commonly smoke-dried over a fire, or hot-air dried in a furnace.

By far the largest copra producer in Melanesia is Papua New Guinea. In 1969 coconut products formed 32 per cent of Papua New Guinea's export earnings. Almost two-thirds of this was in the form of copra, and most of the remainder in the form of coconut oil. Since the development of copper mining in the early 1970s, the relative importance of coconut products to the economy of Papua New Guinea has declined considerably. The most important coconut growing areas are on the northern coast of the Gazelle Peninsula on the island of New Britain, and the narrow littoral from the Gulf of Papua to Milne Bay. There is an oil mill at Raboul.

In the past most of the copra produced in the New Hebrides came from European plantations, the greatest concentration of which is to be found around the shores of the Segond channel. Since before the Second World War, however, there has been little planting or replanting in the plantation sector. Several factors seem to have contributed to the stagnation of the plantation sector, including:

1 the rising cost of labour and the difficulty of obtaining it;
2 the reluctance of the expatriate plantation owner to invest in a very long term crop when the political future is uncertain;
3 the fluctuating and frequently low world market price of copra;
4 the rival attraction of beef cattle rearing, which offers the possibility of a quicker profit.

In the New Hebridean sector, on the other hand, interest in copra production has increased and there has been a great deal of planting in the post-war period. It is estimated that about 60 per cent of the copra produced in the New Hebrides comes from peasant farms. Much of this, however, is sun-dried and is of inferior quality to the plantation product.

The British soap and chemical firm Unilever has several coconut plantations in the Solomon Islands. As in the New Hebrides, however, the amount of copra produced by small-holders now considerably exceeds plantation production. The quality of the small-holders' production tends to be inferior, with only 52,7 per cent classified as Grade 1 in 1973, compared with 92,5 per cent in the case of plantation copra.

About half of Fiji's copra comes from commercial plantations, most of which are located on the coastal fringes of the islands of Vanua Levu and Taveuni. Copra is collected among the islands by a fleet of small copra boats and taken to Suva where there is an oil mill. Since 1953 the rhinoceros beetle has done a great deal of damage to coconut palms in Fiji.

Oil palm

The oil palm is another important source of vegetable oil. It is native to the forests of western tropical Africa, but has been successfully introduced into other parts of the tropical world. The most important oil palm growing areas are all located within 10 degrees of the Equator, in hot, humid lowlands. The oil palm thrives best in areas where:

1 temperatures are high throughout the year. Mean monthly temperatures should be over 21°C.
2 rainfall is abundant and well distributed throughout the year. Ideally the oil palm requires a rainfall of at least 1 500 mm, but it can be grown in areas where it is as low as 1 000 mm per annum, providing that it is well distributed.
3 there is a well drained soil. The oil palm is in fact very tolerant in its soil requirements, and in south-eastern Nigeria grows well on poor sandy soils.

The oil palm usually begins to bear fruit when it is about five years old, and reaches full bearing at eight to ten years, after which there is a tendency for yields to decline. The economic life of the palm is usually about 50 years. The fruit grows in large bunches at

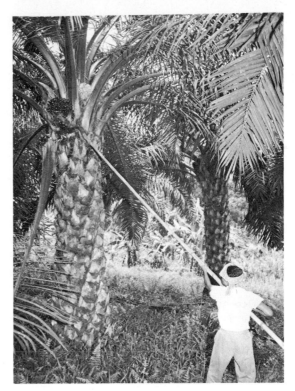

Harvesting oil palm on a land settlement scheme in Malaysia. The improved variety of palms shown here is much shorter than the semi-wild palm of West Africa, and yields more oil. Note the bananas in the background, which are grown as a subsistence crop.

the top of the trunk. Each mature palm usually bears between two and twelve bunches of fruit annually. The individual fruit consists of a fleshy pericarp surrounding a nut, inside of which there is a kernel. Palm oil is obtained from the fleshy pericarp, while the kernel yields palm kernel oil. Both types of oil, and also the kernels themselves, enter world trade. The extraction of palm oil must be carried out in the growing areas, but much of the world's commercial production of kernels are processed in the importing countries. Palm kernel oil is a hard oil, very similar to coconut oil, and is widely used in the manufacture of edible fats and soaps. Palm oil is also used in the making of edible fats and soaps, as well as in the candle and tin-plate industries.

In the past, the entire production of oil palm products came from tropical Africa, but now the oil palm is also grown on a large scale in Malaysia and Indonesia, and on a smaller scale in parts of Central and South America. In West Africa, the bulk of production still comes from semi-wild palms; but in other parts of the tropical world much of the production comes from plantations, which have been established during the last half century. These plantations grow improved varieties of palm, which are shorter than the semi-wild palms of West Africa. Because of this, the task of harvesting the fruit is easier. They also begin to bear fruit at an earlier age than do the semi-wild palms. The fruit of the improved varieties has a much thicker pericarp than that of the semi-wild palm, and consequently yields more oil.

Most plantations have a central factory where the fruit is processed. At the factory the bunches of fruit are first cooked under pressure in large ovens. They then go into threshing machines, which strip the fruit from the bunches. The fruit next goes into

digesters which turn it into a pulp, and is then put through presses which squeeze out the oil. The nuts are sent to cracking machines, which break them open and extract the kernels.

Outside of West Africa, the leading producers and exporters of oil palm products are Malaysia, Indonesia and Zaïre. In the Malay Peninsula, most of the production comes from plantations. In recent years, however, some peasant farmers have also begun to cultivate the oil palm in Malaysia, particularly on the settlement schemes which have been established by the Federal Land Development Authority. In Indonesia, the oil palm is mainly grown on plantations in the Medan district (the Oostkust) of northern Sumatra. Although Singapore exports large quantities of oil palm products, these are in fact produced in Malaysia and Indonesia. In

Table 59 The production of palm oil, 1975 (thousand tonnes)

World total: 2 923					
Leading producers					
Malaysia	1 165	Zaïre	165	Colombia	57
Nigeria	470	Ivory Coast	140	Sierra Leone	55
Indonesia	370	Cameroon	60	Benin	47

Table 60 The production of palm kernels, 1975 (thousand tonnes)

World total: 1 397					
Leading producers					
Nigeria	295	Zaïre	75	Sierra Leone	52
Malaysia	249	Benin	70	Ivory Coast	36
Indonesia	83	Cameroon	60	Guinea	35

Table 61 The export of oil palm products, 1975 (thousand tonnes)

Palm oil *World total:* 2 046		*Palm kernels* *World total:* 339		*Palm kernel oil* *World total:* 259	
Leading tropical exporters					
Malaysia	1 166	Nigeria	173	Malaysia	109
Indonesia	386	Indonesia	32	Zaïre	28
Singapore	140	Sierra Leone	29	Nigeria	19
Sri Lanka	114	Ivory Coast	29	Benin	16

Zaïre, oil palm products are usually the most valuable agricultural export. The oil palm grows wild in the forests of Zaïre, but about three-quarters of the production of oil palm products now comes from plantations.

The oil palm in West Africa

The oil palm is indigenous to the forest zone of West Africa, occurring in a belt of varying width from eastern Nigeria to Guinea Bissau. Although a few plantations now exist, the vast majority of the palms in West Africa are not cultivated, but have simply been left standing when the surrounding land has been cleared for cultivation.

The oil palm is of considerable importance to the peasant farmer in many parts of the forest zone, both for subsistence purposes and as a source of cash income. In West Africa palm oil is used for soup making, and in cooking in general. In the past it was also used as an illuminant, but has now generally been replaced for this purpose by kerosene. Palm kernel oil is used as skin or hair oil, and also as a cooking oil. Considerable quantities of palm oil are consumed within West Africa, and only Nigeria and Benin have any appreciable surplus for export. Several countries, however, export palm kernels. The leaf ribs of the oil palm are used locally for building purposes, and the leaves themselves are used for thatching. The older palms are often felled, and the trunks tapped to yield a popular drink known as palm wine. Palm wine can be distilled to produce a type of gin, which in Ghana is known as akpeteshi.

In West Africa the semi-wild palms grow to heights of 10–20 metres. In order to harvest the fruit, the farmer usually climbs the trunk with the aid of a rope, and cuts down the ripe bunches. The traditional method of obtaining oil from the pericarp is to pick the fruit from the bunch, and then boil it and pound it. When this has been done, the oil can be squeezed out from the pericarp by hand. In some parts of Nigeria the oil is extracted from the pericarp by trampling on the fruit. The nuts are dried, and then cracked by hitting them with a hammer or stone, so that the kernels can be taken out. Much of the work involved in the preparation of palm oil by these simple methods is done by the women of the household, and they are usually allowed to sell the kernels and keep the money for themselves. If palm kernel oil is needed for domestic use, it is obtained by either roasting or soaking the kernels, and then pounding and soaking them in warm water.

By far the most important producer of oil palm products in West Africa is Nigeria. In 1975 Nigeria was the leading producer of palm kernels, accounting for more than one-fifth of the total world production. In the same year, Nigeria ranked second to Malaysia as a producer of palm oil, accounting for about one-sixth of the total world production. Nigeria is the leading exporter of palm kernels, but ranks behind Malaysia, Indonesia and Zaïre in the export of palm oil, mainly because of the large local demand for this commodity. The other leading West African exporter of oil palm products is Benin. In 1971 oil palm products accounted for more than one-third of Benin's export earnings. Most of the other West African countries mainly export kernels. In Sierra Leone, palm kernels are the leading agricultural export. Smaller quantities of kernels are also exported from Togo, Guinea, the Ivory Coast, Guinea Bissau and Liberia.

In Nigeria, the oil palm belt extends right across the southern part of the country, but the most important concentration of production is in the former Eastern Region, in densely populated Igboland. The main oil palm growing area is bounded by the towns of Port Harcourt, Onitsha and Oron. That area now produces almost all of Nigeria's exports of palm oil, and about half of its palm kernel exports. In that area the oil palm occurs in groves, and covers much of the cultivable land.

Although the oil palm bears fruit throughout the year, the main harvest period in Nigeria is between December and April. Various methods are used to extract the palm oil. Many farmers still use simple hand methods, which only succeed in extracting 55–60 per cent of the total oil content of the fruit. Others make use of hand presses, which extract up to 65 per cent. Since the Second World War, a number of small pioneer oil mills have been established in the oil palm growing areas of Nigeria. These are able to extract up to 85 per cent of the oil content. At first these mills met with opposition from the farmers' wives, who feared the loss of their traditional share in the profits of the palm oil industry from the sale of kernels. The commercial production of palm oil and palm kernels is purchased by agents, who are licensed by State Produce Marketing Boards. These Marketing Boards control the export of palm produce from each state. Each licensed buying agent has a number of middlemen, who supply him with produce, which they purchase from individual farmers. The buying agents deliver the oil in large drums to bulk storage plants at Opobo and Port Harcourt, where it is kept awaiting shipment.

The relative importance of oil palm products to the Nigerian economy has declined considerably in recent years, particularly since the development of the petroleum industry. In 1959 oil palm products accounted for 37 per cent of Nigeria's export earnings, but in 1974 they accounted for less than 1 per cent. The Ministry of Agriculture is now attempting to increase the production of oil palm products in Nigeria, by encouraging farmers to replace their semi-wild palms with improved varieties of palm seedlings supplied from the Ministry's nurseries.

Groundnuts

The groundnut is also an important producer of vegetable oil. It is probably native to Brazil, but is now grown in many parts of the tropical world, and also in the sub-tropics. In many tropical countries groundnuts are grown mainly for subsistence, but groundnuts and groundnut products also form an important export item from a number of them. In some cases the groundnuts themselves are exported, but in several countries the nuts are now crushed locally and the oil is exported. The bulk of the groundnuts and groundnut products entering world trade are sold in Europe, with France being by far the largest single importer. Groundnut oil is used as a cooking or salad oil, and also in the manufacture of margarine and compound cooking fat. The residue which is left after the oil has been extracted from groundnuts is known as 'groundnut cake', and is a valuable animal food.

There are two main varieties of groundnuts, the 'bunch' and the 'runner' types. The bunch type is easier to harvest, as the nuts are bunched together in the soil; but the runner type is more common in tropical Africa, and generally yields better there. The flowers of the groundnut are borne aerially, but after fertilisation the flower-stalks bend downwards, and the nuts develop in the soil. The groundnut thrives in a warm climate. It has a short growing period of only three and a half to five months, and so can be successfully grown in areas which lie well outside the tropics. The groundnut prefers:

1 high temperatures throughout its growing period;
2 a mean annual rainfall of 750–1 250 mm. The crop can, however, be grown with as little as 350 mm per annum, providing that it is concentrated in the growing period.
3 a period of dry weather for the ripening and harvesting of the nuts. Groundnuts are commonly grown in areas which have a highly seasonal rainfall.
4 a loose, fertile, and well-drained soil.

India and China are by far the largest producers of groundnuts, but in both countries much of the crop is consumed locally, and only a small part of the total production enters world trade. The USA is also a major groundnut producer. In the USA the crop is mainly grown for direct edible use or for the manufacture of peanut butter, and only a small proportion of the total crop is crushed for oil. Most of the groundnuts and groundnut products which enter world trade are produced in tropical Africa, with the savanna zone of West Africa being the main supplier.

In most tropical countries, groundnuts are mainly grown by peasant farmers, although several attempts have been made to grow groundnuts on a larger scale. Shortly after the end of the Second World War, for example, the British Government attempted to grow groundnuts on a large scale in southern Tanganyika, using modern mechanical methods. Unfortunately the planners were not sufficiently well acquainted with the physical conditions in the area where the groundnuts were to be grown, and the Groundnut Scheme was a dismal failure and had to be abandoned.

The cultivation of groundnuts in West Africa
Groundnuts were first introduced into West Africa by the Portuguese, and are now grown for subsistence in many parts of the region. In some parts of the savanna zone, they have also become an important export crop. In West Africa, groundnuts are grown almost entirely by peasant farmers. In 1973 the countries of West Africa together accounted for

Table 62 The world production of groundnuts, 1975 (thousand tonnes)

World total: 19 117 Leading tropical producers				Other producers	
India	6 600	Zaïre	268	China	2 791
Senegal	1 130	Thailand	260	USA	1 750
Sudan	1 100	Cameroon	165	Argentina	375
Indonesia	541	Malaŵi	165	South Africa	288
Burma	500	Gambia	140		
Brazil	441	Mali	120		
Nigeria	280	Mozambique	120		

Table 63 The export of groundnuts and groundnut oil, 1975 (thousand tonnes)

Groundnuts World total: 886				Groundnut oil World total: 405	
Leading tropical exporters					
Sudan	203	Cameroon	18	Senegal	209
India	70	Senegal	17	Brazil	38
Brazil	54	Upper Volta	15	Nigeria (1974)	24
Gambia	51	Mali	13	Niger	21
Nigeria (1974)	30	Guinea Bissau	9	Gambia	14
Malaŵi	26	Indonesia	8		

about one-third of the world's export trade in groundnuts, and about half of that in groundnut oil.

Within the savanna zone there are two main areas where groundnuts are grown for export. In the east, the main area is centred around Kano in northern Nigeria, and extends north-westwards to Katsina and Kaura Namoda, and also north-eastwards along the railway line to Nguru. This eastern groundnut producing zone also extends into Niger. In Niger groundnuts are mainly grown in a narrow zone along the border with Nigeria, the main centres of production being around Maradi and Magaria. The main problem facing the groundnut industry in Niger, is the high cost of transporting the nuts and oil to the seaports.

The commercial production of groundnuts in northern Nigeria did not begin until about 1912, when the railway line from Lagos was extended to Kano. The completion of this line made it easy to transport groundnuts from northern Nigeria to ports

on the coast. In the area around Kano, physical conditions are highly suitable for the cultivation of groundnuts. The area has a mean annual rainfall of 750–1 000 mm, most of which falls in the five months from May to September. The soils are light and sandy. On most farms in the Kano area groundnuts are the main cash crop, while important subsistence crops are millet and guinea corn. The groundnuts are usually planted in June, shortly after the rains have begun. Sometimes they are grown on their own, but often they are planted between rows of guinea corn.

In the Kano area, harvesting mainly takes place in October and November, after the rains have finished. The plants are usually dug up with the help of a hoe, and are left on the ground to dry for about a week. At the end of this time, the nuts are picked from the plants. Some of the nuts are kept for the use of the farmer and his family, and the surplus sold. Groundnuts for export are bought by the Northern States

Marketing Board. Before the farmer sells the groundnuts, he shells them. In the past this was done by pounding them in a calabash or some other form of container. Today, however, many farmers use simple hand-operated decorticating machines. After shelling, the farmer puts the nuts into sacks, and takes them by donkey or bicycle to the nearest buying station. Here they are sold at a fixed price to an agent of the Marketing Board. When he has bought sufficient nuts, the agent takes them by lorry to Kano, which is the largest groundnut collecting centre in Nigeria. Here the sacks of groundnuts are stored in great pyramids, to await transport by rail or road to the ports. Some of the nuts are crushed at mills in Kano, and exported in the form of groundnut oil and cake.

In the west, the cultivation of groundnuts is of outstanding importance in Gambia and in parts of Senegal. In Senegal groundnut products are by far the most important export item, accounting for about two-fifths of that country's export earnings in the period 1972–4. About half of Senegal's production usually comes from Sine Saloum Cercle, centred on the railhead at Tambacounda. The cultivation of groundnuts for export is also important in Thiès and Diourbel cercles, and in Casamance to the south of the Gambia river. The bulk of Senegal's exports are now in the form of groundnut oil and cake. Dakar is the main oil milling centre, but there are also mills at several other places including Rufisque, Kaolack and Ziguinchor.

The relative importance of groundnuts to the economy of Gambia, is even greater than in Senegal. In 1974–5 groundnuts and groundnut products accounted for about four-fifths of Gambia's export earnings. Although the production of groundnut oil is increasing, the bulk of Gambia's exports are still in the form of shelled nuts.

Sugar cane

Sugar can be obtained from several different plants, of which by far the most important are sugar cane and sugar beet. The bulk of the sugar which enters world trade is made from sugar cane. Sugar cane is believed to have originated in tropical Asia. Although primarily a tropical crop, it is now also cultivated in areas which lie well outside the tropics. For its successful cultivation, it requires:

1 high temperatures throughout its growing period, with mean monthly temperatures not falling much below 21°C;
2 abundant moisture. In areas where cane is grown without irrigation, it requires a mean annual rainfall of at least 1 000 mm.
3 a period of dry, sunny weather for ripening and harvesting;
4 a well drained soil. Cultivation and harvesting is easier if the land is reasonably flat.

Sugar cane is grown from stem cuttings. These are usually planted by hand in furrows, and covered with soil. The first harvest is obtained between 12 and 18 months after planting, depending upon the favourability of the climatic conditions in the area where it is being grown. Cane being cut for the first time is known as 'plant cane'. After the plant cane has been harvested, a new crop is usually allowed to grow up from the old roots. This practice is known as ratooning, and the cane obtained in this way is called 'ratoon cane'. Ratooning can be continued for a great number of years, but with each successive crop the yields decline, and the most common practice is to take only two to four ratoon crops, before removing the old roots and planting new cane.

In most tropical countries the harvesting of cane is still done by hand. The workers cut through the stems close to the ground, and strip off the tops and leaves. In a few parts of the tropical world, mechanical methods of cutting and loading cane have been introduced in recent years. Various methods are used to transport the cane from the fields to the processing plants. In some areas cane is loaded on to carts drawn by oxen or mules, while in other areas it is transported by lorries or tractor-drawn trailers. Some large plantations have their own light railway systems. On plantations in Guyana, the cane is loaded into steel barges known as punts, which are pulled along the irrigation canals to the factories.

In some areas sugar cane is grown in small patches by peasant farmers. Much of this cane is not in fact processed into sugar, but is consumed directly by the local inhabitants, who chew lengths of the stem. In other cases the peasant farmers' cane is processed at small mills, to produce a crude form of sugar, known as 'gur' in India, and as 'jaggery' in East Africa.

Where cane is grown on large plantations, the crop is generally processed by modern methods at large factories. In some cases peasant farmers also sell their cane to factories. In Jamaica, for example, there are thousands of small growers, who send their cane for processing to the factories owned by neighbouring plantations. The cane should be delivered to the factory within 48 hours of being cut, as the sugar content declines rapidly after cutting.

At a modern sugar factory the cane is put through the following processes:

1 *Juice extraction*. The cane is cut into short lengths by revolving knives, and then passed through a series of rollers which squeeze out the juice. The solid matter left after the juice has been extracted, is known as bagasse or megass. In many sugar factories bagasse is fed into the boilers as fuel. It can, however, be used to make wall board and coarse types of paper.

2 *Clarification*. The juice is clarified by adding a small quantity of lime, and then heating it. The juice is then passed over filters, which remove any impurities.

3 *Evaporation*. The juice has a water content of 80–90 per cent. Most of the water is got rid of by boiling in evaporators, which converts the juice into a thick syrup.

4 *Crystallisation*. From the evaporators the syrup goes into vacuum pans, where further evaporation results in the formation of sugar crystals.

5 *Centrifuging*. The vacuum pans discharge massecuite, which is a dense mixture of sugar crystals and molasses. The massecuite is put into a centrifugal machine. This consists of a perforated drum, which rotates within a fixed casing. The sugar crystals remain within the drum, but the molasses drains out through the holes, and is collected by the casing. Molasses can be used as animal food, or can be distilled to produce alcohol. In the West Indies, much of the molasses is used in the manufacture of rum.

Sugar cane is grown in a great many tropical countries, and cane sugar is an important export item from a number of them. Some countries, particularly several of the West Indian territories, also export

molasses and rum. Most tropical countries only produce raw brown sugar, and refining into white sugar generally takes place in the importing countries. The amount of cane which is needed to produce one tonne of raw sugar varies, depending mainly upon the favourability of the climatic conditions under which the cane is grown, and upon the efficiency of the factory which processes it. An average figure is probably about 10 tonnes of cane for one tonne of raw sugar.

India is by far the world's largest producer of sugar cane, accounting for one-fifth of the total production in 1975. In India, cane is mainly grown in small patches on peasant farms, and much of it is processed into gur at numerous small mills. Because of the vast size of its domestic market, in most years India does not export much sugar. The most important sugar exporting country in tropical Asia is the Philippines, where sugar cane is grown both by small-holders and on plantations.

Brazil is the world's second largest producer of sugar cane, but unlike India it is also one of the leading sugar exporters. In the past, sugar cane was mainly grown on plantations in the north-eastern coastal plains of Brazil. Today, however, the production of sugar is also of importance in the states of São Paulo, Minas Gerais and Rio de Janeiro. Other leading producers on the mainland of tropical America are Mexico, Colombia, Ecuador, Peru, Venezuela and Guyana.

Sugar cane has played a very important role in the recent history of most West Indian islands. Cuba is today by far the most important exporter of sugar in the world. Sugar and its by-products are also very important export items from a number of other territories, including the Dominican Republic, Haiti, Jamaica, Puerto Rico, Barbados, Trinidad and Tobago, Guadeloupe, Martinique, and St. Kitts. Because of their small size, however, most of these do not rank among the leading world producers and exporters of sugar.

In tropical Africa, sugar is the outstanding export crop of the islands of Mauritius and Réunion. In 1974 sugar and its by-products accounted for nine-tenths of the export earnings of Mauritius. In Mauritius, cane is grown both on plantations and by small-holders, and occupies about nine-tenths of the total cultivated area. In Réunion, sugar and its by-products accounted for slightly less than nine-tenths of the export earnings in 1974. The cultivation of sugar cane is also of importance in a number of countries on the mainland of Africa, notably in Mozambique, Uganda and Zimbabwe. In Zimbabwe cane is mainly grown on irrigated plantations, which are situated in the Zambezi valley and in the southern lowveld. The production of sugar in Zimbabwe increased from 5 000 tonnes in 1956 to 259 000 tonnes in 1974.

Sugar cane is a very important crop along the east coast of Queensland, and Australia is now one of the world's leading sugar exporters. The main cane growing area extends from Brisbane in the south, to Cairns in the north. In this area, most of the cane is grown on farms of 40–80 hectares in size. In the past, the harvesting of cane on these farms was done by gangs of migratory seasonal workers, but today machinery is being increasingly used in cutting and loading the cane. The cane grown in Queensland is processed at about 35 large factories, some of which are co-operatively owned.

In the tropical Pacific, sugar cane is a very important export crop in both Fiji and Hawaii. In 1974 sugar and molasses accounted for 72 per cent of Fiji's export earnings. In Fiji, virtually all the cane is grown by Indian tenant farmers, who supply the factories operated by the Australian owned Colonial Sugar Refining Company.

The Cuban sugar industry

Throughout the twentieth century, the Cuban economy has been based primarily upon sugar cane. Although Cuba ranks a long way behind India in the amount of cane produced, it is by far the most important sugar exporting country in the world. In 1975 more than one-quarter of the raw sugar which entered world trade was produced in this West Indian island. More than half the cultivated land in Cuba is devoted to the growing of cane, and sugar and its by-products usually account for about four-fifths of the island's export earnings.

The development of the Cuban sugar industry has been favoured by the following factors:

Table 64 The production of sugar cane, 1975 (thousand tonnes)

World total: 637 427					
Leading tropical producers				Other producers	
India	140 196	Indonesia	14 306	China	42 140
Brazil	89 935	Dominican Rep.	9 436	USA	25 854
Cuba	53 500	Peru	9 000	Australia	22 160
Mexico	32 000	Ecuador	5 500	Pakistan	21 242
Philippines	24 616	Venezuela	5 321	S. Africa	18 000
Colombia	19 411	Guatemala	4 900	Argentina	16 000

Table 65 The export of raw sugar, 1975 (thousand tonnes)

World total: 21 661					
Leading tropical exporters					
Cuba	5 744	Mauritius	464	Colombia	198
Brazil	1 750	Peru	422	Mexico	178
India	1 125	Guyana	289	Réunion	135
Philippines	972	Jamaica	254	El Salvador	128
Dominican Rep.	950	Fiji	250	Zimbabwe	116
Thailand	595	Guatemala	204	Trinidad	109

136

Fig. 9.6 Cuba – the sugar industry

1 Cuba is the least mountainous of the bigger West Indian islands, and has large areas of flat or gently rolling land. The gentleness of the terrain facilitates the cultivation and harvesting of the cane, and also its transport from field to factory.

2 In many parts of the island soils are suitable for cane growing. Of particular importance are the productive Matanzas red clay soils, which are composed of residues from dissolved limestone.

3 Temperatures are high throughout the year. Havana has a mean January temperature of 22°C and a mean July temperature of 28°C.

4 The rainfall is generally adequate for it to be possible to grow cane without irrigation. Most parts of the island have a mean annual rainfall of at least 1 000 mm, and there is a relatively dry period during the early part of the year when the crop can be harvested.

5 The long narrow shape of the island means that all the cane growing areas are within easy reach of the coast, with its numerous good harbours. Most sugar factories are not more than 100 km from a port, and consequently the cost of transporting the finished product is low.

6 In the past, the development of the Cuban sugar industry was stimulated by the fact that the island is situated close to the United States, which in pre-Castro times was the main market for Cuban sugar.

In spite of these advantages, the expansion of the sugar industry began at a later date in Cuba than in most other parts of the West Indies. Up until the latter part of the nineteenth century, the cultivation of cane was limited to a few parts of the island. The most important centres of production were in the west, particularly in the provinces of Havana, Matanzas and Las Villas. During the nineteenth century, the cultivation of cane was mainly carried out on small or medium sized farms, most of which were operated by their owners. These farmers set their cane for processing to a large number of relatively small mills, known as *ingenios*.

During the early part of the twentieth century, the Cuban sugar industry underwent a rapid transformation. In 1901, following the end of the civil war in which the island gained its independence from Spain, the United States signed a treaty with Cuba. Under the terms of this treaty, the American Government reserved the right to intervene in Cuban domestic affairs, and in return granted a preferential tariff to Cuban sugar. Following the signing of this treaty, American investors began to pour vast amounts of capital into the Cuban sugar industry. American companies bought up large areas of land in Cuba, for the purpose of growing cane. On this land, they built modern large-scale mills known as *centrales*. They also laid down extensive light railway systems, to facilitate the movement of cane from the fields to these centrales. Cheap labour was brought from the neighbouring territories of Haiti and Jamaica, to work in the canefields and factories. During the early part of

137

the twentieth century, the cultivation of cane spread outwards from the old centres of production. The main direction of advance was eastwards into the provinces of Camaguey and Oriente, which together now account for more than half of the island's total annual production.

In 1860, there had been some 2 000 small ingenios engaged in the manufacture of sugar. By 1959, however, the whole of the Cuban crop was being processed by about 160 centrales. The amount of cane land which was needed to feed these large factories varied, but the average centrale controlled about 16 000 hectares, while the largest serviced 67 000 hectares. The sugar companies themselves grew some cane, with the help of hired labour. Probably about three-quarters of the Cuban crop, however, was grown by tenant farmers known as *colonos*. The sugar companies allocated land to the colonos, on which they grew cane. In return for the cane which they delivered to the centrale, the colonos received a share of the sugar production. In the period immediately before 1959, about 60 per cent of the capital invested in the Cuban sugar industry was American, 22 per cent Cuban, 15 per cent Spanish, with the remainder coming from Canada and other countries. After Fidel Castro seized power in 1959, all the sugar companies were expropriated, and the centrales are now run by the state. Under the Agrarian Reform Law of 1959, large agricultural holdings were prohibited. By the end of 1963, the state owned 57 per cent of the arable land in Cuba. Since Castro came to power, the United States has ceased to trade with Cuba, and the bulk of Cuba's sugar is now sold to the USSR, China and other communist countries.

One of the major problems which has faced Cuba throughout the twentieth century, has been that of fluctuations in the world price of sugar. In 1920, for example, the average price was 11,95 cents per pound (26,3 cents per kg), and yet in 1932 sugar sold for only 0,71 cents per pound (1,57 cents per kg). Because sugar and its by-products usually account for about four-fifths of Cuba's export earnings, the prosperity of the island's economy depends very largely on the state of the sugar market. On account of the large proportion of arable land devoted to the cultivation of sugar cane, in the past Cuba has had to import large quantities of foodstuffs. Since 1959, however, attempts have been made to diversify Cuban agriculture by reducing the area under cane, thus releasing land for the cultivation of food crops. Another problem associated with the Cuban sugar industry, is that of seasonal variations in the demand for labour. During *zafra* (harvest) there is a very heavy demand for labour, both in the fields and in the factories. The zafra lasts for less than half of the year, however, and during the out-of-crop period between June and December the sugar industry requires comparatively little labour. This period is locally known as the *tiempo muerto* (dead season).

Cotton

Cotton is by far the most important of the vegetable fibres. The cotton plant is a flowering shrub, which is usually grown annually from seed. It is cultivated in a great many tropical countries, as well as in several parts of the sub-tropics. For its successful cultivation it requires:

1 warm temperatures during its growing period. Mean temperatures should be over 25°C during part of the year;
2 a period of 180–200 days in the year without frosts, as the cotton plant is highly susceptible to damage by frost;
3 a moderate rainfall, with at least 600–750 mm falling during the growing period. In some parts of the tropical world, cotton is grown under irrigation.
4 a period of dry weather for ripening and harvesting. Heavy rainfall after the bolls have opened is likely to cause discoloration of the fibre.
5 good drainage. The cotton plant tolerates a wide range of soils, but growth is retarded if drainage is poor.

Cotton is commonly sown on ridges, which are about a metre apart. Several seeds are planted together, and when the young cotton is a few centimetres high the surplus plants are pulled out. A great deal of weeding is necessary during the early part of the growing period. Flowering usually begins two to three months after planting. The flowers are replaced by seed pods known as bolls, which burst open on ripening. Inside the bolls are fluffy white fibres known as lint, which are attached to cotton

Picking cotton in Uganda

Cotton may be divided into four main classes, on the basis of length and quality of the fibre. The *short staple* cottons are those which have a fibre length of less than 22 mm; they are mainly grown in India and in other Asian countries. The *medium staple* cottons have a fibre length ranging from 22 to 29 mm; these are the principal kinds of cotton grown in the Americas and in parts of tropical Africa. The *long staple* cottons have a fibre length of 30 to 33 mm, while *extra-long staple* cottons have a fibre length of more than 33 mm. The extra-long staple and long staple cottons are used in fine spinning, and are mainly grown in arid or semi-arid areas. The main producers of these high quality cottons are Egypt, Sudan and Peru.

The cotton plant is subject to the attacks of a great number of insect pests. One of the most important is the pink bollworm, which was first reported in India in 1842, and which has since become established in many other countries. It is estimated that in the past the pink bollworm has caused an annual loss of 15–25 per cent of the Indian cotton crop. Another important insect pest is the boll weevil, which is restricted to the northern hemisphere of the Americas, although closely related species occur in South America. Other pests include the American bollworm, spiny bollworm, stainers and jassids. Control measures which are applied against insect pests include spraying or dusting with insecticides, and the enforcement of a close season for cotton growing. One of the most important of the diseases affecting the cotton plant is bacterial blight, which in one phase is known as blackarm disease. In the early days of cotton growing in the Gezira Scheme of Sudan, outbreaks of blackarm disease were partly responsible for sharp declines in cotton yields. Considerable progress has now been made in the breeding of disease-resistance varieties of cotton.

The most important cotton producing areas of the world all lie well outside the tropics, in the USSR, the USA, and China. Of the countries which lie wholly or largely within the tropics, India is by far the most important producer. In India cotton is mainly grown on peasant farms. The bulk of the Indian cotton crop is grown without irrigation, in areas where the rainfall is 600–1 000 mm per annum and is concentrated in the summer months. The main cotton areas are on the Deccan plateau. In this

seeds. The cotton is usually ready to be harvested between five and seven months after planting. In most tropical countries the bolls are picked from the plant by hand. This is a very labour consuming operation, and in some parts of the tropical world migrant workers are employed by the cotton farmers during the harvest period. After picking, any dirty or stained cotton must be removed. The clean cotton is put into sacks, and transported to factories known as ginneries. Here it is put through machines called gins, which remove the lint from the seeds. The lint is compressed into large bales, and is sent to the textile factories. Although the lint is by far the most important product of the cotton plant, the seed is also useful. By crushing the seeds, cotton seed oil can be extracted. This is widely used as salad and cooking oil, and also in the making of soap and margarine. The residue which is left after the oil has been extracted is known as cotton seed cake, and is a valuable animal food.

region cotton is mainly grown on deep, heavy, moisture-retentive black soils, which in English are commonly known as 'black cotton soils' and in India as 'regur'. In the past India was an important exporter of raw cotton, but because of the growth of the domestic cotton textile industry the country is now on balance an importer.

Cotton is an important export crop in several of the countries of tropical America. Raw cotton is one of Mexico's leading exports, with much of the production coming from irrigated lands in the northern part of the country. In Central America, the leading producers are Nicaragua, El Salvador and Guatemala. The development of cotton growing on a large scale in those countries did not begin until after the Second World War. Unlike in most other parts of the tropical world, the bulk of the cotton production in Central America comes from estates, and considerable use is made of machinery. In South America, Brazil is the largest producer, with more than half of the cotton output now coming from the central plateau area. In spite of substantial demand for raw cotton by its domestic textile industry, Brazil has a considerable surplus for export.

Cotton is now grown in a large number of tropical African countries, with the bulk of the region's production coming from peasant farmers. Sudan is by far the largest producer and exporter. Cotton ranks second to coffee among the export crops of East Africa. Both Uganda and Tanzania are important producers and exporters, but cotton is of only minor importance in Kenya, most parts of which are either too cool or too dry for its successful cultivation.

Although cotton is grown on a small scale in many parts of the savanna zone of West Africa, no West African country ranks as a major world producer. Much of West Africa's production is consumed by the local cloth-making industries, but there is a small export of cotton and its by-products from several countries, including Nigeria, Mali, Benin and Upper Volta. The most important West African cotton growing area is in north-central Nigeria, extending along an axis from Kaura Namoda southeastwards through Zaria towards the Jos Plateau. In this area the rainfall is sufficient to permit the cultivation of cotton without irrigation. Part of Mali's production, however, is grown on the irrigated lands of the Office du Niger in the Inland

Table 66 The production of cotton lint, 1975 (thousand tonnes)

World total: 12 006 Leading tropical producers				Other producers	
India	1 225	Guatemala	105	USSR	2 500
Brazil	515	El Salvador	78	China	2 168
Sudan	229	Peru	73	USA	1 813
Mexico	180	Chad	65	Pakistan	510
Colombia	139	Nigeria	46	Turkey	477
Nicaragua	121	Zimbabwe	43	Egypt	392

Table 67 The export of cotton lint, 1975 (thousand tonnes)

World total: 3 879 Leading tropical exporters					
Mexico	151	Colombia	86	Zimbabwe	33
Sudan	141	El Salvador	78	Mozambique	31
Nicaragua	133	Chad	40	Paraguay	26
Brazil	107	Peru	40	India	25
Guatemala	90	Tanzania	40	Uganda	25

Delta of the Niger. Elsewhere in tropical Africa, cotton is an important export crop in Mozambique, Chad, Central African Republic and Malawi.

Cotton growing in Sudan

Sudan is still predominantly an agricultural country, and its economy is at present dominated by the production of cotton for export. During the years 1971–3, for example, cotton and its by-products accounted for three-fifths of Sudan's export earnings. Sudan ranked ninth as a producer of cotton lint in 1975, accounting for almost 2 per cent of the total world production. In 1975 Sudan ranked sixth in the world as a cotton exporter, accounting for 4 per cent of the total export trade.

Although a small amount of cotton is grown in areas of rain cultivation, the present position of Sudan as a major producer and exporter of cotton can largely be attributed to the development of irrigation during the last half century. More than half of Sudan's annual production of cotton at present comes from the Gezira. The word Gezira means island in Arabic, and is applied to the triangle of land lying between the White Nile and the Blue Nile to the south of their confluence at Khartoum. The Gezira consists of a gently sloping clay plain. The rainfall ranges from about 450 mm per annum in the south, to 175 mm in the north. There are at least five months in the year without rain. In the past the Gezira was sparsely inhabited by semi-pastoral people, who used the scanty rainfall of the area to rear livestock, and to plant crops of drought-tolerant grains. In at least two years out of five the crops were very poor.

The development of the Gezira as a major cotton growing area dates back to the construction of the Sennar Dam, which made possible the irrigation of a large part of the plain. The Gezira Scheme was first proposed in 1904. Work began on the construction of the Sennar Dam in 1913, and was completed in 1925. The Sennar Dam serves partly as a storage dam, holding back water for use after the Blue Nile flood has passed; and partly as a barrage, raising the water to the level of the main canal. The construction of irrigation canals across the flat plains was a fairly easy task. The main canal runs along the eastern edge of the plain, and carries water northwards. From the main canal, the water passes into branch canals, from

Fig. 9.7 Sudan – the Gezira Scheme

which distributing channels lead to the individual fields. Because the land slopes gently towards the west, the water can be distributed by gravity. Between 1958 and 1962, the area under irrigation was extended as a result of the construction of the Managil Branch Canal.

The total area now irrigated by the Gezira Scheme and its Managil Extension amounts to about 1,8 million feddans (1 feddan = 0,42 hectares), of which more than 0,5 million are devoted to the cultivation of cotton each year. One adverse effect of the development of irrigation in the Gezira, has been the spread of the disease bilharziasis. The snail which carries bilharziasis is not able to survive in the fast-flowing Blue Nile, but the irrigation canals provide an ideal habitat for it. The problem of bilharziasis in the Gezira has been partially overcome by treating the water in the infected canals with copper sulphate.

The irrigated land on the main Gezira Scheme was divided up into farms of 40 feddans. This is very large by African peasant standards, and some of the holdings have since been sub-divided. On the Managil Extension the size of holdings was reduced to 15 feddans, in order to provide farms for a greater number of people. On the main Gezira Scheme, the farmers follow an eight year rotation. Every year each farmer has a quarter of his land under cotton, a quarter under food and fodder crops, with the remaining half being kept fallow. On the Managil Extension a six year rotation is used, with one-third of the land being under cotton, one-third under food and fodder crops, and one-third left fallow. One of the most important food crops grown by the farmers of the Gezira is dura, a type of sorghum-millet. Other important food crops are wheat and groundnuts. The main fodder crop of the area is lubia, a type of bean which is mainly grown to feed livestock, but which can also be used for human consumption.

The number of tenant farmers on the Gezira Scheme with its Managil Extension is now about 86 000. A very interesting feature of this scheme is the fact that it involves a three-way partnership between the Sudan Government, the tenant farmers and the managing body. Originally the managing body was a privately owned company, the Sudan Plantation Syndicate. The tenant farmers were allowed to keep all the food and fodder crops they produced, and in addition received 40 per cent of the proceeds from the sale of their cotton crop. The government, which provided the land and the water, also received 40 per cent. The remaining 20 per cent went to the Sudan Plantations Syndicate, which supervised the collection, transport, ginning and marketing of all the cotton grown on the Gezira. In 1950 the concession of the Sudan Plantations Syndicate was terminated, and it was replaced as the managing body by the Sudan Gezira Board. Recent legislation has revised the distribution of profits, so that the managing body now receives 10 per cent of the total, the government 42 per cent, the tenants 44 per cent, local councils 2 per cent and the social development fund 2 per cent.

Some of the farming processes on the Gezira are now mechanised, including much of the preparation of the land and the spraying of the crop. Most of the other work, however, is still done by hand. August is the main month for the sowing of the cotton crop in the Gezira. During the months of September, October and November the farmer is engaged in thinning out the young plants, and hoeing down weeds. Every 10–20 days the cotton is watered. The picking of the crop begins in January, and continues until mid-April. During the harvest season there is a considerable movement of migrant workers into the Gezira, from other parts of Sudan. After picking, the sacks of cotton are taken by lorry, trailer or camel to one of the main collecting centres. The Sudan Gezira Board maintains a light railway network, which is used to transport the cotton from the collecting centres to the Board's ginneries at Meringan and Hassa Heissa.

Although the Gezira is the main cotton area in Sudan, the cultivation of cotton is also of considerable importance in several other parts of the country. Important irrigation schemes include those of the Tokar Delta, the Gash Delta and Khashm el Girba. The Tokar Delta is situated on the Red Sea coast to the south of Suakin, and is formed by alluvial deposits laid down by the Baraka river. The Tokar Delta covers 400 000 feddans, although the average area flooded each year is only about 60 000 feddans. The Baraka river is dry for most of the year, but from mid-July to mid-September the annual floods arrive. The cotton is sown as soon as the flood waters subside in September.

The Gash Delta is situated near the town of Kassala, to the east of Khartoum. It is watered by the Gash river, which rises in Ethiopia and floods between mid-July and early September. The flow of the river is variable, and the area irrigated annually varies from 35 000 to 75 000 feddans.

The Khashm el Girba Dam was built across the Atbara river between 1961 and 1965, and will eventually make possible the irrigation of some 500 000 feddans. Wheat and groundnuts are grown as well as cotton on the Khashm el Girba Scheme, and there is also a large sugar plantation. The Khashm el Girba Scheme has provided a home for about 40 000 people from around Wadi Halfa, whose land was flooded following the construction of the new Aswan Dam in Egypt.

The Roseires Dam built across the Blue Nile upstream from Sennar, was completed in 1966 and holds three times as much water as the Sennar Dam. The Roseires Dam provides some additional water for the Gezira Scheme and the Managil Extension, but most of its water is reserved for the new El Rahad Scheme.

In addition to the large irrigation schemes already discussed, there are a considerable number of both privately-owned and government-owned pump irrigation schemes along the Blue Nile and White Nile, which provide water for cotton growing. A small amount of cotton is also grown by rain cultivation, mainly in the Nuba Mountains, the Gedaref area, and Equatoria Province.

In the past the bulk of the cotton grown in the Sudan was of the extra-long staple type, although some short staple cotton was grown in areas of rain cultivation. Sudan ranks second to Egypt as a producer of extra-long staple cotton, usually accounting for about one-third of the world's production. Because of the lessened demand for extra-long staple cottons, the government of Sudan is now pursuing a policy of diversification in cotton growing. As the extension of irrigation makes new lands available, farmers in these areas are being encouraged to grow medium-staple cottons.

Although there are several textile factories in Sudan which produce cotton cloth for local needs, the bulk of the Sudanese crop is exported. The Sudan Gezira Board holds cotton auctions in Khartoum. From Khartoum the cotton is railed to Port Sudan for shipment overseas. Important purchasers of Sudan's cotton are West Germany, Italy, the United Kingdom, Japan, India, China and the USSR.

Exercises

1 Write a detailed account of the production of export crops in either West Africa or East Africa.
2 Write brief accounts of any two of the following: the Brazilian coffee industry; rubber growing in Malaysia; tea growing in Kenya; cocoa growing in West Africa.
3 Write a detailed account of the Gezira irrigation scheme.
4 a) What are the major plant pests and diseases of the tropical world?
  b) Discuss the effects of plant pests and diseases upon the production of export crops in any one tropical country.
5 a) Name some of the tropical countries which are heavily dependent upon the production of a single export crop.
  b) Discuss the problems which can arise because of excessive dependence upon one export crop.
6 a) Write a brief account of the development of the Cuban sugar industry.
  b) What factors favour the growth of sugar cane in Cuba?

Suggested reading

See Chapter 11.

Table 68 Cotton production in Sudan (thousand bales)

	1968–9	1969–70
Gezira	775	624
Private estates	220	226
Khashm el Girba	119	119
Nuba Mountains	37	39
Gash and Tokar Deltas	9	4
Total	1 160	1 012

CHAPTER TEN

Agriculture: livestock rearing

In most parts of the tropical world, livestock rearing is both small in amount and poor in quality, with the result that there is a marked deficiency of animal protein in the diet of many tropical peoples. Although in parts of tropical Asia cattle or water buffaloes are reared by many peasant farmers, they are kept mainly for the purpose of ploughing and pulling carts. In spite of the fact that India has more cattle than any other country in the world, Indians generally eat very little meat, the Hindus regarding cattle as sacred animals and refusing to kill them.

Mixed farming is not generally a very common practice within the tropics, the two outstanding systems of livestock management being nomadic herding and livestock ranching.

A: Nomadic herding

Nomadic herding is the simplest form of pastoralism. The nomadic herder makes use of natural pastures for the extensive grazing of his livestock, which are reared primarily for his own subsistence. Nomadic herding is mainly practised in areas of low and unreliable rainfall, which experience a marked dry season. In such areas, the cultivation of crops is difficult, unless irrigation is practised. Within the tropics, nomadic herding is an important way of life in the drier grassland areas of East Africa and West Africa; in parts of the Sahara Desert; and in parts of the Arabian peninsula.

Amongst the pastoral peoples of these areas a distinction can be made between true nomads and transhumants. The true nomads are on the move almost continuously with their flocks and herds, whereas the transhumants migrate seasonally between wet-season and dry-season pastures. The movements of the pastoralists are determined by a number of factors, of which the most important are the seasonal availability of water and pasture. Other factors affecting their movements include the incidence of fly-borne and tick-borne diseases, and the prevalence of biting insects. The nomadic pattern of the pastoral Fulani in West Africa, for example, generally involves a southward movement during the dry season, as the northern pastures and water supplies dry up; and a return northwards with the rains, to avoid the seasonal advance of the tsetse fly. The Baggara Arabs of the Sudan also move southwards during the dry season and return northwards when the onset of the rains brings a plague of biting insects to the southern pastures.

The type of livestock reared by the nomadic herders varies. In the grassland areas of tropical Africa, peoples such as the Fulani, the Baggara Arabs and the Masai are primarily cattle rearers, although they often keep large numbers of sheep and goats as well. In very arid areas, camels replace cattle as the most important type of large stock. Camels are useful animals in arid areas, because they are able to go several days without water, and can live on thorny bushes. Camel rearing peoples in tropical Africa include the Somalis of the Eastern Horn, and the Northern Tuareg of the Sahara Desert. In the dry areas of north-western Kenya, the Turkana rear both camels and cattle.

The nomadic herders obtain a great deal of their food from their flocks and herds. Amongst most of these peoples, meat forms only a small part of the diet. The slaughter of livestock represents a reduc-

Nomadic herders: inside a Masai enkang in East Africa. Note the low huts, the thorn bush stockade, and the cattle, goats and donkeys.

tion in the family's capital assets, and killings are usually restricted to special occasions such as weddings and festivals. Animals are also slaughtered when it is felt that they are about to die. Milk invariably forms a very important part of the diet of the nomadic herders. Some peoples, such as the Masai and the Turkana, practise the custom of bleeding their animals.

Although pastoral peoples generally dislike the hard, monotonous work and the settled way of life associated with the growing of crops, many do in fact have some small dependance upon cultivation. The Baggara Arabs, for example, plant crops of millet at the start of the rainy season, leaving them to grow while they move with their livestock to more northerly pastures. At the end of the rainy season they return to harvest the crops. Even the pure nomad must obtain some grain, usually exchanging animal products for it in the markets of the neighbouring tribes of cultivators.

Generally the land used by the nomadic herders is held and grazed communally, although livestock are usually owned on an individual or family basis. Each owner usually aims at keeping as many livestock as possible, regardless of their quality or the availability of pasture. This urge to build up large flocks and herds can be attributed to several factors:

1 Amongst the nomadic herders livestock are regarded as wealth, and a man's social position and prestige depends upon the size of his flocks and herds, rather than upon money or other possessions.

2 Many pastoral peoples use livestock for the payment of 'bride price', the bridegroom's family being required to make a present of animals to the

family of the bride, before the ceremony of marriage can take place.

3 Large numbers of livestock are also kept as a form of insurance policy against drought and famine, on the mistaken assumption that the more animals a man has, the greater the number that are likely to survive a bad year.

Because of their traditional attitudes towards livestock, the nomadic herders have in the past been reluctant to sell their surplus animals. Some change, however, is now gradually taking place in this respect. The Fulani, for example, have for a long time been accustomed to selling considerable numbers of their livestock, to supply the peoples of the forest zone of West Africa with meat.

The nomadic herders of tropical Africa are faced with numerous problems. Many of these problems are the result of the physical environment in which the pastoralists live:

1 Climatic difficulties are amongst the most severe handicaps to livestock rearing in most parts of tropical Africa. Because of the seasonal nature of the rainfall, drinking water for livestock is in short supply for part of the year. During the dry season the pastures become parched and brown, and the condition of the livestock deteriorates. The rainfall is very unreliable, and during unusually dry years the pastoralists often lose a considerable number of livestock.

2 The natural pastures are usually of poor quality. Many of these pastures are dominated by coarse grasses, which are only nutritious when young.

3 The livestock are affected by a large number of diseases and insect pests. In the past, outbreaks of rinderpest often caused heavy losses of livestock, but vaccination campaigns have now largely brought this disease under control. The most limiting of the animal diseases in tropical Africa is bovine trypanosomiasis or *ngana*. This disease is

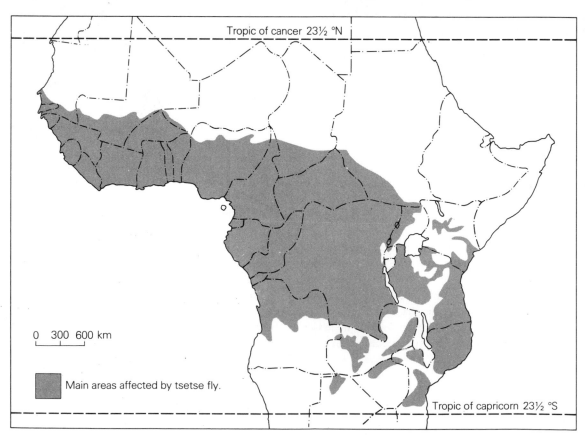

Fig. 10.1 Tropical Africa – main areas affected by tsetse fly

transmitted by the tsetse fly. Various species of tsetse fly are found in a broad belt across Africa, from about 12°N to 15°S. Certain areas within this belt are free from tsetse, however, particularly the highland areas. Numerous techniques have been tried against the tsetse fly. One way of dealing with this pest is to clear away all the bush, so that it has no shade in which to rest. Unfortunately, bush clearing on a large scale is expensive. Spraying the bush with insecticides seems to offer the most effective means of dealing with the tsetse problem, and large areas in northern Nigeria have been cleared of tsetse fly by this method.

4 The native breeds of livestock are generally of poor quality. Although hardy, they are slow to mature. They are also inefficient producers of meat and milk, compared with temperate breeds of livestock.

In addition to the physical problems outlined above, there are also important man-made problems which influence the livestock industry of tropical Africa:

5 One of the most important of these is the widespread practice of overstocking. The communal ownership and grazing of the land, coupled with the lack of any restriction on the amount of livestock an individual can own, often results in the pastoralists keeping far more animals than the available pasture can adequately support. The keeping of excessive numbers of livestock results in the destruction of the grass cover, and ultimately leads to soil erosion.

6 The practice of burning off dead grass during the dry season is also very widespread. Although burning is believed to have some beneficial effects upon the vegetation, uncontrolled fires can do a great deal of damage. They leave the soil bare, exposing it to erosion when the next rains begin. Burning also favours the spread of fire-resistant bushes and poorer grasses, thus resulting in a deterioration in the quality of the grazing.

The Masai of East Africa

The Masai occupy a vast area of dry grassland in East Africa. Their territory extends from just south of Nairobi in Kenya, into the northern part of Tanzania. The Masai in Kenya numbered about 155 000

Fig. 10.2 East Africa – the Masai

in 1969, while there were a further 80 000 living in Tanzania in 1967. The rainfall over most of Masailand averages less than 750 mm per annum, and is highly unreliable. The year is divided into two wet and two dry seasons. The 'short rains' usually occur in November-December, and the 'long rains' in March–May. The Masai are transhumants, their movements being closely related to the seasonal pattern of rainfall distribution. During the dry periods the Masai congregate around sources of permanent water, such as the permanent streams which flow down from the hills, and areas of permanent swamp. When the rains begin, and surface water becomes more readily available, they disperse with their flocks and herds to find fresh grazing, and to allow the pastures near the permanent water supplies to recover.

Because of their semi-nomadic way of life, the homes of the Masai are very temporary structures. They live in low huts, which are made of a

147

Masai cattle gather at a watering place during the dry season, near Narok in Kenya

framework of sticks, plastered over with a mixture of mud and cow dung. Several Masai families live together in a small settlement, known as an *enkang*. The huts in the enkang are arranged in a large circle, and are surrounded by a thorn bush stockade. The livestock are driven inside the stockade at night, to protect them from wild animals. Each family has its own entrance in the stockade, through which its animals enter and leave. When the occupants of the enkang find it necessary to move in search of fresh pasture and water supplies, they usually leave the huts and stockade standing, returning to occupy them again some months later.

The most important animals of the Masai are their cattle, although goats and sheep are usually kept as well. Donkeys are often kept as beasts of burden, being particularly useful when the Masai are moving from one site to another. As with other African pastoral peoples, the Masai try to keep as many livestock as possible. The livestock are owned on an individual basis, but the land is communally grazed. During the day, the main herds are driven out to pasture by the young men and older boys, but young animals usually remain around the settlement and are tended by the women and younger children. During the dry periods of the year, the main herds may have to walk 15–25 km to water.

Traditionally the diet of the Masai is derived entirely from their livestock, although in times of drought they may eat some maize meal to augment the milk supply. Milk from their cattle forms the most important item in the diet of the Masai, and is drunk either fresh or curdled. Each morning and evening, the women milk the cows inside the stockade. The slaughtering of animals for meat is only carried out when some ceremony is being celebrated, such as a wedding, or the birth of a child. Meat is also eaten when an animal dies, or is killed by wild predators. In times of drought and milk shortage, blood forms a part of the Masai diet. To obtain blood from their cattle, the Masai tie a leather thong around the animal's neck causing the jugular vein to swell. This vein is then pierced with a special arrow, and the blood is collected in a gourd. A good deal of blood can be obtained in this way, without doing the animal any permanent harm, provided that it is not carried out at too frequent intervals. Although Masailand abounds in wild game, the Masai have never eaten game meat, with the exception of eland meat which they consider to resemble beef.

The most important of the problems facing the Masai are drought and disease. Important livestock diseases in East Africa are rinderpest, bovine pleuro-pneumonia, east coast fever, trypanosomiasis and anthrax. In the past outbreaks of rinderpest helped to keep the livestock population in check, but since the 1940s vaccination campaigns have practically eliminated this once important disease. As a result, the number of livestock kept by the Masai has tended to increase rapidly and overstocking has become a serious problem in many areas. There has been a considerable deterioration in the quality of the pasture in several parts of Masailand, particularly around the permanent water holes. The folly of keeping more livestock than the available pasture can adequately support was well brought home to the Masai during the severe drought of 1960–1, when several hundred thousand head of cattle died of starvation, and many Masai were left destitute.

In the past the Masai were unwilling to part with their livestock, but in recent years some change has taken place in this respect. The Masai are beginning to enter increasingly into the cash economy, selling some surplus livestock, and using the money to buy blankets, maize meal, tea, sugar and tobacco. Some Masai also now make and sell handicrafts to tourists.

It has become obvious that a change in the way of life of the Masai is necessary. In particular they will have to be encouraged to sell more livestock, not only to make the range lands economically more productive, but also in order to prevent overstocking. One suggested remedy is the modification of the traditional semi-nomadic way of life, to something resembling modern ranching. In parts of Kenya, particularly in the Narok and Kajiado districts, several group ranches have already been established. This has involved the grouping together of a number of Masai families on ranches large enough to support their combined herds. On these group ranches the livestock continue to be individually owned, but the ranch itself is managed on a corporate basis.

B: Livestock ranching

Unlike nomadic herding, livestock ranching is not an

Modern ranching in tropical Australia. Stockmen driving a herd of cattle to the railhead. Note the windpump for raising water from a borehole.

indigenous system of livestock management in tropical areas. It has been introduced by Europeans and modified to suit tropical conditions. Cattle ranching is carried out on a large scale in the grassland areas of tropical South America and Australia. It is also of importance in parts of East Africa, particularly in Tanzania and Kenya; in parts of Central Africa, particularly in Zimbabwe and Zambia; and in parts of Central America and the West Indies. Ranching within the tropics is mainly concerned with the commercial production of beef, but in parts of Africa, South America, and the island of Puerto Rico, herds of dairy cattle are also ranched. In Venezuela, for example, much of the fresh milk supply for the capital city of Caracas is produced on ranches in the dry lowlands around Lake Maracaibo. The milk produced in this area is transported some 500 km to Caracas by refrigerated tankers.

Both nomadic herding and livestock ranching involve the use of natural pastures for the extensive grazing of livestock; and both are mainly practised in areas where the rainfall is light, seasonal in distribution, and highly unreliable. There are, however, several important differences between these two systems of livestock management:

1 The nomadic herder rears livestock primarily for his own subsistence, and is very often reluctant to dispose of them, whereas the livestock rancher rears livestock primarily with the intention of selling either the animals themselves, or their products.
2 In the case of nomadic herding the land is held and grazed communally, but in the case of ranching it is usually held and grazed on an individual basis.
3 In the case of ranching the movement of livestock is usually confined to the ranch, which forms a permanent base. Nomadic herding, on the other hand, usually involves the movement of livestock over a much wider area.
4 The rancher usually concentrates on the rearing of one type of livestock, whereas the nomadic herder often rears several different types.

The carrying capacity of most range land is extremely low, several hectares being required to feed each animal. In the Rupununi Savannas of south-western Guyana, for example, the overall stocking density is between four and eight cattle per square km. Because of this low carrying capacity, an efficient cattle ranch has to be very large indeed.

The tropical rancher is faced with many of the same problems as the nomadic herder. Foremost amongst these problems is the seasonal shortage of pasture and water. During the dry season the cattle generally lose weight, and in exceptionally bad years severe losses of livestock commonly occur. The natural pastures are generally of poor quality. In some areas attempts have been made to improve the quality of the pasture, by introducing improved species of grasses. In Central America and the West Indies, for example, Pangola grass which is native to South America, has been found to form very productive pastures in areas where the rainfall is adequate.

One of the most acute problems facing many tropical ranchers is that of poor communications; for unlike the nomadic herder, the rancher is highly concerned with the marketing of his livestock or their products. Unfortunately, many ranching areas are geographically remote, with the result that cattle often have to be transported long distances to market. In some cases, the lack of roads or railways in the ranching areas means that the cattle have to be driven long distances overland on foot. In Guyana, for example, the cattle reared in the remote interior savannas are mainly consumed in the densely populated coastal strip. Before 1940, cattle from these savannas were driven overland for almost 300 km along a cattle trail, to Paradise on the Berbice river. At Paradise they were loaded onto a steamer and sent down the river to Rosignol, and thence to Georgetown by rail. This was a long journey, and many cattle died on the way. A possible alternative to transporting live cattle to market, is to build slaughter houses and refrigeration plants in the ranching areas, and to send out the meat by aeroplane. This in fact is what is now done in Guyana. The cattle reared on the Rupununi savannas are slaughtered at a modern plant at Lethem and the meat is flown to Georgetown.

Tropical ranchers also often suffer from the lack of good local markets for meat. Many of the ranching areas are situated in countries which have a fairly small human population, with the result that the local market is limited, and production must be aimed at the export market. The production of meat for export is, however, more complicated than production for local consumption. There must be facilities for deep freezing the meat, and furthermore, most importing countries impose rigid disease control regulations.

Cattle ranching in northern Australia

The rearing of beef cattle is the main agricultural activity in the savanna lands of the northern parts of Western Australia, Northern Territory and Queensland. In these cattle rearing areas the rainfall is generally between 400 and 1 000 mm per annum, and is highly seasonal in its distribution. The year in northern Australia is divided into two seasons, which are commonly known as the Wet and the Dry. The wet season begins in November or December, and continues until March or April. During the wet season there is a rapid growth of grass, and the rivers often flood wide areas. During the dry season, however, there is frequently a serious shortage of both pasture and drinking water.

The cattle ranches, which in Australia are known as cattle stations, are very large indeed, many of them covering several thousand sq km. The Barkly Tableland, which is one of the better cattle rearing districts in northern Australia, has about 18 cattle stations which occupy a total area of more than 100 000 sq km. The main homestead, where the station owner or manager lives, is frequently the only permanent habitation on the whole station. At the main homestead there are usually quarters for the stockmen, cattle dips, water storage facilities and a landing strip for light aircraft. Because of the vast size of the station the stockmen, many of whom are aborigines, spend much of the year away from the main homestead, moving around the station and camping out.

The cattle stations in northern Australia have very few fences, and the cattle graze in an uncontrolled fashion. Once or twice during the year the cattle are mustered (rounded up). At muster time they are dipped to control cattle ticks, and the calves are branded to distinguish them from the animals belonging to neighbouring stations. The mature bullocks are taken away from the main herd, and are paddocked ready to be sent to the fattening areas or to the meatworks on the coast. The main breeds of cattle reared in northern Australia are Aberdeen Angus, Devon, Hereford, Shorthorn, and crossbreeds of these.

In many cases the cattle stations in the interior of northern Australia are only used for rearing the cattle, which are then sent elsewhere to be fattened

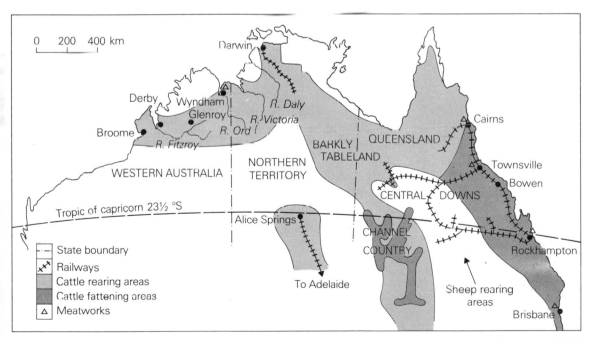

Fig. 10.3 Tropical Australia – cattle ranching

151

before they are slaughtered. The cattle are often driven long distances on foot along stock roads to the fattening areas. The main fattening areas are along the coast of Queensland, and in the Channel Country. The Channel Country provides excellent pastures for fattening during the summer months, when widespread flooding occurs. Unfortunately, in about four years out of ten, the summer floods fail and fattening cannot be carried out. Most of the abattoirs and meat processing plants are situated on the coast, and a large part of the meat which is produced in northern Australia is exported to Britain and elsewhere. Important centres of the meat industry are Wyndham in the north, and Townsville, Bowen, Rockhampton, Brisbane and Cairns in the east.

The cattle ranching industry of northern Australia is faced with many problems:

1 The most serious problem is the shortage of water and pasture at the end of the dry season. Most cattle stations expect to lose about 10 per cent of their stock each dry season. The condition of the cattle which survive generally deteriorates.

2 The cattle are affected by many diseases and insect pests, including pleuro-pneumonia, cattle ticks and the buffalo fly.

3 The cattle ranching areas are very poorly served by roads and railways. As a result the cattle often have to be driven long distances on foot to the nearest road or rail head. On these long drives, which frequently take several weeks, the cattle lose weight. In unusually dry years, drives cannot be undertaken, because of the shortage of water along the stock roads. With the construction of new roads in northern Australia, however, the trucking of cattle is now on the increase. A possible solution to the transport problem is to construct abattoirs in the ranching areas, and to fly the carcasses to the meatworks on the coast. A slaughterhouse has in fact already been established at Glenroy, some 240 km to the south of Wyndham. At Glenroy the carcasses are loaded into air freighters, which are able to make two trips a day to Wyndham.

4 In this sparsely populated part of Australia, it is often difficult to obtain sufficient labour.

Exercises

1 a) In which parts of the tropical world is nomadic herding an important way of life?

b) Illustrating your answer with examples from the tropical world, show how the way of life of the nomadic herders is related to the physical environment in which they live.

2 a) Write a detailed account of livestock ranching in any one tropical area.

b) Outline the problems faced by ranchers in the area you have chosen.

3 a) Discuss the problems facing the pastoral peoples of tropical Africa.

b) To what extent are these problems of their own making?

Suggested reading

See Chapter 11.

CHAPTER ELEVEN

Agriculture: increasing production

In most tropical countries there is a real need to increase agricultural production, for two main reasons. Firstly, large numbers of the inhabitants of the tropical lands are at present either under-nourished or malnourished, and increased agricultural production is necessary if the standard of living of the existing population is to be raised. Secondly, the population of most tropical countries is expanding rapidly, and consequently it will be necessary to increase production in order to feed these extra mouths.

It is possible to increase the agricultural production of the tropical lands in two different ways:

1 by extending the area of land which is at present used for agriculture;
2 by increasing the output per unit area of existing agricultural land.

Expanding the agricultural area

The extent to which it is possible to expand the existing agricultural area varies considerably from one part of the tropical world to another. In most parts of South Asia and in many of the West Indian territories, for example, nearly all of the best agricultural land is already under cultivation. On the other hand, in tropical South America and to a lesser extent in parts of Central America, tropical Africa and Southeast Asia there are still vast areas of land which are virtually uninhabited, and which offer possibilities for agricultural development. In most cases, however, formidable problems will have to be overcome before such lands can be developed for agriculture.

In the Amazon basin, in the Caribbean lowlands of Central America and in the islands of Borneo and New Guinea, there are vast areas of tropical rain forest which are very sparsely peopled. These forests, however, are difficult to clear, and many of the forest soils quickly lose their fertility once they are brought under cultivation. Furthermore, these areas at present lack adequate means of communication with the outside world, and roads or railways will have to be built in order to enable agricultural settlers to dispose of their surplus production. In spite of the problems involved, a certain amount of agricultural settlement has taken place in recent decades in the rain forest areas of Southeast Asia and South America.

In some parts of the tropical world there are extensive areas of swampland. Notable examples occur around the mouth of the Amazon river, along the east coast of Sumatra, in western and southern Borneo and in the Niger Delta. At some future date, parts of these swamplands could be reclaimed for agricultural purposes, although such reclamation schemes would doubtless be very expensive. The reclamation of swampland for agricultural purposes has already taken place on a relatively small scale in several parts of the tropical world. In Guyana, for example, much of the existing cultivated land has been reclaimed during the last two or three centuries from coastal swamps. This reclamation has involved the building of walls to keep out the sea, and the digging of canals for drainage purposes. In West Africa during the last few decades some areas of mangrove swamp have been reclaimed for rice growing, particularly in Gambia, Guinea Bissau, Guinea and Sierra Leone.

153

In other parts of the tropical world there are extensive areas which are at present unsuitable for cultivation on account of their extreme aridity. The provision of irrigation water is essential if such areas are to be made more productive. It should be noted that irrigation is useful not only in areas which are too dry for any sort of cultivation, but also in areas where the unreliability of the rainfall at present causes crop yields to be uncertain. A major problem in the development of large-scale irrigation schemes, is the massive outlay of capital which is needed for the construction of dams and distributary canals.

Irrigation is already of considerable importance in several parts of the tropical lands. Probably the best known irrigation scheme in tropical Africa is the Gezira scheme in Sudan. Smaller schemes include that of the Office du Niger in the middle section of the Niger valley in Mali, the Richard Toll scheme in Senegal, the Mwea-Tebere scheme in Kenya, and the various schemes in the lowveld of Zimbabwe. The Office du Niger scheme has involved the building of a barrage across the Niger at Sansanding, to raise the level of the river by four metres. The Sansanding barrage was begun in 1937 and completed in 1941, and is nearly a kilometre long. By 1971 some 42 000 hectares had been irrigated by the Office du Niger, supporting some 30 000 people. Most of the early settlers on this scheme came from southern and eastern Mali. Originally it was intended that the scheme would produce vast quantities of cotton for sale to France, but the early settlers had no experience of irrigated farming and allowed the cotton to degenerate. The emphasis has changed away from cotton, and much of the irrigated land is now being used for rice growing.

In tropical Asia irrigation is of considerable importance in several countries, particularly in India. In 1973 some 21 per cent of India's net cultivated area was irrigated. In tropical America irrigation is of particular importance in Mexico and Peru. In Mexico it was estimated that in 1967 about 18 per cent of the cultivated area was irrigated. In Peru the bulk of the country's major export crops of cotton and sugar cane are grown on irrigated land in the coastal oases.

Increasing output per unit area

Considerable opportunities exist in many parts of the tropical world to increase production per unit area. In most tropical countries production per unit area is still relatively low, when compared with that of the more developed countries of the temperate lands. There are various possible means by which greater production could be achieved, including:

1 the introduction of improved varieties of crops;
2 the greater use of artificial fertilisers;
3 the more effective control of pests and diseases;
4 the use of better cultural methods;
5 improved methods of animal husbandry;
6 improvements in the transport and marketing of farm produce;
7 the provision of credit facilities;
8 changes in land tenure.

Improved varieties of crops

Scientific plant breeding has greatly helped to increase crop production in many of the developed countries of the temperate lands, but in the past has been of much less importance in the tropical world. The scientific plant breeder is primarily concerned with the production of new varieties of crops which will give higher yields per unit area than do existing varieties. The plant breeder may also be interested in producing varieties of crops which are resistant to various diseases, or varieties which are more drought-resistant and which consequently can be grown in areas of lower or more unreliable rainfall.

Progress has already been made in introducing improved varieties of crops into some parts of the tropical world. For example, improved varieties of oil palm are now grown on plantations in Southeast Asia and Zaïre. These give far higher yields of oil than do the semi-wild palms of West Africa. In tropical America varieties of banana have been developed which are resistant to Panama disease. In tropical Asia some success has been achieved in breeding high-yielding varieties of cereals, particularly rice. In 1949 the Food and Agricultural Organisation (FAO) of the United Nations established the International Rice Commission, to study the problems involved in increasing rice production. The FAO financed a rice hybridisation project, starting in 1950. The object of this project was to combine the desirable characteristics of both the Indica and the Japonica types of rice. In India the so-called green revolution which consists of using high-yielding crop varieties in conjunction with irrigation and fertilisers, has already changed the appearance of many rural areas. By the early 1970s some 15 per cent of India's cultivated area was under high-yielding crops.

Artificial fertilisers

Most farmers in the developed countries of the temperate lands now greatly increase their crop yields by heavy applications of suitable artificial fertilisers. There seems little doubt that crop yields in most tropical countries could also be greatly increased by this means. So far, in most tropical countries relatively little use is made of artificial fertilisers. The greatest use of fertilisers is generally made on plantations and on large farms producing export crops. The least use is generally made on small peasant farms producing subsistence crops. One of the main reasons for this is the fact that artificial fertilisers tend to be expensive, particularly as few tropical countries have as yet developed their own chemical industries, and

so have to rely upon imports. There is also a need for more experimental work to be done, in order to ascertain the response made to artificial fertilisers by various crops under different physical conditions.

Control of pests and diseases

In many parts of the tropical world a great deal of damage is done each year to farm crops by various pests and diseases. Some of the more important diseases of tropical crops have been mentioned in Chapter 9. Agricultural pests include not only animals, but also birds and insects. In parts of Africa, large animals such as elephants and baboons are responsible for a great deal of crop damage. Elephants for example, not only eat farm crops, but also uproot and trample them. This type of problem is not always easy to overcome, as in attempting to control wild animals, the interests of the cultivator may well conflict with those of the wild life conservationist. Smaller animals such as rats, frequently cause considerable losses to food crops during stor-

Grain storage bins in Northern Ghana. In areas of highly seasonal rainfall it is necessary to store food from one annual harvest to the next. Pests may cause severe losses of food crops during storage.

155

age. This problem can be reduced by the provision of better food storage facilities. Birds are particularly harmful in areas where cereal crops are grown, especially at harvest time. In the Senegal Delta for example, the quelea bird is often responsible for heavy losses in the rice crop. Insects may be harmful to the farmer not only by eating his crops, but also by assisting in the spread of plant and animal diseases. One of the most destructive of the insect pests of the tropical lands is the locust, great plagues of which have at times destroyed crops over a very wide area, particularly in the drier parts of tropical Africa.

There are various possible methods of controlling plant pests and diseases. One of these is biological control, which involves making use of the natural enemies of the pest concerned. For example the moth *Levuana iridiscens* whose larvae formerly caused considerable damage to coconut palms in Fiji, has been controlled by the introduction of a type of parasite from Malaysia. In using the biological method of control, however, care must be taken to ensure that the introduced predators are not themselves harmful to crops or to domestic animals. A second method of control is to breed for resistance to diseases. A third method involves spraying or dusting with chemicals. There are limitations to the use of chemical control, however, as care has to be taken that the chemicals used do not damage the crop itself, nor do they destroy beneficial insects such as predators or pollinators. A considerable degree of success has already been achieved in the chemical control of some pests and diseases. Locusts for example, can be controlled by aerial spraying once the swarms have been located. Leaf spot disease of the banana can now be controlled by spraying with Bordeaux mixture and the capsid insect which attacks the cacao tree can be controlled by spraying with Gammalin 20. On the other hand, attempts to control such diseases as Panama disease of the banana, and swollen shoot disease of the cacao tree have so far met with very little success.

Better cultural methods

In many of the developed countries of the temperate lands crops are grown and livestock are reared on the same farm. Mixed farming has the great advantage that the animal dung helps to maintain the organic content of the soil. At present mixed farming is not common in most parts of the tropical world. Even where livestock are kept on crop farms, the two activities are rarely integrated. In some tropical countries, notably in India, animal dung is dried and used for fuel, rather than being applied to the soil. The increased use of animal manure on tropical farms would help to maintain soil fertility, and would reduce the need for prolonged periods of fallow.

In many parts of the tropical world the risk of soil erosion would be greatly reduced, if the farmers were to use better cultural methods.

Improvements in animal husbandry

In many parts of the tropical world there is considerable scope for improvements in the standard of animal husbandry. The productivity of native breeds of cattle is generally low, in terms of both meat and milk. Exotic breeds of cattle from North America and Europe, however, do not generally do well in the tropics, except in some highland areas. They have difficulty in standing the constantly high temperatures, and do not thrive on the poor natural pastures. Improvements in tropical livestock can be made either by crossbreeding native females with imported males, or alternatively up-grading the local animals by selective breeding.

In addition to the diseases of the temperate lands, livestock in the tropical lands are subject to a number of tropical diseases. Large areas of tropical Africa are at present rendered useless for cattle rearing because they are infested with tsetse fly, which transmits bovine trypanosomiasis. Most breeds of cattle, with the exception of dwarf breeds such as the Ndama of West Africa, are susceptible to trypanosomiasis. Pests and diseases of livestock can be controlled in a number of ways. Dipping or spraying with insecticides is useful in the control of certain insect pests, such as ticks. Inoculation has proved effective in controlling virus diseases such as foot and mouth disease and rinderpest, and bacterial diseases such as anthrax.

Another major problem facing animal rearers in many parts of the tropical world is the seasonal shortage of water and pasture. In parts of tropical Africa much is now being done to overcome the problem of water shortage in stock rearing areas, by the sinking of boreholes to tap underground supplies of water, and by the construction of concrete or earthen dams to make it possible to store surplus water during the rains for use during the dry season.

In many cases there is also a need for change in the attitudes of the animal rearing peoples of the tropical lands. In particular there is a need for the livestock rearers to adjust the size of their flocks and herds to what the available pasture is capable of supporting, and also to develop a greater willingness to sell off surplus animals.

Transport and marketing

In many tropical countries the transport of surplus farm produce to market provides a problem, because of the inadequacies of the existing road and railway systems. In areas where transport facilities are poor it is difficult for the farmer to engage in the commercial production of such perishable commodities as meat, milk, fruits and vegetables.

In some parts of the tropical world the actual selling of surplus farm produce is also a problem. This is particularly the case in areas where large numbers of peasant farmers are engaged in the small-scale production of export crops. Various methods have been tried in an attempt to alleviate the marketing problems of the peasant farmers. In Ghana, Nigeria and Uganda, for example, government-sponsored marketing boards have been set up. These boards purchase the peasant farmers crops at fixed prices, and then organise their resale on the world market. In other countries such as Kenya, some success has been achieved by co-operative marketing boards.

In the past the tropical farmer has suffered greatly as a result of short-term fluctuations in the world market prices of his crops. In recent years some attempt has been made to overcome this problem by the establishment of commodity agreements.

Agricultural credit

Many tropical farmers are handicapped by the shortage of capital needed for the purchase of such things as fertilisers, improved varieties of seed and better farm implements. In countries such as India agricultural indebtedness has for a long time been a great problem. In the past many Indian farmers have had to obtain credit from village money lenders, often at exorbitant rates of interest. In some countries attempts have been made to overcome the problem of the shortage of agricultural credit, by the formation of co-operative credit societies.

Changes in land tenure

In many parts of the tropical world the way in which land is distributed and owned has tended to make it difficult to increase agricultural productivity. In tropical America in particular, in the past land was very unevenly distributed. Characteristically much of the best agricultural land was held in the form of a small number of very large properties (*latifundios*), while a much smaller proportion was held in the form of a large number of tiny holdings (*minifundios*). It is claimed, for example, that in 1910 in Mexico 1 per cent of the population held 97 per cent of the land, while 96 per cent of the population owned only 1 per cent. It was argued that such an uneven distribution of land was both socially and economically harmful. It was socially harmful because it left the mass of the population without the means of making an adequate living from the land, and thus resulted in them becoming discontented. Indeed, discontentment about land distribution was one of the important factors which led to the Mexican Revolution of 1910–15. It was also considered to be economically harmful, as many of the large properties were not intensively worked, as their owners were able to make a good living without farming the land efficiently.

During the present century a considerable amount of agrarian reform has been undertaken in some parts of tropical America, particularly in such countries as Mexico and Bolivia. The object of these reforms has been to bring about a more even distribution of the country's land resources, by breaking down the very large properties, and redistributing the land amongst small farmers or landless labourers. Experience has shown, however, that on its own land reform does not necessarily bring about an increase in agricultural productivity. For the latter to occur, it is usually necessary for land reform to be accompanied by other measures, such as the introduction of better varieties of seed, the increased use of fertilisers and the provision of agricultural credit.

In some parts of the tropical world, farmers suffer not only from the shortage of good land, but also from the fact that their holdings are highly fragmented, consisting of several different plots of land

157

which are often situated some distance apart. For example, there is a record of one farmer in the Kikuyu area of Kenya who had 29 different plots of land, adding up to a farm of less than 4 hectares in size. Such fragmentation generally comes about as the result of inheritance practices, whereby when the head of family dies, his land is subdivided between his male heirs. The fragmentation of holdings has several drawbacks. Firstly, the farmer wastes a great deal of time in travelling between his various plots; secondly, an unusually high proportion of his land is taken up by field boundaries; and thirdly, the small size of the plots makes it difficult for him to use modern farm machinery.

In areas where holdings are highly fragmented, land consolidation schemes can help to make farming more efficient. Schemes of this type have been successfully carried out in some areas, notably in parts of the Kikuyu area of Kenya. Following the Mau-Mau rebellion of 1952–6, the scattered homesteads of the Kikuyu were grouped into villages. The farm land was then redistributed in such a way that in place of his numerous scattered plots, each farmer received a single piece of land which he could surround with a fence.

ALAN GILBERT: *Latin American Development* – Chapter 5

PIERRE GOUROU: *The Tropical World* – Chapters 4–6

DAVID GRIGG: *The Harsh Lands*

R. J. HARRISON CHURCH: *West Africa* – Chapters 6 and 7

B. W. HODDER: *Economic Development in the Tropics* – Chapters 6 and 7

W. B. MORGAN AND J. C. PUGH: *West Africa* – Chapters 2 and 3

A. M. O'CONNOR: *An Economic Geography of East Africa* – Chapters 2–6

A. M. O'CONNOR: *The Geography of Tropical African Development* – Chapter 2

M. C. POLLOCK: *Studies in Emerging Africa* – Chapters 3 and 4

J. M. PRITCHARD: *Africa – A Study Geography for Advanced Students* – Chapters 4, 5 and 6

M. F. THOMAS AND G. W. WHITTINGTON, Ed.: *Environment and Land Use in Africa* – Chapters 9, 10 and 17

C. C. WEBSTER AND P. N. WILSON: *Agriculture in the Tropics*

H. P. WHITE AND M. B. GLEAVE: *An Economic Geography of West Africa* – Chapters 4 and 5

Exercises

1 a) In which parts of the tropical world are there still extensive areas of sparsely inhabited land, which offer possibilities for agricultural development?

  b) What problems will have to be overcome before these areas can be brought under cultivation?

2 In many parts of the tropical world agricultural output per unit area is relatively low.

  a) suggest reasons for this low productivity;

  b) discuss the possible means by which productivity could be improved.

Suggested reading

W. ALLAN: *The African Husbandman*

JOHN I. CLARKE, Ed.: *An Advanced Geography of Africa* – Chapter 10

CHAPTER TWELVE

Fisheries

A: General

Fish is a very important item in the diet of many tropical peoples. In several parts of the tropical world fish is the most cheaply produced form of animal protein, being of particular importance in areas where the rearing of livestock is difficult. Most of the fish consumed within the tropical world is caught in the sea, but in some countries fresh-water fisheries are also of considerable importance. In some parts of the tropical world fishing is still undertaken primarily for subsistence purposes, but in others it is now highly commercialised.

Methods of fishing

Many different methods are used to catch fish, only a few of which are discussed here. In some countries modern fishing vessels and equipment are used, but in most parts of the tropical world the methods employed are still very simple. The exact method of fishing used depends upon several factors, important among which are the depth of the water in which fishing takes place, the type of fish sought, and the level of development of the peoples involved.

Some simple methods

Very simple methods which are sometimes used to catch fish in shallow waters include spearing, shooting with bows and arrows, and the use of poisons. In most countries the use of poisons is now illegal, but it is still a common method of catching fresh-water fish in some parts of the tropical world. The Amerindians of Guyana, for example, use a poison called *curare*. This is thrown into shallow pools in the rivers during the dry season. The fish in the pools rise to

Hauling in a beach seine net near Cape Coast, Ghana. Note the heavy surf, which is typical of this section of the West African coastline.

159

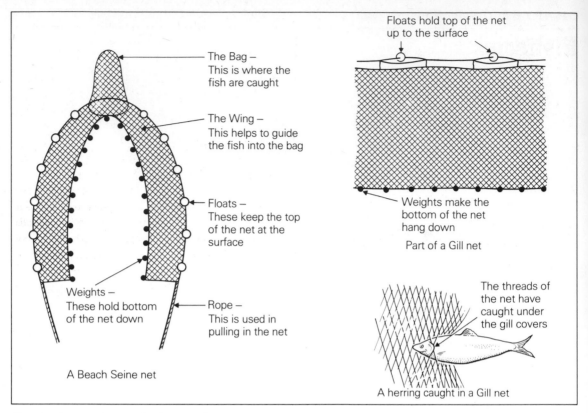

The Bag –
This is where the
fish are caught

The Wing –
This helps to guide
the fish into the bag

Floats –
These keep the top
of the net at the
surface

Weights –
These hold bottom
of the net down

Rope –
This is used in
pulling in the net

A Beach Seine net

Floats hold top of the net
up to the surface

Weights make the
bottom of the net
hang down

Part of a Gill net

The threads of
the net have
caught under
the gill covers

A herring caught in a Gill net

Fig. 12.1 Some simple methods of catching fish

the surface, either dead, or so drugged that they can be taken by hand.

In the shallow waters of coastal lagoons, lakes, rivers and seasonal swamps, various types of fish baskets and fish traps are used. These devices vary considerably in size and design. In the Tonlé Sap in the Khmer Republic, for example, the most important fishing device is the barrage. Barrages are made of split bamboo fencing, mounted on poles driven into the bed of the lake. They are laid out in such a way that they either confine the fish in a certain space, or lead them into various kinds of non-return traps.

Other common methods of catching fish in shallow water, include the use of scoop nets and cast nets. In using the scoop net, the fisherman lays the net down in the water, and either lifts it up at intervals, or whenever he sees fish passing over it. If the scoop net is used at night, lights are commonly used to attract the fish. The cast net is a circular net,

to the middle of which is attached a cord. The fisherman either holds this cord in his hand, or attaches it to his wrist. The periphery of the net is weighted, so that when the fisherman throws it in front of him with a slight twist, it spreads out and falls on the water in a circle. The weights carry it to the bottom, and the fish beneath it are trapped when the net is pulled in by its cord. If the water is extremely shallow, the fisherman often wades when using the cast net, but in deeper water he usually works from a canoe.

In some sandy coastal areas, the beach seine net or haul net is used. This consists of a bag-shaped net, to the mouth of which two wings of netting are attached. The wings serve to prevent the fish from escaping, and to guide them towards the bag. Several hundred metres of rope are attached to each of the wings. A canoe is used to set the beach seine net in the water, at a short distance from the shore. Two teams of fishermen then haul in the ropes, until the

160

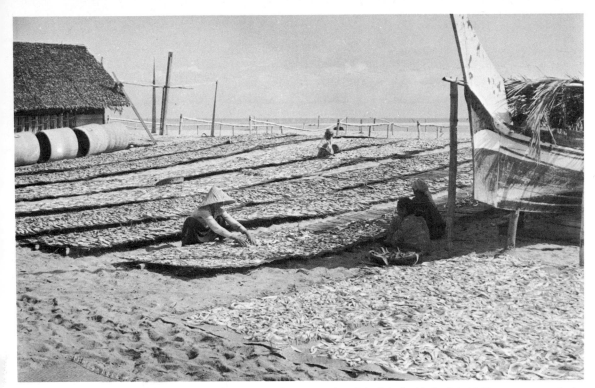

Drying fish on the beach in Malaysia. The gills and entrails have been removed, and the fish salted before being laid out on mats to dry in the sun.

bag with its catch of fish can be drawn up on to the beach. The beach seine net is also sometimes used in fishing from the shores of lakes.

In many parts of the tropical world, inshore fishermen (those who fish within a few kilometres of the shore) operate from canoes or from other types of small craft. In fishing for pelagic fish (those which live near to the surface) the inshore fishermen often use some form of gill net. This consists of a long piece of netting, which is usually laid down in the water and left in position for several hours at a time. The top of the gill net is held at or near to the surface by floats, while weights at the bottom cause the net to hang down straight in the water. The mesh of the net (the space between the threads) is of such a size that the type of fish which is being sought can get its body part of the way through, but can then go no further. When the fish tries to wriggle out backwards, it is held by the threads of the net which catch under its gill covers. Demersal fish (those which usually live near to the sea bed) are often caught by using baited hooks on the end of long lines.

More modern methods

More modern methods of fishing using motorised vessels are now employed in some tropical countries. Important among these are trawling and purse seining. Trawling is mainly used in the catching of demersal fish, and involves dragging a cone-shaped bag (a trawl) over the sea-bed behind the boat. The mouth of the trawl is kept open by wooden boards, which pull outwards as they are towed through the water.

The purse seine net is used in the catching of pelagic fish. Unlike the gill net, the purse seine net is laid out in a circle to enclose a shoal of fish. At the bottom of the net there are rings, through which passes a rope. When the circle has been completed, the rope is pulled to close the bottom of the net, thus trapping the fish inside it. The fish can then be scooped out of the net into the boat.

Trolling is a method which is sometimes used in fishing for larger pelagic fish such as tuna. Trolling involves towing lines behind a vessel moving at moderate speed. Very often no bait is used in

161

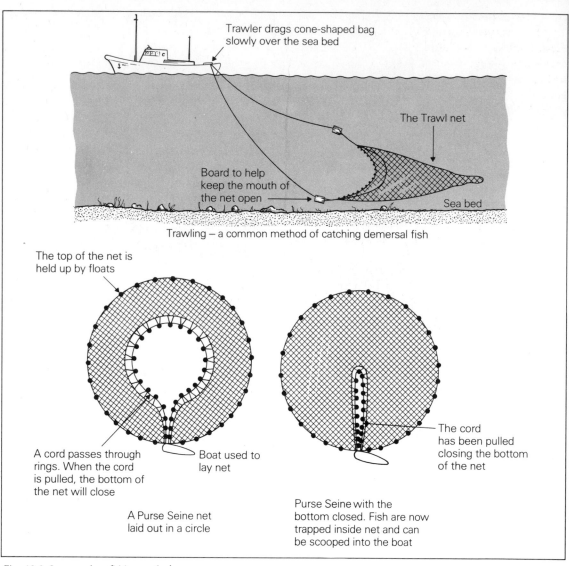

Trawler drags cone-shaped bag
slowly over the sea bed

The Trawl net

Board to help
keep the mouth of
the net open

Sea bed

Trawling – a common method of catching demersal fish

The top of the net is
held up by floats

A cord passes through
rings. When the cord
is pulled, the bottom of
the net will close

Boat used to
lay net

The cord
has been pulled
closing the bottom
of the net

A Purse Seine net
laid out in a circle

Purse Seine with the
bottom closed. Fish are now
trapped inside net and can
be scooped into the boat

Fig. 12.2 Some modern fishing methods

trolling, the hooks being attached to a metal lure. The lure is agitated by the water flow, and its movement and the reflection of light from it attract the fish to the hooks.

Processing the catch

Some of the fish caught in tropical countries is consumed fresh, but as fish spoils very rapidly under hot conditions, if the catch is not to be consumed immediately, it must be preserved in some way. In most tropical countries, very simple methods of fish preservation are still used. Common among these are sun-drying, salting, and smoking.

Very small fish can be spread out whole and left to dry in the sun, but larger fish must first be split open and gutted. In some areas, where salt is readily available and where salt-fish is acceptable to the consumer, the fish may first be salted before it is dried. In very humid conditions the heat of the sun alone may not be sufficient to ensure rapid drying, and so the fish is spread out over or before a fire. Along the coast of West Africa, circular fish ovens

162

are a very common sight in many fishing villages. These are usually made of clay, although sometimes metal drums are used instead. Near to the top of the oven there is a gridwork of sticks or metal, upon which the fish is laid. There is an opening at the bottom of the oven, so that firewood can be put inside. A fire is lit, and the smoke from it rises around the fish. Fish preserved by smoking will only keep good for a few days. In parts of Southeast Asia, fish is preserved by converting it into a highly spiced, partly fermented fish paste.

In some tropical countries, more modern methods of fish preservation are now used. These include canning and deep freezing. In some countries there are also factories which produce fish meal and fish oil.

Platform of sticks or metal grid near top of oven. The fish is placed here. The smoke from the fire below rises through the grid.

Hollow circular oven usually made of clay

Wood or other fuel which is burned to make the smoke

Fig. 12.3 An oven used for smoking fish in Ghana

B: The fisheries of selected areas

In 1975 the tropical world accounted for just over one-quarter of the world's total catch of fish. Six tropical countries each had a catch of more than 1 million tonnes, while 11 non-tropical countries exceeded this figure.

The Peruvian fishing industry
In 1975 tropical America accounted for 29 per cent of the tropical world's fish catch, and 8 per cent of the total world catch. By far the largest fish producer in tropical America is Peru.

The growth of a large scale fishing industry in Peru is a comparatively recent development. In 1949, for example, the Peruvian catch amounted to only 45 000 tonnes, but in 1970 it was almost 12,5

million tonnes. In that year Peru was the world's leading fish producer, accounting for 18 per cent of the total world catch.

The growth of the Peruvian fishing industry has been favoured by the fact that the country's more than 2 000 km long coastline is washed by the cool waters of the equatorwards-flowing Peruvian current (Humboldt current). These waters support vast quantities of plankton (minute plants and animals which float in the upper layers of sea water, and which directly or indirectly form the food for most marine life).

Fishing is now carried on from some 50 ports along the Peruvian coastline, of which the most important are Chimbote and Callao. The methods of fishing employed are modern and efficient. The bulk of the catch is made up of anchoveta, a small pelagic fish of the herring family. Most of the anchoveta

Table 69 Fisheries: nominal catches, 1975 (thousand tonnes)

World total: 69 732 *Leading tropical producers*		*Other leading producers*			
Peru	3 447	Japan	10 508	S. Korea	2 133
India	2 328	USSR	9 876	Denmark	1 767
Indonesia	1 390	China	6 680	Spain	1 533
Thailand	1 370	USA	2 799	S. Africa	1 314
Philippines	1 342	Norway	2 550	Chile	1 128

Fig. 12.4 The Peruvian fishing industry

catch is processed into fish meal (used for animal feed and fertiliser) and fish oil, at factories which until recently were owned by the same companies as the fishing fleets. In 1971 anchovetas constituted 96 per cent of the Peruvian catch by weight. Other important species of fish landed in Peru are tuna, and bonito, both of which are mainly processed by canning and freezing. In 1971 there were 109 fish meal factories in operation, employing some 3 000 workers. There were also several fish freezing and canning plants.

The bulk of Peru's production of fish meal and fish oil is exported to the USA, the USSR, China and Europe. In 1970 Peru accounted for more than six-tenths of the world's export trade in fish meal, and was also the world's leading exporter of fish oil, accounting for more than three-tenths of the total export trade. In 1971 fish and fish products accounted for 38 per cent of Peru's export earnings.

Millions of sea-birds also feed on the fish which live in the cool waters off the coast of Peru. These birds nest on the off-shore islands where their droppings collect as guano in the dry climate. Guano is rich in nitrogen, potassium and phosphorous, and is therefore valuable as fertiliser. In the past the guano accumulated to form deposits which were several metres in thickness. During the nineteenth century, however, these deposits were intensively exploited, and guano formed an important export item from Peru. Today guano is mainly collected for use in the coastal oases of Peru. Its collection is carefully controlled by the government, in order to avoid excessive exploitation.

Every year, sometime between December and March, winds from across the equator bring an eddy of warm water southwards along the coast of northern Peru. The warm water spreads over the cool waters of the Peruvian current. This invasion of warm water is known by the Peruvians as El Nino, and in normal years it is soon dissipated. At irregular intervals, however, and for reasons which are not fully understood, the north wind is stronger, and warm water covers the cool waters all the way to northern Chile. In years when this happens, the fish go further out to sea in search of food, and it becomes difficult for the Peruvian fishermen to locate them. Not only is there a drastic reduction in the fish catch in such years, but also vast numbers of sea-birds die of starvation.

During the early 1970s the Peruvian fish catch declined drastically. In 1973 2 299 million tonnes were landed, representing only 18 per cent of the 1970 catch. This decline can partly be attributed to the temporary disappearance of the anchoveta shoals due to the arrival in 1972 and 1973 of the warm nino current, and partly to the effects of overfishing. In an attempt to conserve fish stocks, in recent years the Peruvian Government has restricted the length of the local fishing season. In order to protect their fishing industry from the fleets of other nations, the Peruvians have recently claimed sovereignty over the sea for a distance of 200 nautical miles (370 km) from their coastline, instead of the traditional 12 nautical miles (22 km). Fishing within this zone is now restricted to Peruvian boats. In an effort to rationalise the processing side of the fishing industry, in 1973 the government expropriated all the private firms producing fish meal and its derivatives, and created a state corporation known as Pescaperu to control the processing of fish meal and oil. In 1974 there were signs of the beginning of a recovery in the Peruvian fishing industry.

The fisheries of Southeast Asia

Fishing is of considerable importance in Southeast Asia. In most parts of this region fish is a staple food, being eaten as a complement to rice. The methods of fishing employed in Southeast Asia are still for the most part very simple, and the average output of the fishermen is very small. Some of the fish caught in the area is eaten fresh by the fishermen themselves, but much of the catch is preserved by smoking, sun-drying or by conversion into one of the highly-spiced, partly fermented fish pastes which are very popular with the peoples of Southeast Asia. Large quantities of fish in these forms are moved inland within each country, and there is also a considerable movement of preserved fish between the various countries of Southeast Asia.

In many parts of Southeast Asia inland fisheries are of very great importance, with fish being caught in rivers, lakes, flooded rice fields and irrigation canals. In many areas fish are also cultivated in artificial fish ponds.

The most productive of the natural fresh-water fisheries of Southeast Asia is that of the Tonle Sap in the Khmer Republic. The amount of water in the Tonle Sap varies considerably throughout the year. During a large part of the year the lake is very shallow, being everywhere less than 2 metres in depth, and covering an area of some 2 500 sq km. The Tonle Sap usually drains into the Mekong river, but during the period from June to October the Mekong floods, and the flow of water in the outlet river is reversed. Water from the Mekong then flows into the Tonle Sap, causing the water level in the lake to rise, and flooding the surrounding forest land. The most productive fishing occurs when the flood waters begin to recede. Many full-time fishermen live around the shores of the Tonle Sap, in villages of pile dwellings. In addition to the full-time fishermen, a considerable number of migrant fishermen move temporarily into the area during the peak fishing period, which extends from October to January. Much of the fish which is caught is dried for export. Some fish is sent alive towards the estuary of the Mekong, in floating cages made of bamboo.

Inland fisheries are also important in Indonesia, in 1975 accounting for three-tenths of that country's total catch. Around the towns of Djakarta, Surbaya and Semarang in northern Java, there is a considerable demand for fish, and to help meet this demand coastal mangrove swamps have been partially enclosed to control the flow of tidal water. Into these enclosures are placed fish spawn and young sea fish. The young fish are left to fatten on algae, and on water weeds which are cultivated for them. One of the most popular species in these brackish ponds is milkfish, which reaches a marketable size within a year. Coastal fish ponds of this type are also found in other parts of Southeast Asia. On the island of Singapore, for example, reclaimed mangrove swamps are used for the cultivation of prawns. In many parts of Southeast Asia, artificial fish ponds have been constructed. In these ponds, fish of the carp family are reared and fattened throughout the year.

In many parts of Southeast Asia, flooded rice-fields also yield fish. In some areas the fish are reared in the rice fields as a second crop, the fields being specially flooded for this purpose after the rice crop has been harvested. More commonly, however, the fish are reared at the same time as the rice is growing. Where this is the case, the rice fields may be deliberately stocked with young fish shortly after the rice has been transplanted, or the fish may simply enter the fields with the irrigation water. The fish in the rice fields mainly feed on algae and other vegetable matter. In the Malay Peninsula the farmer often digs a sump-pond in the lowest part of his rice field. When the fields are drained to allow the rice to ripen, the fish collect in these sump-ponds, where there is still water for them. The farmer is then able to scoop them out.

Of the marine fisheries, inshore fishing is by far the most usual in Southeast Asia. Much of Southeast Asia's marine fishing is in fact done where the sea is less than 3 metres deep. In some cases sea fishing is done without the use of boats, the fishermen either wading in the shallow water near to the shore, or setting fish traps of various types. Where boats are used they are generally very small, and rarely move far from shore. They are usually propelled by paddles or sails, although in recent years there has been some mechanisation of fishing boats in some areas.

Table 70 Fisheries of Southeast Asia: nominal catches (thousand tonnes), 1975

Burma	485	Malaysia	474
Hong Kong	151	Philippines	1 342
Indonesia	1 390	Singapore	18
Khmer Rep.	85	Thailand	1 370
Laos	20	Vietnam	1 014

The West African fisheries

Fish forms an important item in the diet of many of the peoples of West Africa, particularly in the forested areas of the south, where meat is expensive and in short supply. Fishing is an important occupation along most parts of the West African coastline, and many of the rivers and lakes are also intensively fished. The Ivory Coast, Mali, Mauritania and Senegal are able to produce a small surplus of fish for export, but most other West African countries have to import substantial quantities of fish to supplement their own catch.

The bulk of West Africa's annual catch of fish comes from the sea. The methods of fishing used in West Africa are still for the most part very simple. In the shallow waters of coastal lagoons, cast-nets and various types of fish traps are commonly employed. Beach seine nets are operated from sandy beaches along some parts of the coast. Much of the fishing in the open sea is carried out from large dug-out canoes. Until recently these canoes were propelled only by paddles and sails, but an increasing number of canoe fishermen are now fitting out-board motors to their craft. These motors reduce the time spent in travelling to and from the fishing grounds, and also enable the fishermen to operate further from the shore. Even with out-board motors, the canoe fishermen rarely travel more than a few kilometres from land, and usually only stay at sea for a few hours at a time. The methods of catching fish used by the canoe fishermen

Smoke drying fish near Cape Coast, Ghana. The fish are laid on a gridwork near the top of the oven, and smoke from the fire below rises around them.

vary. In Ghana, a type of gill net known as the *ali* net is used in fishing for pelagic fish such as herrings, while hand lines are used to catch those kinds of fish which feed at greater depth. When the canoes are not in use, they can be drawn up onto the beach. This is a great advantage, as sheltered harbours are few along most parts of the West African coastline.

Small motorised fishing vessels now operate from a few centres such as Takoradi, Tema and Elmina in Ghana. Vessels of this type are built in Ghana by the State Boatyards Corporation at Sekondi. Although these motorised vessels are able to travel further out to sea than the canoes, they do not usually have any

Table 71 West African fisheries: nominal catches (thousand tonnes), 1975

Benin	29	Ivory Coast	63	Nigeria	507
Gambia	11	Liberia	17	Senegal	362
Ghana	255	Mali	100	Sierra Leone	68
Guinea	5	Mauritania	34	Togo	14
Guinea Bissau	2	Niger	15	Upper Volta	4

means of refrigerating their catch, and so rarely stay at sea for more than a few hours at a time. The methods of fishing used by these vessels include trawling, purse seining and hand-lining.

Deep-sea fishing is still in its infancy in West Africa, and so far has been best developed in Senegal, Ghana and the Ivory Coast. Deep-sea fishing vessels have refrigerated holds in which they can keep their catches, and so they are able to stay at sea for several days or even weeks at a time.

The West African countries which at present have the largest marine catches are Senegal, Ghana, Nigeria, the Ivory Coast and Mauritania. The coast-line of Mauritania and the northern part of Senegal is washed by the cool waters of the equatorwards-flowing Canary Current, which provide a favourable environment for fish. Although much of Senegal's catch is still produced by canoe fishermen, in recent years there has been a notable development of large-scale off-shore tuna and sardine fisheries. The main fishing centres in Senegal are St. Louis, Dakar, Mbour, Joal and Sangomar. In 1974, fish accounted for 7 per cent of Senegal's export earnings.

Fishing is important in Mauritania, both as a source of fish for local consumption and for export. Until the development of iron ore mining during the 1960s, salted and dried fish formed one of Mauritania's leading export items. In the past, river fishing was of particular importance. The coastal waters were mainly fished by Canary Island fisher-men, who landed only part of their catch in Mauritania. More recently, vessels from such countries as France, Spain, the USSR, and Japan have been exploiting the rich fishing grounds off the coast of Mauritania. In recent years, attempts have been made to develop a modern sea-fishing industry in Mauritania itself. In the period 1966–8, the Société Mauritanienne de Pêche (SOMAP) built up a fleet of eight trawlers and six other vessels. SOMAP is trying to build up Mauritanian crews under Breton (French) captains. Nouadhibou is now a well equipped fishing port. In 1974, fish accounted for only 1 per cent of Mauritania's export earnings.

In the Ivory Coast, in addition to the traditional canoe fishery, there is an expanding fleet of modern tuna and sardine fishing vessels. These vessels are based on the port of Abidjan, and are mainly owned by French companies. In recent years there has also

been a marked development of the fishing industry in Liberia. The local canoe fishermen are now mainly equipped with out-board motors. The Liberian-owned Mesurado Fishing Company operates a fleet of about 30 trawlers from the port of Monrovia, and about half of these are now engaged in shrimping. The shrimps are mainly frozen for export, while the other kinds of fish which are caught are sold in Monrovia or up-country.

In Ghana canoe fishing continues to play a significant role in the fishing industry, but a number of small motorised vessels are also now in operation. A small fleet of deep-sea fishing vessels is based at the port of Tema. Some of these vessels are operated by the State Fishing Corporation, while others belong to private companies. These deep-sea vessels go as far as the waters off Senegal, Mauritania and the Canary Islands, and catch fish by trawling and purse-seining. There are also now a number of Japanese tuna fishing vessels which operate from Tema, but most of their catch is not sold in Ghana. Until recently Nigeria imported large quantities of fish annually to supplement the local catch, but is now trying to build up a modern fishing industry. A fleet of trawlers operates from Lagos. Prawns are caught in large quantities in the shallow waters off the Niger Delta, and limited quantities are now exported.

Many West African rivers are intensively fished, especially the Senegal and the middle section of the Niger. Lake Chad is also a very important source of fish, and it is hoped that sizeable fishing industries will develop in Lake Volta and in Lake Kainji. In 1975, almost one-sixth of Ghana's domestic catch came from Lake Volta.

Fresh-water fisheries are of particular importance in Mali. Although it is a land-locked country, Mali is estimated to have an annual fish catch of about 100 000 tonnes. Most of Mali's catch comes from the river Niger and the adjoining lakes. As well as providing an important source of protein for the local population, considerable quantities of smoked and dried fish are exported from Mali to neighbouring West African countries, particularly to Ghana and to Upper Volta.

Part of West Africa's fish catch is consumed fresh, but a large part is preserved by such simple methods as smoking, salting and sun-drying. Modern fish processing plants have so far been established in only

167

a few West African countries. There are canneries for sardines and tuna at Abidjan and Dakar, while at Monrovia there are facilities for freezing and packaging shrimps. In Mauritania, the Industrie Mauritanienne de la Pêche Complex (IMAPEC) has recently opened plants at Nouadhibou for the canning and freezing of fish, and also for the production of fish meal.

The East African fisheries
It is estimated that about 378 000 tonnes of fish were landed in East Africa in 1975. Uganda and Tanzania were the largest producers, while Kenya was by far the smallest. The bulk of the East African catch comes from the region's many lakes.

The marine fisheries of East Africa are at present very poorly developed. Although East Africa has almost 1 000 km of coastline, only 9 per cent of the region's total catch came from the sea in 1975. Fishing is very unevenly distributed along the East African coast. It is of most importance on the islands of Zanzibar and Pemba, which account for about one-third of East Africa's marine catch. In Kenya the greatest interest in sea fishing is shown around Malindi and Lamu. Most of East Africa's marine fishermen operate from small canoes, and their activities are limited to within a few miles of the shore.

Lake Victoria contributes by far the largest share of East Africa's fresh-water catch. It is the largest of East Africa's lakes, and contains many species of economic value. Around much of its shores the population is both dense and relatively prosperous, and there is a ready local market for fish. Fishing is carried out from a large number of landings around the lake shore, and is mainly done from canoes, many of which are now propelled by out-board motors. Most of the fishing takes place within a short distance of the shore, as the local fishermen do not

have the capital to buy larger boats with refrigeration facilities, which would enable them to fish the deeper waters near the middle of the lake. Gill nets are mainly used in canoe fishing, while beach seine nets are operated from the shores of the lake. The most important species caught in Lake Victoria are Tilapia, Haplochromis and Bagrus. Some of the catch is sold fresh, but much of it is preserved on the lake shore by smoking, salting and sun-drying.

Lake Tanganyika provides the second largest catch. The main species taken in Lake Tanganyika is the Dagaa, a small pelagic fish which rises to the surface only at night. Fishing for Dagaa is only undertaken on moonless nights. Lights are used to attract the Dagaa to the boats, and scoop nets are used to lift them out of the water. Most of the commercial catch is taken in a small area around Kigoma and Ujiji, and dried fish is dispatched by rail to other parts of Tanzania.

Lake Kyoga has a very irregular outline, and all parts of the lake are within easy reach of the shore. Consequently Lake Kyoga is more intensively fished than Lake Victoria. A large part of the catch consists of Protopterus, most of which are caught in very shallow water by using fish traps and hand lines. Fishing in Lake Kyoga is mainly done by the Bokenyi, a small group who live around the eastern shores of the lake.

Other lakes which are important sources of fish include Mobutu (formerly Albert), Idi Amin Dada (formerly Edward), and George in Uganda. In all three cases marketing the catch is a major problem, as they are distant from the main centres of population. Until 1960 much of the fish caught in these lakes was sold in Zaïre, but this trade has almost disappeared because of currency problems. The Uganda Fish Marketing Corporation (TUFMAC) has a freezing plant beside Lake George, where it produces frozen Tilapia fillets which are sold both in

Table 72 East African fisheries: nominal catches (thousand tonnes), 1975

	Kenya	*Tanzania*	*Uganda*	*East Africa*
Marine	4,5	30,2	—	34,7
Fresh-water	22,8	150,5	169,7	343,0
Total	27,3	180,7	169,7	377,7

Uganda and in Kenya. Private firms have also established freezing plants near Lakes George and Idi Amin Dada. Fishing is also of considerable importance in Lake Rukwa in Tanzania. Although it is a very shallow lake, Rukwa contains large stocks of Tilapia and other species. In Kenya, Lakes Baringo, Naivasha and Rudolf are minor sources of fish. Lake Rudolf is well stocked with fish, but the population around its shores is sparse, and it is remote from potential markets. The Kenya Fisheries Department has recently trained some of the Turkana people living in the Ferguson Gulf area in fishing methods.

Sport fishing is a considerable tourist attraction in East Africa. Along the coast there is game fishing for marlin, shark, tuna, sailfish, etc. In the interior, Lakes Rudolf and Naivasha are important sports fishing resorts, while many of the streams in the Aberdare Range and the Mount Kenya area offer excellent fishing for trout.

Other tropical African fisheries

Of the other tropical African countries, fishing is of particular importance in Angola and Namibia. The coastline of both these countries is washed by the cool waters of the equatorwards-flowing Benguela current, which support large quantities of plankton. There are numerous coastal settlements in Angola from which fishing is carried out, the most important being Mocamedes, Porto Alexandre, Benguela, Baia dos Tigres and Luanda. The most important species landed in Angola are maasbanker (horse mackerel), pilchard and tuna. More than three-quarters of Angola's annual catch is processed into fish meal and fish oil, most of which is exported to countries outside of Africa. Much of the rest is sun-dried and sold in the interior of Angola and in neighbouring countries such as Zaïre. In 1973, fish and fish products accounted for 7 per cent of Angola's export earnings.

Namibia (South West Africa), which lies only partly within the tropics, also has an important fishing industry. The Namibian fisheries are largely controlled by South African companies. The main fishing centres are Luderitz and Walvis Bay. The latter is an integral part of the Cape Province of the Republic of South Africa, although it is administered as part of Namibia. The catch consists largely of pilchards although rock lobsters are also of importance. A large part of the catch is canned, or processed into fish meal or fish oil. In 1972 fish and fish products accounted for 19 per cent of Namibia's export earnings.

Other tropical African countries which have a sizeable fish catch include Chad, Cameroon and Zaïre. As Chad is a land-locked country, the whole of its catch comes from lakes and rivers. Fishing is of importance in Lake Chad, and also in the Logone and Chari rivers. A large part of the catch is preserved by drying or smoking, and there is a small export of fish to neighbouring countries. Part of Cameroon's catch also comes from the rivers of the Logone-Chari system. In Zaïre a large part of the fish catch is taken from the lakes which border the Zaïre river, although sea fishing is also growing in importance.

Exercises

1 Compare the fishing industry of West Africa with that of East Africa.
2 Write a detailed account of the fishing industry of any one tropical country.

Suggested reading. See Chapter 13

Sources of statistics. See Chapter 13

Table 73 Fisheries: nominal catches for selected countries (thousand tonnes), 1975

Angola	184	Congo	16	Namibia	87
Burundi	15	Ethiopia	27	Somalia	33
Cameroon	72	Madagascar	56	Sudan	23
C.A.R.	21	Malaŵi	71	Zaïre	125
Chad	115	Mozambique	13	Zambia	50

CHAPTER THIRTEEN

Forestry

A: General

There are almost 40 million sq km of forest in the world, of which roughly half are found within the tropics. The forests which occur in the tropical world are of several different types, the most important being tropical rain forest and tropical monsoon forest.

The importance of tropical forests

As well as providing wood for fuel and for building purposes, tropical forests and woodlands yield a wide variety of other useful products. These are mainly gathered in fairly small quantities by the local inhabitants, and include gums, resins, fibres, fruits, nuts, medicinal plants and tanning materials. Although much of what is gathered from the tropical forests and woodlands is consumed locally, in some parts of the tropical world forest products are gathered for export. Tropical forests also play an important role in controlling the run-off of water over the land surface, thus helping to protect the soil from erosion.

Fuel and building materials

Within the tropics, vast quantities of wood are cut annually for fuel. In many parts of the tropical world wood is still the main domestic fuel, being consumed either directly in the form of firewood, or indirectly in the form of charcoal. In some areas, wood is also an important industrial fuel. In the coastal areas of West Africa, for example, large quantities of firewood are burned in the ovens which are used for smoking fish.

In countries such as Zimbabwe, wood is used in the firing of tobacco-curing kilns. In a few countries, wood is still the major fuel used by the railways.

Wood is also widely used for building purposes. In many parts of tropical Africa, for example, poles are used to make the framework for houses. On this framework the mud walls are built, and the roof laid. In coastal areas, wood is widely used in boat building. The large canoes used by the fishermen of Ghana, for example, are made by hollowing out the trunks of the obeche tree.

Gums and resins

Tropical forests and woodlands yield a wide variety of useful gums and resins. Although the importance of wild rubber production has declined considerably since the end of the first decade of this century, some rubber is still collected from trees which grow wild in the forests of the Amazon basin. Balata, a substance somewhat similar to rubber, is obtained from the sap of the bulletwood tree which grows wild in the rain forests of South America. In Guyana, balata collecting is mainly carried out by the Amerindians in the interior of the country. Gutta percha, which is almost identical in nature to balata, is obtained from the sap of a tree which grows wild in the forests of the Malay Archipelago. Balata and gutta percha are used in the making of such things as machine belting, electrical insulation, and the casings of golf balls.

Chicle, which is used in the manufacture of chewing gum, is the coagulated juice of the sapodilla tree. This tree grows wild in the rain forests of Central America. Although chicle has largely been supplanted by synthetic products as the basic ingredient of chewing gum, small quantities are still collected for export in the forests of the Petén lowland of northern Guatemala, the adjacent Yucatan Peninsula of Mexico, and the interior of Belize. The swamp forests of the Malay Archipelago yield jelutong, which is also used in the manufacture of chewing gum.

Gum arabic which is used in confectionary and in the making of inks, is obtained from several species of acacia tree, which grow wild in the drier woodland areas of tropical Africa. Gum arabic is an important export item from Sudan, accounting for 6 per cent of that country's export earnings in 1974. Gum arabic is also exported in smaller quantities from several other African countries, including Mauritania, Senegal, and Tanzania.

Fruit and nuts

Wild fruit and nuts are gathered in many parts of the tropical world. Part of West Africa's production of palm oil and palm kernels, for example, still comes from palms which grow wild in the forest. In the savanna woodland areas of West Africa, the shea tree (known as *karite* in French) is important as a source of vegetable oil. The kernel from the nut of the shea tree yields shea butter, which is widely used for cooking purposes in the savanna zone of West Africa. There is also a small export of shea products from several West African countries, particularly from Upper Volta and Benin.

In north-eastern Brazil, the nuts of the babassu palm are collected. The kernels contain an oil which has somewhat similar properties to those of coconut oil, and which can be used in the manufacture of soap, margarine and cooking oils. Vegetable oil can also be obtained from the kernel of the cohune palm, which is found in the wetter parts of Central America from the Yucatan Peninsula to Belize. Unfortunately commercial production is hampered by the extreme hardness of the nut which contains the kernel. Brazil nuts are gathered for export in many parts of the Amazonian forests, particularly in the basin of the Tocantins river. The nuts are shipped from the ports of Manaus and Belém to Europe and North America, where they are eaten as whole nuts or used in confectionary. Ivory nuts, which come mainly from Ecuador, are the fruits of the tagua palm. These hard nuts provide the so-called vegetable ivory, which was once much used in the making of buttons. The

development of plastics has, however, resulted in a considerable decline in the demand for ivory nuts. Illipé nuts are gathered in the forests of the Malay Archipelago, and are mainly exported to Europe. The vegetable fat extracted from illipé nuts is used as a substitute for cocoa butter in the manufacture of chocolate.

Fibres

Many different kinds of fibre are gathered from tropical forests and woodlands. Piassava fibre, for example, is obtained from the leaf stalks of the raphia palm. The best quality fibre is obtained from palms growing in the fresh-water swamps of the Bonthe district of Sierra Leone. Piassava fibre is used in the making of stiff brushes.

Kapok, which is the name given to the moisture-resistant fibres obtained from the seed pod of the silk cotton tree, is used in the making of such things as life preservers and sleeping bags. The silk cotton tree grows in many parts of the tropical world, but the bulk of the world's commercial production of kapok comes from Asia, with the most important producer being Indonesia.

Toquilla fibre, which is obtained from the leaves of the toquilla palm, is used in the making of the so-called Panama hats. The Panama hat-making industry is still of some importance in the coastal lowlands of Ecuador, particularly near the small towns of Chone, Jipijapa and Manta.

Tanning materials

Tannin, a substance widely used in the production of leather, is obtained from a number of different tropical plants. One source of tannin is the heartwood of the quebracho tree, which grows wild in the woodlands of the Parana–Paraguay basin of South America. Quebracho extract is a significant export item from Paraguay. Other sources of tannin include the bark and leaves of the mangrove, and the bark of the wattle tree. The wattle tree is native to Australia, but it is now grown in highland areas in several parts of East Africa and Central Africa. The wattle tree thrives in fairly cool conditions, and in East Africa it is mainly grown at heights of over 1 500 metres. When the wattle tree is about eight years old, it is cut down and the bark is dried, and then sent for processing to wattle extract factories. The trunk of

171

the tree is commonly used for fire wood, or for the making of charcoal.

Miscellaneous products

The carnauba palm is a drought-resistant tree, which grows wild in north-eastern Brazil. The most valuable part of this tree is the wax which coats the underside of the leaf. This wax has a wide range of uses, being employed in the manufacture of such things as floor and furniture polishes, gramophone records and carbon paper.

The cinchona tree is of importance for its bark, which is the natural source of the drug quinine used in the treatment of malaria. Cinchona grows wild in the forests of the Amazonian slopes of the Andes from Colombia to Bolivia, and in the past the collection of cinchona bark was of some importance in those areas. During the nineteenth century, however, plantations of cinchona were established in tropical Asia, and these now produce most of the world's supply of cinchona bark.

The protective role of forests

In addition to their direct economic value, tropical forests are of considerable importance for the role which they play in the protection of water catchment areas. Forest provides the most effective anti-erosion control of any type of vegetation. The forest canopy breaks the force of falling rain, before it reaches the ground. Furthermore, the litter of decaying leaves on the floor of the forest acts as a huge sponge, absorbing a large part of the water falling on it, and releasing it slowly and harmlessly to the underlying soil. It is particularly important that the forest cover should be maintained on steep watershed areas, especially in regions where the rainfall is heavy and of a torrential nature.

Commercial timber production

The commercial timber production of the tropical

Making an access road into the forest in southern Ghana. Logging companies in West Africa often have to construct their own roads, before they can extract the timber.

172

forests as a whole is quite small, compared with that of the forests of higher latitudes. In 1974, the tropical world accounted for only one-eighth of the total world production of industrial roundwood. A number of tropical countries do, however, export timber in substantial quantities.

Most of the timbers extracted from the tropical forests are hardwoods, whereas those from the temperate forests are predominantly softwoods. Tropical hardwoods have a number of important uses. They are much in demand for the making of high-quality furniture, where the need is for a wood which has an attractive appearance. Because of their durability, they are also widely used for boatbuilding, and for heavy construction work of various kinds. In 1974, the tropical world accounted for about four-fifths of the total value of the non-coniferous logs which entered world trade, and almost half of that of non-coniferous sawnwood.

In the past, nearly all timber exported from tropical countries was shipped in the form of whole logs. An increasing amount of the timber which is felled in the tropical world is, however, now being processed into sawnwood or into wood-based panels (mainly plywood and veneers) before being shipped overseas. The value of the timber to the exporting country is greatly increased, if some processing takes place before shipment.

At present the tropical world's production of woodpulp and paper is very small. In 1974 the tropical world accounted for under 2 per cent of the world's production of woodpulp, and under 4 per cent of that of paper. Most tropical countries import substantial quantities of paper and paper products. The demand for paper products is likely to rise sharply in most tropical countries, because of the rapid population growth which is now taking place, and because of improvements in literacy and in living standards in general. Unfortunately, most tropical woods are much less suitable for the production of pulp, than are the softwoods of the temperate forests. Experience obtained from operational plants in Brazil and Colombia, and from a pilot plant in the Ivory Coast has, however, shown that it is possible to produce pulp and paper from many species of trees which grow in the tropical rain forests. Bamboo forests may also become an important source of raw material for pulp and paper making in the future.

Problems of production

The lumbermen of the tropical forests are faced with a number of problems:

1 The trees of the tropical forests rarely grow in pure 'stands' of the same species. Valuable timber trees are generally widely scattered, and are interspersed with other species which are at present of no commercial value. Consequently it is often difficult to locate the valuable species, and also to remove them from the forest once they have been felled.
2 In many parts of the tropical world, much of the best timber is inaccessible because of the lack of roads and railways in the forest areas. Although in some areas use can be made of rivers to float the logs to the sawmills or to the ports, not all kinds of timber can be transported in this way. Some tropical hardwoods have such a high specific gravity that they either float so low in the water that they become grounded, or do not float at all.
3 In some of the most densely forested parts of the tropical world, such as the Amazon basin and the island of Borneo, the population is extremely sparse. In such areas logging companies often find it difficult to obtain sufficient labour.

Tropical Africa

In tropical Africa by far the most important area for commercial timber production is the coastal zone of West Africa. Outside of West Africa the most important timber producer is Gabon, which until the mid-1950s was the leading exporter of timber in the whole of tropical Africa. More than four-fifths of Gabon is covered with tropical rain forests, and until the commencement of mineral exploitation during the early 1960s, the economy of the country was virtually dependant upon timber. Even in 1973, timber was the second most valuable export item, accounting for 43 per cent of Gabon's export earnings.

The exploitation of timber in Gabon is carried out both by large European firms using mechanical methods of extraction, and by Gabonese enterprises of various sizes. Until a few years ago, lumbering was largely confined to areas near to the coast or near to rivers, in the so-called first zone. A great deal of felling has already taken place in Gabon, with the result that the most accessible areas of forest have already been depleted. An increasing amount of lumbering is now taking place in the second zone in the interior of the country. In the first zone, timber was mainly transported to the coast down the rivers in rafts. In the second zone, however, the existence of rapids makes river transport difficult, and further development of timber resources in the interior is dependent upon the construction a road network.

The principal species of timber exported from Gabon is okoume, which is particularly suitable for peeling to produce plywood. Other useful species of timber at present exploited include ozigo and azobe. A large part of Gabon's export of timber is still in the form of logs. There is, however, a large plywood factory at Port Gentil, and some plywood is exported. In 1975 work began on the construction of a cellulose factory in Gabon.

Timber is also the leading export of the neighbouring People's Republic of Congo, accounting for 42 per cent of that country's export earnings in 1972. The leading species exported from Congo are okoume and limba (known as ofram in Ghana). In the past timber for export came mainly from the Moyambé region near the coast, but as in Gabon, the depletion of the coastal forests has resulted in the extension of lumbering into the interior. The bulk of Congo's export of timber is in the form of logs, although there is also a small but growing export of sawn timber and veneers. There are plans to restore the country's limba forests by replanting, and to develop plantations of eucalyptus to provide the raw material for a cellulose industry.

Cameroon also has an important timber industry, and in 1972 timber accounted for 10 per cent of its export earnings. Logging activities in Cameroon are still largely in the hands of European companies. Important species at present being exploited include

Table 74 The timber production and export trade of selected countries, 1974

Country	Volume of timber felled (thousand m³)	Value of timber exports (million $)		
		Logs	Sawn wood and sleepers	Wood-based panels
Tropical Africa	30 431	583,3	118,2	69,5
Angola	1 201	8,5	2,0	0,5
Cameroon	1 375	54,0	5,3	4,4
C.A.R.	466	1,0	0,9	—
Congo	671	37,0	3,0	9,0
Ethiopia	1 220	—	—	—
Gabon	1 647	125,0	0,4	20,1
Ghana	1 459	49,0	32,6	9,5
Guinea	465	—	3,7	—
Ivory Coast	5 695	277,0	50,2	11,8
Kenya	790	—	1,2	0,2
Liberia	603	13,0	0,4	—
Madagascar	1 513	0,2	0,1	—
Mozambique	835	0,4	7,4	0,1
Nigeria	2 960	16,0	3,4	9,5
Zimbabwe	502	0,1	2,4	0,9
Sudan	1 278	—	—	—
Tanzania	1 172	0,3	1,1	0,3
Uganda	1 075	—	0,4	—
Zaïre	1 883	1,3	3,3	3,2
Zambia	165	—	—	—

obeche, iroko and mahogany. The Central African Republic (C.A.R.) has large timber resources, which at present are under-exploited. A major problem facing the timber industry in the C.A.R. is the high cost of transporting the timber to the coast. The production of timber for export has, however, expanded rapidly in recent years, and in 1971 timber accounted for 11 per cent of the C.A.R.'s export earnings. The production of timber has also expanded rapidly in Equatorial Guinea.

Tropical Asia

Timber is an important export item from a number of tropical Asian countries, particularly from the Philippines, Indonesia, Malaysia and Burma. In the Philippines nearly two-fifths of the total land area is covered with commercially exploitable forests, the greatest reserves of timber being in the interior of the islands of Mindanao, Negros, Samar, Palawan and Mindoro. In the period 1969–72 timber was the leading export item from the Philippines, accounting for 23 per cent of its export earnings. The best known of the Philippine timbers is lauan (sometimes called Philippine mahogany, although it is not a member of the true mahogany family). Lauan is very much in demand for cabinet and furniture making. The bulk of the Philippine's export of timber is in the form of logs, although there is also an appreciable trade in plywood and veneers.

The timber industry is also of considerable importance in Malaysia, particularly in East Malaysia (Sabah and Sarawak). In 1969 timber accounted for 73 per cent of the export trade of Sabah, and 38 per cent of that of Sarawak. The development of the timber industry on a large scale in East Malaysia only dates back to the 1950s and 1960s. One of the most important timbers exported from East Malaysia is ramin, which occurs in the swamp forests of the lowlands. Ramin is used mainly for furniture making. Other important export timbers include jongkong and meranti. Most of the timber is exported in the form of logs, but there is also a significant export of sawn timber from Sarawak. One of the largest customers for East Malaysia's timber is Japan. About three-fifths of West Malaysia is covered with tropical rain forest. A considerable amount of timber is extracted from West Malaysia's forests for local consumption, and there is now a surplus for export.

In recent years there has been a phenomenal rise in log exports from Indonesia, particularly from Kalimantan. In 1973 timber accounted for 18 per cent of Indonesia's export earnings. Much of Indonesia's timber exports go to Japan, with other important customers being South Korea and Taiwan.

Timber usually ranks second to rice as Burma's leading export, and in the period 1969–72 accounted for an average of 24 per cent of its export earnings. Forests cover almost seven-tenths of Burma's surface, but the wasteful methods of the indigenous cultivators have resulted in the destruction of vast areas of valuable timber resources. The most important of the timbers extracted from the monsoon forests of Burma is teak. This is noted for its hardness and durability, and is greatly used in the ship-building industry for decking and similar work. After felling, the teak logs are usually hauled to the water's edge by elephants or tractors, and then floated downstream. Great rafts of teak logs are floated down such rivers as the Irrawady, Sittang and Salween during the rainy season from July to October. The rafts are assembled at such places as Mandalay, Pakokku and Prome on the Irrawady, and at Toungou on the Salween. Some of the teak is sawn into lumber before it is shipped overseas, but in 1972 about two-thirds of the total value of Burma's export timber was in the form of logs. The main saw-milling centres in Burma are Rangoon and Moulmein. Large quantities of teak are exported to India, and the United Kingdom is also an important customer. In recent years, the volume of other kinds of timber extracted from the Burmese forests has exceeded that of teak. Much of the production of these other timbers, however, tends to be consumed within Burma. Another important timber which is exported from Burma is pyinkado (also known as ironwood). Pyinkado is noted for its great hardness, and is much used for railway sleepers. Pyinkado is a difficult timber to exploit, because it is heavier than water, and can therefore only be floated down rivers if it is buoyed up with lighter woods.

The timber industry is also of some importance in Thailand. Teak is cut in the monsoon forests of the northern mountains, and individual logs are floated down the northern tributaries of the Menam. At places such as Uttaradit, Raheng and Sawankalok, the logs are assembled into rafts, before continuing their journey downstream to the sawmills at Bang-

175

Table 75 The timber production and export trade of selected countries, 1974

Country	Volume of timber felled (thousand m³)	Value of timber exports (million $)		
		Logs	Sawn wood and sleepers	Wood-based panels
Tropical Asia	86 592	1 400,1	298,2	194,1
Burma	2 611	29,2	14,3	2,3
India	11 922	35,6	0,3	10,8
Indonesia	27 331	670,0	7,8	—
Khmer Rep.	490	0,1	—	—
Malaysia	25 018	433,6	213,2	59,9
a) Sabah	12 595	365,6	0,4	6,0
b) Sarawak	3 354	45,4	24,3	1,8
c) West Malaysia	9 069	22,6	188,5	52,1
Philippines	10 500	216,3	30,1	44,7
Sri Lanka	904	—	—	—
Thailand	5 388	12,1	20,0	3,3

kok. Lack of effective conservation measures has been responsible for a serious decline in the extent of Thailands reserves of commercial timber.

Tropical America

Although forests occupy vast areas in tropical America, exports of timber from most countries are small. The largest producer and exporter of commercial timber is Brazil. Although Brazil has vast forest resources, the more accessible of these have been badly depleted as a result of cutting for charcoal and for firewood. The forests of the Amazon basin contain a vast variety of hardwoods, but these as yet are very little exploited. Small quantities of mahogany, rosewood and balsawood are cut in the Amazonian forests, and rafted down to the port of Belem for export. The greatest development of lumbering in Brazil has in fact taken place to the south of the Tropic of Capricorn, in the states of Paraná, Santa Catarina and Rio Grande do Sul. The predominant tree in this area is the araucaria pine (also known as Paraná pine), which yields a soft, easily worked timber. There are now more than 3 000 saw-mills in southern Brazil. Softwoods constitute the bulk of Brazil's timber exports.

Timber ranks second to meat as the leading export from Paraguay, accounting for 19 per cent of its export earnings in 1970. The eastern part of Paraguay is largely covered with semi-deciduous forests, and these yield a variety of hardwoods. The exploitation of Paraguay's forest resources is handicapped by the inadequacy of transport facilities.

Although forests cover more than four-fifths of the total area of Guyana, the timber resources of that country have as yet been relatively little developed. In 1972, timber accounted for only 1 per cent of Guyana's export earnings. Because of the difficulties involved in transporting the logs from the forest, timber cutting is mainly confined to areas which are close to navigable rivers. The bulk of Guyana's commercial production at present comes from the area known as the Bartica Triangle which is between the Mazaruni and the Essequibo rivers. Although the rain forests of Guyana contain hundreds of different species of tree, only a few are exploited for their timber. The best known of Guyana's timber is greenheart. Greenheart does not rot in water, and resists the attacks of marine borers, and for this reason it is greatly in demand for marine construction work. Unfortunately the cost of extraction is high. Greenheart occurs in small pockets of forest, and it is necessary to construct a large distance of timber roads in order to be able to haul the logs to the banks of the rivers. Furthermore, greenheart will not float, and so it has to be loaded on to pontoons for transport down the river. Other species which are at present exploited include purpleheart, mora and crabwood. Purpleheart is used for flooring and for ornamental work; mora is used for railway sleepers; and crabwood is used locally for furniture-making.

The neighbouring territories of Surinam and French Guiana also have considerable timber resources, which are as yet little developed. There is, however, a significant export of timber from Surinam, mainly in the form of plywood. In 1973 timber accounted for 4 per cent of Surinam's export earnings.

The timber resources of Central America have already been considerably depleted, as a result of cutting in the past. The most important timber exporting country is at present Honduras. In the past Honduras was noted for its fine mahogany which came from the rain forests in the Caribbean lowlands. As a result of the unwise exploitation of these forests in the past, the mahogany trade is now insignificant.

Most of Honduras' export of timber is now made up of pine, which grows in the mountainous interior of the country. The bulk of the timber exported from Honduras is in the form of sawn timber, most of which is sold to the territories of the West Indies and to neighbouring El Salvador. In 1974, timber accounted for 17 per cent of the export earnings of Honduras. The rain forests of the Caribbean lowlands of Nicaragua and Guatemala produce some tropical hardwoods.

In the past the economy of Belize was largely based upon its forest resources. Nearly nine-tenths of Belize is covered with forest, and forest products have formed a very important export item from the time of the earliest European settlement. During the seventeenth century, the most important export from Belize was logwood. The logwood tree yielded a dye which was used in the British woollen textile industry. As a result of the discovery of synthetic dyes, however, the export of logwood has declined considerably, and is today negligible. The most important

Table 76 The timber production and export trade of selected countries, 1974

Country	Volume of timber felled (thousand m³)	Value of timber exports (million $)		
		Logs	Sawn wood and sleepers	Wood-based panels
Tropical America	45 366	10,9	202,5	60,9
Bahamas	400	—	—	—
Belize	47	0,1	2,5	—
Bolivia	266	—	4,9	—
Brazil	23 800	6,8	116,1	48,7
Colombia	4 940	1,9	6,1	0,7
Costa Rica	1 180	—	—	1,7
Ecuador	1 868	—	6,3	0,1
Fr. Guiana	37	0,3	0,2	—
Guatemala	431	—	3,7	0,1
Guyana	256	0,4	1,4	—
Honduras	1 334	0,7	26,4	—
Mexico	6 227	—	4,7	0,5
Nicaragua	810	0,4	6,7	1,4
Paraguay	1 178	—	21,0	2,1
Peru	854	—	1,0	1,0
Surinam	158	0,1	1,3	4,1
Venezuela	613	—	—	—

of the timbers of Belize is now mahogany. Mahogany cutting is most intensive in the north-west of the country. A short railway line carries logs from Gallon Jug to Hill Bank on the New river. Here the logs are fastened into rafts and floated down the river to Corozal, and then towed along the coast to Belize City where there is a large sawmill. Other timber trees which are exploited in Belize are pine and cedar. Intensive exploitation over a long period of time has considerably depleted the forest resources of Belize. In 1974 timber accounted for only 4 per cent of the country's export earnings, although in 1958 it accounted for 43 per cent.

In many of the densely populated West Indian islands, the original forest cover has largely been removed. Most West Indian territories now have to import a great deal of their requirements of timber. A notable exception is the island of Dominica, which still has extensive timber resources. The lack of roads in the mountainous interior of the island, however, makes it difficult to exploit Dominica's forest resources. In several of the islands of the Bahamas, particularly in Andros, Grand Bahama and Great Abaco, there are extensive stands of pine.

B: Forestry in West Africa

The tropical rain forests of West Africa contain a vast number of different species of trees. In Nigeria, for example, as many as 300 species of trees which yield timber are known to exist, but of these only about 30 are at present exploited.

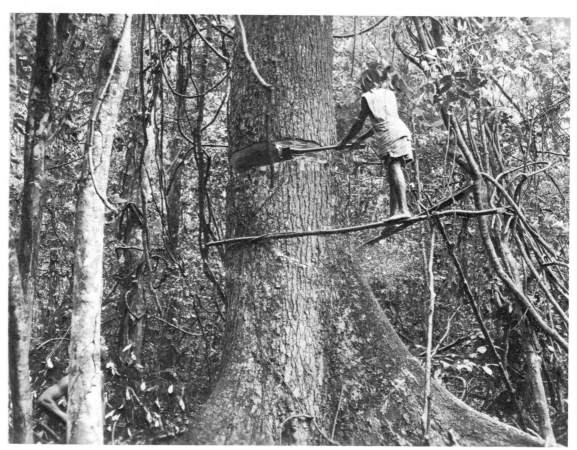

Felling a tree in the forest zone of Ghana. Note the large trunk and buttress roots. The worker is standing on a low platform to avoid having to cut through the buttresses.

178

A logging arch hauling out a log

Timber production and transport

Much of the timber produced in West Africa is still felled by axe and hand saw, although the use of power driven saws is increasing. Many of the trees of the West African rain forests have buttresses extending outwards from the base of the trunk, and this makes the task of felling more difficult. To avoid having to cut through the buttresses, the fellers usually work from platforms which they build around the trunk of the tree, at a height of about 3–5 metres from the ground. After the tree has been felled, the branches are cut off, and the trunk is sawn into manageable lengths. The bark is also usually stripped off.

The logs are hauled by tractor or 'logging arch' to the nearest road, railway or river, for transport to the saw mills or to the ports. In Ghana timber is moved entirely by road and rail, but in Nigeria a great deal of timber is floated down rivers, or along coastal creeks or lagoons. Those logs which are too heavy to float, are usually buoyed up by fastening them to

lighter logs. In the Ivory Coast also, some logs are transported by water.

Processing and export

An appreciable amount of the timber which is felled in the forests of West Africa is exported, most of it going to countries in Europe. In 1971, for example, Italy, West Germany, the Netherlands, Belgium and the United Kingdom between them purchased 82 per cent of Ghana's export of logs.

Before the Second World War, mahogany was the only West African timber which was exported in substantial quantities, accounting for over 90 per cent of the total timber exports. Since the war, however, timber merchants in Europe have begun to accept a much wider variety of timber. Now more than 25 different West African timbers are regularly marketed abroad, about 10 of which are sold in substantial quantities. In 1971 mahogany accounted

179

for only 7 per cent of the total value of Ghana's timber exports.

Although the greater part of West Africa's timber is still shipped overseas in the form of logs, an increasing amount of timber is now processed locally before shipment. In addition to the export of sawn timber, there is also a growing export trade in plywood and veneers.

The main producers

At present only the Ivory Coast, Ghana, Nigeria and Liberia export substantial quantities of timber.

The Ivory Coast

Until the mid-1950s the Ivory Coast was a relatively minor timber producer, but since that time the development of the timber industry has been very rapid. The value of the logs and sawn timber exported from the Ivory Coast increased tenfold between 1956 and 1967. In 1974 the Ivory Coast was the leading timber producer in tropical Africa, with timber exports far surpassing those of Ghana and Nigeria combined. Timber accounted for 24 per cent of the Ivory Coast's export earnings in 1971.

Several large logging companies, both from France and from other European countries, are engaged in timber extraction in the Ivory Coast. Felling operations have been extended from the more accessible areas of forest around Abidjan, into the more remote areas further west, particularly around Daloa, Gagnoa, Issia, Sassandra, Bereby and Tabou. Most of the timber exported from the Ivory Coast is still in the form of logs, although the value of sawn timber exports is increasing. Several logging companies have established sawmills in the Ivory Coast, and there are also a number of plywood and veneer factories in operation.

Ghana

Ghana ranks second amongst the West African timber exporters. In 1971 timber accounted for about one-tenth of Ghana's export earnings. The export of timber from this part of the West African coast began as early as the end of the nineteenth century. The forest resources of Ghana have been depleted to a far greater extent than have those of the neighbouring Ivory Coast, and in recent years timber production has expanded at a less rapid rate.

In 1969 Ghana exported 28 different species of timber. The most important of these were obeche (which is known locally as wawa), utile, sapele, mahogany, makore, edinam, kokrodua and mansonia, which together accounted for 90 per cent of the total export of timber. Well over half the timber shipped from Ghana is in the form of logs, although substantial quantities of sawn timber are also exported. Plywood and veneers are produced at factories at Samreboi and at Sefwi Wiawso, both for local use and for export. Most of the timber exported from Ghana comes from the Western Region, Ashanti Region, the western part of Brong-Ahafo Region and the western part of Central Region. All of Ghana's exports of timber are handled by the port of Takoradi.

Nigeria

Although Nigeria's timber exports are at present surpassed by those of both the Ivory Coast and Ghana, its resources of timber are greater than those of either country. The bulk of the timber for export comes from the forests of Bendel State, which supplies more than 80 per cent of Nigeria's commercial production of timber. A timber producing area of lesser importance is that which lies to the east of the Cross river, in Cross River State.

The development of the timber industry in Bendel State has been favoured by the ease of access to the main lumbering areas, and by the relative wealth of economic species found there. The main centre of the Nigeria timber industry is the town of Sapele. There are a great many sawmills in and around Sapele, as well as a very large plywood and veneer factory. The port of Sapele, which is situated on the Benin river, handles a great deal of Nigeria's timber exports. Some timber is also exported through Lagos. Obeche is the most important of the timbers which are exported from Nigeria, accounting for over half of the volume and value of log exports, and about one-third of the volume and value of sawn timber exports. Other important export timbers include abura, agba, mansonia and mahogany.

Liberia

There are extensive reserves of timber in Liberia,

Unloading railway wagons at the port of Takoradi, Ghana. The lighter logs are put into the water, and towed out to the ships waiting at the moorings.

particularly in the eastern part of the country. In the past these have been relatively little exploited, because of their inaccessibility. In recent years there has been an increase in timber production in Liberia, particularly following the opening in 1967 of a new 170 km long road from the port of Greenville to Tchien. An agreement with one of the iron ore mining companies which permits the use of its railroad for the transport of logs to the port of Buchanan, has also stimulated timber production.

The future

In many parts of the forest zone of West Africa the timber resources have already been seriously depleted, as a result of the activities of the lumberman and the cultivator. In the past lumbering operations in West Africa have generally been of a very wasteful nature, with little or no attempt being made to plant trees to replace those which have been felled.

The cultivator has also been responsible for the destruction and degradation of vast areas of forest in West Africa, particularly in recent years, when the rapid growth of population has led to an ever increasing demand for agricultural land. The removal of the forest for farming has gone especially far in the Yoruba and Igbo areas of Nigeria, in the Ashanti and Eastern Regions of Ghana, and in Sierra Leone. The once extensive forests of Sierra Leone have now largely disappeared, only about 5 per cent of the total area now supporting true high forest. The rest has degenerated into various forms of bush, largely as a result of the activities of slash and burn cultivators.

The urgent need to conserve forest resources is now widely recognised in West Africa. In the Ivory Coast, for example, a state company (SODEFOR) was established in 1966 to develop forestry and its connected industries. SODEFOR has a reafforestation programme covering more than 400 000 hectares. The first plantings under this programme were made in 1968.

C: Forestry in East Africa

Forestry is of much less importance in East Africa than in West Africa. Clearing for cultivation has greatly reduced the area of natural forest in East Africa. Although about 10 per cent of the region's land surface is scheduled as Forest Reserve, only 1½ per cent in fact carries true high forest, much of the remainder being open woodland.

Large quantities of wood are cut annually in East Africa for fuel and for building purposes. In most parts of East Africa wood fuel is used for cooking purposes, and in the highland areas it is also needed for heating. Wood fuel is also still used for some industrial purposes. Large quantities are used in tobacco curing and in the smoking of fish, and some sugar factories, vegetable oil mills and tea factories also use wood fuel. Poles are widely used in East Africa to form the framework of houses.

The production of commercial timber is adequate to satisfy most local needs, and to sustain a small export trade. All three East African countries, however, import large quantities of wood products, especially paper and paperboard manufactures. The value of these imports at present considerably exceeds the value of the region's timber exports.

The main objectives of forestry development in East Africa are:

1 to satisfy as far as possible the local demand for forest products of all kinds;
2 to protect the main water catchment areas from erosion. Protection forests are carefully maintained on watersheds in such wet, steep upland areas as the Usumbara, Uluguru and Pare Mountains in Tanzania; the Aberdare Range and the slopes of Mount Kenya in Kenya; and Mount Ruwenzori in Uganda.

Timber production

Although natural forests still provide much of the timber cut in East Africa, the importance of recently established softwood plantations is steadily increasing. Even before the Second World War, it was recognised that the natural forests of East Africa could not supply all the region's future needs in timber, and because of this large areas of forest have recently been planted, especially in Kenya and Tanzania. These plantations consist largely of exotic softwoods, with cypress and pine being of particular importance.

Kenya

In Kenya the main areas of forest are largely confined to the well-watered highlands, most of the country's productive forests occurring at heights of between 1 500 and 2 750 metres. Until the mid-1950s nearly all of Kenya's timber came from natural forests, but by 1969 exotic plantations were supplying nearly two-thirds of the country's commercial log output, and this proportion is likely to increase considerably in the future. Lumbering is of particular importance in Rift Valley Province, especially in the forests to the west of the rift, where settlements such as Elburgon, Londiani and Timboroa are largely dependant upon logging and saw-milling. The forest in this area largely consists of the indigenous conifer, podocarpus; but there are also plantations of cypress. There are a large number of small sawmills in the forested areas of Kenya, and in 1972 there were also two plywood factories in operation. A large afforestation programme centered around Turbo is intended to supply the raw material for the pulp and paper mill which was opened in 1975 at Webuye (formerly Broderick Falls).

Tanzania

Tanzania has a far larger area of Forest Reserve than either Kenya or Uganda, but most of this consists of open woodland which is of little value for timber. Most of Tanzania's commercial timber production is confined to patches of true forest in the north and the east of the country. The natural hardwood forests of the Usumbara Mountains are intensively exploited for camphorwood and muhuhu. These forests have a relatively high proportion of useful trees, and are conveniently situated in relation to internal markets and also to the coast for export. Camphorwood is used mainly in furniture-making, while the exceptionally hard muhuhu is used for flooring. The forests of the higher and cooler slopes of Mount Kilimanjaro provide softwoods, mainly natural podocarpus but also some planted cypress. There are also forests of softwoods in the southern highlands, but these are as yet relatively little exploited on account of their remoteness.

Uganda

Large areas of the once extensive forests of Uganda have been cleared for cultivation. The largest remaining blocks are in Western Region, but there are also numerous smaller remnants in Buganda and Eastern Regions. The commercial exploitation of timber is of most importance in Bunyoro District in the west, where the rainfall is sufficient to support high forest, and where because of the relatively sparse population much of this forest has remained uncleared. Important timber trees in this area include mvule (known as iroko or odum in West Africa) and mahogany. In Busoga District in the east, most patches of forest are very small, but because of their accessibility and because they contain much mvule, they are intensively worked. Jinja is the main centre of Uganda's timber trade.

Exercises

1 Discuss the importance of tropical forests to man.
2 Write a detailed account of commercial timber production in either West Africa or East Africa.
3 Discuss the problems which are involved in the exploitation of tropical forests.

Suggested reading

E. H. G. DOBBY: *Southeast Asia* — Chapter 23
C. F. HICKLING: *Tropical Inland Fisheries*
A. M. O'CONNOR: *An Economic Geography of East Africa* — Chapters 7 and 8
A. M. O'CONNOR: *The Geography of Tropical African Development* — Chapter 3

H. P. WHITE AND M. B. GLEAVE: *An Economic Geography of West Africa* — Chapter 6

Sources of statistics

F. A. O.: *Yearbook of Fishery Statistics*
F. A. O.: *Yearbook of Forest Products Statistics*
UNITED NATIONS: *Statistical Yearbook*

CHAPTER FOURTEEN

Mining

A: General

In most parts of the tropical world, only a very small proportion of the economically active population is engaged in mining. The extraction of minerals, however, does play an important role in the economic life of many tropical countries. In countries such as Nigeria, Brunei, Liberia, Mauritania, Venezuela and Zambia, for example, minerals account for the bulk of the export earnings. In some parts of the tropical world, the development of mining has been associated with sizeable movements of population. The occurrence of valuable mineral deposits has also sometimes stimulated the development of transport facilities, particularly the building of railways.

Methods of mining

A wide variety of different mining methods are employed in the tropical world, some of the more important of which are discussed below. In some cases the mineral or mineral-bearing rock is easily accessible, and can be worked by simple hand methods. Under such circumstances, mining may be carried out by individual miners, working either alone or in small groups. In other cases the mineral deposits are much less accessible, and expensive equipment is needed in order to work them. Under these circumstances mining is usually in the hands of large companies, which have the necessary capital and technical expertise.

Many of the large mining companies at present operating in the tropical world are foreign-owned. The companies often pay substantial amounts of money in the form of income taxes and royalties, to the governments of the countries in which they operate. These governments, however, are aware that their mineral resources are a wasting asset (once they have been used, they cannot be replaced), and in many cases they are now anxious to maintain a closer control over their exploitation than has been the case in the past. The governments of several countries have in recent years nationalised the whole or part of the mining industry.

Much of the mineral production of the tropical world is at present exported to the highly industrialised nations of the temperate lands. In many cases the minerals are exported either in completely raw form, or after only a limited amount of processing has taken place. The governments of many countries would like to see more processing taking place locally, as this would increase their foreign exchange earnings, and also create new employment opportunities.

Opencast mining

In some cases the mineral deposit which is to be worked lies within a few metres of the surface. Under these circumstances it can be mined by opencast (also known as open-pit) methods. In opencast mining, the few metres of overburden (the unwanted material lying on top of the mineral deposit) is stripped off, and is dumped nearby. If the mineral-bearing rock is soft, it can be removed by digging. Where it is harder, however, it may first have to be loosened with explosives. In the past gangs of labourers using picks and shovels were employed, but in most large opencast mines modern machines such as mechanical shovels and dragline excavators are now used to remove the overburden and dig out the mineral-bearing rock. If the land being mined by opencast methods is valuable for agriculture, the overburden may be replaced, once the mineral-bearing rock has been extracted.

Underground mining

If the mineral deposit is covered by a great thickness of other rock, opencast methods of mining become expensive, and therefore some form of underground mining may have to be resorted to. Where the mineral occurs in gently sloping veins or seams which outcrop on the side of a hill or valley, it may be possible to work it from adits. These are horizontal or gently inclined tunnels, which are driven into the hillside. Where, on the other hand, the mineral-bearing rock does not come to the surface, or where it occurs in very steeply inclined seams, vertical shafts have to be sunk. These may extend downwards for several thousand metres. From the shafts, horizontal tunnels are driven outwards, until the vein of mineral-bearing rock is reached. The mineral-bearing rock is usually blasted loose with the aid of explosives, and then transported along the tunnel to the shaft by light railway or conveyor belt. It is then brought to the surface in a type of lift, called a cage, which moves up and down the shaft. The cages are also used in transporting the miners and their equipment to and from the working levels.

In the case of the production of petroleum and natural gas, the deposit is reached by sinking wells, some of which are of very considerable depth. The petroleum or gas is brought to the surface either under its own pressure, or by pumping. In some parts of the tropical world, oil wells are drilled in the sea bed. In this case the drilling equipment is either mounted on a floating platform, or on a platform which stands on the sea bed on telescopic legs.

Placer mining

In some cases minerals occur as placer deposits, the original mineral-bearing rock having been broken down by the natural processes of erosion, and transported and redeposited by running water. Thus, for example, particles of gold, tin or platinum may occur in the sands and gravels in the beds of some rivers.

The simplest method of recovering these deposits is by panning. This involves digging out the sand or gravel from the bed of the river, and swirling it around with water in a shallow pan. The pan is tilted in such a way that the lighter sand or gravel is washed over the side, leaving the heavier mineral at the bottom of the pan. This type of mining requires very little in the way of equipment, and is usually carried out by individual prospectors. A much more advanced form of placer mining is known as dredging.

B: Some important minerals

Petroleum and natural gas

In 1975 the tropical world accounted for about one-seventh of the world's production of petroleum, but for only one-twenty-seventh of its natural gas production. A large part of the petroleum produced in the tropical world is still exported in crude form, although many tropical countries now have oil refineries which produce refined products for the domestic market. Because the local demand for natural gas tends to be very small, a large part of the tropical world's production is not at present collected, but is flared off (disposed of by burning).

By far the largest petroleum producer in tropical America is Venezuela. Other significant producers are Mexico, Brazil, Trinidad, Colombia and Ecuador, with smaller quantities coming from Bolivia and Peru. The Mexican oilfields are located in the lowlands bordering the Gulf of Mexico, and are a southern extension of the Gulf coast fields of the USA. The exploitation of Mexico's oil deposits began in the early part of the twentieth century. They were first developed by North American and British companies, but in 1938 the Mexican petroleum industry was nationalised and is now controlled by a government agency known as Petroleos Mexicanos (PEMEX). The most productive of the Mexican fields are centred around Tampico, which is the main refining centre and oil port. Although there are several refineries on the coast, substantial quantities of crude oil are transported by pipeline to Mexico City for refining. Besides petroleum, Mexico produces large quantities of natural gas, some of which is also piped to the interior of the country.

The oilfields of the West Indian island of Trinidad

Fig. 14.1 The Mexican oil industry

are a continuation of those of eastern Venezuela. Because of the complex geology of the area, the cost of producing oil in Trinidad is high. Part of Trinidad's production comes from wells which have been sunk several kilometres offshore, in the shallow waters of the Gulf of Paria. There are two oil refineries in operation in Trinidad, and in order to keep these working economically, it is necessary to supplement local production of petroleum with substantial imports from such countries as Venezuela and Saudi Arabia. Many of the oil wells in Trinidad also yield natural gas. This is used locally for the generation of electricity, and also for making artificial fertilisers and other petrochemicals. Petroleum and petroleum products usually account for about nine-tenths of Trinidad's export earnings.

Although the Dutch West Indian islands of Aruba and Curacao do not themselves produce petroleum, the economy of both is heavily dependent upon oil refining. In 1973 crude oil accounted for 82 per cent of the import spendings of the Netherlands Antilles (Aruba, Curacao, Bonaire, St. Eustatius, Saba and

St. Maarten), while refined petroleum products accounted for 95 per cent of export earnings. Large oil refineries were established in 1916 on Curacao, and in 1925 on Aruba. These islands were selected as sites for refineries because of their nearness to the Maracaibo oilfields of Venezuela, and because they possessed harbours which were capable of handling large tankers. The development of oil refining attracted large numbers of workers from other West Indian islands to Aruba and Curacao. Since about 1950, however, the automation of the oil industry has resulted in a drastic reduction in the number of workers needed in the refineries, and unemployment has become a serious problem.

The leading oil producer in tropical Asia is Indonesia. The most important Indonesian oilfields are on the island of Sumatra. In 1973 crude petroleum and petroleum products together accounted for half Indonesia's export earnings. Other significant tropical Asian producers are Brunei and India, with smaller quantities coming from Malaysia and Burma.

The large-scale production of petroleum did not

Table 77 Petroleum: Leading producers, 1975 (thousand tonnes)

World total: 2 646 290 Leading tropical producers				Other producers	
Venezuela	122 150	Brunei	8 639	USSR	491 000
Nigeria	88 440	Brazil	8 459	USA	413 000
Indonesia	64 116	India	8 700	Saudi Arabia	352 394
Mexico	36 456	Ecuador	8 155	Iran	267 623
Gabon	11 375	Colombia	8 102	Iraq	111 168
Trinidad	11 125	Angola	8 027	Kuwait	105 232

begin in tropical Africa until the 1950s. The outstanding producer is now Nigeria, with smaller quantities coming from Gabon, Angola and Congo. Oilfields were discovered near Port Gentil in Gabon in 1953, and production began there in 1956. Since 1966 oil production has been extended to richer fields further to the south, particularly around Gamba. In 1973 crude petroleum accounted for about half Gabon's export earnings.

The first shipment of oil from Angola was made in 1956, and production increased rapidly after 1961. The main oilfields are located to the south of the town of Luanda, where there is now a large oil refinery. New oilfields are being developed both on land and off-shore in the Cabinda Enclave, to the north of the mouth of the Zaïre river. The development of these oilfields is likely to result in a large increase in Angola's oil production. In 1973 crude petroleum and petroleum products accounted for about one-third of Angola's export earnings.

In recent years the search for oil has been extended to many other countries in tropical Africa. Exploratory wells have been drilled both on land and in the shallow waters off the coast, but as yet no major new oilfields have been discovered.

Coal

Very few tropical countries produce coal, and in 1975 the tropical world accounted for less than one-twentieth of the world's total production.

The only important tropical producer is India, which in 1975 ranked seventh in the world. India has fairly large reserves of poor and medium quality coal, but much smaller reserves of good quality coking coal. Most of India's production comes from coalfields in the Damodar valley, in the states of Bihar and West Bengal. In the Damodar valley the coal seams are of considerable thickness; seams of 15 metres are often found, with occasional ones of up to 25 metres in thickness. The railways are the largest single consumer of coal in India. Substantial quantities of coal are also used by the Indian iron and steel industry, and by thermal power stations.

The largest producer in tropical Africa is Zimbabwe, which is fortunate in possessing large reserves of good quality coking coal. These are mined at Wankie, on the main railway line to the south-east of the Victoria Falls. Mining began at Wankie in 1903. Much of the coal at Wankie lies close to the surface, and is easily worked from inclined shafts, at depths of from 25 to 60 metres. The costs of production are extremely low. Since 1959 there has been a lessened demand for coal from Wankie. Until the opening of the Kariba power stations in 1959, large quantities of coal were needed by thermal power stations in both Zimbabwe and Zambia. Coal was also in the past greatly used as a fuel on the railways, but these have now increasingly turned to the use of diesel locomotives.

Before 1966, all the coal needed in Zambia was carried by rail from Wankie in Zimbabwe. Since that time, however, Zambia has started to develop its own coal deposits in the Gwembe valley. Opencast methods were used to work low-grade coal deposits at Nkandabwe. The Nkandabwe mine, however, has now been closed, after being in operation for only two years. Underground methods of mining are at present being employed at nearby Maamba, where the coal is of a somewhat higher calorific value than that found at Nkandabwe.

Table 78 Coal production, 1975 (thousand tonnes)

World total: 2 367 900					
Leading tropical producers				Other producers	
India	95 890	Brazil	2 717	USA	568 158
Mexico	5 128	Zambia	814	USSR	484 668
N. Vietnam	4 250	Mozambique	500	China	470 000
Zimbabwe	3 500	Nigeria	237	Poland	171 625
Colombia	3 200	Indonesia	206	United Kingdom	128 616

Small quantities of coal are produced in Nigeria, Mozambique, Zaïre and Tanzania. In Nigeria, coal has been mined at Enugu since 1915. The deposit at Enugu is virtually the only source of coal in West Africa. At Enugu mining is carried out by driving horizontal tunnels or adits into the Enugu escarpment at the level of the coal seams. The exploitation of the Enugu coal deposits was taken over by the Nigerian Coal Corporation, which was formed in 1950. In the past a great deal of the coal produced at Enugu was used by the Nigerian railways, and some was exported to Ghana for use on the railways there. Large quantities were also used in the generation of electricity. In recent years the conversion of the railways to diesel locomotives, and the increasing use of oil, natural gas and running water for the generation of electricity, has resulted in a sharp decline in the demand for coal. From the peak year of 1958 when some 940 000 tonnes of coal were mined, production at Enugu fell to 640 000 tonnes in 1966. During the Nigerian civil war the mines at Enugu were closed for a short period, but coal production started again in 1969.

Large deposits of coal are known to exist in southern Tanzania, but these have as yet been little developed on account of their remoteness and the lack of local markets. The main deposits are in the Songwe-Kiwira coalfield at the north-west corner of Lake Malaŵi, and in the Ruhuhu coalfield just to the east of Lake Malaŵi.

The largest producers in tropical America at present are Colombia, Brazil and Mexico. Colombia has large deposits of coal, but as yet these have not been very much developed. The bulk of Colombia's production at present comes from near Belencito. In Brazil coal is mainly mined in the southern states of Río Grande do Sul, Santa Catarina and Paraná. The

coal occurs in thin seams, and is of low-grade quality. Part of the production is sent to Volta Redonda for use in the iron and steel industry. The bulk of Mexico's production comes from the Sabinas Basin in the state of Coahuila.

Iron ore

In 1975 the tropical world accounted for about one-quarter of the world's production of iron ore. Although a number of tropical countries are important producers of iron ore, relatively few have as yet established their own modern iron and steel industry. In many cases one of the major obstacles to such a development has been the lack of adequate local supplies of coking coal.

In tropical America the largest producers are Brazil, Venezuela, Peru and Mexico. Brazil is extremely rich in iron ore, and in 1975 ranked as the world's fourth largest producer of this mineral. The most important of the Brazilian iron ore resources are the haematite deposits in the state of Minas Gerais. These ores are of exceptional purity with an iron content of about 68 per cent, and less than 0,002 per cent of phosphorous. The Minas Gerais deposits are mined by opencast methods near the headwaters of the Rio Doce at Itabira and Lafaiete. The ore from Itabira is railed to the ports of Vitoria and Tuabarao for export. The ore from Lafaiete, on the other hand, is railed to the large modern iron and steel works at Volta Redonda.

By far the largest producer in tropical Asia is India, which ranked seventh in the world in 1975. India possesses some of the world's largest deposits of iron ore. These are mainly haematites and magnetites, with an iron content of 60–70 per cent. The

Fig. 14.2 West Africa – Mining and mineral localities

most important deposits are in the north-eastern part of the Indian peninsula, in the states of Bihar, Orissa and Madhya Pradesh. There are also large deposits in Goa, on the western side of the peninsula. Much of India's iron ore production is consumed by the domestic iron and steel industry, but there is also some export to such countries as Japan.

In the last few decades there has been a rapid expansion in the production of iron ore in tropical Africa. The largest producer is Liberia, but Mauritania, and Angola are also important. Lesser producers include Zimbabwe and Guinea.

Although the existence of vast deposits of iron ore in Liberia was known well before the start of the Second World War, mining did not actually begin until 1951. Since that time, however, production has expanded rapidly, and in 1974 iron ore accounted for

two-thirds of Liberia's export earnings. There are four large companies engaged in the mining of iron ore by modern opencast methods in Liberia. The oldest of these is the American-owned Liberian Mining Company (LMC). The LMC mines in the Bomi Hills and rails its ore to the port of Monrovia. The Liberian-American-Swedish Minerals Company (LAMCO) began its operations in 1963. LAMCO has its mines in the Nimba Mountains on the border with Guinea, and rails its ore to Buchanan. The National Iron Ore Company (NIOC) is owned mainly by the Liberian Government and by Liberian shareholders. NIOC began its operations in 1961 at Mano river, close to the border with Sierra Leone, and rails its ore to Monrovia. The German-Liberian Mining Company (DELIMCO) is a consortium of four German and one Italian steel companies. It

189

began its operation in the Bong Range in 1965 and also rails its ore to Monrovia.

The mining of iron ore in Angola began in 1956. The Companhia Mineira do Lobito mines ore at Cuima, Teixeira da Silva, Andulo and Cassinga. The Cassinga mines have proven reserves of more than 1 000 million tonnes, and a railway spur has been built to link the mines with the Mocamedes to Serpa Pinto railway. Much of Angola's production is exported to West Germany and Japan.

In Guinea iron ore was mined during the 1950s and 1960s on the Kaloum Peninsula near Conakry, but the workings were abandoned in 1967. There are vast deposits of high-grade iron ore in the interior of Guinea, in the Mount Nimba and Mount Simandou areas. The main problem involved in the development of these deposits is their remoteness from coastal ports. The Mount Nimba deposits could have been developed in the 1960s, if Guinea had been willing to see the ore exported through the port of Buchanan in Liberia. At present the government of Guinea plans to develop both the Mount Nimba and Mount Simandou deposits in partnership with a number of foreign iron and steel companies. Such a development will probably involve building a branch line to the main Guinea railway, and the construction of a new deep-water harbour near Conakry.

In the Ivory Coast there are vast deposits of iron ore at Bangolo near Man, but as in the case of the Guinean deposits, the major problem is that of finding the most suitable means of transporting the ore from the interior to the coast for shipment.

Zimbabwe is fortunate in possessing not only high-grade iron ore, but also excellent supplies of coking coal and limestone. Iron ore has been mined since the 1940s, to supply the iron and steel works at

Redcliff. In 1962 a new opencast mine near Que Que began producing iron ore for export to Japan. Iron ore is also mined south of Shabon.

Deposits of iron ore are known to exist in several other African countries. These are not at present worked, mainly on account of their remoteness. They include deposits at Liganga to the south of Njombe in Tanzania, at Belinga in north-eastern Gabon, and in northern Mozambique.

In tropical Australia iron ore is mined in the Hamersley and the Ophthalmia Ranges, and also on Cockatoo Island in Yampi Sound. The iron ore mined on Cockatoo Island is shipped to the east coast of Australia, where it is used in the iron and steel works at Port Kembla and Newcastle. The ore mined in the Hamersley and the Ophthalmia Ranges is shipped through the ports of Dampier and Port Hedland, and is mainly sold to Japan.

Bauxite

In 1975 the tropical world accounted for well over half of the world's production of bauxite. Bauxite is a reddish coloured ore, most of which is used in the manufacture of aluminium, although large quantities are also used in the manufacture of abrasives, refractories (heat resistant materials used in lining the insides of furnaces, etc.), cement and chemicals. The metal aluminium is noted for its exceptional lightness, and when it is suitably alloyed (mixed with other metals) it is also very strong. It resists rust and corrosion, and is an efficient conductor of electricity. Aluminium has a very wide range of uses. Large quantities of this metal are used in the manufacture of the bodies of railway carriages, automobiles, buses

Table 79 Iron ore production, 1975 (thousand tonnes)

World total: 500 200 Leading tropical producers				Other producers	
Brazil	46 621	Peru	5 067	USSR	129 483
India	26 002	Angola	3 388	Australia	60 860
Liberia	16 923	Mexico	3 369	(partly from tropical north)	
Venezuela	15 425	Sierra Leone	916	USA	48 881
Mauritania	5 646	Philippines	839	China	32 500

and lorries. Aluminium is also used in the manufacture of the wings and fuselages of aeroplanes, door and window frames, small boats and kitchenware. It has also become a serious competitor to copper in the transmission of electricity.

Most bauxite occurs close to the surface, and can be mined by opencast methods. After mining the bauxite is usually washed, crushed, and dried. In the manufacture of aluminium, the bauxite is first converted into a white powder called alumina. This is usually done by using the Bayer process, in which finely ground bauxite is mixed under pressure with caustic soda in large tanks called digesters. The impurities form a sludge, and can be filtered off. Some 2–3 tonnes of bauxite are needed to produce 1 tonne of alumina, and in order to reduce the cost of transport there is a growing tendency to manufacture the alumina as close to the bauxite mines as possible. The production of aluminium from alumina is a reducing process, done by electrolysis. To make 1 tonne of aluminium requires about 2 tonnes of alumina, and also about 18 000 kilowatt hours of electricity. Consequently aluminium smelters are generally located in areas where large quantities of cheap power are available. In 1975 the tropical world accounted for less than one-twentieth of the world's aluminium production.

The world's largest producer of bauxite is now Australia. A large part of Australia's production comes from the tropical north, the main centres of production being Weipa on the western coast of the Cape York Peninsula, and Gove on the north-eastern tip of Arnhem Land.

The largest producers in tropical America are Jamaica, Surinam and Guyana, with lesser quantities coming from the Dominican Republic, Haiti and Brazil. In Surinam the bauxite deposits occur inland from the zone of coastal lagoons. Mining began in 1916, and at present bauxite is produced at Moengo on the Cuttica river, and near Paranam on the Suriname river. Part of Surinam's production is converted into alumina before being exported. There is now also an aluminium smelter at Brakopondo Falls on the Suriname river, which is supplied with power by a new hydro-electric station. In 1973 bauxite, alumina and aluminium accounted for 87 per cent of Surinam's export earnings. Extensive deposits of bauxite are also known to exist in neighbouring French Guiana, but as yet these have not been developed.

Vast deposits of bauxite occur in tropical Africa, where the leading producer is Guinea. Significant quantities are also produced in Ghana and Sierra Leone. In Guinea bauxite deposits occur in several places. Until recently bauxite was mined on Kassa Island, which is one of the Iles de Los. The deposits on Kassa Island have almost been exhausted, and the workings there were abandoned in 1966. Since 1968 bauxite has been mined on Tamara Island, another of the Los group. Now, however, the bulk of Guinea's bauxite production comes from the mainland. Since 1960 an international company has been mining at Fria, 145 km to the north-east of Conakry. This company operates a large alumina plant at Fria. One of the world's largest and richest deposits of bauxite occurs at Sangaredi, inland from Boke in the north of Guinea. Since 1973 this deposit has been worked by an international company, in which the government of Guinea holds a 49 per cent interest. Before mining operations could begin at Sangaredi, it was necessary to build a 136 km long railway line to the new port of Kamsar. In 1974 some 5 million tonnes of bauxite were exported from Kamsar, and annual production from the Sangaredi deposit is expected to reach 9 million tonnes by 1979. The government of Guinea also has plans to develop other bauxite deposits at Togue and Dabola. At some future date the Souapiti Falls on the Konkoure river near Fria may be harnessed to generate electricity, thus making it possible to produce aluminium within Guinea. At present the alumina produced at the Fria plant is exported, part of it going to Cameroon. Although Cameroon does not itself produce bauxite, an aluminium smelter was built in 1957 at Edea hydro-electric station.

In Ghana, bauxite is mined by the British Aluminium Company near Awaso. The ore is railed to the port of Takoradi for export. Several other extensive deposits of bauxite are known to exist in Ghana, including those around Yenahin to the west of Kumasi, those at Ejuanema near Mpraeso, and those at Kibi. At present there is no factory in Ghana for the conversion of bauxite into alumina, and the alumina needed by the Volta Aluminium Company at Tema has to be imported, while Ghana's bauxite is exported.

Fig. 14.3 Ghana – Mineral deposits and mining

Table 80 Bauxite production, 1975 (thousand tonnes)

World total: 75 180 *Leading tropical producers*					*Other producers*	
Jamaica	11 304	Indonesia	993		Australia	22 205
Guinea	7 420	Dominican Rep.	785		(largely from tropical north)	
Surinam	4 751	Malaysia	704		USSR	4 400
Guyana	3 198	Sierra Leone	645		Hungary	2 890
Brazil	1 277	Haïti	523		Greece	2 850
India	1 273	Ghana	325		France	2 563

Tin

In 1975 the tropical world accounted for about nine-tenths of the free world's production of tin. The most important use for tin is in the coating of steel to make tinplate. Tin resists corrosion and is non-toxic, and for these reasons tinplate is used in the manufacture of cans for the preserving of food. Significant quantities of tin are also used in the manufacture of various alloys, including bronze (tin and copper) and solder (tin and lead). Most of the world's production of tin comes from placer deposits, although in a few areas it is mined from lodes.

In 1975 about three-fifths of the free world's production of tin came from Southeast Asia, with Malaysia being by far the most important producer.

Other important producers were Thailand and Indonesia, with Laos and Burma producing smaller quantities. Thailand's tin comes mainly from the peninsula to the south of the Kra Isthmus. Here alluvial gravels are worked by dredges, including large sea-dredges, which operate in the shallow waters off the coast. Some tin is also produced by Chinese miners using the gravel pumping method. Until recently tin concentrates were shipped to Penang in West Malaysia or to Singapore for smelting, but Thailand now has its own smelter.

The entire Indonesian production of tin comes from the islands of Bangka, Billiton and Singkep, which are situated just off the south-east coast of Sumatra. Alluvial deposits are mainly worked by dredges, and some lode tin is mined on Billiton. Large numbers of Chinese labourers have settled in the tin mining areas. The tin concentrates produced on Billiton and Singkep are still shipped to Penang for smelting, but in 1967 a tin smelter was established on Bangka Island.

The free world's second largest producer is Bolivia. The Bolivian tin mining industry is very different from that of Southeast Asia. In Bolivia mining is underground, and the mines themselves are situated at altitudes of more than 3 500 metres and are several hundred kilometres inland. The large scale mining of tin began towards the end of the nineteenth century, and the first export took place in 1895. The production of tin increased until 1929, the peak year for production in Bolivia, when some 45 000 tonnes were produced. Since then production has declined, and in 1974 only 29 000 tonnes were produced. The tin ore bodies occur in the Eastern Cordillera, with the most important mining centres lying between La Paz and Uyumi. In the period before 1952, about three-quarters of Bolivia's tin production was in the hands of three families. These 'tin barons' were enormously wealthy, and exerted considerable political influence. In 1952 the National Revolutionary Movement took over the government of Bolivia, and one of its first tasks was to nationalise the tin mines. The mines belonging to the large companies were confiscated, and the state-controlled Mining Corporation of Bolivia was formed. The cost of producing in Bolivia is high, as the best and most easily worked lodes are now exhausted. The cost of transport is also high. Until recently the tin concentrates made the long journey by rail to the Chilean ports of Arica and Antofagasta. In 1971, however, a smelter was opened at Vinto, and this has helped to reduce transportation costs. In 1974 tin accounted for 42 per cent of Bolivia's export earnings.

The only important tin producers in tropical Africa are Nigeria and Zaïre, with smaller quantities coming from Rwanda, Namibia and Rhodesia. In Zaïre tin is mined in the east of the country, particularly around Manono and in the Maniema district. There is a tin smelter at Manono, and part of Zaïre's production is exported in the form of metal. Although Rwanda is a relatively minor producer, tin concentrates rank as the country's second most valuable export.

Copper

In 1975 the tropical world accounted for more than a quarter of the world's production of copper ore. Copper is resistant to many forms of corrosion, and can easily be alloyed with other metals. It has a high conductivity of electricity, and a great deal of the

Table 81 Tin concentrates production, 1975 (thousand tonnes)

World total (excluding communist countries): 175 600 Leading tropical producers				Other producers	
Malaysia	64 364	Nigeria	4 652	Australia	9 310
Bolivia	28 328	Zaïre	4 400	U.K.	3 330
Indonesia	25 346	Rwanda	1 250	S. Africa	2 771
Thailand	16 406	Namibia	700		
Brazil	5 000	Laos	518		

world's copper production is used as wire in electrical equipment. Most of the rest is used in the manufacture of copper alloys, such as brass (copper and zinc) and bronze (copper and tin).

A large part of the tropical world's production of copper ore comes from African countries. Most of tropical Africa's copper comes from a 500 km long belt which begins in northern Zambia, and extends north-westwards into the Shaba Province of Zaïre. Copper mining began in Zaïre in 1906, when the Belgian-owned Union Miniere du Haut-Katanga was granted a concession covering some 34 000 sq km, which was to last until 1990. In 1967, however, the government nationalised the Union Miniere, and the mining industry of Zaïre is now controlled by a wholly state-owned company known as La Generale des Carrieres et Mines du Zaïre (GECAMINES).

In Shaba Province there are three main groups of copper mines. These are centered around Kolwezi in the west, around Likasi (formerly Jadotville) in the centre, and around Lubumbashi (formerly Elizabethville) in the east. Two types of copper ore occur in Zaïre, the sulphides and the oxides. The sulphides come mainly from the Kipushi mine to the west of Lubumbashi. At Kipushi mining extends underground to a depth of about 500 metres. Associated with copper at Kipushi are zinc, lead, cadmium and geranium. The oxides come mainly from the western group of mines around Kolwezi, and are mainly mined by opencast methods. Associated with the copper from these mines is cobalt. Zaïre usually accounts for well over half of the world's cobalt production. This metal is used in the manufacture of alloys for use under high temperature conditions, such as in the various parts of gas turbine engines. Cobalt alloys are also used in the manufacture of permanent magnets. Because of the long distances involved in transporting the copper to the seaports for export, the ores are concentrated, smelted and refined in the mining areas. There are large metallurgical plants near Likasi, and at Luilu near Kolwezi. In 1974 copper accounted for almost two-thirds of Zaïre's export earnings.

Other tropical African producers of copper ore include Zimbabwe, Namibia, Mauritania and Uganda. In Mauritania a deposit of copper ore is worked by opencast methods at Akjoujt, 270 km inland from Nouakchott. In Uganda mining of copper ore began in 1956 at Kilembe, in the foothills of the Ruwenzori Mountains. At Kilembe the copper ore is extracted from both surface and underground workings, and is concentrated near the mine. The concentrates are railed to Jinja, where there is a smelter which uses electricity from the Owen Falls hydro-electric station. From Jinja the copper is railed to the port of Mombasa in Kenya for export to Japan. In addition to copper, the ore from Kilembe has a fairly high cobalt content. At present cobalt concentrates are not exported, but are stockpiled at the railhead.

The most important copper producer in tropical America is Peru. Before 1960 the largest copper producer in Peru was the American-owned Cerro de Pasco Corporation which has its mines in the highlands of central Peru, particularly around the town of Cerro de Pasco. The export of copper from the rich Toquepala deposits in southern Peru did not begin until 1960. These deposits are amongst the richest in the world, and are situated near the Chilean frontier at a height of more than 3 000 metres. Mining is undertaken by the Southern Peru Copper Corporation, which is a consortium of several American companies. The development of the Toquepala deposits involved a vast outlay of capital. In order to get at the 400 million tonnes of ore, some 120 million tonnes of overburden had first to be removed. The small fishing port of Ilo had to be developed into a port suitable for the shipment of copper, and more than 200 km of railway line had to be built to link the mines with this port. A large copper smelter was built a few kilometres to the north of Ilo. Because southern Peru is extremely arid, the water needed at the mines had to be brought by a 77 km long pipeline from Lake Suche in the Western Cordillera. A sea-water desalting plant was built on the coast near Ilo.

The only important copper producer in tropical Asia is the Philippines. Copper is mined in several parts of the Philippine Islands, particularly in Cebu, Negros Occidental, and south-eastern Luzon. In tropical Australia copper is mined at Mount Isa near Cloncurry, and at the Mount Morgan mine near Rockhampton.

A very recent, although already major development, has been the exploitation of a large deposit of copper ore on Bougainville Island in Papua New

Table 82 Copper ore production, 1975 (thousand tonnes)

World total: 7 630 Leading tropical producers				Other producers	
Zambia	806	Mexico	78	USA	1 282
Zaïre	500	Rhodesia	30	USSR	1 100
Philippines	226	Namibia	25	Chile	831
Peru	174	India	24	Canada	724
Papua New Guinea	173	Mauritania	16	Australia	236

Guinea. Production only began in 1972, but by 1974 copper had become Papua New Guinea's main export, accounting for about two-thirds of the country's export earnings. The copper is mined by opencast methods, and after crushing, grinding and flotation the concentrate is pumped as slurry through a 25 km long pipeline to the port of Anewa Bay for export. The mining company concerned has long term contracts to supply copper concentrates to smelters in Spain, Japan and West Germany.

Manganese

In 1975 the tropical world accounted for about one-third of the world's production of manganese ore. Most manganese is used in the making of steel. Small quantities are used in practically all steels, to eliminate the brittleness caused by sulphur. Larger amounts are added to produce manganese steel, which is very hard and tough, and which is used in making such things as rock-crushers, sprockets, clutches and railway point-blades.

One of the most important tropical producers of manganese ore is Brazil. In Brazil manganese for the domestic iron and steel industry comes from a number of small mines in the states of Minas Gerais, Goias and Bahia. There are also vast deposits of manganese at Serro do Navio, just to the north of the mouth of the Amazon river. Ore from Serro do Navio is exported through the port of Santana, the main importers being the USA, Norway and the Netherlands.

Several tropical African countries are important producers and exporters of manganese ore. Gabon has some of the world's largest deposits, and in 1974 accounted for over one-tenth of the world's production. Gabon's deposits are located at Moanda, and are mined by opencast methods. A 75 km long cableway transports the ore from the mine to M'Binda in the Congo, and from there it is railed to Pointe Noire for export.

Other important producers are Ghana and Zaïre. In Ghana the ore is worked by opencast methods at Nsuta, near Tarkwa. After washing the ore is railed to the port of Takoradi. In Zaïre manganese ore is mined in the area to the west of Kolwezi in Shaba Province. Until recently manganese ore was mined at Grand Lahou in the Ivory Coast. The low quality of the ore, together with poor world market prices made the operation of the Grand Lahou mine unprofitable, and it was closed in 1970.

In tropical Asia the outstanding producer is India.

Table 83 Manganese ore production, 1975 (thousand tonnes)

World total: 9 320 Leading tropical producers				Other producers	
Gabon	1 116	Ghana	199	USSR	2 951
Brazil	820	Zaïre	160	S. Africa	2 006
India	575	Mexico	154	Australia (largely from tropical north)	673

Manganese ores are widely distributed in peninsular India. The main mining centres at present are in the states of Orissa, Mysore and Madhya Pradesh. India exports some manganese ore, mainly to Japan. In tropical Australia large quantities of manganese ore are mined on Groote Eylandt in the Gulf of Carpentaria.

Diamonds

A very large part of the world's total production of natural diamonds comes from tropical countries. Diamonds are the most highly valued of all the precious stones. The largest and most perfect stones, which are known as gem diamonds, are used in jewellery. When they have been cut and polished, they are remarkable for their brilliance and sparkle. Very small, discoloured, or otherwise imperfect stones are generally used in industry, and are known as industrial stones. Because they are harder than any other naturally occurring substances, diamonds are useful in making many types of modern industrial equipment, such as drill bits, lathe tools, and abrasive drilling wheels.

Nearly all of the tropical world's production of diamonds now comes from Africa. In terms of weight, Zaïre is the leading diamond producer in the world. In terms of value, however, Zaïre is surpassed by the Republic of South Africa, whose production contains a far higher proportion of gem stones. In Zaïre diamonds are mined in two main zones, one around Tshikapa on the Kasai river, and the other around Mbuji Mayi (formerly Bakwanga) on the Bushimaie river. Some of the diamonds recovered at Tshikapa are of gem quality; but the Mbuji Mayi deposits, which usually account for about 95 per cent of the total weight of diamonds produced in Zaïre, yield almost entirely industrial stones.

In Ghana diamonds are the second most important mineral produced. Almost the whole production consists of industrial stones. Most of Ghana's diamonds come from alluvial deposits in the valley of the Birim river. These are worked by a British company known as Consolidated African Selection Trust (CAST), whose mining operations are centered around the village of Akwatia. At Akwatia draglines strip off a few metres of overburden, and then dig out the diamond-bearing gravel. The gravel is loaded into large earth-moving vehicles, which carry it to the company's washing plants, where the diamonds are removed. Small quantities of diamonds are recovered by African miners, using simple hand methods. These miners dig shallow pits, and remove the diamond-bearing gravel. The gravel is then washed, and the diamonds are picked out by hand. The main area of African mining is in the valley of the Bonsa river, to the south of Tarkwa.

In Angola diamonds are mined by the Companhia de Diamantes de Angola (DIAMANG). This company mines near Dundo in the north-east of the country. The Angolan fields are a continuation of the Kasai fields of Zaïre. A large part of Angola's production consists of gem stones. Namibia's diamond production comes from the coastal area near to the mouth of the Orange river. Until recently part of the production was obtained by dredging the sea bed, but this proved uneconomic and offshore operations ceased in 1971. Most of Namibia's production consists of gem stones.

Diamonds are by far the most important mineral at present produced in Tanzania. Production comes entirely from the Mwadui deposit, near Shinyanga. This deposit is worked by Williamson Diamonds Limited, which is jointly owned by the Tanzanian Government and De Beers. The diamonds occur in a kimberlite pipe, which reaches the surface and covers an area of about 150 hectares. At present all the mining at Mwadui is done in open pits. About half the production consists of gem stones. Unfortunately the highest grade material at Mwadui is rapidly being worked out, and at the present rate of extraction it seems likely that mining operations there will come to an end by the late 1970s.

A number of other tropical African countries produce diamonds. By far the most important of these are Sierra Leone and Botswana. Others include the Central African Republic (C.A.R.), Liberia, the Ivory Coast and Guinea. In Botswana diamond mining only began in 1971, but since then production has expanded rapidly. The main mining centre is Orapa, to the west of Francistown. Before 1960 diamond production in the C.A.R. was entirely in the hands of expatriate companies, but by 1970 the whole production came from individual African prospectors of whom there were some 45 000. In

Fig. 14.4 East Africa – Mining and mineral localities

1973 diamonds were C.A.R.'s leading export, accounting for about a third of total export earnings. Large quantities of the diamonds mined in the C.A.R. are smuggled into the Congo. In Liberia diamonds are mainly mined by small operators in the valley of the Lofa river. A large proportion of the diamonds exported from Liberia, however, have in fact originated in Sierra Leone, and have been smuggled into the country. In the Ivory Coast diamonds are mined in two areas. The more important of these is around Tortiya, in the valley of the Bou river to the south of Korhogo. The other diamond mining area is near

Table 84 Diamond production, 1975 (thousand metric carats)

World total: 30 830 Leading tropical producers				Other producers	
Zaïre	12 810	Venezuela	819	USSR	9 800
Botswana	2 414	Angola	460	S. Africa	7 502
Ghana	2 298	Liberia	406		
Namibia	1 740	C.A.R.	339		
Sierra Leone	1 650	Ivory Coast	209		
Tanzania	896				

Seguela. In Guinea diamonds are mined in the Kissidougou and Beyla areas in the south-east of the country.

C: Mineral production in selected areas

Mining in Sierra Leone

The economy of Sierra Leone is heavily dependant upon mining. In 1974 minerals accounted for about three-quarters of Sierra Leone's export earnings.

Diamonds

Diamonds are by far the most important of the minerals at present mined in Sierra Leone. Diamonds occur in alluvial deposits in several parts of the country. A large part of Sierra Leone's production consists of gem stones. The recently discovered Star of Sierra Leone is reputed to be the world's third largest diamond, measuring some 64 mm in length and 38 mm in width. In 1974 diamonds alone

Diamond diggers at work in Sierra Leone. Note the simple equipment being used.

198

Fig. 14.5 Sierra Leone – Mining and mineral localities

accounted for 61 per cent of Sierra Leone's export earnings.

Diamonds were discovered in commercial quantities in 1930, and in 1933 the Sierra Leone Selection Trust (SLST), a subsidiary of the Consolidated African Selection Trust, was granted an exclusive 99 year diamond prospecting licence for the whole country. The company's operations became centered in two main areas, one near Yengema to the west of Sefadu, and the other at Tongo to the south of Sefadu. In those areas the diamond bearing gravel is mined by opencast methods, and taken to the company's washing plants for processing. In 1969 it was announced that the government proposed to take a 51 per cent interest in the mining companies operating in Sierra Leone. It was agreed that the Sierra Leonean assets of the SLST should be vested in a new company called

the National Diamond Mining Company (DIMINCO).

Because the diamond bearing gravels occur very close to the surface, and because a high proportion of the diamonds which they contain are valuable gem stones, the diamond fields of Sierra Leone have in recent years attracted a large number of illicit miners. During the 1950s large numbers of independent prospectors, not only from Sierra Leone, but also from other West African countries, began digging for diamonds on the SLST's concession. The methods used by these miners are similar to those used in the Bonsa valley in Ghana. The miners dig shallow pits until they reach the diamond-bearing gravel, and then use pans to sift through this gravel, picking out by hand any diamonds which they find there. This method of mining is relatively wasteful, as a fairly

199

high proportion of the diamonds contained in the gravel are not recovered. Unfortunately, once an area has been worked over by diamond diggers, it is seldom economic to rework it by modern mechanical methods.

In order to try to overcome the problem of illicit diamond mining, it was decided that in 1956 the SLST should surrender the right to all but 1 165 sq km of its original concession. The remainder of the country was opened up to Sierra Leonean miners, who can now obtain a licence from the government to dig for diamonds. The output of these licensed diggers now exceeds that of DIMINCO. The main area for the hand mining of diamonds is along the banks of the Sewa river.

Another problem which has faced the Sierra Leonean diamond industry in recent years has been that of smuggling. All the diamonds produced in Sierra Leone must be sold through the Government Diamond Office, and the government imposes a duty of $7\frac{1}{2}$ per cent on diamond exports. In order to avoid the payment of this duty, some diamonds are smuggled out through neighbouring countries, particularly through Liberia, where the export duty on diamonds is only 3 per cent.

Iron ore
In 1974 iron ore accounted for 10 per cent of Sierra Leone's export earnings. It was mined near Marampa by the British-owned Sierra Leone Development Company (DELCO). The first shipment of iron ore was made in 1933. Before exports could begin, a port had to be built on the coast at Pepel, and a 90 km long railway constructed to link the port with the mine. The ore was mined by opencast methods, and was crushed and washed at the mine before being railed to Pepel. By the early 1970s the most easily worked ore at Marampa had already been exhausted. For a number of years Delco made little profit from the Marampa mine, and closed it down in 1975. There are other deposits further north at Tonkilili, but these are of lower grade ore than those at Marampa, and at present it is considered that it would be uneconomic to work them.

Bauxite
Bauxite is mined by opencast methods in the **Mokanji Hills**, in the south-west of Sierra Leone.

Although mining did not begin until 1963, in 1974 Sierra Leone's output was 650 000 tonnes, considerably exceeding that of Ghana. The bauxite is taken by road to Point Sam, and then sent in lighters down the Bagru Creek, to be transferred to ocean-going vessels which anchor near Bonthe. There are also extensive deposits of bauxite in the Port Loko area, which may be developed in the near future.

Others
There are extensive deposits of rutile in the southern coastal areas of Sierra Leone. Rutile is a titanium oxide mineral, which is used in the manufacture of paint pigments, etc. The world's largest proven reserves of rutile occur in a 40 km long by 25 km wide belt in the vicinity of Gbangbama. Mining began near Gbangbama in 1965. The company originally involved was Sherbro Minerals Limited, which employed dredging techniques. Because of heavy financial losses, however, Sherbro Minerals ceased mining operations in 1971. Another company has since taken over the rutile workings, and plans to begin production in the near future.

In the past chromite was mined near Hangha in Kenema District, but because of the high production costs involved, mining operations ceased in 1962.

The Jamaican bauxite industry

The West Indian island of Jamaica is the world's second largest producer of bauxite, in 1975 accounting for almost one-seventh of total world production. The first shipment of Jamaican bauxite was made in 1952. Since that time the island's bauxite production has increased tremendously, and in 1974 bauxite and alumina accounted for 74 per cent of Jamaica's export earnings.

Factors influencing its development
The Jamaican bauxite deposits occur as a layer of varying thickness, on top of the white limestone rock of the centre and south of the island. Several factors have favoured the development of the bauxite industry:

1 The reserves of bauxite in the island are enormous.
2 Although the alumina content of Jamaican bauxite

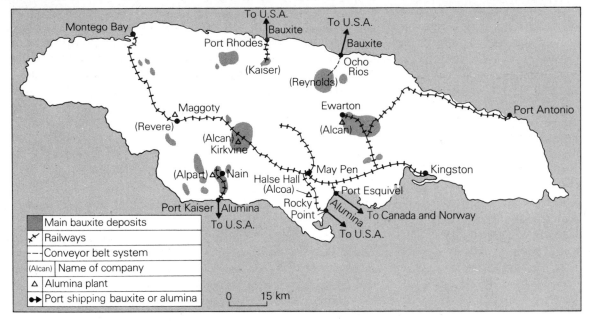

Fig. 14.6 Jamaica – Bauxite industry

is lower than that of Guyanese bauxite (it takes 3 tonnes of Jamaican bauxite to produce 1 tonne of alumina, as compared with only 2 tonnes of Guyanese bauxite), the way in which bauxite occurs in Jamaica makes it much cheaper to mine. In Jamaica the bauxite lies close to the surface, and the ore itself is soft. Once a few centimetres of overburden has been stripped off, the bauxite can be dug out without having to be blasted.

3 As Jamaica is a narrow island, all the bauxite deposits are within a few kilometres of the coast, thus facilitating export.

4 Jamaica is situated relatively near to the USA and Canada, which provide a large market for bauxite and alumina.

Methods of production

In Jamaica bauxite is mined entirely by opencast methods. The topsoil is first removed from a few hectares of land, and the bauxite is dug out by large mechanical shovels and draglines, and then loaded into earth-moving vehicles which carry it to the processing plants. After the bauxite has been removed, the topsoil is replaced, and the land is reclaimed for agricultural purposes. Some of the reclaimed land is farmed by the mining companies themselves, and some is rented to tenant farmers.

Some of the bauxite produced in Jamaica is dried in large rotating ovens, and shipped overseas in this form. An increasing amount of bauxite, however, is now being processed locally into alumina before shipment. In 1973, for example, out of a bauxite production of 13 386 000 tonnes, 7 273 000 tonnes (54 per cent of the total) was exported as dried bauxite, and the remainder was converted into alumina in Jamaica.

The economic impact of the bauxite industry

The bauxite and alumina industry is Jamaica's largest source of foreign exchange. In 1974 Jamaica's domestic exports were valued at J$653 million, of which J$347 million (or 53 per cent of the total) came from the sale of alumina, and J$135 million (21 per cent) from the sale of bauxite.

Although the Jamaican bauxite industry is largely in the hands of North American companies, the Jamaican Government receives a great deal of money from the industry in the form of income taxes and royalties. In 1973 these amounted to more than J$41 million. In addition, the bauxite industry has created a great deal of relatively well paid employment.

201

The bauxite companies

In 1973 six companies were involved in the Jamaican bauxite industry, of which five were American and one was Canadian. The Canadian company, Alcan Jamaica Limited, mines in the parishes of Manchester, St. Catherine and St. Ann. The whole of Alcan's production is processed into alumina at the company's two plants, one located at Kirkvine near Mandeville, and the other at Ewarton. The alumina from these plants is sent by rail to Port Esquivel, for shipment to Canada. Reynolds Jamaica Mines Limited mines in the parish of St. Ann. The bauxite is dried at the company's plant at Claremont, and transported by a 10 km long conveyor belt system to the port of Ocho Rios for shipment to the USA. Kaiser Bauxite Company mines in the parish of St. Ann, and has facilities for the storage and loading of bauxite at Port Rhoades near Discovery Bay. Recently Kaiser, Reynolds, and another American company called Anaconda have formed Alumina Partners of Jamaica (Alpart), and have built an alumina plant at Nain in St. Elizabeth. Alpart is now Jamaica's largest alumina producer. The alumina produced at Nain is shipped through Port Kaiser. Alcoa Minerals of Jamaica mines in the parish of Clarendon, and has an alumina plant at Halse Hall. Alcoa's production is shipped through Rocky Point. The last company, Revere Jamaica Limited mines in St. Elizabeth, and has an alumina plant at Maggotty. Revere ships its production through Rocky Point. In 1974 and 1975 the government of Jamaica acquired a 51 per cent share in Kaiser and Reynolds.

The possibility of producing aluminium

At present no aluminium is manufactured in Jamaica, although the government would like to see an aluminium smelter established in the island. The development of an aluminium industry would increase the amount of foreign exchange earned from bauxite, and would also create badly needed new employment.

The major obstacle to the establishment of an aluminium industry is the lack of adequate supplies of cheap power. Recently the governments of Jamaica, Guyana and Trinidad and Tobago have been examining the possibility of jointly establishing an aluminium industry. It has been suggested that a smelter could be located in Trinidad, where it could make use of local supplies of natural gas as its source of power. Such a smelter could process the alumina production of both Jamaica and Guyana. The governments of Jamaica and Mexico also have plans for the establishment of an industrial complex which will produce bauxite, alumina and aluminium on a joint venture basis, with a smelter to be sited in Mexico.

Mining in Guyana

In 1973 minerals accounted for almost half Guyana's export earnings.

Bauxite

Bauxite is by far the most important mineral at present mined in Guyana. The Guyanese deposits occur in a belt about 25 km in width, which runs roughly in a north-west to south-east direction, from a point on the Essequibo river near Bartica, practically to the Courantyne river. Whereas the Jamaican bauxite deposits occur very near to the surface, in Guyana they are buried beneath a considerable thickness of sand and clay. The removal of this thick overburden adds greatly to the cost of mining, but fortunately the Guyanese bauxite has a higher alumina content than the bauxite which is found in Jamaica.

Before mining can begin, the tropical rain forest must first be cleared. The overburden, which in places is more than 30 metres in thickness, is then dug away by large walking draglines, or washed away by powerful jets of water. Once the overburden has been removed, the bauxite is loosened by blasting with explosives.

Before 1971, bauxite was produced and exported by two North American companies. The Demerara Bauxite Company Limited (DEMBA) was by far the larger producer, accounting for more than nine-tenths of the total output. The DEMBA mines were located mainly around the town of Linden (formerly Mackenzie) 100 km up the Demerara river, and at Ituni 55 km to the south-east of Linden. DEMBA operated two plants, one for processing the ore into dried bauxite for export, and the other for the manufacture of alumina. In 1971 the Bauxite Nationalisation Act was passed, and DEMBA was

Bauxite mining using open-cast methods near Linden, Guyana. A mechanical shovel loads the bauxite in railway wagons for transport to the processing plant. Note the dense forest in the background.

taken over by a state-owned company known as the Guyana Bauxite Company Limited (GUYBAU).

The other bauxite company operating in Guyana is Reynolds Guyana Mines Limited, whose operations are centred around Kwakwani, 190 km up the Berbice river. Bauxite from the mines at Kwakwani is taken by barge to Everton at the mouth of the Berbice river, where it is dried and then loaded into ocean-going vessels for export. In 1973 bauxite and alumina accounted for 47 per cent of Guyana's export earnings.

Other minerals

The other minerals which are at present mined in Guyana are gold and diamonds. Gold occurs in scattered deposits throughout the north-western part of Guyana, and also in the Rupununi District.

Alluvial deposits are worked by small independent producers, who are locally known as 'porknockers'. Individual miners use shallow wooden or metal pans to sift through the gravel which they take from the river bed. In some cases several miners join together to work the area, using a sluice box.

Diamonds are recovered from the beds of many streams, particularly those which flow down from the Pakaraima Plateau. Of particular importance for diamond mining are the tributaries of the Mazaruni and the Potaro rivers. Mining is mainly carried out by porknockers, using simple methods.

Until recently manganese ore was mined at Matthews Ridge, in the north-western part of Essequibo. The ore was dug out by mechanical shovels, and then loaded into railway waggons which carried it 50 km to Port Kaituma. At Port Kaituma it was loaded into

203

ocean-going vessels. Production of manganese ore ceased in 1968, as a result of a sharp drop in world market prices.

Iron ore from Mauritania

Since the early 1960s, the development of iron ore mining has transformed the economy of Mauritania. A large part of Mauritania consists of desert, and is very sparsely populated by nomadic pastoralists. Before 1963 Mauritania's export trade was extremely

Fig. 14.7 Mining in Mauritania

small, and was largely composed of livestock, with fish, gum arabic, dates and salt being of lesser importance. In 1972, however, iron ore accounted for 74 per cent of Mauritania's export earnings.

The Mauritanian iron ore deposits occur in the heart of the western Sahara, in the Khedia d'Idjil range. This range is 25 km long, and has a maximum width of 10 km. It rises abruptly from the surrounding plains, and reaches a height of about 900 metres. The Khedia d'Idjil range was estimated to contain more than 200 million tonnes of iron ore, with an iron content of over 60 per cent. The iron ore occurs in three main ore bodies, at Tazadit in the east of the range, at Rouessa in the centre, and F'Derik in the extreme west.

The existence of iron ore deposits in the Khedia d'Idjil range was known in the 1930s, but it was not until 1952 that the Société des Mines de Fer de Mauritania (MIFERMA) was formed to develop the deposits. French, British, West German, Italian and Mauritanian capital were involved in this great undertaking. Mining started at Tazadit in 1961, but the first normal shipment of iron ore from Mauritania was not made until 1963. During the period from 1960 to 1963 MIFERMA built a railway line 635 km in length, from F'Derik (formerly Fort Gouraud) to the coast at Nouadhibou (formerly Port Étienne). An iron ore loading terminal was built at Point Central, just to the south of Nouadhibou.

The building of the railway line provided many problems. The shortest route from the mines to the coast would have been through Spanish Sahara (now Western Sahara), to the port of Villa Cisneros (now Dakhla). Because of silting, however, Villa Cisneros was found to be unsuitable for development as a mineral port. Furthermore, MIFERMA was unable to reach a satisfactory agreement with the Spanish Government. In order to avoid passing through Spanish Sahara, the railway line had to make a large loop southwards, before going westwards to the coast at Nouadhibou. At one place it was necessary to make a tunnel about 2 km in length through a granite escarpment. In other places moving sand dunes had to be stabilised by treating them with heavy oil.

In the Khedia d'Idjil range the iron ore is mined by opencast methods. The ore is blasted loose by explosives, and then taken by lorry to the crushing plants at Tazadit and F'Derik. After crushing, it is railed to Nouadhibou for export. The leading importers of Mauritanian iron ore have been the United Kingdom, France, Italy, Belgium, Spain, Japan and West Germany. In 1974 the government of Mauritania nationalised the iron mining industry.

Tin mining in West Malaysia

Tin is by far the most important of the minerals at present mined in West Malaysia. In 1975 West Malaysia accounted for over one-third of the free world's production of tin concentrates. In 1974 tin accounted for 15 per cent of Malaysia's export earnings.

Most of the tin mined in the Malay Peninsula comes from alluvial deposits, which occur on both sides of the Main Range. Most of the production in fact comes from tin fields which lie on the western side of this range. The most important of these fields is that of the Kinta valley in the state of Perak, which has so far accounted for about 45 per cent of West Malaysia's recorded production of tin.

Tin has been mined in the Malay Peninsula for several centuries. During the seventeenth century the Chinese established trading stations in the Malay Peninsula, to collect the tin produced by Chinese miners working there. During the latter half of the nineteenth century the Chinese began working new tin fields in the states of Perak and Selangor. Fighting broke out between rival clans of Chinese miners for the possession of mining land, and this led to British intervention in the Malay Peninsula in the

Fig. 14.0 Tin mining in West Malaysia

Dredging for tin in West Malaysia. The dredge is floating on a pond which it has excavated for itself. Note the water and waste material being dumped back into the pond behind the dredge.

205

1870s. Although European-owned companies now produce a great deal of West Malaysia's tin, the Chinese have continued to play a very important role in the tin industry.

Methods of production

Various methods of tin mining are employed in the Malay Peninsula, of which by far the most important ones are gravel pumping and dredging. Other methods include hydraulicking, underground mining, opencast mining and dulang washing.

Dredging was first introduced into the Malay Peninsula in 1912, and in 1974 was responsible for about one-third of West Malaysia's tin production. Dredging is a method which is particularly suitable for working deposits in swampy or very wet ground. The capital cost of installing a dredge is enormous, and this method of mining is mainly employed by European-owned companies. Most of the dredges used in the Malay Peninsula are bucket dredges. These consist of an excavator and a concentrating plant, which are mounted on a floating platform. The dredge is installed in an artificial pond or paddock. The paddock is formed by the dredge itself, as it digs up the tin-bearing gravel in front of it, by means of buckets mounted on an endless band. The buckets deposit the excavated material on the dredge, where it is washed and screened and the crude ore recovered by means of a palong. The tailings (the waste material which is left after the tin ore has been removed) are discharged back into the paddock behind the dredge.

In 1974 gravel pumping accounted for more than half of West Malaysia's tin production. In this type of mining, the tin-bearing ground is broken down by a high pressure jet of water from a monitor nozzle. It is then raised by means of a gravel pump to a palong. This is a high, trestle-like structure, on which there

The gravel-pumping method of mining tin in West Malaysia. Note the powerful jets of water which loosen the tin-bearing material. This material flows into a sump, and is then pumped up to a palong (the trestle-like structure in the background) where it passes through sluice boxes to separate the tin from the waste material.

are a series of sluice boxes. At intervals baffles are placed across the sluice boxes. The slope of the palong is such that the water and waste material are able to flow over the baffles, but the tin ore which is heavier is trapped by them. From time to time the tin ore is removed from the sluice boxes.

Hydraulicking is similar to gravel pump mining, but whereas in the latter water is supplied by pumps, in hydraulicking it is supplied by a natural head which is obtained by damming a stream some hundreds of metres above the mine. This type of mining is only possible near a suitable source of water.

In opencast mining the tin-bearing gravel is excavated in a dry state, and then mixed with water before being sent to palongs for the ore to be extracted. The largest opencast tin mine in the Malay Peninsula is the Hong Fatt mine at Sungei Besi in the state of Selangor. The largest underground tin mine in the Malay Peninsula is the Sungei Lembing mine in the state of Pahang.

Dulang washing is a method of recovering tin from waste material, rather than of actually mining it. The technique involved is similar to that used in panning for gold, and is carried out by individual operators, most of whom are Chinese women. Dulang washers usually operate in the tailings left behind by other mining operations, or in streams near to tin mines.

The tin concentrates which are produced by these various methods in the Malay Peninsula are smelted at Penang and Butterworth. The tin concentrate is mixed with limestone and coal, and smelted at high temperatures in a furnace. The metal is then refined, and moulded into ingots.

Some problems

One of the major problems facing the Malaysian tin mining industry is that of market stability. In the past the world market price of tin has been subject to sharp fluctuations. There is also the problem of finding new commercial deposits of tin ore, to replace those which are being worked out. Another problem is the fact that tin mining, by the methods used in the Malay Peninsula, is a very destructive form of land use. Land which has been used for tin mining is generally difficult to rehabilitate for agriculture after mining has ceased.

Petroleum and iron ore from Venezuela

Petroleum

Venezuela is by far the largest tropical producer of petroleum. In 1975 it ranked fifth in the world, accounting for 5 per cent of the world's production. In 1973 petroleum and petroleum products accounted for 94 per cent of Venezuela's export earnings.

Venezuela's production of petroleum comes from three main areas:

1 the lowlands around Lake Maracaibo;
2 eastern Venezuela in the states of Monagas and Anzoategui;
3 the Apure-Barinas basin in the western Llanos.

Of these three oil producing regions, that around Lake Maracaibo is at present by far the most important, accounting for about three-quarters of Venezuela's total production of crude oil. The production of petroleum in this part of Venezuela began in 1918. Production comes particularly from the eastern side of the lake, where Lagunillas is the main centre. Rows of oil derricks extend along the shore of the lake, and a large number of oil wells have been sunk in the soft bottom of the lake itself. Some of the oil produced in this area is transported by pipeline to Amuay and Cardón on the Paraguaná Peninsula, where there are refineries and deep-sea oil terminals.

About one-fifth of Venezuela's petroleum production at present comes from eastern Venezuela. The oilfields in this area were discovered in 1928 and in 1931 a large refinery was established at Caripito, which can be reached by ocean-going tankers through the Gulf of Paria and the San Juan river. Crude oil is also piped to Puerto La Cruz, which is another important refining centre. The third petroleum producing region in the state of Barinas was opened in 1958, following the completion of an oil pipeline to Puerto Cabello on the Caribbean coast.

Until 1976 the petroleum industry in Venezuela was mainly in the hands of large foreign companies. Although there were quite a number of these in operation, three of them were of outstanding importance, namely Creole, Royal Dutch/Shell, and Gulf. The Venezuelan Government was also involved in the production of oil. In 1960 the government-owned Corporación Venezolana del Petroleo (CVP) was

Fig. 14.9 The oil industry of Venezuela and the adjacent islands

created, and this company was given exclusive rights to new concessions. The CVP, however, accounted for less than one-third of Venezuela's petroleum production. In 1976 the Venezuela oil industry was nationalised, and a new body known as Petrovén was established to administer it.

In the early days of the Venezuelan petroleum industry, all the oil produced around Lake Maracaibo was shipped overseas in crude form. Because of the shallowness of the water at its entrance, large tankers were unable to enter Lake Maracaibo. Consequently the crude oil was shipped in shallow-draught tankers to the Dutch West Indian islands of Aruba and Curacao. The oil was refined in Aruba and Curacao, and the refined products shipped in large ocean-going tankers to the mainland of North America and Europe.

Since the Second World War, the Venezuelans have insisted that a larger share of their crude oil production should be refined within the country. Creole built a large new refinery on the Paraguaná Peninsula, at a place which could be easily reached by deep-draught tankers, and in 1949 the refinery was connected to the oilfields of the Maracaibo basin by means of a pipeline. In 1956 a newly dredged

channel, 10 metres deep, made it possible for tankers of up to 28 000 tonnes to enter Lake Maracaibo.

In 1972 Venezuela exported 111 363 000 tonnes of petroleum, valued at 7 537 million bolivares; and 50 171 000 tonnes of petroleum products, valued at 3 765 million bolivares. The leading importers of Venezuelan petroleum are the USA, the Netherlands Antilles, Canada, the United Kingdom, and Trinidad and Tobago.

Natural gas is produced with petroleum in Venezuela. Before 1950 the oil companies flared (burned off) the natural gas produced from their oil wells, but now a great deal of it is distributed by pipeline to various centres, to serve as a fuel for the generation of electricity and as a raw material in the new petrochemical industries which have been established. Some gas is exported.

Iron ore

Iron ore is the other outstanding mineral at present produced in Venezuela, although ranking far behind petroleum in importance. In 1974 iron ore accounted for 2 per cent of the country's export earnings. In 1975 Venezuela ranked as the world's tenth largest

208

producer of iron ore, accounting for 3 per cent of the total production.

The existence of extensive iron ore deposits in Venezuela was known as early as the nineteenth century, but their development did not begin until after the Second World War. At this time, the tremendous demands which the war had made upon the iron ore resources of the USA caused that country to seek foreign supplies. From 1950 to 1974 two large American companies were engaged in mining iron ore in Venezuela. In 1974 both of these companies were nationalised.

The iron ore deposits occur in a 480 km long belt along the northern fringe of the Guiana Massif, to the south of the Orinoco river. The deposits at present being worked are those at Cerro Bolivar to the west of the Caroni river, and those at El Trueno and El Pao to the east of the Caroni. Mining is by opencast methods, using huge mechanical shovels, which are capable of removing 20 tonnes of ore at one time. The ore is crushed at the mines, and then railed to the Orinoco river. The deposits at Cerro Bolivar and El Trueno are connected by rail to the wharves at Ciudad Guayana, near the confluence of the Caroni and Orinoco rivers. One of the many distributaries of the Orinoco has been dredged to enable large ore carriers to reach Ciudad Guayana. The ore mined at El Pao is railed to Palua on the Orinoco. From Palua barges carry it to Puerto de Hierro on the Paria Peninsula, where it is transhipped into ocean-going vessels. A state-owned iron and steel works has been built on the Orinoco river, not far from Ciudad Guayana.

Copper mining in Zambia

The economy of Zambia is dominated by copper mining. In 1973 copper accounted for 94 per cent of Zambia's export earnings. In 1975 Zambia ranked behind the USA, the USSR and Chile as the world's fourth largest producer of copper, accounting for more than one-tenth of the total production.

Zambia's copper production comes mainly from the Copperbelt, an area of gently undulating country, 150 km long and 50 km wide, extending roughly from Luanshya to Chililabombwe. Although the existence of copper in this area was known as

Fig. 14.10 The Zambian Copperbelt

early as 1902, commercial mining there did not begin until the 1920s.

The organisation of the mining industry

Before 1970, the copper mining industry of Zambia was controlled by two large companies, the Anglo American Corporation and the Roan Selection Trust. The former is now called Nchanga Consolidated Copper Mines Limited (NCCM), and the latter Roan Consolidated Mines Limited (RCM). In 1970 the state took a 51 per cent share in the mining industry, and the Mining and Industrial Development Corporation of Zambia (MINDECO) was set up. The original companies still continue to provide the management services.

A large part of Zambia's copper production comes from underground mines, although there are also a number of open-pit workings. The mines operated by RCM in 1973 were the Roan Antelope mine at Luanshya, the Mufulira mine, the Chibuluma mine, the Chambishi mine, the Baluba mine, and the Kalengwa mine. The mines at Luanshya, Mufulira and Chibuluma are entirely underground workings. At Chambishi there is a small open-pit working, which will eventually be developed into an underground mine. The Baluba mine is recently opened, and is a large open-pit mine which is only likely to be worked for a very few years. The Kalengwa mine is also an open-pit working.

The mines operated by the NCCM were the Nchanga mine near Chingola, the Rokana mine at Kitwe, the Konkola mine at Chililabombwe, the Mindola mine, the Bwana Mkubwa mine near Ndola, and the Kansanshi mine near Solwezi. The Nchanga mine is the largest in the whole Copperbelt, and comprises an underground mine and several open-pit workings. The Rokana mine is mainly underground, but also has a small open-pit working. The Konkola and Mindola mines are entirely underground workings, while the Bwana Mkubwa mine is an open-pit mine which was recently reopened. The Kanshanshi mine is an underground mine which was opened very recently, and is situated at a considerable distance to the west of the main Copperbelt.

Methods of production

About three-quarters of Zambia's copper production comes from underground mines. In these mines, vertical shafts are sunk to the appropriate levels. From the shafts, horizontal tunnels are driven towards the orebody. Holes are drilled in the copper-bearing rock, and these are filled with explosive charges. Blasting causes the solid rock to shatter. The broken rock can then be hauled to the surface for processing.

After mining, the ore is taken to concentrators, which are located near the mines. Each of the larger mines has its own concentrator. The ore mined in Zambia has an average copper content of about 3,4 per cent. At the concentrators, the ore is crushed into a fine powder, and then concentrated by the flotation process. This involves mixing the finely powdered ore with water and special chemicals. Air is blown through the mixture, and the copper-bearing particles cling to the bubbles which float to the surface, and can be skimmed off and dried. The copper concentrates, which consist of copper minerals together with a small amount of waste material, are

Underground mining for copper in the Zambian copperbelt. The miners are drilling holes in the rock face which they will later fill with explosives. Note the safety helmets and battery-powered lamps.

210

then sent to the smelters which are located at the Rokana, Mufulira, and Luanshya mines. Here they are mixed with limestone, and put into a furnace, into which coal and pre-heated air are also fed. The intense heat inside the furnace, causes the concentrates to melt, and to separate into two layers. The heavier, lower layer near the bottom of the furnace consists of a mixture of copper and iron sulphide, which is known as matte. The lighter upper layer consists of waste material, which is known as slag. The slag is skimmed off, and the molten matte is poured into converters. In the converter, air is blown through the matte to remove the sulphur impurities, raising the copper content to about 99,4 per cent. About one-sixth of the Copperbelt's production of copper is at this stage cast into slabs of blister copper (so called because as it solidifies the residual gases raise blisters on the surface), and is exported in this form. The rest is electrolytically refined. During the refining process, small quantities of other metals such as gold, silver and cobalt are recovered as by-products. At Rokana mine there is a cobalt refinery.

Export routes

In the past, most of Zambia's copper production was sent by rail through Zimbabwe to the port of Beira in Mozambique. Recent political differences with Zimbabwe, however, have led to Zambia seeking alternative export routes. In 1973 part of Zambia's production went by road to the ports of Dar-es-Salaam in Tanzania, and Mombasa in Kenya; part went by rail to the port of Lobito in Angola; and part went by a combination of road and rail through Malawi to the port of Nacala in Mozambique. The completion of the Tazara Railway in 1975 should prove to be a great boon to the Zambian copper industry. In 1974 the leading importers of Zambian copper were the United Kingdom, Japan and West Germany.

Tin and petroleum from Nigeria

Tin

Before the development of the petroleum industry, tin was Nigeria's leading mineral export. Extensive alluvial deposits of tin are found on and near the Jos Plateau. The mining and smelting of tin by primitive methods was undertaken by the peoples of the Jos Plateau long before the arrival of the Europeans in West Africa, but the modern Nigerian tin mining industry only dates from about 1903. In 1975 Nigeria ranked as the free world's seventh largest producer of tin concentrates, accounting for 3 per cent of total production.

The production of tin in Nigeria is undertaken both by large companies and by private individuals. Many of the tin mining companies are British owned. The most important company is the Amalgamated Tin Mines of Nigeria, which at one time was the largest single tin producer in the world. Tin is mined at the surface by a variety of methods. In some cases the tin-bearing gravel is dug out by hand. Many companies, however, now use draglines. After removing the overburden, the draglines dig out the tin-bearing gravel, and pile it into heaps. Strong jets of water are then used to wash the gravel through a series of sluice boxes. The tin-bearing particles, together with some other minerals such as columbite, sink to the bottom of the sluice boxes, while the lighter unwanted material is carried away by the water.

Until 1961 the tin produced on the Jos Plateau was exported in the form of tin concentrate, which had a metal content of about 74 per cent. In 1962, however, a tin smelter was opened at Makeri, a few kilometres to the south of the town of Jos. This now processes all the tin concentrates produced in Nigeria. It has also recently begun to process tin concentrates imported from the neighbouring country of Niger, where small quantities of tin are mined in the Air Plateau region. After smelting the tin is cast into ingots, and exported in this form.

Columbite, the ore of niobium, is an important by-product of tin mining in Nigeria. Niobium is a rare element which is used in the production of heat-resisting steels for jet engines, gas turbines, etc. Nigeria is one of the world's most important producers of columbite.

In recent years the Nigerian tin mining industry has been faced with a number of problems. One of the main problems has been the fact that the unfavourable price of tin on the world market, has been coupled with rising costs of production. In particular the cost of labour has risen considerably, because of recent wage awards. As a result, profit margins have become very small. Furthermore, the reserves of the grades of tin ore which are at present being exploited are dwindling.

Petroleum

Fortunately for Nigeria, large deposits of petroleum have been discovered beneath the sedimentary rocks of the Niger Delta, and the neighbouring coastal plains. Oil production in Nigeria only began in 1956, but since that time the industry has expanded rapidly. Although the oil industry suffered a severe set back during the Nigerian Civil War, recovery has been rapid since the cessation of hostilities. Nigeria's annual production of petroleum increased from 262 000 tonnes in 1958 to 111 578 000 tonnes in 1974.

Nigeria's first commercial oil well began production in 1956 at Oloibiri, to the west of Port Harcourt. Soon after this, other wells around Port Harcourt itself began producing oil. In 1964 oil fields around Ughelli in Bendel state began production, while in 1965 production began from off-shore fields at the mouth of the Escravos river. An extensive system of pipelines has been laid down for the transport of oil. In 1975 Nigeria's pipeline network had a total length of about 2 800 km. The first crude oil pipeline, some 100 km in length, was built from Oloibiri to Port Harcourt, and later a pipeline network was developed to connect the oilfields in the Port Harcourt area. The first shipment of crude oil from Nigeria was made from Port Harcourt in 1958. Because of the shallowness of the Bonny river at Port Harcourt, this port was unable to handle large tankers, and in 1961 it was replaced as an oil exporting port by a modern oil terminal which was built further downstream at Bonny. A second oil terminal was opened at Escravos in 1968, and other terminals have since been built.

In 1972 there were six foreign owned companies actually producing oil in Nigeria, while a number of others held prospecting licences. The producing companies were Shell/BP, Gulf, Mobil, Agip/Phillips, Safrap and Texaco. In late 1972 Shell/BP alone was accounting for about two-thirds of Nigeria's oil production, the other leading producers being Gulf and Mobil. These three companies together were

Table 85 Nigeria: Production of petroleum and natural gas

Year	Petroleum (thousand tonnes)	Natural gas (million cubic metres)
1958	262	—
1960	857	—
1962	3 391	2
1964	6 046	54
1966	20 989	176
1968	7 148	145
1970	54 506	111
1972	91 609	273
1974	111 578	574

accounting for well over nine-tenths of the country's total oil production. In the case of both Gulf and Mobil, a large part of the oil production comes from off-shore fields. In 1971 the Nigerian National Oil Corporation was established, and it is expected that this company will exploit several off-shore concessions which have been reserved for the government. Since 1973 the Nigerian National Oil Corporation has compulsorily taken a share in several of the companies which are at present producing oil in Nigeria.

Before 1964 the whole of Nigeria's production was exported in crude form. Since the completion of the oil refinery at Port Harcourt, however, a small proportion of the total output has been processed locally, to supply Nigeria's domestic needs for refined petroleum products. The Port Harcourt refinery is owned jointly by the Nigerian Government and Shell/BP. There are plans to establish two more oil refineries in Nigeria, and these will probably be located at Warri and Kaduna. Unlike the refinery at Port Harcourt which was established primarily to supply the Nigerian market, the proposed new refineries are expected to export part of their production. At present, however, the bulk of the petroleum produced in Nigeria continues to be exported in its crude form. In 1974 petroleum accounted for 93 per cent of Nigeria's export trade.

A considerable quantity of natural gas is produced with the crude oil in Nigeria. There are also reserves of natural gas which are not associated with oil wells. More than nine-tenths of Nigeria's natural gas production is at present flared off, because of the lack of an adequate local market for it. The remainder is mainly used for the generation of electricity by the power stations at Afam and Ughelli, and by the oil companies themselves who use it as a fuel. A number of industries in the area have also begun to use natural gas. In future natural gas could become the basis of a petrochemical industry.

Exercises

1 Write a detailed account of the tropical world's production of any one of the following minerals: petroleum, coal, iron ore, bauxite, copper, tin.
2 Compare and contrast tin mining in Malaysia with tin mining in Bolivia.
3 Describe the mineral resources of either West Africa or East Africa, and discuss the extent to which these resources have been developed.
4 Write a detailed account of mining in either Sierra Leone and Mauritania, or Jamaica and Guyana.
5 Write a detailed account of one of the following: copper mining in Zambia, petroleum production in Venezuela, iron ore mining in Liberia, petroleum production in Nigeria.
6 Assess the contribution made by the mining industry to the economy of any one tropical country.

Suggested reading

J. P. COLE: *Latin America — An Economic and Social Geography* — Chapter 8
WILLIAM A. HANCE: *The Geography of Modern Africa* — Chapter 12
R. J. HARRISON-CHURCH: *West Africa* — Chapter 8
W. B. MORGAN AND J. C. PUGH: *West Africa* — pp. 542–55
A. M. O'CONNOR: *An Economic Geography of East Africa* — Chapter 9
A. M. O'CONNOR: *The Geography of Tropical African Development* — Chapter 4
P. R. ODELL: *An Economic Geography of Oil*
OOI JIN-BEE: *Peninsular Malaysia* — Chapter 11
J. M. PRITCHARD: *Africa. A Study Geography for Advanced Students* — Chapter 9

H. P. WHITE AND M. B. GLEAVE: *An Economic Geography of West Africa* — Chapter 6

Source of statistics

UNITED NATIONS: *Statistical Yearbook.*

CHAPTER FIFTEEN

Power

The tropical world at present accounts for only a very small part of the world's production of electricity. In nearly all tropical countries the average per capita production and consumption of electricity is small, compared with those of the highly industrialised countries of Western Europe and North America.

Many tropical countries have an enormous potential for the generation of hydro-electric power. The Kaieteur Fall of the Potaro river in Guyana is five times the height of the Niagara Falls.

Table 86 Electricity in selected countries, 1975

	Installed capacity (thousand kW)	Total production (million kWh)	Production per capita (kWh)
World		6 245 400	1 605
Tropical America			
Barbados	67	214	873
Bolivia	346	1 000	177
Brazil	19 588	78 068	728
Colombia	4 495	14 100	598
Dominican Rep.	443	1 632	347
Ecuador	407	1 290	192
El Salvador	306	1 068	266
Honduras	144	480	158
Jamaica	677	2 331	114
Mexico	11 052	43 288	719
Peru	2 354	8 300	532
Puerto Rico	3 946	16 203	5 249
Venezuela	4 705	21 179	1 766
Tropical Asia			
Brunei	81	230	156
Burma	263	773	25
Hong Kong	2 274	7 373	169
India	22 172	85 613	143
Khmer Rep.	50	150	18
Malaysia	1 117	5 487	46
Philippines	3 019	12 359	290
Singapore	1 115	4 176	1 866
Sri Lanka	281	1 149	82
Thailand	2 500	7 910	189
Tropical Pacific			
American Samoa	13	62	2 138
Fiji	83	241	421
Fr. Polynesia	29	95	742
Papua New Guinea	250	969	352
Tonga	3	5	49
N. America and W. Europe			
Canada	59 886	272 624	11 940
Norway	17 090	77 564	19 357
Switzerland	12 816	42 282	6 603
United Kingdom	78 900	272 219	4 864
USA	524 270	2 000 916	9 367
W. Germany	74 356	301 802	4 881

In most parts of the tropical world it is not the lack of physical resources which is primarily responsible for the present low level of electric power development. Although few tropical countries produce coal in abundance, a number of them are now important producers of petroleum and natural gas, while in many parts of the tropical world there exists an enormous potential for the generation of hydro-electric power.

The factors which contribute most to the low level of electricity production in the tropical world are economic rather than physical. Of particular importance is the fact that in most countries the demand for electricity is at present relatively small. The domestic consumption of electricity is generally low, as many of the inhabitants of the tropical world cannot afford to use electricity in their homes. Furthermore, because in most countries the manufacturing sector of the economy is as yet little developed, the industrial demand for electricity is also generally small. It seems likely, however, that in the future, improvements in living standards and the development of manufacturing industry, will lead to an enormous increase in the demand for electricity in many parts of the tropical world. Already in some countries, the development of new manufacturing industry is being hampered by the lack of adequate and cheap sources of power.

Power production in tropical Africa

Before the Second World War, electricity production in tropical Africa was on an extremely small scale. Even in 1948 tropical Africa's production of electricity was little more than 2 000 million kilowatt hours (kWh). During the 1950s and 1960s, however, there was a considerable increase in the amount of electricity generated, and by 1974 annual production amounted to over 33 000 million kWh. In spite of

Fig. 15.1 Tropical Africa – important hydro-electric power schemes, 1972

this increase, the per capita production and consumption of electricity in tropical Africa remains very much lower than in the countries of North America and Western Europe.

During the 1940s, the bulk of tropical Africa's electricity was produced at thermal power stations. In the past most thermal stations used coal as a fuel, but today many of them use oil, while a few such as the ones at Afam and Ughelli in Nigeria use natural gas. Although in several countries the amount of thermal power generated has increased considerably in recent years, it is hydro-electric power which is today of much more importance in tropical Africa as a whole.

It is thought that tropical Africa possesses 30–40 per cent of the world's total potential for the production of hydro-electric power. As yet, however, only a very small part of this potential has been developed. Running water has several advantages over other sources of power. Of particular importance is the fact that it is a renewable resource, whereas coal, oil and natural gas are non-renewable. Although hydro-electric stations are often expensive to build, they are generally relatively cheap to run. Providing that a hydro-electric station is kept working at near full capacity, it will normally supply electricity at a lower cost than will a thermal station.

There are several factors which favour the production of hydro-electric power in tropical Africa:

1 Africa as a whole is a continent of plateaux, each plateau usually having well-marked edges. Where

Table 87 Electricity in selected countries, 1964–75

	Installed capacity (thousand kWh)		Total production (million kWh)		Production per capita (kWh)
	1964	1975	1964	1975	1975
Angola	265	509	260	1 305	193
Benin	8	15	20	57	18
Cameroon	165	225	1 068	1 190	186
Ethiopia	119	320	208	665	24
Gambia	4	10	7	27	56
Ghana	147	995	489	4 050	411
Ivory Coast	52	350	183	860	176
Kenya	101	282	323	971	72
Liberia	118	300	212	870	509
Malaŵi	20	79	42	292	58
Mauritius	96	121	93	320	356
Mozambique	209	393	242	717	78
Niger	6	20	15	70	15
Nigeria	272	860	1 024	3 211	51
Senegal	69	120	197	389	94
Sudan	59	120	167	350	20
Tanzania	70	160	205	636	42
Togo	11	25	27	118	53
Uganda	151	163	521	830	72
Upper Volta	8	18	19	53	9
Zaïre	766	1 217	2 618	3 440	138
Zambia	216	1 031	713	6 191	1 264
Zimbabwe	1 177	1 192	3 801	6 131	972

Table 88 The relative importance of thermal and hydro-electric power in selected countries, 1975

Country	Percentage of total electricity production	
	Hydro	Thermal
Angola	73	27
Cameroon	95	5
C.A.R.	94	6
Congo	55	45
Ethiopia	53	47
Gambia	0	100
Ghana	99	1
Ivory Coast	33	67
Kenya	67	33
Liberia	37	63
Malaŵi	86	14
Mauritius	13	87
Mozambique	41	59
Niger	0	100
Nigeria	99	1
Senegal	0	100
Tanzania	88	12
Uganda	98	2
Upper Volta	0	100
Zaïre	98	2
Zambia	96	4
Zimbabwe	87	13

rivers flow across these breaks of slope, they are usually interrupted by falls or rapids, and it is there that the best sites for power production are to be found.

2 The predominance of old, hard rocks means that firm foundations for dams are often available, and also that most rivers carry relatively little silt.

3 Unlike in the case of such countries as Canada and Sweden, there is no problem of the rivers freezing over in winter.

The main physical problem for water power development in tropical Africa is the fact that most of the rivers have highly seasonal régimes. Because of marked seasonal fluctuations in the flow of rivers, it is often necessary to undertake the construction of large, expensive dams. These dams not only create

the head of water which is necessary for power generation, but also result in the formation of large storage lakes which make it possible to regulate the flow of water throughout the year. As in other parts of the tropical world, however, the factor which at present contributes most to the lower level of power production in tropical Africa is the smallness of the demand for electricity.

The Volta River Project

The most important single source of electric power in West Africa is the Volta River Project in Ghana. This project involved the construction of a huge dam across the Volta river, where it cuts through the Akwapim Hills at Akosombo. The construction of the Akosombo dam began in 1962, and the first phase of the project was completed in 1966. The cost of the project amounted to about US $200 million, of which half was provided by Ghana. The completion of the dam changed the map of Ghana very considerably. It resulted in the formation of Lake Volta, with a surface area of 8 482 sq km. The lake stretches for 400 km behind the dam, and has flooded 3,5 per cent of Ghana. It is one of the largest man-made lakes in the world.

In the first stage of the project, four generators with a combined capacity of 512 000 kilowatts (kW), were installed in the power house at Akosombo. In 1972 two more generators were added, bringing the total capacity to 768 000 kW. In 1971 Akosombo accounted for almost 99 per cent of Ghana's total electricity production. The remainder was produced by a number of small thermal power stations operated by the Electricity Corporation of Ghana (ECG) and by various mining companies. Since the Akosombo station came into operation, the amount of electricity generated by thermal stations has declined, as the table below shows.

A large proportion of the electricity generated by the Volta River Authority (VRA) at Akosombo is consumed by the aluminium smelter of the Volta Aluminium Company (VALCO) at Tema. Indeed, if it had not been for the possibility of setting up an aluminium industry in Ghana, the vast hydro-electric power project at Akosombo would not have been economically viable. In 1971 VALCO purchased almost two-thirds of the electricity generated at Akosombo. The bulk of the remainder of the

Akosombo Dam and power station, Ghana. Note the main dam with Lake Volta behind. The penstocks (pipes down which the water drops on to the turbines) are on the left of the photograph, and the spillways (through which the surplus water is allowed to escape) are on the right.

VRA's production is sold to the Electricity Corporation of Ghana and to the mining companies.

A 161 kilovolt (kV) transmission line has been built to link Akosombo with the main towns in southern Ghana, including Accra, Tema, Kumasi and Takoradi. Long-term plans envisage the construction of transmission lines to carry power from Akosombo to the Northern and Upper Regions of Ghana, but at present the demand for electricity in the north of the country is extremely small. A transmission line has been built from Akosombo to

the Togo border, and Ghana has an agreement with Togo and Benin to sell them electricity.

The Volta River Project has had a number of important consequences for Ghana:

1 It has made possible the production of large quantities of relatively cheap electricity, both for consumption within Ghana, and for export to neighbouring countries. The availability of this cheap electricity has favoured industrial development in Ghana, and in particular made possible

Table 89 Generation of electricity in Ghana (million kWh)

	1965	1967	1969	1971
Total	528	1 560	2 772	2 941
Thermal				
ECG	336	30	21	20
Mines	192	34	22	12
Hydro-electric				
Volta River Authority	—	1 496	2 729	2 909

219

Table 90 Electricity from Akosombo (thousand kWh), 1966–71

	1966	1968	1970	1971
Total generated	475 600	2 523 600	2 881 000	2 909 290
Total sold	449 700	2 473 400	2 806 000	2 834 600
Main customers				
VALCO	13 900	1 865 900	2 012 400	1 919 090
ECG	300 900	420 100	546 800	659 250
Mines	127 200	177 400	206 800	226 500
Akosombo Township	2 700	6 800	7 200	8 809
Akosombo Textiles	—	2 000	14 800	20 815

the establishment of an aluminium smeltin industry at Tema.

2 As Ghana does not at present produce any coal, petroleum or natural gas, the generation of electricity by running water has greatly reduced the need to import fuel for thermal power stations, thus saving foreign exchange. At the same time Ghana is able to earn foreign exchange from the sale of electricity to its neighbours.

3 The formation of Lake Volta caused some disruption of road transport. In particular the main north–south road from Tamale to Kumasi was cut, necessitating the use of a ferry at Yeji. Vehicles using this road are now sometimes subject to long delays at Yeji. At the same time, the lake itself provides a new routeway, linking southern Ghana with the less developed northern part of the country. The Volta Lake Transport Company operates regular passenger and freight services between Akosombo at the southern end of the lake, and the new lake ports of Kpandu, Kete Krachi, Yeji and Yapei further north.

4 Lake Volta has become an important source of fish. The fish catch from the lake increased from 8 000 tonnes in 1965 to 39 000 in 1971. In the latter year Lake Volta accounted for almost one-fifth of Ghana's domestic fish catch. In the past Ghana has had to import substantial quantities of fish to supplement the domestic catch, and the development of this important fresh-water fishing could bring about a welcome saving of foreign exchange.

5 It may in future be possible to use water from Lake Volta to irrigate parts of the Accra Plain, which is one of the driest areas along the Ghana coast.

6 A less fortunate result has been the fact that the formation of Lake Volta has increased the possibility of the spread of bilharzia, as it provides a suitable breeding ground for the snails which carry this disease. Also, onchoceriasis (commonly known as 'river blindness') has spread to the Volta river below the dam, where the water now flows more rapidly. The simulium fly, which is the vector of onchoceriasis, only proliferates in fast-flowing water.

7 The formation of the lake made necessary the resettlement of 78 000 people, who previously lived in those parts of the Volta valley which are now beneath the waters of the lake. The VRA has tried to make the new settlements better places to live in, by the provision of social amenities and such basic facilities as good drinking water and latrines. Improved methods of agriculture are being encouraged in the settlement areas.

Power production in Nigeria

Until the late 1950s, coal from the mines at Enugu provided the main fuel for power generation in Nigeria, but as the oil deposits in the Niger Delta began to be exploited, a gradual shift to oil and later to natural gas took place. New thermal stations have been built on the gasfields at Afam and Ughelli.

Hydro-electric power was generated on the Jos Plateau as early as the 1920s, to supply the tin mines. The first major hydro-electric power project in Nigeria, however, was not undertaken until 1964, with the building of a dam across the Niger river at Kainji. The first phase of the Kainji project was completed in 1967, when four generators with a total capacity of 320 000 kW were installed in the power station. As the demand for electricity in Nigeria increases, a further eight generators will be added, to bring the final capacity of the Kainji station to 960 000 kW. In 1969 1 300 km of transmission lines carried electricity from Kainji to the main towns of Nigeria.

The construction of the Kainji Dam resulted in the formation of Lake Kainji, which covers a total area of about 1 300 sq km, and extends behind the dam for some 137 km. The formation Lake Kainji has been of considerable assistance to navigation of the Niger river. A system of locks has been installed, to enable boats to by-pass the dam itself. The Awuru rapids have also been by-passed by a lock, and the Bajibo rapids have been cleared. River craft of 1–1½ metres draught can now travel throughout the year from the Niger Delta to beyond Yelwa. The large storage capacity of Lake Kainji makes it possible to maintain full flood control in the Niger valley as far downstream as the confluence of the Kaduna river, while partial flood control can be maintained from the Kaduna confluence to the confluence of the Benue river at Lokoja. One effect of this will be to reduce the flooding of the fadamas downstream from Jebba, thus allowing the expansion of agriculture in this area. Furthermore, the Nigeria Sugar Company at Bacita will be able to irrigate its sugar cane plantations throughout the year. The lake itself will provide a valuable fishing ground, whose potential catch is estimated to exceed 10 000 tonnes per annum. The formation of Lake Kainji made it necessary to resettle some 60 000 people.

In order to meet the even greater demands for electricity which are expected in the 1980s, there are plans for the construction of another dam and power station on the Niger at Jebba, some 103 km downstream from Kainji. This is likely to have a capacity of 500 000 kW. There are also plans for a third hydro-electric power project in the Shiroro Gorge on the Kaduna river. At the Shiroro Gorge there is an estimated potential of 480 000 kW.

Other West African countries

In the other countries of West Africa, electricity production is at present on a very much smaller scale than in Ghana and Nigeria. In some of these countries, such as Senegal, Gambia and Upper Volta,

power is supplied entirely, or almost entirely by thermal power stations burning imported fuels. In other countries there are also hydro-electric plants.

Until recently the Ivory Coast depended upon thermal power stations for its electricity, but in recent years several hydro-electric projects have been inaugurated. The first hydro-electric development was at Ayame on the Bia river, where there are two small stations with a total capacity of 50 000 kW. A more recent development is the Kossou dam and power station on the Bandama river, with a capacity of 171 000 kW. The building of the Kossou dam necessitated a great deal of resettlement. In 1976 work began on the 900 000 kW scheme at Buyo on the Sassandra river, and this is expected to become operative by 1980. Another scheme likely to become operative at about the same time is that at Taabo on the Bandama river in central Ivory Coast.

In Liberia there are thermal power stations at Monrovia, and also at the iron mines. There is a hydro-electric station at Mount Coffee on the St. Paul river. Because of the abundant rainfall, and the many steep gorges in the Fouta Djalon which provide suitable dam sites, Guinea has a very considerable hydro-electric power potential. The first hydro-electric station in Guinea was finished in 1965 at Grandes Chutes on the Samou river. The Kinkon dam and power station in the Pita region were completed in 1967. At some future date the Konkoure river might be harnessed, to provide electricity for aluminium smelting. In Sierra Leone there is a small hydro-electric plant on the Guma river near Freetown. There are also plans for a hydro-electric scheme at Bumbuna Falls on the Rokel river. Such a scheme might be associated with the development of the bauxite deposits of the Port Loko area.

Power production in East Africa

The production of electricity in East Africa is not handicapped by the lack of physical resources. Although the region produces very little coal and no petroleum or natural gas, petroleum can easily be imported from the countries of the Middle East, and there are many opportunities for the harnessing of water power. As in other parts of tropical Africa, the production of electricity in East Africa is mainly limited by the relative smallness of the local demand. Before 1954 most of the electricity produced came from thermal stations located in the main towns. Today, however, hydro-electric stations provide most of the power generated in East Africa.

The outstanding source of electricity in Uganda, and indeed in the whole of East Africa, is at present the Owen Falls hydro-electric station. This station was opened in 1954, and is situated where the Victoria Nile flows out of Lake Victoria. The lake itself acts as a vast natural reservoir, which ensures an ample supply of water throughout the year. At first the demand for electricity within Uganda was very small, and it was not until 1968 that the Owen Falls station was brought to its full capacity of 150 000 kW. One of the major problems in Uganda, as indeed in many parts of tropical Africa, is the high cost of transmitting electricity to a poor and scattered rural population. Fortunately, Uganda has been able to sell a large proportion of the electricity produced at Owen Falls to neighbouring Kenya. A 132 kV transmission line carries electricity from the power station at Owen Falls to the Eldoret, Kisumu, Nakuru and Nairobi areas of Kenya. The export of electricity began in 1958, and in 1973 about a third of the electricity generated at Owen Falls was sold to Kenya.

In 1974 the Owen Falls power station accounted for more than nine-tenths of Uganda's total production of electricity. The rest was produced by a number of small hydro-electric and thermal stations. A small hydro-electric plant on the Kagera river in south-western Uganda has for a long time supplied power to the tin mines in that area, and now also provides the public supply for the Ankole District. An even smaller hydro-electric plant was opened in 1964 to serve Kabale. The Mobutu power station in Toro only supplies the copper mine at Kilembe.

In spite of the developments which have already taken place, the water power resources of Uganda have as yet scarcely been touched. The total potential of the Victoria Nile between Lake Victoria and Lake Mobutu is alone estimated at 1½ million kW. Suitable sites for the construction of new dams exist at Bujagali some 8 km downstream from Owen Falls, and also at both the Karuma Falls and the Kabalega Falls (formerly the Murchison Falls) further to the north. Because of fears that the natural beauty of the Kabalega Falls would be spoiled if a power station were constructed there, the Kabalega Falls power

scheme has been abandoned. A suggested alternative was for the construction of a power station at the Aru Falls, at the junction of the Aswa and the Agogo rivers, to the north-east of Kabalega Falls. This scheme, however, proved to be impracticable, because of the marked seasonal fluctuation in the volume of water which passes over the Aru Falls.

Although Uganda is at present the largest producer of electricity in East Africa, Kenya is by far the largest consumer. Kenya is the most industrialised of the three countries, and there is a relatively large demand for electricity, particularly in the Nairobi area. In 1975 Kenya imported 261 million kWh of electricity, to supplement the domestic production of 901 million kWh. Part of Kenya's domestic production of electricity comes from thermal stations, the largest of which are the oil-fired plants in Nairobi and Mombasa. Investigations are being made into the feasability of generating electricity from geothermal steam in the Lake Naivasha and Lake Hannington areas.

Kenya has a very much smaller hydro-electric power potential than Uganda, the only sizeable rivers being the Tana and the Athi, both of which are subject to marked seasonal fluctuations in flow. Kenya is, however, now developing its water power potential, in order to reduce its dependence upon electricity imported from Uganda, and also to reduce the need to import fuel for thermal power generation. Several small hydro-electric stations on the rivers to the north of Nairobi have supplied power to central Kenya for many years. The most important hydro-electric development, however, has been the recent scheme for harnessing the Tana river at Seven Forks, 160 km to the north-east of Nairobi. The first stage of this scheme involved the construction of a dam and power station at Kindaruma. The Kindaruma power station was opened in 1967, with a capacity of 40 000 kW. The second stage involves the construction of a dam and power station at Kamburu, a few kilometres upstream from Kindaruma. The Kamburu power station began operation in 1975, with a capacity of 200 000 kW. The third stage of the Seven Forks scheme will involve the construction of a power station at Gtaru. This is scheduled for completion in 1978.

Tanzania is at present both the smallest producer and the smallest consumer of electricity of the three

East African countries. Part of Tanzania's production comes from thermal stations, the most important of these being in Dar-es-Salaam. A thermal station also supplies the island of Zanzibar. There are several small hydro-electric stations at present in operation. The first of these was built at Pangani Falls on the Pangani river in 1938, and has a capacity of 17 500 kW. In 1964 another station was built at nearby Hale, with a capacity of 21 000 kW. This supplies electricity to Dar-es-Salaam. In 1968 a third station was opened higher up the Pangani river at Nyumba ya Mungu. This has a capacity of 8 000 kW, and supplies the towns of Aursha and Moshi. There are also two small hydro-electric stations on the Rufiji river. In 1975 the first phase of a much larger hydro-electric project came into operation at Kidatu on the Great Ruahu river. This has a capacity of 50 000 kW, and supplies electricity to Dar-es-Salaam.

Zimbabwe, Zambia and Malaŵi

Before 1960 the major sources of electricity in Zimbabwe were thermal power stations, of which the most important were those at Salisbury, Umniati and Bulawayo. All depended upon coal brought by rail from the mines at Wankie. In 1955, however, work began on the construction of a dam across the Zambezi river in the Kariba Gorge. At the time of the construction of the Kariba Dam, Zimbabwe (then called Southern Rhodesia), Zambia (Northern Rhodesia) and Malaŵi (Nyasaland) together formed the Federation of Rhodesia and Nyasaland, and the Kariba project was intended to provide for the power needs of both Zimbabwe and Zambia. In both countries the demand for electricity is relatively large, the main consumers being the mines of the Zambian Copperbelt, and the mines and factories of Zimbabwe.

The completion of the Kariba Dam in 1958 resulted in the formation of Lake Kariba, which covers an area of 5 200 sq km, and extends for 280 km behind the dam. An underground power station was built on the south bank of the Zambezi river in Rhodesia, and this came into operation in 1960. The south bank power station has a capacity of 705 000 kW. 1 600 km of transmission lines were constructed, to carry electricity from Kariba as far north as Kitwe in the Zambian Copperbelt, and as far south as Bulawayo in Zimbabwe.

After the breakup of the Federation of Rhodesia and Nyasaland in 1963, and the Unilateral Declaration of Independence by the Rhodesian Government in 1965, Zambia continued to receive a large part of its electricity from Kariba. Even in 1971 about three-quarters of the electricity consumed in Zambia was imported from Zimbabwe. By far the largest consumer is the mining industry, which accounts for some four-fifths of the country's total electricity consumption.

In order to reduce its dependence upon electricity imported from Zimbabwe, Zambia has recently undertaken the development of its own water power resources. In 1969 a 60 000 kW hydro-electric station was completed at Victoria Falls, higher up the Zambezi from Kariba. A dam and power station have also recently been completed on the Kafue river, some 50 km to the south of Lusaka. The Kafue station came into operation in 1972, with an initial capacity of 600 000 kW. Work is now nearing completion on the second stage of the Kafue project, which involves the construction of a storage dam at Iteshi Teshi near the head of the Kafue Flats, and the installation of additional generators in the Kafue Gorge power station, to bring its total capacity to 900 000 kW. The Iteshi Teshi dam will also provide all the year round irrigation water for the Kafue Flats. In 1970 work was begun on the construction of a second power station at Kariba, this time on the north bank of the Zambezi in Zambia. The north bank station began producing electricity in 1976.

Before 1966 most of Malaŵi's electricity was generated by thermal stations, which used imported fuels. Malaŵi has, however, a very considerable hydro-electric potential, it being estimated that the Shire river alone has a potential of 500 000 kW. The first major hydro-electric station in Malaŵi was built at Nkula Falls, on the middle section of the Shire river. It was opened in 1966 with an initial capacity of 16 000 kW. In 1967 another generator was added, bringing Nkula Falls' capacity to 24 000 kW. The demand for electricity in Malaŵi increased more rapidly than was expected, as a result of the development of new industries, and by 1970 the full capacity of Nkula Falls was approached. A start was therefore made on the construction of another station at Tedzani Falls, 8 km downstream from Nkula. The Tedzani Falls station had an initial capacity of 16 000 kW.

Some other African countries

In 1974 4 000 000 kWh of electricity were generated in Zaïre, making it the third largest producer in tropical Africa. Virtually all of Zaïre's electricity production now comes from hydro-electric stations, but so far only a fractional part of Zaïre's enormous water power potential has been harnessed. Zaïre has the largest hydro-electric power potential of any country in the world. A large part of this potential occurs in the 350 km stretch of the Zaïre river between Kinshasa and Matadi. In this section the Zaïre drops a total of 270 metres in 30 falls and rapids. One great advantage of the Zaïre for power generation is the fact that, as the bulk of its basin is located in the equatorial climatic region, the river has a much more even flow than most other large rivers of tropical Africa.

Before 1972 there were already a number of hydro-electric stations in operation in Zaïre, mainly in Shaba Province. The largest of these was Le Marinel plant on the Lualaba river, with a capacity of 276 000 kW. Other smaller plants in Shaba include the Francqui plant near Likasi, where the Lufira river drops 110 metres in the Cornet Falls; the Bia plant a few kilometres downstream from this; and the Delcommune plant on the Lualaba river, a few kilometres upstream from Le Marinel. The electricity needs of the town of Kinshasa and the province of Bas Zaïre were partly catered for by the 12 000 kW Sanga station, and the 75 000 kW Zongo station, both on the Inkisi tributary of the Zaïre.

In 1968 work began on the giant Inga scheme, about 145 km from the mouth of the Zaïre. This project, which is by far the largest in Africa, has an ultimate potential of 30 million kW. This vast potential is due to the fact that the water level in this section of the river drops more than 67 metres in only 26 km. The first phase of the Inga project involved the construction of a dam across a dry valley, the Nkokola valley, which is almost as deep as the main river itself, and runs parallel to it. The dam was completed in 1972, and channels were cut to divert water to it from the main river. Because the dam was built on a dry site, construction work was very much easier than was the case in many other large power projects in tropical Africa.

The amount of power Inga Phase 1 should be capable of producing far exceeds the present demand for electricity in Kinshasa and Bas Zaïre, but several new industries are now being established in the area. Industries which will use large quantities of power from Inga include a steelworks at Maluku, the Lukala cement factory, and the oil refinery at Moanda. In Shaba Province, which in 1970 consumed four-fifths of Zaïre's electricity production, the copper industry is becoming concerned about the possibility of a shortage of power in the near future. In order to supply Shaba with additional power, it is planned to construct some 1 800 km of high tension power lines from Inga to the mining area.

In 1974 40 per cent of the electricity produced in Mozambique was supplied by hydro-electric stations, the largest of these being the Mavudzi station on the Revue river. The electricity production of Mozambique will, however, be greatly increased when the Cabora Bassa scheme is completed. This scheme involves the building of a dam across the Zambezi, 480 km from its mouth. The site of the dam is the Cabora Bassa Gorge, which is very narrow, and which has almost vertical walls of granite and gneiss. When finished the main dam will be over 150 metres high, and will impound waters which will stretch back for 240 km. Grandiose plans have been made to irrigate a vast area of land in the lower Zambezi valley, and the river itself could become navigable from Tete to the sea. The first phase of Cabora Bassa should make 1 200 000 kW available. The amount of electricity which Cabora Bassa will be capable of producing is far more than Mozambique itself is likely to need in the immediate future, and much of its production will be sold to the neighbouring Republic of South Africa. It will be carried by a 1 400 km long transmission line to a point near Pretoria in the Republic.

Several hydro-electric stations have been built in Angola in recent years. The most important of these projects is the Cambambe station on the Cuanza river, which was opened in 1963 with an initial capacity of 130 000 kW, which will later be raised to 260 000 kW. There are smaller stations at Biopio and Lumaum on the Catumbela river.

During the 1960s the governments of Portugal and South Africa reached an agreement on the joint use of the waters of the Cunene river, the lower part of whose course forms part of the boundary between Angola and Namibia. The proposed Cunene scheme

Fig. 15.2 Proposed Cunene River Scheme, 1975

Power station under construction
Possible power station sites(potential in thousand kw)

1 Calueque (20) 2 Jacavele (60) 3 Luandega (195)
4 Ondorusu (70) 5 Zebra (60) 6 Epupa (445)
7 Baynes (260) 8 Marien (300) 9 Hartman (260)
10 Hombolo (195)

Brazil's deposits of coal are small and are generally of poor quality, and the country's known reserves of petroleum are only moderate. Fortunately, however, Brazil possesses a very large potential for the generation of hydro-electric power. The rivers which possess the greatest potential for power generation are the Amazon, the Paraná, and the São Francisco. The greatest demand for electricity at present is in the mining and industrial areas of the south-east, and particularly in the area between the towns of Rio de Janeiro, São Paulo and Belo Horizonte. During the 1960s and the early 1970s great efforts have been made to develop Brazil's water power potential, by the construction of dams and hydro-electric power stations.

is a multi-purpose one, and involves damming the river in several places for the generation of electricity and the storage of water for irrigation purposes. In 1973 a dam was completed at Gove, and a canal system was developed to provide irrigation water for farmers in Ovamboland. Work in progress in 1975 included the construction of a power station at Ruacana Falls with an initial capacity of 80 000 kW, later to be increased to 240 000 kW; and the building of a regulating dam at Calueque which should provide sufficient irrigation water for the immediate needs of Ovamboland, as well as for parts of Damaraland and the coastal desert. When fully developed there could be no less than 11 power stations on the Cunene river, between Calueque and the Atlantic Ocean. Whether or not this ambitious scheme will ever be fully realised, will clearly depend upon the kind of relationship South Africa is able to establish with newly independent Angola.

Table 91 Electricity in Brazil, 1948–75

Year	Installed capacity (thousand kW)		Production (million kWh)	
	Total	Hydro	Total	Hydro (as % of total)
1948	1 625	1 334	6 797	NA
1954	2 774	2 156	11 871	84
1960	4 800	3 642	22 865	83
1962	5 729	4 126	27 158	76
1964	6 840	4 894	29 094	76
1966	7 566	5 524	32 654	85
1968	8 555	6 183	38 181	80
1970	11 233	8 829	45 460	88
1972	13 715	10 979	56 295	90
1974	16 807	13 762	70 480	95
1975	19 588	16 193	78 068	72

Power production in Brazil

Since the end of the Second World War there has been a remarkable expansion of electricity production in Brazil. During the period between 1948 and 1975 Brazil's installed capacity was increased from 1 625 000 kW to 19 588 000 kW. In spite of this greatly increased capacity for power generation, in recent years Brazil's industrial expansion has been hampered by the shortage of cheap supplies of electricity.

During the first half of the twentieth century a number of hydro-electric power projects were undertaken in Brazil, mainly to supply electricity to the towns in the south-east of the country. These projects were small in size, in comparison with those which were later to be undertaken during the 1960s and early 1970s.

The first sizeable hydro-electric plant to be built in tropical South America was at Juiz de Fora, to the north of Rio de Janeiro. In the period between the two world wars, a number of hydro-electric plants were also built near to São Paulo. Several of these plants were located on the headwaters of the Tiête river. The most impressive of the early projects was located on the crest of the Serra do Mar escarpment, overlooking the port of Santos. This project involved the damming of several of the rivers which rise to the east of São Paulo. By 1927 two large storage reservoirs had been created in the Serra do Mar. Water from these reservoirs is led through a tunnel to the Cubatão power house, situated 720 metres below.

In recent years a number of dams and power stations have been built on the Rio Grande. One such power station was opened at Peixoto in 1957. The much larger Furnas Scheme, which is situated further upstream was completed in 1965. The Furnas Dam is located where the Rio Grande and its principal tributary the Sapucai meet, and its construction has resulted in the formation of an artificial lake with a surface area of 1 600 sq km. The Furnas station is almost equidistant from the three important power consuming centres of Rio de Janeiro, São Paulo and Belo Horizonte. The transmission line which carries power from the Furnas station to São Paulo passes via Pocos de Caldas, and supplies electricity to the aluminium works there.

A number of hydro-electric projects have recently been completed in the valley of the São Francisco river. Important among these are the Tres Marias and the Paulo Alfonso schemes. The Tres Marias dam and power station are located to the north-west of Belo Horizonte, and supply electricity to the mining and industrial areas of the state of Minas Gerais. The Paulo Alfonso power project is situated much further north, at the Paulo Alfonso Falls. Here the São Francisco river passes through a narrow gorge, and drops 85 metres in a series of cascades. The Paulo Alfonso project supplies electricity to the underdeveloped north-eastern part of the country. Transmission lines carry electricity from the Paulo Alfonso station to several towns on the north-east coast, including Salvador and Recife. The dams which have been constructed in the valley of the São Francisco are intended to provide an example of complete river basin control, including not only the generation of power, but also flood control, irrigation and improvements in transportation.

In the late 1960s work began on the giant Urubupungá hydro-electric complex on the Paraná river. When it is completed this will be one of the largest hydro-electric schemes in the world, with a capacity of 4,6 million kW. The Urubupungá complex consists of two power stations. The Jupiá power station has recently been completed, and the larger Ilha Solteira plant should be completed by 1977. The Jupiá dam is supplied by the waters of the Paraná river and two of its tributaries, the Tiête and the Sucuriá. The Jupiá station has 14 generators, with a combined capacity of 1,4 million kW. The Ilha Solteira dam and power station are situated 50 km upstream from Jupiá. The dam at Ilha Solteira is supplied by the waters of the Paraná river, and from two of the rivers which meet to form the latter, the Grande and the Garanaíba. The Ilha Solteira station will eventually have 20 generators, with a combined capacity of 3,2 million kW. When it is completed this station will be the largest in the western world.

Even larger than the Urubupungá complex, however, will be the proposed Itaipu project, which is planned for lower down the Paraná. This will be built near to a series of falls called the Sete Quedas. The Paraná river here forms the boundary between Brazil and Paraguay, and the Itaipu project will be undertaken jointly by the two countries. It is estimated that the Itaipu project will have a final capacity in the order of 13 million kW.

Table 92 Electricity in India, 1948–75

Year	Installed capacity (thousand kW)		Production (million kWh)	
	Total	Hydro	Total	Hydro (as % of total)
1948	1 809	507	5 725	42
1954	3 229	796	9 669	39
1960	5 580	1 846	20 123	39
1962	6 925	2 939	26 227	45
1964	8 458	3 392	33 149	45
1966	11 376	4 760	40 512	41
1968	14 296	5 910	51 642	40
1970	16 429	6 458	59 975	41
1972	17 990	6 788	70 516	39
1973	18 410	6 970	72 753	40
1974	20 130	7 520	75 704	36
1975	22 172	8 442	85 613	39

Fig. 15.3 Major power projects of India, 1972

fired. Thermal stations are found in most areas of India, but they are particularly important in the north-east of the country, within relatively easy reach of the coalfields of the Damodar valley.

The power potential of India's rivers is estimated to be in the order of 41 million kW. In 1974 less than one-sixth of the total potential had been harnessed.

Table 93 The distribution of water power potential

	Potential (million kW)	% of total
West-flowing rivers of Western Ghats	4,3	10,4
East-flowing rivers of southern India	8,6	21,0
River of central India	4,3	10,4
Ganga (Ganges) basin	4,8	11,7
Brahmaputra, Manipur and Tyao	12,5	30,4
Indus	6,6	16,1
Total	41,1	100,0

Power production in India

Since the time of independence, India's capacity to generate electricity has expanded enormously. In 1975 the amount of electricity generated was more than 15 times as great as that generated in 1948. In spite of this, India's output of electricity is still very small, in relation to the size of the country's population. In 1975, for example, the United Kingdom, with less than one-tenth of India's population, generated over three times as much electricity. In the same year India's electricity production was only slightly larger than that of Norway, although its population was almost 150 times as large.

Thermal power

In 1974 61 per cent of India's electricity production came from thermal stations. In this respect India is markedly different from Brazil, the bulk of whose electricity comes from hydro-electric stations. India is fortunate in possessing very large deposits of coal, and most of the thermal stations in India are coal-fired.

In western India, the heavy rainfall and the often precipitous edge of the Western Ghats provide favourable conditions for the generation of hydro-electric power. There are three particularly important centres of hydro-electricity production along this western mountain edge. Behind Bombay City in the north there are three power stations which are fed by large storage reservoirs located on the reverse slopes of the Western Ghats. Water from these reservoirs is led through the crest of the Ghats by tunnels, and the head at the three stations ranges from 506 to 530 metres. In the central area there is an important hydro-electric power station at the Gersoppa Falls (Jog Falls) on the Sharavati river. Further south there are several power stations in the Nilgiri Hills.

On the peninsula proper there are extreme variations in the river regimes, with many rivers drying up entirely during the dry season. In these areas water has to be impounded behind large dams, such as those which have been built at Mettur on the Cauvery river, at Hirakud on the Mahanadi river, and at Tungabhadra on a tributary of the Krishna

227

(Kistna) river. Many of these dams are in fact multi-purpose projects, intended not only for the supply of power, but also for the storage of water for irrigation purposes.

The third main area of hydro-electric power production in India is in the north, where use is made of the rivers which rise in the Himalayas. Hydro-electric projects which are already in operation here include the Nangal Dam on the Sutlej river, and the Bhakra Dam a few kilometres further upstream.

India is today taking an active interest in the development of nuclear energy. The country's first nuclear power station, with a capacity of 400 000 kW, was opened in 1969 at Tarapur near Bombay. More recently a second nuclear station with a capacity of 220 000 kW has been opened at Kofa in Rajasthan. In 1974 nuclear power accounted for 3 per cent of India's total production of electricity.

In 1974–5 industry accounted for 65 per cent of India's electricity consumption, while domestic consumers only accounted for 9 per cent. There has, however, been an increase in the consumption of electricity by domestic consumers in recent years. In 1947 only 0,27 per cent of villages in India were supplied with electricity, but by 1975 29,2 per cent received the benefits of electrification. In spite of this, cow dung still remains the principal fuel in many of India's villages. Since 1966–7 the rural electrification programme has been re-oriented. The emphasis is now on the energisation of pumps and wells to supply water for irrigation purposes.

Table 94 Electricity consumption, 1974–5

Nature of use	% of total consumption
Industrial power	65,3
Agricultural	12,6
Domestic	9,1
Commercial	5,5
Railway traction	3,2
Public lighting	1,1
Other uses	3,2
Total	100,0

Exercises

1 Describe the potential power resources of either West Africa or East Africa, and comment on the extent of their development.
2 With the aid of a sketch-map, locate the major hydro-electric power schemes in tropical Africa. How have these schemes contributed to the economic development of the area?
3 Write an account of the production of electricity in either Brazil or India.
4 What have been the major consequences of the construction of any one of the following dams: Akosombo, Kainji, Kariba?
5 'In tropical Africa it is not the lack of physical resources which is primarily responsible for the low level of electric power development.' Discuss this statement.

Suggested reading

JOHN I. CLARKE, Ed.: *An Advanced Geography of Africa* – pp. 394–409
B. W. HODDER: *Economic Development in the Tropics* – pp. 46–8
A. M. O'CONNOR: *An Economic Geography of East Africa* – Chapter 11
A. M. O'CONNOR: *The Geography of Tropical African Development* – Chapter 6
M. C. POLLOCK: *Studies in Emerging Africa* – Chapter 8
NEVILLE RUBIN AND WILLIAM M. WARREN, Ed. *Dams of Africa*
H. P. WHITE AND M. B. GLEAVE: *An Economic Geography of West Africa* – pp. 151–6

Source of statistics

UNITED NATIONS: *Statistical Yearbook*

CHAPTER SIXTEEN

Manufacturing

A: General

In most tropical countries the manufacturing sector of the economy is as yet little developed. In the tropical world as a whole a very high proportion of the economically active population continues to be engaged in agriculture, while the proportion engaged in manufacturing remains extremely small. Much of the manufactured goods needed by the

A very simple form of manufacturing. Making a rope from coir (coconut fibre) on the beach near Cape Coast, Ghana.

peoples of the tropical world still have to be imported from countries which lie outside the tropics.

Until comparatively recently a large part of the tropical world was subject to the rule of countries in Europe. These economically more developed European countries tended to regard their colonial possessions mainly as markets for their own manufactured goods, and as suppliers of foodstuffs and raw materials. Consequently, they generally did little to encourage the development of manufacturing industry in the tropical world.

Motives for industrialisation

In recent years the governments of many of the newly independent countries of the tropical world have begun to show a great interest in the development of the manufacturing sector of the economy, and a number have in fact embarked upon ambitious industrialisation programmes. These programmes have a number of objectives, some of the more important of which are:

1 to diversify and strengthen the country's economy, and thus make it possible to raise the standard of living of its inhabitants;
2 to create opportunities for employment;
3 to improve the country's balance of trade.

The governments of the developing countries of the tropical world can see that on the whole the most prosperous nations of the world are the ones which are highly industrialised, and consequently they tend to associate prosperity with industrial development. The governments of most tropical countries would like to broaden the economy, by reducing its dependence upon agriculture. Furthermore, they realise

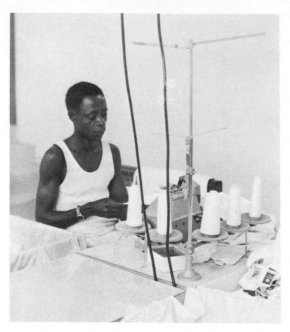

Modern factory industry. Inside a shirt factory in Accra, Ghana.

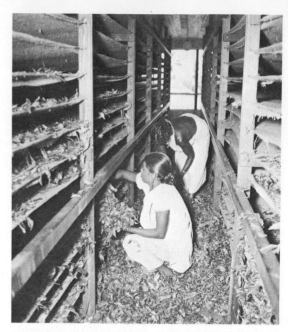

Many industrial establishments in the tropical world are concerned with the processing of local agricultural products. Spreading out leaves to wither at a tea factory in West Malaysia.

that it is usually easier to increase productivity in manufacturing than it is in agriculture.

In many parts of the tropical world, the rapid growth of population which has taken place in recent years has led to serious problems of unemployment and underemployment. In some countries there is the problem of too many people dependent upon too little land. It is argued that if some of the surplus labour at present engaged in agriculture were to be absorbed in manufacturing, there need be no decline in the level of agricultural production, and the standard of living of those remaining on the land could be raised. The importance of industry as a provider of employment should not, however, be overestimated, as relatively small numbers of workers are in fact required to operate a modern factory. Nevertheless, in countries such as Hong Kong, and to a lesser extent Singapore, Puerto Rico and Jamaica, the establishment of new factories has created many job opportunities.

A great many tropical countries have a highly unfavourable balance of trade. The development of manufacturing can help to improve a country's balance of trade in two important ways. Firstly, by

the further processing of locally produced raw materials before they are exported, the value of the country's export trade can be increased. For example, far more foreign exchange can be earned if timber is exported in the form of sawn timber, plywood or veneer, than if it is shipped overseas in the form of logs. In most tropical countries the older-established industries are in fact mainly concerned with the primary processing of locally produced raw materials for export. Secondly, by substituting locally manufactured goods for imported ones, the cost of a country's imports can be reduced. Many of the industries recently established in tropical countries are of the 'import-substitution type. Although in the long term the development of manufacturing is likely to improve a country's balance of trade, in the short term it may in fact cause a sharp deterioration in it, as in order to set up new industries it is usually necessary to import expensive machinery.

Obstacles to industrialisation

In attempting to develop the manufacturing sector of the economy, the governments of tropical countries

230

A canning factory in West Malaysia. Stacking sealed tins of pineapple for cooling, prior to packing them into cardboard boxes for export.

Other industries are concerned with the processing of local minerals. Kilns for drying bauxite at Linden, Guyana.

find themselves faced by numerous problems, among the more important of which are:

1 the shortage of capital;
2 the shortage of skilled labour;
3 the narrowness of market opportunities.

One of the major obstacles to industrial development in most tropical countries has been the shortage of capital, large amounts of which are needed if factories are to be built, and machinery is to be purchased. Because of the general poverty of the majority of the inhabitants, in most countries the level of domestic savings is low. Furthermore, the inhabitants of these countries often prefer to invest such savings as they are able to make in land or in jewellery, rather than in new industrial enterprises, where the risks involved are generally greater. In those countries where a large part of the national income is concentrated in the hands of a relatively few people, the wealthy few often dissipate much of their money in ostentatious living, instead of channelling it into productive enterprises.

If sufficient capital is not available locally for the establishment of new manufacturing industries, a possible alternative is to attract investment from outside sources. This has been successfully done in recent years in several of the territories of the West Indies. In Puerto Rico and Jamaica, for example, a large number of new industries have been established since the end of the Second World War. The governments of these two territories have attracted outside investors by offering them special incentives. The Jamaican Government, under the Industrial Incentives Law, offers approved new industries relief from income tax for the first 10 years of their existence, or for the first 15 years in the case of manufacturers who are willing to locate their factories in special development areas. Approved new industries in Jamaica are also permitted to import their raw materials free of duty. In other countries, however, the idea of obtaining capital from outside sources has proved to be very much less popular, and foreign investors have not always been encouraged.

Although in many countries a great deal of unemployment exists, there is often at the same time a severe shortage of skilled and even semi-skilled labour. With the present level of education and training, the productivity of the tropical factory worker is often much lower than that of his European or North American counterpart. Given time and proper training, however, there is absolutely no reason why this situation should not be remedied. In addition to the lack of skilled manpower, there is also often a shortage of experienced management and technical personnel. At present many tropical countries have to rely to a large extent upon expatriate managers and technicians for the running of their newly established industries. This tends to make management costs higher than in the manufacturing countries of the temperate lands.

Many countries are also handicapped in their industrialisation programmes by the small size of the domestic market. The size of a country's domestic market depends not only upon the size of its total population, but also upon the standard of living enjoyed by its inhabitants. Some countries, particularly many of the ones in the West Indies and Africa, have extremely small populations. In 1975, for example, 10 of the West Indian territories each had a population of less than 100 000, and a further six each had less than 1 million. Only Cuba, the Dominican Republic, Haiti, Jamaica, Puerto Rico, and Trinidad had a population of more than 1 million, and the combined population of these six territories was only 25 million. In the same year there were 13 tropical African countries each with less than 1 million inhabitants, while a further 16 countries each had less than 5 million. Only Ethiopia, Kenya, Nigeria, Sudan, Tanzania, Uganda and Zaïre had a population of more than 10 million. Even in some tropical countries which have large populations, the domestic market for the more expensive kinds of manufactured goods is small, because of the low purchasing power of most of the inhabitants.

The size of the market for manufactured goods can, however, be increased by the formation of various kinds of regional groupings, such as customs unions and free trade areas. The object of the formation of such groupings is to encourage trade between the various member states. Manufacturing industry in Kenya has greatly benefited from the setting up of the East African Common Market, which has given the Kenyan manufacturer access to a market comprising Tanzania and Uganda, as well as Kenya itself. The combined population of the three

An aerial view of an alumina factory at Ewarton, Jamaica

An aerial view of a copper smelter at Kitwe, Zambia.

East African Common Market countries is three times as great as that of Kenya alone. Similarly, manufacturing industry in Jamaica has benefited from the setting up of the Caribbean Free Trade Association (CARIFTA).

There is also the possibility of tropical countries producing manufactured goods for export. It is, however, usually difficult for tropical countries to establish export markets for their manufactured goods. Newly established industries tend to be relatively inefficient, and therefore find it difficult to compete in terms of quality and price with the older established manufacturing industries of the temperate countries. Furthermore, the more highly developed countries of the world tend to protect their own manufacturing industries by the imposition of tariffs or import quotas. Nevertheless, a few tropical countries such as Hong Kong and Puerto Rico have succeeded in establishing large export markets for their manufacturing industries.

B: Selected manufacturing industries

West Africa

Craft industry and modern industry
The manufacturing industry of West Africa can be broadly divided into African craft industry and modern industry. Craft industries have been important in West Africa for many centuries, and in spite of competition from factory produced goods, a wide range of hand-made articles is still produced. The type of handicraft work produced in West Africa varies from one area to another, and also from tribe to tribe. Important craft industries include the spinning, weaving and dyeing of cotton cloth, tanning and leather making, wood carving, basket making, the making of pottery, and gold and silver smithing.

The development of modern manufacturing industry in West Africa is a very recent occurrence, only dating back to the period between the two world wars. In spite of the fact that some new industries have been established in every West African country since the end of the Second World War, only a very small proportion of the economically active population is engaged in manufacturing, and a large part of West Africa's needs in manufactured goods still has to be imported.

The extent to which modern manufacturing industries have already been established, varies considerably from one country to another. The greatest amount of industrial development has so far taken place in Nigeria, Ghana, Senegal and the Ivory Coast. Nigeria is very favourably placed for industrial development, in comparison with most other West African countries. It has a large domestic market, its population exceeding that of all other West African countries combined; it has a wide range of raw materials; and it has abundant power resources in the form of coal, petroleum, natural gas and running water. Very little industrial development has so far taken place in the land-locked countries of Mali, Niger and Upper Volta, all of which have small and very poor populations, and limited natural resources.

A number of different factors play a part in influencing the location of industry, including:

1 the availability of raw materials;
2 the availability of power;
3 proximity to markets;
4 the availability of suitable labour;
5 transport facilities;
6 government policy.

The relative importance of each of these locational factors does, however, vary from industry to industry, and also from region to region. According to the major factor which has influenced their siting, modern West African industries can be divided into the following broad groups:

1 raw material oriented industries;
2 power oriented industries;
3 market oriented industries.

Raw material oriented industries
The oldest, and still the most important group of modern West African industries, is that which is concerned with the processing of local raw materials. Very often these local raw materials are processed for export, but in other cases they are intended for the domestic market. Examples of the latter include the processing of sugar cane and the milling of rice. Raw

234

materials tend to be processed close to where they are produced, if processing:

1 makes the finished product less perishable;
2 reduces the bulk or the weight of the product, thus saving on transport costs.

A great number of industries in West Africa are concerned with the primary processing of locally produced agricultural raw materials. Foremost among them, are those concerned with the extraction of vegetable oil. Factories for the extraction of groundnut oil are of particular importance in Senegal and in northern Nigeria, but there are also groundnut oil mills in Gambia, Mali, Niger and Upper Volta. There are modern factories for the extraction of palm oil in several countries, particularly in Nigeria and Dahomey. A great deal of West Africa's palm oil, however, still continues to be extracted by the farmers themselves, using simple hand methods. Other mills are concerned with the extraction of coconut oil and cotton seed oil. Locally produced vegetable oils are in several countries used in the manufacture of soap and margarine, but the factories engaged in the manufacture of these products tend to be located close to their market, rather than at the source of raw material.

The processing of latex and the manufacture of sheet rubber is of importance, particularly at Harbel in Liberia; at Bingerville and Pakidié in the Ivory Coast; and at Sapele, Calabar, Benin City, Warri, Hagbo-Uno, Owerri and Elele in Nigeria. Cotton ginning is of particular importance in the northern part of Nigeria, but there are also ginneries in Benin, the Ivory Coast, Mali, Senegal, Togo and Upper Volta. There are several factories which produce sugar from locally grown sugar cane, including the ones at Komenda and Asutsuare in Ghana, and at Bacita in Nigeria.

There are several meat canneries in West Africa, most of them located in the Sudan savanna zone. At Vom on the Jos Plateau in Nigeria, milk is collected and a powdered form is produced. Butter and cheese are also made at Vom. The canning of fruit and fruit juice is of some importance in the forest zone of Nigeria, the Ivory Coast, Guinea and Ghana. Many of the larger fruit canneries, however, have suffered in the past from inadequate and irregular supplies of fruit. A factory near Cape Coast in Ghana extracts lime juice and lime oil for export to the United Kingdom.

As already mentioned in Chapter 12, the bulk of the fish landed in West Africa is either consumed fresh, or is preserved by such traditional methods as smoking and sun-drying. A number of fish canneries and cold storage plants have, however, been established. At Dakar in Senegal and Abidjan in the Ivory Coast there are canneries, which produce canned tuna fish for export. There are fish freezing plants at Nouadhibou in Mauritania, Lagos in Nigeria, and Monrovia in Liberia. At Tema in Ghana there is a cold store and cannery complex.

The processing of timber is of considerable importance in the forest zone, particularly in the Ivory Coast, Ghana, Nigeria and Liberia. In all of these countries there are a large number of saw mills, most of which are quite small. They produce sawn timber for the domestic market, and also for export. There are factories producing plywood and veneers at Sapele in Nigeria, Samreboi and Sefwi Wiawso in Ghana, and also in the Ivory Coast.

The primary processing of minerals before export is carried out in a number of countries. Most ores contain only a relatively low percentage of metal, and consequently the cost of transport can be greatly reduced if some concentration is done as close to the mine as possible. There are a number of plants for the crushing, washing, sorting or concentration of minerals in West Africa. There are gold extraction plants at Obuasi and Tarkwa in Ghana, and plants for the washing of diamonds at Akwatia in Ghana and Yengema in Sierra Leone. There is a tin smelter at Makeri in Nigeria. Iron ore beneficiation plants are found in Liberia, Sierra Leone and Mauritania, and alumina is produced from bauxite at Fria in Guinea. Both Togo and Senegal have plants for the processing of phosphate rock. At M'Bao near Dakar, phosphate rock is used in the manufacture of fertilisers. There are several factories which use local limestone for the manufacture of cement, including those near Abeokuta, Calabar, Enugu and Sokoto in Nigeria; and near Rufisque in Senegal. At Aboso near Tarkwa in Ghana, there is a glass factory which uses local glass sand as its raw material. At Port Harcourt in Nigeria there is an oil refinery which processes locally produced petroleum into petroleum products for the domestic market.

Several of the more important minerals produced in West Africa are, however, still shipped either in their raw form, or after only simple washing and crushing has taken place. These include much of the region's iron ore, bauxite and manganese ore. Most of Nigeria's petroleum is also still exported in crude form. Although several countries are now important producers of iron ore, there is no iron and steel industry in West Africa, apart from steel rolling mills using scrap metal. Although Ghana has sizeable deposits of bauxite, the alumina needed for the aluminium smelter at Tema has to be imported.

Power oriented industries

Industries are attracted to low-cost sources of power if the cost of energy represents a considerable part of the total cost of the finished product. The most notable of the power oriented industries in West Africa is the smelting of aluminium at Tema in Ghana. The electricity used by the smelter is produced at Akosombo, some 80 km away to the north. Although the availability of an abundance of cheap electricity is the main reason for the existence of an aluminium smelting industry in Ghana, the choice of Tema rather than Akosombo as the exact location of the smelter was influenced by the fact that the alumina has to be imported.

Market oriented industries

Most of the remaining West African industrial establishments can be classified as market oriented industries. There has been an appreciable development of this group of industries in recent years. Most of the new market oriented industries have been established either in the capital cities or at the main ports. Industries tend to be located at ports if they use bulky imported raw materials. Examples of such industries include the refining of imported petroleum, and the manufacture of cement from imported clinker. The main centres where market oriented industries have already been established are Accra, Tema and Takoradi in Ghana; Lagos, Port Harcourt, Kano and Kaduna in Nigeria; Abidjan in the Ivory Coast; and Dakar and Rufisque in Senegal. Manufacturing industries tend to be located near their market if:

1 the product is made more perishable or more fragile by manufacturing;
2 the product is much bulkier than the raw materials from which it is made;
3 the industry is a service industry.

A large number of industrial establishments in West Africa are concerned with the manufacture of food, beverages and tobacco products. Baking and ice cream making are examples of industries whose products are more perishable than the raw materials from which they are made, and which are therefore located close to their market. There are bakeries in a great many West African towns, and ice cream is made in a number of larger ones. There are breweries using imported raw materials at Lagos and Aba in Nigeria; Lomé in Togo; Accra and Kumasi in Ghana; Abidjan in the Ivory Coast; Monrovia in Liberia; Wellington just outside Freetown in Sierra Leone; and at Dakar in Senegal. Because of the large water content in beer and carbonated beverages, considerable savings in transport costs can be made if these products are manufactured close to their main market. There are distilleries in several of the larger towns, and modern cigarette factories at Port Harcourt, Oshogbo, Ibadan, Zaria and Ilorin in Nigeria; Takoradi and Tema in Ghana; Bouaké in the Ivory Coast; Wellington in Sierra Leone; Bamako in Mali; Dakar in Senegal and Monrovia in Liberia. Other market oriented industries include flour milling, and the manufacture of chocolates and sweets. In West Africa flour mills are usually dependent upon imported grains, and therefore tend to be located at the main ports.

Other market oriented industries are concerned with the production of cloth, clothing and footwear. There is a large market for cotton cloth in West Africa, and modern textile industries have been established in a number of countries. Important centres for the spinning, weaving and finishing of cotton cloth include Dakar and Rufisque in Senegal; Abidjan and Bouaké in the Ivory Coast; Tema and Akosombo in Ghana; and Lagos, Kano and Kaduna in Nigeria. There are modern clothing factories in a number of countries. Although many sandals are still produced by artisans in West Africa, there are now also a number of modern footwear factories, including those at Accra, Abidjan, Kano, Lagos and Rufisque.

Fig. 16.1 Ghana – location of major manufacturing industries

237

At present there are only a few large metal manufacturing establishments in West Africa. At Tema in Ghana and at Emene near Enugu in Nigeria, there are steel rolling mills which use scrap metal as their raw material. There are a growing number of industrial establishments which are engaged in the assembly of motor vehicles and electrical appliances. These include the assembly of motor vehicles at Accra, Tema, Abidjan, Lagos and Kaduna; the assembly of bicycles; and the assembly of radios and television sets. There are also a number of factories which produce metal sheets, drums, cans, pipes, wire, etc.

In addition to those cement factories which use local limestone as their raw material, there are a number which depend upon imported clinker, and which consequently are located at ports. Examples of these are at Tema, Takoradi, Abidjan, Wellington, Lagos and Port Harcourt. Asbestos cement sheets are produced at Ikeja near Lagos, and at Emene near Enugu. There are numerous small establishments which are engaged in the production of cement building blocks.

There are also a number of relatively recently established chemical industries, of which the most important is the refining of petroleum. In addition to the refinery at Port Harcourt which processes a small part of Nigeria's petroleum production for the local market, there are several other refineries which depend upon imported petroleum. These are located at Tema, Abidjan, Monrovia, Wellington and M'Bao. There are motor vehicle tyre factories at Ikeja and at Port Harcourt in Nigeria, and at Bonsaso in Ghana. Other chemical products which are manufactured include paints, varnishes, matches, insecticides, pharmaceuticals and explosives.

Because of the great increase in bulk after manufacture, household articles are usually produced in the market areas. Wooden furniture is made in small workshops in many towns, and there are also a number of factories which produce metal furniture and metal doors and window frames. A wide variety of both metal and plastic household utensils are also manufactured in West Africa, there being a large market for such products.

Service industries include the repair of railway locomotives and rolling stock, the repair of motor vehicles, the retreading of tyres, printing and ice-making. There are large railway workshops near Lagos and near Takoradi.

Kenya

Before the Second World War there was very little manufacturing in Kenya, and such industrial establishments as did exist were largely concerned with the processing of local agricultural products for export. Although agriculture still remains the mainstay of the country's economy, during the 1960s and early 1970s there was a considerable expansion of manufacturing industry in Kenya.

Manufacturing industry is in fact much more highly developed in Kenya, than in either Tanzania or Uganda. The manufacturing sector in Kenya not only employs a larger number of people, but also produces a much wider range of products than is the case in either of the other East African countries. There seem to be several reasons for this greater development of manufacturing in Kenya, one of the most important of which is related to the size of the market. Because of its larger Asian and much larger European population, there is a bigger market in Kenya for the more expensive types of manufactured goods than in either Tanzania or Uganda. Furthermore, a factory in central Kenya is better located to supply the whole of the East African market than is one in Tanzania or Uganda. Kenya has also benefited from the greater availability of local capital.

The distribution of manufacturing

By far the most important manufacturing centre in Kenya, and indeed in the whole of East Africa, is Nairobi. The city of Nairobi, with its large and relatively prosperous population, itself provides a substantial market for manufactured goods, and the country to the north of the city also supports a dense population. A very wide range of manufactured goods are produced in Nairobi. Many of the manufacturing establishments are located in a well-developed industrial area in the south-east of the city.

The second most important industrial centre in Kenya is Mombasa. The importance of Mombasa as a centre for manufacturing is largely related to its function as the chief port of the country. Several of Mombasa's largest industrial establishments, such as the oil refinery and the steel rolling mill, are dependent upon imported raw materials. Other centres with a substantial number of industrial establishments are Thika, Nakuru, Kisumu and Eldoret. Outside of these main centres, Kenya's manufacturing establishments tend to be widely dispersed, and are mainly concerned with the processing of agricultural and forestry products.

Raw material oriented industries

As is the case in West Africa, a large number of industrial establishments in Kenya are concerned with the primary processing of local agricultural products. Coffee processing does not require very expensive equipment, and is carried out in a large number of relatively small establishments. These are mainly concentrated in the highlands to the east of the Rift Valley, particularly in the Kiambu and Nairobi districts. The processing of tea requires a far greater capital outlay, and is carried out in a much smaller number of relatively large establishments. The main centres of tea processing are in the Kericho and Kiambu districts, although this industry is now spreading into other districts in the highland areas largely as a result of the government's encouragement of tea growing among small farmers. The Kenya Tea Development Authority (KTDA) has in recent years established a number of new factories, for the processing of tea grown by small farmers.

Factories for the extraction of sisal fibre are mainly located around Thika and Voi. As the fibre only represents about 4 per cent of the total weight of the leaf, sisal processing must be carried out very close to the point of production, in order to minimise transport costs. Although much of the sisal produced in Kenya is shipped overseas in the form of baled fibre, there are also factories which use sisal fibre as their raw material. At Ruiru between Nairobi and Thika, there is a factory which uses local sisal fibre together with some imported jute for the manufacture of sacks for agricultural purposes. Ropes, twines and sisal matting are also produced at the same factory. The cultivation of cotton is of much less importance in Kenya than in either Tanzania or Uganda, and consequently cotton ginneries are less numerous.

The manufacture of sugar from locally grown cane is of increasing importance. Because of the great reduction in bulk which results from sugar manufacture, and because sugar cane needs to be processed within a few hours of being cut, sugar factories are located in the main cane growing areas. In 1975 there were five modern sugar factories in operation in Kenya. Four of these were located in the area to the east of Kisumu at Miwani, Chemilil, Muhuroni and Mumias, while the fifth was at Ramisi on the coast to the south of Mombasa. In addition to these modern factories which depend to a large extent upon cane grown on plantations and large farms, there are also a number of smaller mills which process the cane grown by peasant farmers, to produce a crude form of brown sugar known as 'jaggery'.

Several establishments are concerned with the processing of meat products, dairy products, and fruits and vegetables. The Kenya Meat Commission (KMC) operates a large meat processing plant at Athi River near Nairobi, and a smaller one at Mombasa. In addition to producing fresh meat for the local market and for export, the Athi River plant produces canned meats. At Uplands near Limuru, there is a factory which produces bacon, and a wide range of other pig products. The Kenya Co-operative Creameries operates several milk collection and processing plants, and has a factory near Eldoret which produces milk powder. A number of establishments produce butter, ghee (butter clarified to resemble vegetable oil) and cheese. The canning of fruits and vegetables is of considerable importance, the main centres of this industry being Thika and Machakos.

Other establishments concerned with the processing of local agricultural products include a pyrethrum extract factory at Nakuru, and wattle extract factories at Eldoret and Thika. There are tanneries at Thika, Limuru and Eldoret. On the coast at Kilifi there is a factory for the processing of cashew nuts. The extraction of vegetable oil is of very much less importance in Kenya than in Uganda or Tanzania, although some coconut oil and cotton seed oil is produced.

Although forestry is of much less importance in Kenya than in such countries as Ghana and the Ivory Coast, there are a number of small establishments concerned with the processing of forest products. The greatest concentration of sawmills is in Rift Valley Province, particularly in the forested area to the west of the Rift. In 1975 a large pulp and paper factory was opened at Webuye.

The production of minerals is at present on a very small scale in Kenya, and industries concerned with their processing are consequently of only minor importance. At Magadi there is a factory for the processing of soda ash and salt obtained from Lake Magadi. Cement factories using local limestone are located at Athi River, and at Bamburi near Mombasa. In addition to supplying the local market, the cement industry produces a considerable surplus for sale to neighbouring countries.

Market oriented industries

In recent years a considerable number of new market oriented industries have been established, particularly in the Nairobi area, and to a lesser extent in the Mombasa, Thika, Nakuru and Kisumu areas.

The grain milling industry in Kenya is partly raw material and partly market oriented. The milling of maize is very widespread in the main grain growing areas of Kenya, and is mainly carried out at very small mills. The largest grain mills in Kenya are those concerned with the production of wheat flour, and are located at Eldoret, Nakuru and Nairobi. Those at Eldoret and Nakuru are located in the centre of important wheat growing areas. Bakeries are found in most of Kenya's larger towns.

The brewing of African beers is widespread. In addition there are large modern breweries producing lager-type beers at Nairobi and Mombasa. There are distilleries in Nairobi, and soft drinks are bottled in a number of towns, including Nairobi, Mombasa and Eldoret. The British American Tobacco Company has a factory at Nairobi, which produces cigarettes and pipe tobacco.

There are several textile factories, and these use both imported and local fibres. There are factories which make cloth from imported rayon at Thika and at Mombasa, and large cotton mill at Kisumu. A factory at Eldoret produces knitting wool, while woollen blankets are made at Nakuru and Eldoret. The grestest concentration of clothing factories is in Nairobi. The Bata Shoe Company has a large factory at Limuru, where both canvas and leather footwear are produced.

There is a large oil refinery at Mombasa, which processes crude oil imported from the Middle East.

In addition to supplying the Kenyan market, this refinery sells large quantities of refined products to Uganda and to a number of other African countries. There are glass factories at Nairobi and Mombasa. The main products are containers, particularly bottles for beer, spirits and soft drinks. A factory at Thika processes waste materials, to produce coarse paper. A large factory making motor vehicle tyres has recently been established at Nairobi, and the Bata Shoe Company produces bicycle tubes at its Limuru factory. The largest soap factories in Kenya are located at Nairobi, and there are others at Mombasa and Kisumu. There are factories producing pharmaceuticals and various kinds of toilet preparations at Nairobi. There are several factories which produce paints and varnishes, and these are also mainly located at Nairobi. There is a match factory at Mombasa.

A growing number of industrial establishments are concerned with metal fabrication and with light engineering. A mill at Mombasa produces rolled steel bars and rods from imported billets, and another steel mill has recently been constructed at Kikuyu near Nairobi. The Metal Box Company has a factory at Thika which produces cans for foods and kerosene, while at Mombasa there is a factory producing steel drums. Some motor vehicles are assembled at Nairobi, although nearly all the vehicles used in Kenya are still imported. There are also factories for the assembly of radios and other small electrical goods. There are other factories producing razor blades, nuts and bolts, door and window frames, tools, etc.

Important service industries include the repair of railway locomotives and rolling stock, the repair of motor vehicles, tyre retreading, and printing and publishing. The main workshops of the East African Railways Corporation are located at Nairobi, while minor repairs to ships are carried out at Mombasa. Nairobi is the main centre of the printing and publishing industry.

Puerto Rico

In 1940 the West Indian island of Puerto Rico was extremely poor. Its economy was largely based upon the cultivation of such traditional export crops as sugar cane, coffee and tobacco, and such industry as did exist was largely concerned with the processing of these crops. The island's population was growing rapidly, and there was a serious unemployment problem. Since that time, Puerto Rico's economy has been transformed, largely as a result of a highly successful government-sponsored industrialisation programme. By 1970 manufacturing had come to contribute more to the island's economy than agriculture. In that year Puerto Rico had more than 2 700 manufacturing establishments, which employed 137 000 workers at wage rates considerably higher than those to be found in almost any other country in the tropical world.

The development of manufacturing

The real beginnings of modern manufacturing industry in Puerto Rico date back to 1942, when the government created the Puerto Rican Development Corporation (PRIDCO), which was entrusted with the task of developing new industries in the island. In 1950 the Economic Development Administration (known in Spanish as *Fomento*) was created, and this took over the function of industrial promotion which had previously been performed by PRIDCO.

At first it was felt that the development of manufacturing could best be done by the setting up of factories which would be owned and operated by the state. Factories were established for the manufacture of glass, footwear, paperboard, clay products and cement. It was soon realised, however, that if government funds were to be used to establish and run new industries of this type, they would be completely inadequate for the task. Consequently it was decided that in future the government would concentrate on a programme of encouraging private firms to set up new factories in Puerto Rico, and the factories which had been operated by PRIDCO were sold.

The government realised that a large part of the capital which was needed for industrial expansion in Puerto Rico would have to come from the United States, and North American companies were encouraged to establish branch factories in the island. North American investors were attracted to the island in several ways. In 1947 a law was passed exempting new factories from the payment of Puerto Rican taxes during the early years of their existence. Firms establishing new industries in the island could claim freedom from taxation for periods ranging from 10 to 17 years. Offices were set up in the cities of New York, Chicago, Los Angeles and Miami, to promote new investment in the island. The government itself built a large number of factories, which the industrialists could either buy or lease. The government also offered help in the recruitment and training of labour, and in the granting of credit facilities. These measures proved highly successful, and by 1969 Fomento had promoted 1 800 new factories in the island, which provided employment for 111 000 workers.

Favourable factors

The natural resources of Puerto Rico are somewhat limited. The island possesses no known deposits of coal, petroleum or natural gas, and has only a limited potential for the development of hydro-electric power. A number of factors have, however, helped to make possible the rapid growth of manufacturing which has taken place in the last three decades:

1 Because of Puerto Rico's special relationship with the United States (it is a self-governing commonwealth which is voluntarily associated with the USA), there are no tariff barriers separating the island from the mainland, and consequently goods which are manufactured in Puerto Rico can enter freely into the USA. The island thus has a very large market for its manufactured goods. A large part of the goods which are produced in Puerto Rico's factories are destined for the USA, while many of the raw materials needed by these factories are imported from the USA. In 1971 the USA provided 77 per cent of Puerto Rico's imports, and purchased 93 per cent of the island's exports.

2 The island's proximity to the mainland of North America has meant that the cost of transporting the raw materials and the finished products is relatively low.

3 Although average wage rates are appreciably higher in Puerto Rico than in most other tropical countries, they are lower than those paid to factory workers on the mainland of North America.

4 Because of the existence of a favourable political

241

climate, North American companies have had the confidence to invest in the island.

The nature and distribution of manufacturing

Before 1940 such manufacturing establishments as existed were mainly concerned with the processing of local agricultural products. Of particular importance were the manufacture of sugar, molasses and rum from sugar cane, and the making of cigarettes and cigars from locally grown tobacco. Also of some importance was the needlework industry, which employed a large number of the island's women, who mainly worked in their own homes and were paid according to what they produced.

During the early 1950s many of the new industries which were established in the island were light, labour-intensive industries, taking advantage of the fact that wage rates in Puerto Rico were substantially below those in the USA. Of particular importance were factories producing clothing, footwear, and electrical equipment. These industries were mainly located in the urban centres, particularly in those which had port facilities and other services to offer. The greatest number of new manufacturing establishments were located in the San Juan metropolitan area, while the ports of Mayaguez on the west coast and Ponce on the south coast of the island also attracted many industries.

More recently, however, heavier and more automated industries have begun to be established in Puerto Rico. Of particular importance are oil refineries, fertiliser factories and other chemical plants. There is a large oil refinery near the port of Ponce. This processes crude oil imported from Venezuela and elsewhere, and as well as supplying the domestic market with refined petroleum products, it provides the raw materials for a growing petrochemical industry. There is also a large cement factory at Ponce, while at Santurce near San Juan there is an iron works.

Hong Kong

The economy of the British colony of Hong Kong now depends very heavily upon manufacturing. In 1971, of the 1 583 000 people employed in Hong Kong, 677 000, or more than two-fifths of the total, were employed in manufacturing. Various types of manufactured goods account for more than nine tenths of Hong Kong's domestic export earnings.

The development of manufacturing

The development of manufacturing on a large scale only began in the 1950s, and was made necessary by the rapid growth of population which took place after the end of the Second World War. At the outbreak of the war the population of Hong Kong was estimated at 1 600 000. During the war the Japanese invasion brought a decline in the colony's population to 600 000, but by the end of 1950 it had risen again to 2 360 000 and had reached 4 345 000 by the end of 1974. This rapid growth of population was partly a result of a decline in the death rate, but to a large extent it came about as the result of a massive influx of refugees from Communist China.

In the post-war period, Hong Kong was thus faced with the problem of providing food and employment for a rapidly expanding population. The total land area of the colony is only 1 045 sq km, of which about 13 per cent is used for agricultural purposes. Local agriculture is unable to feed the whole of Hong Kong's population, and large quantities of foodstuffs have to be imported. Before the Second World War Hong Kong had a very flourishing entrepôt trade, but after the war this declined considerably. It was against this background that Hong Kong began to industrialise.

Hong Kong had virtually no raw materials or power resources with which to develop manufacturing industry. Fortunately, however, among the refugees from China were many businessmen from Shanghai and Canton, who brought with them their capital and business experience. The colony also had a favourable geographical position in relation to world trade routes, a large and hard-working labour force, and modern and efficient port facilities.

At first the newly established industries catered largely for the cheap Asian markets, such as those in India and Malaysia. Later, however, Hong Kong succeeded in establishing markets for its manufactured goods in the highly industrialised countries of the world, where they were able to compete with the locally produced goods on account of their cheapness. Although factory workers in Hong Kong are better paid than are workers in most other countries of tropical Asia, average wage rates in Hong Kong are appreciably lower than those of Western Europe and North America. In 1974 about four-fifths of Hong Kong's manufactured goods were sold in the highly industrialised countries of the world, with the United States, the United Kingdom and West Germany together taking 55 per cent.

The nature of industry

The majority of industries which have so far been established in Hong Kong are light industries. The type of factory involved in manufacturing ranges from the small cottage type, to large and highly complex modern establishments. Because of the shortage of land for building purposes, many of the light industries operate in multi-storey buildings, which have been specially designed for the purpose.

The textile and clothing industries dominate Hong Kong's manufacturing sector, and in 1975 together accounted for 54 per cent of the colony's domestic export earnings, and employed 52 per cent of its manufacturing labour force. The manufacture of cotton cloth is particularly important, although the importance of woollen textiles and of man-made fibres is increasing. The clothing industry employed more workers in 1975, than did the textile industry. A wide variety of ready-made garments are produced, including cotton singlets, slacks, shirts and dresses, and these are exported to countries all over the world.

Of the other light industries, plastics rank second in importance. Plastic products manufactured in Hong Kong include toys, artificial flowers and household utensils. Also of considerable importance is the electronics industry, which turns out a wide range of products including tape recorders, desk calculators, television sets and transistor radios. A wide range of fabricated metal products are also manufactured, including aluminium ware, enamelware, vacuum flasks, pressure stoves and lanterns, tin cans and metal toys. A large number of workers are also engaged in the making of wigs. Most of the wigs are made from synthetic fibre, and are mainly exported to the USA. Other light industries include the manufacture of watches and clocks, cameras, torches, paper products and rubber footwear.

Hong Kong's heavy industries are mainly related to its port facilities and to the construction industry. They include the repair of ships and aircraft, and the

construction of small and medium sized vessels. Steel reinforcing bars for use in the construction industry are produced either from imported steel ingots, or from scrap metal which is mainly derived from ship-breaking.

Table 95 Industry in Hong Kong, 1975

Type of industry	Number of establishments	Number of persons employed
Food processing	1 114	14 347
Textile manufacture	3 411	112 922
Clothing manufacture	7 073	238 958
Footwear manufacture	450	4 335
Paper and paper products	915	7 442
Printing and publishing	1 578	19 812
Rubber products	336	6 101
Plastic products	3 437	63 706
Fabricated metal products	4 974	57 322
Manufacture of machinery	1 228	11 926
Electrical apparatus, etc.	891	66 353
Transport equipment	217	11 133
Scientific, photographic, optical goods	318	13 177
Other industries	5 092	51 323
Total (all industries)	31 034	678 857

Venezuela

Before the Second World War, Venezuela had very little modern manufacturing industry, apart from establishments dealing with the processing of local agricultural products and petroleum. In the last two decades, however, there has been a rapid expansion of manufacturing. In 1972 there were more than 7 500 industrial plants in operation. These plants employed about 24 per cent of Venezuela's total labour force.

In 1958 the government of Venezuela adopted an import-substitution policy. This policy aimed at encouraging the local production of manufactured goods, and thereby:

1 creating additional employment;
2 reducing the amount of money spent on the importation of manufactured goods;
3 diversifying the country's economy, by reducing its dependence upon petroleum.

In order to stimulate the industrial growth, a number of incentives were offered to private investors. These included:

1 the exemption of new industries from certain taxes;
2 the imposition of high tariffs and other restrictions on imported manufactured goods;
3 the duty-free importation of the equipment and raw materials needed by the new industrial establishment.

Favourable factors

Venezuela has a number of advantages for the development of manufacturing industry:

1 It has a good variety of raw materials, of particular importance being the vast deposits of iron ore which occur to the south of the Orinoco river.
2 It has abundant power resources in the form of petroleum and natural gas. The country also has an enormous hydro-electric power potential.
3 There is a considerable domestic market for manufactured goods. Although the population of Venezuela is only about 12 million, the per capita purchasing power of its inhabitants is very much higher than in most other tropical countries.
4 As a result of the development of the country's petroleum resources, there is plenty of capital available locally. Furthermore, in recent years Venezuela has found it relatively easy to attract foreign investment.

The manufacturing industries of Venezuela can be divided into three broad groups:

1 oil refining and associated chemical industries;
2 the production of light consumer goods;
3 the industries associated with the new industrial complex on the lower Orinoco.

Oil refining and petrochemical industries

In the early days of the Venezuelan petroleum industry, all the country's oil production was exported in crude form. The first oil refinery was built in 1917, and since that time the country's oil refining capacity has been expanded tremendously. It increased from 2 700 000 tonnes in 1938, to 76 600 000 tonnes in 1975. In that year, Venezuela ranked as the free world's ninth largest oil refining country. As Table 96 shows Venezuela has a far greater oil refining capacity than any other tropical country.

Table 96 Oil refining: Annual capacity (thousand tonnes) of leading tropical countries, 1975

World total: 3 044 925 (excl. China and USSR)			
Tropical world: 487 950			
Venezuela	76 600	Puerto Rico	17 150
Brazil	51 500	Philippines	9 500
Singapore	45 950	Colombia	8 670
Neth. Antilles	42 450	Thailand	8 310
Mexico	38 720	Malaysia	6 750
US Virgin Is.	36 400	Cuba	5 700
India	27 820	Peru	5 540
Bahamas	26 100	Panama	5 000
Trinidad	23 050	Kenya	4 300
Indonesia	20 840	Nigeria	3 000

In 1974 two-fifths of Venezuela's petroleum production was refined within the country, while three-fifths was exported in crude form. Of the petroleum processed in Venezuela in that year, 69 per cent was refined into fuel oil, 14 per cent into diesel and gas oil, and 13 per cent into gasolene and naptha, and the remainder into kerosene, asphalt and other products. A very large part of the refined petroleum products were themselves exported, only one-fifth of the total being consumed by the domestic market.

The first Venezuelan oil refinery was built in 1917 at San Lorenzo on the eastern shore of Lake Maracaibo. This was followed by two large refineries

244

built on the Paraguaná Peninsula. These were the Compania Shell de Venezuela refinery at Cardón, and the Creole refinery at Amuay. The latter is now the largest refinery in Venezuela. Further east at Puerto Cabello is the Mobil refinery, which gets its crude oil from the Barinas field. At Puerto la Cruz there are two refineries, one belonging to Sinclair Venezuelan Oil Company, and the other to Venezuela Gulf Refining Company. In eastern Venezuela, Creole has a refinery at Caripito, and Texas Petroleum Company has one at Tucupita.

Petroleum and natural gas form the basis of Venezuela's growing petro-chemical industry. In 1958 the Petrochemical Institute was established, and in 1962 a plant to produce fertilisers was completed at Marón some 25 km from Puerto Cabello. In 1968 the Institute began work on another petro-chemical complex, which was located at El Tablazo on the eastern shore of Lake Maracaibo. El Tablazo was chosen as the site for this complex, because of its nearness to the oilfields around Lake Maracaibo, and the availability of water transportation to the Caribbean Sea and Atlantic Ocean. Five petro-chemical plants have already been completed at El Tablazo, and these produce fertilisers both for the home market and for export, and also polyesters. Several more plants producing a wide range of chemicals will be established at El Tablazo, before the project is finally completed in about 1985.

Consumer goods

Today practically every type of consumer goods is made within Venezuela. Most of the industrial establishments which produce light consumer goods are located in the Core region of Venezuela, particularly in and around the towns of Caracas, Maracay and Valencia.

The processing of foodstuffs is the most important of this group of industries, followed by transportation equipment, textiles, clothing and beverages. Establishments which are concerned with the preparation of foodstuffs include slaughterhouses, meat packing plants, milk pasteurisation plants, fruit and vegetable canning plants, fish freezing plants and ice cream making plants.

The Venezuelan textile industry now supplies about 80 per cent of the total domestic demand for textiles, and practically 100 per cent of the demand for cotton textiles. In 1973 there were 76 primary textile mills in operation, and a total of 17 000 people were employed in the textile industry. The clothing industry is also very important, employing 30 000 workers. There are also industrial establishments concerned with the assembly of motor vehicles, and the manufacture of leather, footwear, paper and furniture.

The Guayana industrial complex

Since 1960 the government of Venezuela has invested large sums of the revenue which it obtains from the petroleum industry in the development of the Guayana region. To stimulate the development of this region, the Corporación Venezolana de Guayana (CVG) was created in 1960. The Guayana region has enormous potential. In particular it possesses vast reserves of iron ore, and a tremendous hydro-electric power potential.

The hydro-electric power potential of the Guayana rivers, particularly the Caroní, is now being developed. The 690 km long Caroní is estimated to have a potential of more than 10 million kW. Two dams, the Macagua and the Guri have already been built. In 1973 these had a combined capacity of 900 000 kW. Two high voltage cables carry electricity throughout the Guayana region, and also as far as Caracas. More generators are to be added, and by 1987 the Guri power station will have a potential of more than 6 million kW.

The most important industrial establishment in the region at present is the Siderúrgica del Orinoco (SIDOR) iron and steel works near the confluence of the Caroní and the Orinoco rivers. The Sidor plant turns out pig iron, steel slabs, tools, wire, and seamless pipes. The iron ore comes from the nearby Cerro Bolivar mines, while coking coal is brought from Europe and Japan by returning iron ore carriers. There is an ample supply of electricity from the Guri power station. There are plans to expand the capacity of the Sidor plant from its present 1,2 million tonnes per year to 5 million tonnes by 1978. In the mid-1970s Venezuela was importing about 700 000 tonnes of steel products per year, but once the expanded Sidor plant is fully operational the country should be able to export $2\frac{1}{2}$ million tonnes per year.

The Guayana region's abundance of cheap hydro-electric power has made possible the development of

245

an aluminium smelting industry. The first aluminium smelter was established at Ciudad Guayana in 1967, and obtains its alumina from a plant in the USA, which in turn obtains its bauxite from Jamaica. There are plans for a second smelter, which should become operational by 1978. This is to obtain its raw material from a new alumina plant under construction at Ciudad Guayana, which will process bauxite imported from Jamaica, Guyana, Surinam and Brazil.

The development of new industries in the Guayana region has resulted in a considerable influx of population. The small towns of San Felix and Puerto Ordaz, located at the confluence of the Orinoco and Caroni rivers have been integrated to form the new planned city of Ciudad Guayana. This city has grown rapidly, from 42 000 inhabitants in 1961 when it was first created, to 160 000 in 1972. It is expected to reach 300 000 by the early 1980s. In order to provide for the new residents, it was necessary for massive public works projects to be undertaken. These included the building of 10 500 housing units, the completion of more than 100 km of primary roads, and the installation of a water supply system and drainage and waste disposal system.

C: The iron and steel industry

Although a large number of tropical countries produce iron ore, in most cases their entire production is shipped in an unprocessed form, and very few have as

Table 97 Iron and steel: Leading tropical producers, 1975 (thousand tonnes)

	Pig-iron and ferro-alloys	Crude steel
World total:	448 500	643 000
India	8 558	7 884
Brazil	6 987	8 306
Mexico	3 082	5 196
Venezuela	538	1 075
Peru	307	443
Zimbabwe	310	350
Colombia	300	264

yet succeeded in establishing their own iron and steel industries. In 1975 the tropical world produced about one-quarter of the world's iron ore, and yet it accounted for only 4 per cent of the world's production of pig-iron and ferro-alloys, and less than 4 per cent of its steel.

India

The largest producer of iron and steel in the tropical world in 1975 was India. A number of factors have favoured the development of the Indian iron and steel industry:

1 the country possesses vast deposits of both iron ore and manganese ore;
2 it has large reserves of coal;
3 it has a large and expanding market for iron and steel products.

The earliest attempt to manufacture iron and steel by modern methods was in 1874. The first large iron and steel works, however, was that established in 1907 at Jamshedpur in the valley of the Subar-

Fig. 16.2 The Indian iron and steel industry, 1973

narekha river, by the Tata Iron and Steel Company (TISCO). The choice of location is very important in the development of an iron and steel industry, as both the raw materials and the finished products are bulky. Furthermore, at a modern steelworks large quantities of water are needed in the cooling process. The steel works at Jamshedpur obtain their water from the Subarnarekha river, and all the other raw materials which it needs are found within a radius of about 110 km. Iron ore is railed from the mines at Badampahar, Gurumahisani and Noamundi, which lie to the south of Jamshedpur; coking coal is brought from the Jharia coalfield in the Damodar valley to the north, while limestone is available at Panposh. The engineering industries of Calcutta, some 240 km to the east of Jamshedpur provide a large market for iron and steel.

Other iron and steel works were established by the Indian Iron and Steel Company (IISCO) at Kulti-Asanol in West Bengal, and by Mysore Iron and Steel Limited at Bhadravati in Mysore. The works at Bhadravati obtains its iron ore from the Baba Budan hills, and in the past depended upon locally produced charcoal for the fuel needed in the smelting process.

During the early 1950s, the works which were then in existence proved quite incapable of supplying all the iron and steel needed by India's development programmes, and large quantities of these essential materials had to be imported. During the First Five Year Plan period (1951–6), as a first step towards increasing the country's iron and steel production the existing works were extended and modernised. During the Second Five Year Plan period (1956–61), three new integrated iron and steel mills were established in India at Rourkela, Bhilai and Durgapur. All three of these mills are managed by the state-owned Hindustani Steel Limited, and began operation in 1959. Each of these plants specialises in certain types of products.

The Rourkela plant is located on the upper Brahmani river in the state of Orissa, and was built with financial and technical assistance from West Germany. Iron ore is mined quite close to Rourkela, but coking coal has to be railed some 280 km from the Bokaro coalfield in the Damodar valley. By products of the coke ovens at Rourkela are used in the manufacture of fertilisers.

The Bhilai plant is located to the east of Nagpur in the state of Madhya Pradesh, and was built with assistance from the USSR. The coking coal needed at the Bhilai plant has to be railed more than 600 km, but deposits of iron ore and limestone occur within easy reach. The Durgapur plant was built with British assistance, and is located in the valley of the Damodar river.

A fourth integrated iron and steel works is under construction at Bokaro. The first blast furnace was commissioned in 1972, and the first oxygen converter in 1974. The second stage of the Bokaro works is likely to be completed by 1977. The government has plans to build three more iron and steel works at Salem in Tamil Nadu, at Visakhapatnam in Andhar Pradesh, and near Hospet in Mysore.

Brazil

Brazil has the largest iron and steel industry in tropical America. Brazil has vast deposits of iron and manganese ores, particularly in the state of Minas Gerais. There are deposits of coal in the south of the country, but this is generally of poor quality, and has to be mixed with imported coal before it is suitable for coking. There is also a large and rapidly expanding market in Brazil for a wide range of iron and steel products.

The manufacture of iron in Brazil dates back to the middle of the sixteenth century, but at the start of the twentieth century the country's annual production of pig-iron only amounted to about 2 000 tonnes. During the first three decades of the twentieth century, private enterprises established a number of iron and steel works in the states of Minas Gerais and São Paulo. These were mainly small, and many of them depended on charcoal for fuel. The most important of the iron and steel works to be established during that period was the Companhia Siderúrgica Belgo-Mineira plant at Monlevade near Belo Horizonte, which began production during the mid 1930s. By 1940 Brazil's pig-iron production reached 185 000 tonnes, and its production of steel ingots 141 200 tonnes. Brazil still had at that time, however, to import some 70 per cent of its rolled steel products.

The real expansion of the Brazilian iron and steel industry dates from 1941, when the government established the Companhia Siderúrgica Nacional (Brazilian National Steel Company) for the purpose of building a large integrated iron and steel works. The site chosen for this new project was Volta Redonda, in the valley of the Paraíba river. Volta Redonda is situated on the railway line from São Paulo to Rio de Janeiro, both of which provide a large market for its products. An adequate supply of water for cooling purposes is provided by the Paraíba river. The most important source of iron ore for the Volta Redonda works is at present the Casa de Pedra deposit in the state of Minas Gerais. The limestone needed as flux comes from Arcos, Barroso and Campo Belo, which are also in Minas Gerais. Part of the coal consumed by Volta Redonda's coke ovens comes from the state of Santa Catarina, and part is imported from the United States. The Santa Catarina coal is shipped to the ports of Rio de Janeiro and Angra dos Reis, and then railed to Volta Redonda.

The works at Volta Redonda came into operation in 1946, but have since been considerably expanded. They are fully integrated, comprising coke ovens, blast furnaces, a steel plant, and a steel rolling mill. The rolling mill at Volta Redonda produces a wide range of products: these include rails for the country's railways; heavy plates for use in ship-building, the oil industry, railroad car manufacture, and the manufacture of storage tanks; plates and strips for use in the automotive, mechanical and electrical industries; tubular steel products, such as pipes; galvanised sheets for roofing and other purposes; tinplate for use in the canned food industry; and structural shapes for use in the construction industry. Large quantities of gas are produced by the coke ovens. Several by-products are extracted from this gas, including coal tars, creosotes, napthalene, light oils, and ammonium sulphate for fertilisers.

During the 1960s two new large integrated iron and steel works were established. These were the Usiminas works at Ipatinga in the valley of the Rio Doce, which came into operation in 1962; and the Cosipa works at Pičagueira near Santos, which came into operation in 1963. The Usiminas works was constructed by a Japanese steel consortium, although it is now largely owned by the Brazilian National Economic Development Bank. This bank also has a controlling interest in the Cosipa works. In 1973 two new state-owned mills came into operation. The first

of these, the Aço Finos Piratini works in the state of Rio Grande do Sul, differs from the other Brazilian iron and steel works in that it relies entirely upon Brazilian coking-coal for smelting. The other new mill, the Usina Siderúrgica do Bahía works in the state of Bahía, uses natural gas for smelting. The gas is brought to the works by a pipeline from the Petrobrás refinery in Salvador.

Several other iron and steel works are in the process of being constructed. These include one at Tubarão in the state of Espírito Santos, and another at Itaqui in the state of Maranhão. The Itaqui works will obtain its iron ore from the recently discovered deposits in the Carajá hills in the state of Pará. Both the Itaqui and the Tubarão works are located near to ports which are capable of handling ore-carriers.

Other tropical countries

Mexico is the third largest tropical producer of iron and steel. The modern Mexican iron and steel industry dates from 1903, when an integrated iron and steel works was established at Monterrey in the north-east of the country. The three essential raw materials needed by the iron and steel industry are all found in this part of Mexico. There are deposits of high-grade iron ore at Cerrado de Mercado near Durango; there is coking coal in the Sabinas Basin in the northern part of the state of Coahuila; while limestone for flux is available from the ranges of the Sierra Madre Oriental. In 1944 a Mexican company established a new iron and steel works at Monclava, near the coal deposits of the Sabinas Basin. The works at Monterrey and those at Monclava produce the bulk of Mexico's iron and steel.

Other tropical American countries with iron and steel industries are Venezuela, Colombia, and Peru. In Colombia iron and steel is produced at the Paz del Río plant at Belencito in the department of Boyaca. This plant was completed in 1954, and is situated at a height of more than 2 500 metres. The major raw materials used by the Paz del Río plant are all found within a radius of about 30 km. The large quantities of water needed by the plant are brought through a 29 km long pipeline from Lake Tota.

In 1958 an iron and steel works was established at the port of Chimbote in northern Peru. The iron ore used at Chimbote is shipped from southern Peru, and electricity is supplied by the Cañon del Pato hydro-electric power station on the Santa river.

In tropical Africa the only country with a well-developed iron and steel industry is Zimbabwe, although in recent years steel mills have been established in several other countries. These mills use either scrap metal, or imported steel ingots. Examples of such mills include the ones at Tema in Ghana, Jinja in Uganda, and Mombasa in Kenya.

Zimbabwe is fortunate in possessing not only high-grade iron ore and suitable limestone, but also excellent coking coal. The most important iron and steel works in Zimbabwe is that of the Rhodesian Iron and Steel Company (RISCO), which was established in 1948 at Redcliff near Que Que. The iron ore and the limestone needed by the Redcliff works are obtained locally, while coking coal is brought by rail from Wankie.

Exercises

1 Describe the distribution and nature of the manufacturing industry of any one tropical country.
2 What are the major obstacles to the further development of manufacturing in the tropical world?
3 Illustrating your answer with examples from the tropical world, discuss the major factors which influence the location of manufacturing industry.
4 Describe the extent to which manufacturing is at present developed in any one country in either West Africa or East Africa, and discuss the prospects for its further expansion.
5 Write a detailed account of India's iron and steel industry.
6 Assess the importance of raw materials as a locating factor, in the distribution of manufacturing industry in any one tropical country.
7 Write a detailed account of the manufacturing industry of Puerto Rico or Hong Kong or Venezuela.

Suggested reading

J. I. CLARKE, Ed.: *An Advanced Geography of Africa* – Chapter 11

R. T. COBB AND L. J. M. COLEBY: *Monsoon Lands* – Chapter 9

KWAMINA B. DICKSON AND GEORGE BENNEH: *A New Geography of Ghana* – Chapter 11

WILLIAM A. HANCE: *The Geography of Modern Africa* – Chapter 13

B. W. HODDER: *Economic Development in the Tropics* – Chapter 10

ALAN B. MOUNTJOY: *Industrialization and Underdeveloped Countries* – Chapters 4 and 5

A. M. O'CONNOR: *An Economic Geography of East Africa* – Chapter 10

A. M. O'CONNOR: *The Geography of Tropical African Development* – Chapter 5

R. B. OGENDO: *Industrial Geography of Kenya*

N. C. POLLOCK: *Studies in Emerging Africa* – Chapter 9

CHAPTER SEVENTEEN

The tourist industry

A: General

Since the end of the Second World War, there has been a tremendous increase in the number of people who travel abroad for holidays. This rapid growth of international tourism has been made possible by:

1 improvements in transport, particularly the development of air transport, which has made long-distance travel faster, easier and cheaper;
2 rising standards of living in many parts of the world, which has meant an increase in the number of people who can afford the time and the money to take holidays abroad.

Generally speaking, however, it is still only in the more highly developed countries of the world that any significant proportion of the population can afford to travel for pleasure. For the bulk of the inhabitants of the less developed countries, travel is still largely limited to movements undertaken for purposes of work.

The development of tourism in the tropical world

Although the vast majority of the inhabitants of the tropical world cannot themselves afford the luxury of foreign travel, in recent years several parts of the tropics have become popular as holiday resort areas. Most of the visitors to such areas come from the temperate lands, and in particular from the countries of North America and Western Europe, the majority of whose inhabitants enjoy a relatively high standard of living.

Tropical América

The tourist industry is of outstanding importance in several of the territories of the West Indies and also in Mexico. In some West Indian territories the annual number of visitors now far exceeds the local population. The United States Virgin Islands, for example, with a total population of 83 000, received 1 312 000 visitors in 1973.

The development of the Mexican tourist industry on a large scale began about 1938, with the completion of the highway from the town of Laredo on the United States border, to Mexico City. In 1974 Mexico received 3 361 000 visitors, a very large proportion of whom were from the USA. Factors which have favoured the large scale development of tourism in Mexico include:

1 the country's proximity to the USA;
2 the fact that a large part of the country has a pleasant climate throughout the year;
3 the existence of numerous fine beaches, particularly along the Pacific coast and in the Yucatan peninsula;
4 the varied mountain scenery of the interior;
5 the exotic folk culture of American Indian origin;
6 the abundance of relics of the ancient Mayan and Aztec civilisations, and the numerous fine examples of Spanish colonial architecture.

One of the most popular resort areas of Mexico is found along the south-west coast, which is sometimes referred to as the Mexican Riviera. This section of the coast, from Acapulco northwards to Mazatlan, is one of the world's foremost winter resort areas. The main holiday centres along this part of the coast are

Acapulco, Zihuantanejo, Puerto Vallarta, Manzanillo, Navidad, San Blas and Mazatlan. The major attractions of the Yucatan peninsula are its large Mayan archaeological sites, such as Uxmal and Chichen Itza. Large numbers of American tourists also visit the border towns, such as Tijuana.

Guatemala also has a growing tourist trade. Like its northern neighbour, Guatemala possesses magnificent mountain scenery, and has a great deal of Indian folk culture. In tropical South America, the tourist trade is already of some importance in Peru, which received 262 000 visitors in 1974. Peru possesses spectacular mountain scenery, and is also famous for its relics of Inca and Pre-Inca civilisations. Particularly noteworthy are the ruins of Machu Picchu near to Cuzco. The development of the Peruvian tourist industry is handicapped by the fact that Peru is relatively remote from the main tourist source areas, and hence expensive to reach.

Tropical Asia

The tourist trade of tropical Asia as a whole is relatively small, although countries such as India, Thailand and Hong Kong do attract considerable numbers of tourists. In 1975 Hong Kong, with a population of only 4,4 million, received 1,3 million visitors. The most numerous of the visitors to Hong Kong in 1975 were the Japanese, who accounted for 29 per cent of the total. Also important were visitors from Southeast Asia (25 per cent), the USA (14 per cent) and Australia and New Zealand (11 per cent).

Mention has already been made of Moslem and Hindu pilgrimages. In 1974–5 some 918 000 Moslem pilgrims from outside of Saudi Arabia visited the holy city of Mecca. Particularly numerous were pilgrims from Turkey, Yemen, Pakistan, Iraq, Iran and Nigeria.

In the past the development of the tourist industry in tropical Asia has been handicapped by the region's remoteness from the main tourist source areas in North America and Western Europe. In the future, however, Japan may well become an important source of tourists for parts of tropical Asia.

Tropical Pacific

The islands of the tropical Pacific probably possess as great a tourist potential as do those of the West Indies, but as yet most of them attract far fewer tourists. At present only Hawaii has a really large tourist industry. The number of visitors to Hawaii increased from 110 000 in 1955 to 2 786 000 in 1974. Tourism in now developing rapidly in several of the other territories of the tropical Pacific, notably in Fiji, Guam, French Polynesia and Western Samoa. The number of visitors to Fiji, for example, increased from 24 000 in 1963 to 186 000 in 1973. A high proportion of the visitors to Fiji are from Australia and New Zealand, which are much nearer to Fiji than is the USA. The major tourist attractions of the Pacific islands are their pleasant climate and numerous fine beaches.

Tropical Africa

Tropical Africa's tourist potential has as yet scarcely been touched, although the governments of several countries are now actively trying to promote tourism. So far, it is the countries of East Africa which have been the most successful in attracting visitors from abroad. Kenya already has a thriving tourist industry, and tourism is also of some importance in Tanzania.

Although Tanzania has possibly even greater natural attractions than Kenya, the Tanzanian tourist industry is as yet much less well developed. The number of visitors to Tanzania did, however, increase from 15 000 in 1962 to 118 000 in 1974. As in Kenya, the major tourist attractions of Tanzania are its abundance of wildlife, its mountain scenery, and its coastal beaches. At present, the area which is the most frequented by tourists, is the so-called Northern Circuit, centred on the town of Arusha. This includes the Mount Kilimanjaro and Mount Meru areas, the Serengeti National Park, and the Ngorongoro Crater. Many of the visitors to northern Tanzania used to travel to Arusha from Nariobi by road, and tended to regard a visit to Tanzania simply as an extension of their holiday in Kenya. In order to encourage more tourists to fly directly to northern Tanzania, the government built the new Kilimanjaro International Airport, which is located between the towns of Arusha and Moshi. The lack of adequate accommodation and transport facilities in the Arusha-Moshi area, however, has so far tended to discourage international airlines from using the new airport. In addition, the closure of the border with Kenya has meant that tourists no longer travel overland between the two countries.

Uganda also has a considerable tourist potential, although its tourist trade has only flourished intermittently. Visitors to Uganda are particularly attracted by the abundance and variety of its wildlife. The most important of Uganda's game sanctuaries are the Kabalega National Park (formerly Murchison Falls National Park), with its abundance of hippopotamus, crocodile and elephant; and the Ruwenzori National Park (formerly Queen Elizabeth National Park). In 1970 Uganda received some 80 000 visitors, but in 1972 unfavourable political conditions led to the government temporarily closing the country to tourists.

Ethiopia, with its fine mountain scenery and its rich culture, has a very considerable tourist potential, but the Ethiopian tourist industry is still in its infancy. Further south, Mozambique attracts a considerable number of visitors from the neighbouring Republic of South Africa, particularly during the southern winter. Most of the visitors to Mozambique arrive by road, and the most popular resorts are Beira and Maputo. Prospects for the development of tourism also seem to be fairly good in Malawi.

The islands of the Indian Ocean have a considerable tourist potential, particularly the Seychelles, with their palm-fringed beaches and mountainous interiors. In the past, poor communications have tended to retard the development of tourism in the Seychelles. This problem, however, has now largely been overcome, with the completion in 1971 of a new international airport on Mahé Island. The number of visitors to the Seychelles increased from about 1 000 in 1968 to 26 000 in 1974.

So far, tourism has been very little developed in West Africa. This part of the continent does not have the same great natural attractions as are to be found in East Africa. In West Africa wildlife is now fairly scarce, there are no great mountains, and the climate along the Guinea coast is not particularly congenial. West Africa's tourist attractions lay more in its colourful festivals, and in its places of historical interest. Although West Africa does have some good beaches, the heavy surf which is experienced along much of the coastline makes conditions less favourable for aquatic sports, than in East Africa. Several West African countries, particularly Senegal, Gambia and the Ivory Coast, however, are trying to promote their beaches, in order to attract visitors from Europe during the northern winter.

Factors influencing the development of tourism

Why has the tourist industry developed so rapidly in some parts of the tropical world, while other areas attract so few tourists? Several factors play an important role in the development of tourism, although their relative importance varies from place to place.

Climate
High temperatures and abundant sunshine throughout the year are among the main inducements for people from the temperate lands to spend a holiday within the tropics. Not all parts of the tropical world, however, are equally favoured in this respect. Climatically, the islands of the West Indies and the tropical Pacific, are particularly attractive to visitors from North America and Europe. In those areas, although temperatures are high throughout the year, they are rarely excessively so. Furthermore, the rainfall tends to occur in heavy downpours of relatively short duration, and there is a high incidence of sunshine at all times of the year.

Beaches
Many visitors to the tropics like to spend a large part of their holiday beside the sea. Consequently they tend to be particularly attracted to those coastal areas where there are good beaches, and where conditions are favourable for such aquatic sports as swimming, water-skiing, surf-riding and sailing. Fine sandy beaches, and warm clear waters, are among the main tourist attractions of the islands of the West Indies and the tropical Pacific. In East Africa, both Kenya and Tanzania possess a coastline fringed with fine beaches, and in this respect they have an advantage over land-locked Uganda.

Scenery
Dramatic mountain and coastal scenery also hold great appeal for some tourists. Many of the islands of the West Indies and the tropical Pacific are scenically very attractive. The scenery of East Africa is generally much more varied than that of West Africa, and this is one of the reasons why East Africa has been able to

attract more tourists. The tourist may also be attracted by picturesque local customs, clothing, and festivals; by antiquities; and by wildlife. For example, the magnificent ruins of the ancient Aztec and Mayan civilisations rank among Mexico's major tourist attractions. Tourists are attracted to India by such famous buildings as the Taj Mahal at Agra, and the great Hindu temples at Varanasi (formerly Banaras). Undoubtedly, the abundance of wildlife is East Africa's greatest single attraction for the tourist. In this respect East Africa has a great advantage over West Africa where big game is now scarce.

Accessibility

However attractive an area may be in other respects, it is not likely to develop into a major tourist resort, unless it can be reached fairly easily and cheaply. Those parts of the tropical world which are situated within relatively easy reach of North America and Western Europe, have a decided advantage over those which are more remote. The fact that the islands of the West Indies at present attract more tourists than do those of the tropical Pacific, can largely be attributed to their greater proximity to the mainland of North America. That Hawaii has a far larger tourist trade than any of the other territories of the tropical Pacific, can also largely be attributed to the fact that Hawaii is much closer to the west coast of mainland USA. Because of this greater proximity, the cost of air travel from San Francisco to Hawaii is less than one-third of the cost to some of the other territories of the tropical Pacific. One of the major obstacles to the growth of tourism in the tropical regions of Africa, Asia and South America, is their distance from the major tourist source areas.

The availability of accommodation

In order to be able to attract tourists in large numbers, an area must be able to offer adequate accommodation. In parts of the tropical world, notably in many African countries, the shortage of suitable accommodation has seriously handicapped the growth of the tourist industry. In other areas, particularly in many of the West Indian territories, there has been a considerable expansion of tourist accommodation in recent years. In Jamaica, for example, the number of beds available to tourists was increased from about 3 300 in 1955, to almost 22 000 in 1974, as a result of the construction of new tourist hotels, resort cottages, apartments, etc.

The political climate

Political stability favours the development of the tourist industry, as the average tourist tends to be easily frightened away from an area by any suggestion of violence or unrest. In recent years, in some parts of the tropical world unfavourable political conditions have hampered the development of tourism.

The economic importance of tourism

The tourist industry contributes to the economy of resort areas in several ways. In particular it:

1 provides a means of earning foreign exchange;
2 creates employment.

The money spent in a country by foreign visitors falls into the category of invisible exports. In some tropical countries receipts from tourism are now the main source of foreign exchange and play an important role in helping to offset the unfavourable balance of visible trade. Admittedly, not all the money spent by tourists remains within the country. In some resort areas large foreign loans have had to be obtained for the building of hotels and other tourist amenities, and some of the tourist earnings simply go towards the repayment of these loans. Also, some of the items which are consumed by the tourist usually have to be imported.

The contribution of tourism to the local economy is particularly significant in many of the territories of the West Indies, but it is also of importance in several other areas. For example, in 1974 visitors to Mexico were estimated to spend US$ 2 215 million. During the same year, Mexico's visible exports were valued at US$ 3 420 million, and her visible imports at US$ 6 504 million. Visitors to Fiji were estimated to have spent F$ 60,6 million in 1974. During the same year Fiji's visible exports earned F$ 95,4 million, while her visible imports cost F$ 219,3 million.

In the major resort areas, the tourist industry is also very important as a provider of employment. Not only is a lot of direct employment provided in the hotels and guest houses which cater to tourists, but much additional work is provided in other spheres, such as in transport and entertainment. It is generally considered that money spent by tourists has a very wide circulation, and that many people eventually feel the benefit of it.

Although the tourist industry makes an important contribution to the economy in several parts of the tropical world, it should be noted that the tourist is fickle. A flourishing tourist industry which has taken years to build up can disappear almost overnight, as a result of unfavourable political developments, economic recession in the tourist source areas, outbreaks of disease, natural disasters, etc. Thus, any economy which places too much reliance upon the tourist industry is a singularly vulnerable one.

In addition to its influence on the economy of the receiving area, which is generally regarded as being beneficial, the growth of tourism has been responsible for bringing together peoples whose life style is very different. Not everyone has been happy about the results of this intermixing. Indeed, in some countries it is claimed that the influx of large numbers of relatively wealthy tourists has tended to bring about a breakdown in the traditional values and way of life of the local inhabitants.

B: The West Indian tourist industry

The growth of tourism

The West Indian tourist industry began towards the end of the nineteenth century, when a few wealthy North Americans and Europeans started to take

Fig. 17.1 The number of visitors to the West Indies in 1969

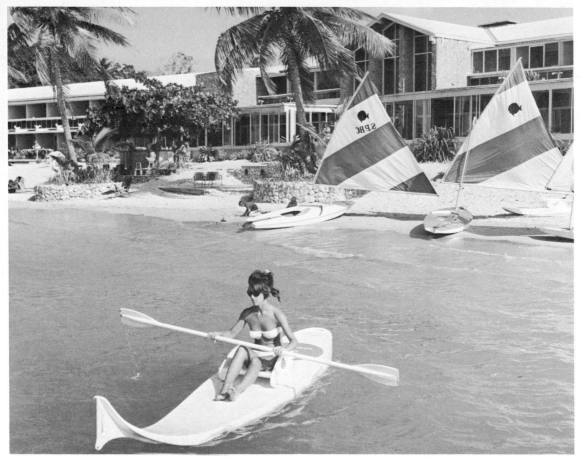

Tourist at beach hotel in Ocho Rios on the north coast of Jamaica. Visitors to the West Indies are particularly attracted by the combination of sun, sea and sand.

winter holidays in the Bahamas and Jamaica. During the early part of the twentieth century the number of visitors increased slowly, and between the two world wars several other islands, such as Barbados and Curacao, were able to build up a modest tourist trade. The real development of the West Indies as a major holiday resort area, however, did not begin until after the end of the Second World War. Since 1950 the number of visitors to the West Indies has increased tremendously, as Table 98 suggests.

In 1974 there were more than 6 million visitors to the region as a whole. Some territories, however, were far more popular with tourists than others, as Table 99 shows.

Table 98 Number of visitors to selected resort areas, 1950–74 (thousands)

Resort area	1950	1955	1960	1965	1970	1974	1974 as % of 1950
Jamaica	75	122	227	317	415	531	708
Bahamas (Nassau)	45	132	306	495	731	926	2 058
Puerto Rico	65	142	389	703	1 088	1 339	2 060

Table 99 Number of visitors to selected resort areas, 1974

Resort area	No. of visitors (thousands)	Total population (thousands)	Visitors per local inhabitant
Antigua	70	70	1,0
Aruba	105	62	1,7
Bahamas	1 388	197	7,0
Barbados	231	244	0,9
Bonaire	11	8	1,4
Cayman Is.	53	11	4,8
Curacao	109	155	0,7
Cuba	15	9 090	0,0
Dominican Rep.	250	4 562	0,1
Grenada	15	96	0,2
Haiti	209	4 514	0,0
Jamaica	526	1 998	0,3
Puerto Rico	1 339	3 031	0,4
St. Lucia	52	107	0,5
St. Vincent	21	107	0,2
UK Virgin Is.	59	11	5,3
US Virgin Is.	1 312 (1973)	83	15,8

Factors favouring the growth of tourism

A variety of factors have contributed to the rapid growth of the West Indian tourist industry, and the more important of these are discussed below.

One of the most important factors which has favoured the growth of tourism is the region's proximity to the main population centres of the eastern United States and Canada. Because of the high living standards which they enjoy, a larger proportion of the inhabitants of those areas can afford to travel abroad for holidays than is the case in any other major part of the world. Because of the relatively short distances involved, air fares to the West Indies are appreciably lower than to most other tourist resort areas, as Table 100 shows.

Although the West Indies are equally close to the northern parts of the mainland of South America, the number of holiday visitors from that area is relatively small. This is partly because the total population is much smaller than that of eastern North America, and also because living standards in South America are generally lower.

For the tourist, one of the most attractive features about the West Indian islands is their climate. Weather conditions are usually particularly pleasant

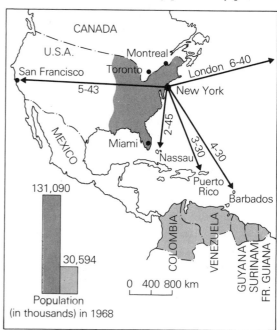

Fig. 17.2 Flying times from New York (hours and minutes)

256

Table 100 Air fares (economy class) from eastern USA in 1977

From	To	Return fare (US$)
New York	West Indies	
	Antigua	288
	Bahamas (Nassau)	242
	Barbados	466
	Jamaica	334
Miami	West Indies	
	Bahamas (Nassau)	64
	Jamaica	200
New York	South America	
	Lima	762
	Rio de Janeiro	984
New York	Africa	
	Accra	1 210
	Nairobi	1 606
New York	Pacific Islands	
	Guam	896
	Hawaii	519
New York	Asia	
	Bangkok	1 832
	Delhi	1 800
New York	Europe	
	Athens	978
	London	626

between December and April, when it is slightly cooler than during the rest of the year, and also rather drier. It is at this time of year that weather conditions are usually at their worst in the areas from which most of the tourists come.

Most of the West Indian islands have excellent beaches, some of them being of pure, white coral sand. The surrounding waters are warm throughout the year, and in many places they are also remarkably clear. Visitors to the West Indies above all enjoy the combination of sun, sea and sand.

While many of the tourist visitors to the West Indies spend much of their time between the beach and the sea, several of the islands also offer magnificent scenery in the interior. This is particularly the case in the more mountainous territories, such as Dominica, Haiti, Jamaica and St. Lucia.

With a few exceptions, the territories of the West Indies have in recent times shown a high degree of political stability. The stable and democratic form of government enjoyed throughout most of the region has certainly been a factor which has favoured the development of tourism. It is noticeable that in territories such as Cuba, the Dominican Republic and Haiti, which have from time to time been subject to political unrest, the tourist trade has flourished only intermittently, and has not shown the same steady growth that has occurred elsewhere. Although at one time Cuba had a flourishing tourist industry, this almost completely disappeared, when the USA broke off diplomatic relations with Cuba in 1961.

Method of arrival

The holiday visitors to the West Indies can be divided into two main categories:

1 passengers on cruise ships;
2 stop-over visitors.

In the early days of the West Indian tourist industry, most of the visitors to the region arrived on cruise ships. Although this is no longer the case, the cruise ship trade is still important in several territories. Most of the cruises start from ports in the USA, although some start in Europe. A typical cruise from the USA lasts between one and three weeks, with several different islands being visited during that period. The cruise ship usually stays one day in each of the ports which it visits, allowing the passengers to go ashore for a few hours of shopping and sight-seeing. During the night the ship moves to its next port of call. The islands which are the most visited by cruise ships are generally those which have the best docking facilities, and also adequate facilities for entertaining the cruise ship passengers.

In many West Indian territories, stop-over visitors are now far more numerous than cruise ship visitors. Although a few stop-over visitors arrive by sea, the vast majority travel by air. The average length of stay varies from about three to four days in some territories, to about two weeks in others.

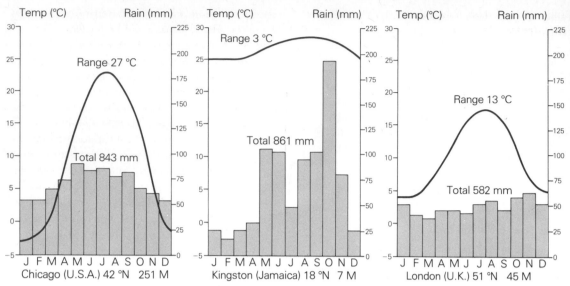

Fig. 17.3 The temperature and rainfall regimes of Chicago, London and Kingston

A calypso band welcomes a cruise ship bringing tourists to Port Antonio, Jamaica

Table 101 Method of arrival in selected resort areas, 1969 (percentage of total)

Resort area	Stop-over visitors		Passengers on cruise ships
	By air	By sea	
Antigua	67	5	28
Barbados	57	1	42
Cayman Is.	94	—	6
Curacao	51	1	48
Grenada	39	4	57
Jamaica	67	9	24
Martinique	20	—	80
Montserrat	90	4	6
Puerto Rico	90	—	10
St. Lucia	35	4	61
US Virgin Is.	71	12	17

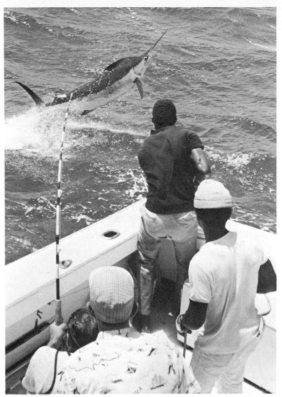

Game fishing is an important tourist attraction in some parts of the tropical world. Hooking a marlin off Port Antonio, Jamaica.

Seasonal distribution

Tourism is now a year-round business in the West Indies. There are, however, two periods when tourists are particularly numerous, a long winter season from December to April, and a shorter summer season in July and August. The popularity of the winter season is largely explained by the fact that it is at that time of year that there is the greatest difference in temperature between the West Indies and the areas from which most of the tourists come. During the winter season, however, most tourist hotels charge appreciably higher rates than during the rest of the year, and for this reason the less affluent tourist tends to prefer the summer season.

The origin of the tourists

By far the greatest number of tourist visitors to the region as a whole come from the mainland of North America. Residents of the USA constitute more than two-thirds of the total arrivals in many of the major resort areas, including the Bahamas, Jamaica, Puerto Rico, and the United States Virgin Islands. In 1974, for example, 78 per cent of the visitors to Jamaica were from the USA. Canadians are also frequent visitors to several of the West Indian territories.

Because of the greater travel costs involved, visitors from Europe tend to be much less numerous. The more southerly islands, such as Aruba and Curacao, attract some visitors from the mainland of South America.

Table 102 Jamaica, stop-over visitor arrivals by country of origin, 1974

Country of origin	Percentage of total
USA	78,4
Canada	8,6
United Kingdom	4,0
Europe	2,3
Commonwealth Caribbean	2,9
Latin America	1,9
Other countries	1,9
Total stop-overs	100,0

The economic importance of tourism

The tourist industry now makes a very important contribution to the economy of the region as a whole, although its relative importance does vary a great deal from one territory to another. In several territories, including the Bahamas, the British Virgin Islands, the Cayman Islands, and the United States Virgin Islands, the tourist industry forms the mainstay of the local economy. Tourism also plays a very important although lesser role in the economic life of a large number of the other territories. Even many of the territories which have in the past attracted few holiday visitors now feel that the development of the tourist industry offers them the quickest means of strengthening their economy. This is particularly so in the case of many of the smaller territories, which are generally lacking in mineral resources, and in which the prospects for the development of manufacturing industry are poor.

The number of visitors to the individual territories of the West Indies varies considerably, but numbers alone do not give any true indication of the importance of tourism to the local economy. Reference must also be made to the size of the local population. Thus, although in 1974 Haiti received a greater number of visitors than did the British Virgin Islands, the number of visitors per local inhabitant was very much smaller.

Even more important than the number of visitors a territory receives, is the amount of money which these visitors spend. This is dependent upon a number of factors, but particularly upon the average length of stay. For example, cruise ship visitors generally make a smaller contribution to the local economy than do stop-over visitors, because they stay for a shorter period of time, and also because they are generally accommodated aboard their cruise ship. Thus, those territories in which cruise ship visitors form a large proportion of the total visitors, can be expected to gain less economic benefit from tourism, than those in which stop-over visitors predominate.

In many West Indian territories earnings from tourism now play a very important role in the balance of payments situation. In 1974 Barbados was estimated to have earned EC$ 156,6 million from tourism. During the same year visible exports earned EC$ 172,3 million, while visible imports cost EC$ 418,3 million. In 1974 visitors to Jamaica were estimated to have spent J$ 121,2 million. During the same year Jamaica's visible exports were valued at J$ 653, 1 million, and visible imports at J$ 850,8 million.

The tourist industry also provides a great deal of employment in many of the territories of the West Indies. This is of particular importance in the more overcrowded territories such as Barbados, where unemployment is a very serious problem. In 1971 the tourist industry was estimated to provide jobs for about 12 000 people in Barbados, out of a total working population of 85 000.

Tourism also makes other less obvious contributions to the economy of the West Indies. In some instances it has provided a valuable stimulus to local agriculture and fisheries, as the tourist hotels provide a ready market for fresh vegetables, fruits, flowers, dairy produce, fish, etc. Local handicraft industries have also benefited from the growth of tourism. The manufacture of handicrafts in sisal, straw and wood has become important in several territories, notably in the Bahamas, Haiti and Jamaica.

C: The Kenyan tourist industry

The growth of tourism

Kenya has the best developed tourist industry of any country in tropical Africa. The number of holiday visitors arriving in Kenya increased from 6 000 in 1952, to 291 000 in 1975. In the past, only the affluent few could afford the high cost of travel from North America or Europe to Kenya. More recently, however, the development of low-cost charter flights and package tours has made it possible for a much larger number of people to visit Kenya on holiday.

The government of Kenya is now taking an active part in the development of the country's tourist trade. Many main roads have been greatly improved for the benefit of tourists, and access roads have been built in parks and game reserves. The Kenya Tourist Development Corporation (KTDC) has taken a financial interest in several hotels in the Nairobi and coastal areas, and also in several game lodges. It has a

SUDAN

ETHIOPIA

UGANDA

To Addis Ababa

Lake Rudolf Sport fishing

To Kampala

SOMALI
REPUBLIC

Lake
Victoria

□ Kisumu

10

9

11

8

7

5

4

16

Nairobi —
Main centre of tourist
industry in East Africa.
Many hotels becoming important
as international conference centre

3

1

2

□ Embakasi international
airport — most tourists arrive here

To Serengeti
National Park

TANZANIA

17

To Arusha

12

13

Lamu — Developing
as tourist centre

Malindi — Several beach
hotels
sport fishing

15

14

Mombasa — Many beach hotels,
both north and south
of town
sport fishing

To Tanga

National Parks and
game reserves

1 Nairobi National Park
2 Olorgesailie National Park
3 Masai Mara Game Reserve
4 Olambwe Valley Game Reserve
5 Lake Nakuru National Park
6 Mount Elgon National Park
7 Aberdare National Park
8 Mount Kenya National Park
9 Samburu Game Reserve and
  Buffalo Springs Game Reserve
10 Marsabit National Reserve
11 Meru National Park
12 Tsavo National Park East
13 Tsavo National Park West
14 Shimba Hills National Reserve
15 Malindi Marine National Park and
   Watamu Marine National Park
16 Ol Doinyo Sapuk National Park
17 Masai Amboseli Game Reserve

○   Game lodges

●   Airfields suitable for light aircraft (only some shown)

□   Airports used by East African Airways

■   Main centres of tourist industry

——— Roads

—·—·— International boundaries

0 20 40 60 80 km

Fig. 17.4 Tourism in Kenya — mid-1970s

Table 103 Number of holiday visitors arriving in Kenya, 1952–75

Year	1952	1957	1962	1967	1972	1973	1974	1975
No. (thousands)	6	10	16	133	328	292	277	291

share in a local charter airline, and has undertaken the construction of a 'traditional' village on the outskirts of Nairobi. The KTDC spends a considerable amount of money each year on official publicity intended to promote Kenya's tourist industry, maintaining Tourist Offices in London, Frankfurt, Stockholm and New York.

The main tourist attractions

The major attractions of Kenya are the great abundance of wildlife, and coastal beaches, the fine mountain scenery in the interior of the country, and the generally pleasant and healthy climate.

In order to preserve the country's wildlife, extensive parts of Kenya have been set aside as wildlife sanctuaries. In 1973 the country had 10 National Parks, and also two National Reserves and three Game Reserves. There are plans for the creation of new parks, and also for the extension of some of the existing ones. Most of the parks and reserves are particularly noted for their abundance of large animal life, such as elephant, rhinoceros, hippopotamus, lion, leopard, cheetah, zebra, giraffe, buffalo and many species of antelope. The Lake Nakuru National

The major tourist attraction of East Africa is the abundance of wild life

262

Climbing Mount Kenya. The mountains of East Africa are a great attraction for the hardier tourists.

Park, however, is more noted for its abundance of wild bird life, and in particular for its vast flocks of flamingo. On the coast, the Malindi Marine National Park and the Watamu Marine National Park are noted for their beautiful coral reefs, where more than 200 species of tropical fish can be seen in the clear, warm waters.

Wildlife sanctuaries, of course, have to compete with the demands of agriculture for land. The rapid growth of population at present taking place in Kenya, is leading to an increase in the demand for land for agricultural purposes. Because of this, it may in future become difficult to preserve all the present wildlife sanctuaries. Fortunately Kenya's parks and reserves are mainly located in those parts of the country which receive a fairly low and unreliable rainfall, and which consequently are not very attractive to the cultivator.

The climate of Kenya is varied. Along the coast temperatures are high throughout the year, with mean monthly temperatures in Mombasa ranging from 24°C in July to 28°C in March. In the highlands temperatures are modified by altitude, mean monthly temperatures in Nairobi ranging from 15°C in July to 19°C in March. In most parts of Kenya there is an abundance of sunshine throughout the year. Mombasa, for example, has a mean of 6,9 hours of sunshine per day in July, and 9,2 hours per day in February.

There are many fine beaches along the coast of Kenya. A large part of Kenya's coastline is protected by fringing coral reefs, which are situated about half a kilometre offshore. Because the beaches are generally situated on the landward side of lagoons which are protected from the open sea by the reefs, the water is rarely rough. In addition to the usual aquatic sports, the coast of Kenya is noted for its excellent big-game fishing.

In the interior of Kenya there is some very striking scenery, particularly in the Mount Kenya area, and in the Rift Valley. Mount Kenya offers excellent walking and climbing to the hardier tourist.

The nature of the tourist trade

The origin of the tourists

Table 104 shows that in 1975 about three tenths of the holiday visitors to Kenya were from other African

Table 104 Holiday visitors departures by country of residence, 1975

Country	Percentage of total
Europe	47,9
United Kingdom	12,7
West Germany	11,9
Switzerland	6,2
Italy	5,2
France	3,1
Others	8,8
North America	14,5
USA	12,6
Canada	1,9
Africa	30,0
Tanzania	15,3
Uganda	5,9
Zambia	2,2
Others	6,6
Other areas	7,6

countries, particularly from the neighbouring countries of Tanzania and Uganda. Almost half of the holiday visitors were from Europe, particularly from the United Kingdom and West Germany, while about one-eighth of the total were from the USA.

Method of arrival

The vast majority of visitors from outside of Africa travel to and from Kenya by air. A large number of international airlines operate regular scheduled flights to Embakasi Airport on the outskirts of Nairobi, and in addition many visitors arrive by special charter flights. The majority of holiday visitors from neighbouring African countries arrive by road, often travelling in their own vehicles.

Distribution of tourism

The majority of the overseas visitors to Kenya divide their holiday between the capital city of Nairobi, the

beach hotels along the coast, and the game lodges in the parks and reserves. In 1975, 42 per cent of Kenya's available tourist hotel accommodation was in Nairobi, and 38 per cent was in the coastal area. Along the coast, the main tourist hotels are centred around Mombasa and Malindi. Further north, the old town of Lamu, with its numerous old mosques and fine beaches, is of growing importance as a tourist centre. Most of the game parks and reserves now have well-equipped lodges, where the tourist can view the game in considerable comfort.

While they are in Kenya, many of the overseas visitors travel by road, either in minibuses operated by the various tour companies, or in vehicles which they hire and drive themselves. Some of the wealthier visitors charter light aircraft, to transport them to and from the more remote parts of the country. Tourism is now an all year round business in Kenya, although the period from December to March is generally the most popular. This corresponds with

The remains of Mayan and Aztec civilisations are one of Mexico's greatest tourist attractions.

264

the climatically most unpleasant period in the main tourist source areas.

The importance of tourism to Kenya

In 1974 tourists were estimated to spend K£ 26,5 million in Kenya, thus making tourism the country's third largest earner of foreign exchange. In 1974 Kenya's leading visible export was coffee which earned K£ 35,2 million, followed by petroleum products with K£ 31,7 million.

As in other resort areas, the tourist industry of Kenya provides much employment. In addition to those who work in hotels and lodges, many people are employed in the transport of tourists, while others work in the game parks. Tourism has also done a great deal to stimulate the local handicraft industry, which has expanded greatly in recent years.

The entrance fees paid by tourists help towards the upkeep of the game parks. Indeed, the fact that wild life is such a major tourist attraction, is an important factor in ensuring its conservation.

Exercises

1 With reference to actual examples, discuss the factors which have influenced the development of the tourist industry in the tropical world.
2 Which parts of the tropical world at present attract large numbers of tourists? Suggest reasons why the tourist industry has become more highly developed in some parts of the tropical world than in others.
3 Analyse the contribution made by the tourist industry to the economic life of the West Indies.
4 Write a detailed account of the tourist industry of Kenya.

Sources of statistics

Information on tourism can be obtained from the various publications of Barclays Bank International Limited. These include *Barclays Overseas Review* (monthly); *Barclays Overseas Surveys* (annual); and the Economic Surveys for individual countries. Statistical information can also be obtained from *Whitaker's Almanack*, *The Statesman's Yearbook* and *The Europa Yearbook: A World Survey*.

CHAPTER EIGHTEEN

International trade

A: General

The trading which takes place between different countries is known as international trade or external trade.

Visible trade

If this trading involves the movement of goods it is known as visible trade, as these items can be seen and recorded as they cross frontiers. The goods which a country sells to other countries are known as its visible exports, while the goods which it buys from other countries are its visible imports. The difference between the value of a country's visible exports and that of its visible imports, is known as its balance of visible trade. If a country earns more money from selling its goods to other countries than it spends on buying goods from them, it is said to have a favourable balance of visible trade. If, on the other hand, a country spends more on its visible imports than it earns from its visible exports, it is said to have an unfavourable or adverse balance of visible trade.

Table 105 shows that in 1963 Guyana earned £36,4 million from the sale of goods to other countries, but spent only £24,5 million on purchasing goods from them. Thus in 1963 Guyana had a highly favourable balance of visible trade, its surplus for that year being £11,9 million. In 1970, on the other hand, visible imports cost Guyana £55,9 million, while visible exports only earned £55,8 million. Thus in 1970 Guyana had a slightly unfavourable balance of trade, its deficit being only £0,1 million. Calculate Guyana's balance of visible trade during each of the other years which are listed in the table.

Invisible trade

The fact that a country has an unfavourable balance of visible trade does not necessarily mean that it is falling into debt, as the transfer of goods is only one aspect of the international balance of payments. A country receives payments not only for the goods which it sells to other countries, but also for the services which it renders them. The services which are performed for people of other countries, and for which payment is received, are known as invisible exports. A country also has to pay for the services

Table 105 Guyana's visible trade, 1963–70 (£ million)

Year	1963	1964	1965	1966	1967	1968	1969	1970
Exports	36,4	33,9	34,7	38,8	41,1	45,1	50,4	55,8
Imports	24,5	31,2	37,3	42,1	46,9	45,7	49,1	55,9
Balance	+11,9	?	?	?	?	?	?	−0,1

Table 106 Visible trade of selected countries, 1973 (US$ million)

Country	Imports	Exports	Balance	Exports as % of imports
Tropical Africa				
Angola	542	778	+236	144
Benin	112	45	−67	40
Chad	82	38	−44	46
Gabon	133	287	+154	216
Ivory Coast	710	857	+147	121
Liberia	193	319	+126	165
Mali	105	57	−48	54
Malaŵi	142	96	−46	68
Mauritania	128	155	+27	121
Nigeria	1 862	3 462	+1 600	186
Senegal	362	195	−167	54
Sierra Leone	158	132	−26	84
Togo	101	61	−40	60
Zaïre	604	850	+246	141
Zambia	532	1 142	+610	215
Tropical America				
Barbados	170	54	−116	32
Brazil	6 848	6 199	−649	91
Colombia	1 062	1 164	+102	110
Ecuador	532	561	+29	105
Guadeloupe	202	65	−137	32
Mexico	4 146	2 452	−1 694	59
Netherlands Antilles	1 600	1 376	−224	86
Trinidad and Tobago	787	694	−93	88
Tropical Asia				
Brunei	129	335	+206	260
India	3 066	2 946	−120	96
Indonesia	2 347	3 211	+864	137
Laos	57	5	−52	9
Sri Lanka	421	389	−32	92
Thailand	2 046	1 531	−515	75
Vietnam (S.)	618	59	−559	10
West Malaysia	2 086	2 460	+374	118
Tropical Pacific				
Fiji	205	79	−126	39
French Polynesia	221	19	−202	9
Papua New Guinea	297	512	+215	172
Western Samoa	21	6	−15	29

Table 107 The export trade of selected countries, 1974

Country	Major export items as % of total exports (by value)
Tropical Africa	
Burundi	Coffee 84; hides and skins 4; cotton 4
Cameroon	Cocoa 34; coffee 21; timber 11; aluminium 5
C.A.R. (1973)	Cotton 63; meat and live animals 14
Gabon (1973)	Petroleum 41; timber 41; manganese 15
Gambia	Groundnuts and products 81
Liberia	Iron ore 66; rubber 16; diamonds 7
Malawi	Tobacco 39; tea 17; sugar 9; groundnuts 5
Mauritania (1972)	Iron ore 69; fish and preparations 11; copper 10
Mauritius	Sugar and molasses 89; clothing 2
Nigeria	Petroleum 93; cocoa 3
Senegal	Phosphates and fertilisers 31; groundnuts and products 31; fish 7
Sierra Leone	Diamonds 61; iron ore 10; palm kernels 6; cocoa 6; bauxite 3
Sudan	Cotton and products 67; groundnuts 11; sesame 9; gum arabic 6
Zaïre	Copper 63; cobalt 5; diamonds 4; coffee 4; oil palm products 4
Zambia (1973)	Copper 94; zinc 2
Tropical America	
Bolivia (1973)	Tin 53; petroleum 15
Colombia	Coffee 46; cotton 7; petroleum and products 7
Dominican Rep.	Sugar and molasses 51; cocoa 7; coffee 6; tobacco 6
Ecuador	Petroleum 59; bananas 11; cocoa 10; coffee 6
Guyana	Sugar, rum and molasses 51; bauxite and alumina 33; rice 8
Honduras	Bananas 32; coffee 18; timber 17
Jamaica	Bauxite and alumina 74; sugar, rum and molasses 5; bananas 2
Netherlands Antilles (1973)	Petroleum products 95; chemicals 2
Panama	Petroleum products 42; bananas 22; sugar 14; fish 8
Trinidad & Tobago	Petroleum and products 90; chemicals 3
Tropical Asia	
Brunei (1972)	Petroleum and products 99
Indonesia	Petroleum and products 50; timber 18; rubber 12
Khmer Rep. (1973)	Rubber 93; beans 4
Philippines	Sugar 27; coconut products 21; copper 14; timber 10
Sri Lanka	Tea 39; rubber 21; coconut products 12
Tropical Pacific	
Fiji	Sugar and molasses 72; gold 9; coconut oil 11
Papua New Guina	Copper 55; coffee 10; coconut products 6; cocoa 5

performed for it by the people of other countries, and these are known as invisible imports. There are several sources of invisible earnings and payments, important ones being:

1 foreign travel;
2 remittances from migrant workers;
3 government transactions;
4 international transportation;

5 insurance;
6 income on investments.

In those tropical countries which have become important as holiday resort areas, the tourist industry is an important source of invisible earnings. Although the inhabitants of such countries themselves spend a certain amount of money on foreign travel, this is generally only a fraction of the amount spent by foreign visitors to these countries. In 1974, for example, Jamaicans spent J$ 18,8 million on foreign travel, while visitors to Jamaica spent J$ 121,2 million in the island. Thus in 1974 Jamaica had a favourable balance of J$ 102,4 million on foreign travel. In several tropical countries the money sent or taken home by migrant workers forms another important source of invisible earnings. These remittances are particularly important to the economic life of several of the smaller West Indian islands. They are also important to the economies of some of the countries of tropical Africa, particularly to Malawi, Mozambique and Upper Volta. Many tropical countries also receive substantial sums of money in the form of aid, from the governments of the more highly developed countries of the world.

Of course, tropical countries also have to pay for the services performed for them by people of other countries. Many of them, for example, have to make substantial payments to foreign shipping and air transport companies for the carriage of goods and passengers. Although some tropical countries now have their own fleets of merchant vessels and their own airlines, many others still depend largely upon the ships of other nations, for the transport of their bulky overseas exports and imports. Many tropical countries also have to make payments to foreign banking and insurance companies for their services. Countries in which a great deal of foreign capital has been invested, have to pay interest and dividends on this capital.

The balance of trade

A great many countries of the tropical world have an unfavourable balance of visible trade in most years. The countries which regularly have highly favourable balances of visible trade are for the most part the ones which are rich in minerals, such as Gabon, Mauritania, Nigeria, West Malaysia, Venezuela, Zaïre and Zambia.

Export trade

With very few exceptions the export trade of tropical countries is made up almost entirely of primary commodities, with agricultural products and minerals being of particular importance. In only a few countries, such as Hong Kong and Puerto Rico, do manufactured goods form a substantial part of the export trade. Furthermore, as Table 107 suggests, most tropical countries depend very heavily upon a limited number of major export items.

Import trade

As already noted in Chapter 16, manufacturing industry is not as yet very highly developed in most of the countries of the tropical world, and because of this fact the import trade of these countries is largely composed of a wide range of manufactured goods. Important items imported into most countries include textiles, clothing, footwear, manufactured metal, machinery, electrical equipment, motor vehicles, chemicals and paper products.

Most tropical countries do not produce either petroleum or coal, and consequently they have to import mineral fuels. Some countries have their own refineries and import crude petroleum, while others import refined petroleum products.

A number of countries are also obliged to import large quantities of foodstuffs. This is particularly the case in those countries where in the past excessive emphasis has been placed on the production of export crops, at the expense of the production of local food crops. Table 108 shows the composition of the import trade of Zambia and Jamaica.

The direction of trade

Except in the case of Southeast Asia and East Africa, trade between the various countries of the tropical world is at present on a very small scale. Many

Table 108 The import trade of Zambia and Jamaica by main commodity group, 1973

Commodity group	% of total imports (by value)	
	Zambia	Jamaica
Food & live animals	7,0	19,3
Beverage & tobacco	0,3	1,4
Inedible crude materials	1,6	4,1
Mineral fuels, lubricants etc.	9,6	10,9
Animal & vegetable oils & fats	1,2	1,0
Chemicals	10,1	9,8
Manufactured goods, classified by materials	22,3	23,3
Machinery & transport equipment	40,1	22,9
Miscellaneous manufactured goods	7,3	7,3
Miscellaneous items	0,5	0,2

tropical countries have similar primary commodities to sell, and need to buy a similar range of manufactured goods. Consequently much of their trade is with the highly industrialised nations of the temperate lands.

Trade problems

The fact that the export trade of most tropical countries is largely composed of a limited range of primary commodities has often been the cause of economic instability, as the world market price of ·these commodities has tended to fluctuate sharply over short periods of time. This has been particularly so in the case of such commodities as sisal, for which synthetic substitutes have been developed. In the case of commodities such as coffee, overproduction has often been the cause of falling prices.

In recent years the world demand for manufactured goods has tended to increase more rapidly than the demand for most primary commodities. Because of this fact, recent trends in the pattern of international trading have tended to favour the highly industrialised nations of the temperate lands, whose export trade is largely composed of various kinds of manufactured goods, at the expense of the develop-

ing nations of the tropical world, whose export trade is to a large extent composed of foodstuffs, agricultural raw materials and minerals.

There are various possible ways of attempting to alleviate the international trading problems of the countries of the tropical world. These include the diversification of agriculture, the establishment of commodity agreements to regulate production, and the development of manufacturing industry. In many tropical countries greater emphasis could be placed on the cultivation of food crops for the local market, thereby reducing the need to import foodstuffs. A policy of agricultural diversification could, for example, be profitably pursued in many of the territories of the West Indies, where in the past excessive concentration on the cultivation of export crops such as sugar cane, resulted in the neglect of local food crop production, thus necessitating the importation of large quantities of foodstuffs.

The problem of short-term fluctuations in the price can be tackled by the establishment of commodity agreements, such as the International Coffee Agreement and the International Sugar Agreement. Under such agreements, each of the member producing countries is allocated an export quota. These quotas can, however, be adjusted from time to time. The International Coffee Agreement was established in 1962, and its membership now covers practically the whole of world coffee production, and also the bulk of the major coffee consuming countries. This agreement serves to keep surplus coffee off the world market in years when exceptionally good harvests result in overproduction of this commodity, and thus helps to prevent sharp declines in world market price.

The establishment of manufacturing industry can also help to alleviate the trading problems of tropical countries. Firstly, the further processing of locally produced primary products before they are shipped overseas increases their value, and hence the amount of foreign exchange which they earn. Secondly, foreign exchange can be saved by substituting domestically manufactured goods for those which are at present imported. There is also the possibility of tropical countries producing manufactured goods for export. A few countries have in fact already succeeded in building up export markets for their manufactures. The establishment of export markets for manufactured goods is often difficult, however, as the developed countries of the world often tend to impose tariff barriers designed to keep out manufactures originating in countries where wage rates are very low.

B: The external trade of selected countries

Ghana

In the years from 1960 to 1967 Ghana had a very unfavourable balance of visible trade. From 1968 to 1970, however, Ghana had a favourable balance, largely due to higher prices for cocoa beans and gold on the world market. In 1971 the price of cocoa beans dropped sharply, and once again Ghana had an unfavourable balance.

As is the case in most tropical countries, Ghana relies very heavily upon a limited number of export items. Cocoa, mainly in the form of beans, usually accounts for about two-thirds of Ghana's export earnings. Other agricultural exports are of very minor importance, and include small quantities of coffee, lime juice and oil, yams and kola nuts. The most important of Ghana's mineral exports is gold, followed by diamonds, manganese ore and bauxite. Timber exports are also of importance. Most timber is exported in the form of logs or sawn timber, but there is also some export of plywood and veneer sheets. Since the establishment of the aluminium smelter at Tema, Ghana has been able to export aluminium.

In 1973 about three-fifths of the total value of Ghana's import trade consisted of a wide range of manufactured goods. Of particular importance were machinery and transport equipment which accounted

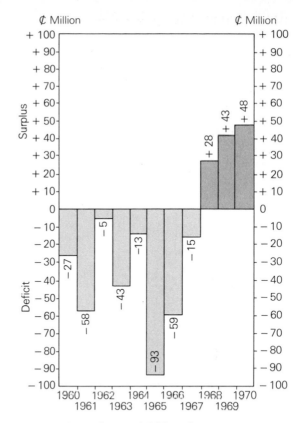

Fig. 18.1 Ghana's balance of visible trade

for 21,3 per cent of the total. Large quantities of textiles were also imported (6,0 per cent of the total), with cotton yarns and fabrics being of particular importance. Other manufactured goods imported included iron and steel (2,9), paper and paper products (2,8) and manufactures of metal (2,6).

Mineral fuels and lubricants accounted for 8,9 per cent of the import trade. Almost three-quarters of that consisted of crude petroleum for the refinery at Tema, with much of the remainder being refined petroleum products. Chemicals accounted for 17,4

Table 109 Ghana's visible trade, 1960–71 (N₵/thousands)

Year	1960	1964	1968	1970	1971
Exports	231 979	229 279	342 040	467 378	373 896
Imports	259 235	243 184	314 032	419 047	443 142
Balance	−27 256	−13 095	+28 008	+48 331	−69 246

271

Table 110 Ghana's export trade, 1967–71

	Major export items as % of total exports (by value)			
	1967	1969	1970	1971
Cocoa beans	54,5	55,9	65,3	57,6
Cocoa paste & butter	10,4	7,0	6,8	7,7
Kola nuts	0,2	0,2	0,1	0,1
Timber (logs)	5,3	6,2	4,3	5,7
Timber (sawn)	4,0	3,8	3,9	3,4
Bauxite	0,7	0,4	0,4	0,6
Manganese ore	3,9	1,8	1,6	1,8
Diamonds	5,3	3,5	3,1	3,2
Gold	8,7	7,6	5,6	7,8
Aluminium	3,5	11,3	6,7	8,2

per cent of the total imports, with medicinal and pharmaceutical products, and dyeing, tanning and colouring materials being of particular importance.

Ghana imports large quantities of foodstuffs, and in 1973 these accounted for 21,4 per cent of the import bill. Of particular importance were imports of cereals and cereal preparations (7,5 per cent), which were mainly in the form of wheat and rice. Considerable quantities of fish and fish preparations were also imported. Other important foodstuffs included sugar (4,0 per cent), dairy produce (1,5 per cent), live animals (1,0 per cent) and meat (0,5 per cent).

In 1973 the United Kingdom was Ghana's leading trading partner, purchasing almost one-fifth of the country's exports, and supplying about one-sixth of its imports. The second most important trading partner was the USA. Ghana also traded a great deal with several of the countries of Western Europe, particularly West Germany, the Netherlands, Italy and France. Of the Asian countries, Japan was Ghana's most important trading partner. All of the above countries imported large quantities of Ghana's cocoa, and in return supplied a wide range of manufactured goods. The USSR, Poland and Yugoslavia all purchased large quantities of cocoa from Ghana, but were less important as suppliers of imports.

In 1973 the countries of West Africa supplied only 6 per cent of Ghana's imports, and in return purchased 2 per cent of its exports. The leading West African supplier of goods was Nigeria, followed by Ivory Coast, Upper Volta, Togo, Mali, Benin and Niger. Ghana's import trade with Nigeria was largely composed of petroleum, while Upper Volta, Mali and Niger mainly supplied live animals. Ghana's main West African customer in 1973 was Mauritania.

Table 111 Ghana's main trading partners, 1973

Country	Destination of exports (% of total)	Origin of imports (% of total)
United Kingdom	18,4	16,5
USA	14,6	15,6
West Germany	8,7	12,1
Japan	8,8	7,2
Netherlands	9,0	3,7
Italy	5,5	2,1
USSR	5,9	1,4
France	0,7	5,6
Poland	3,1	0,7
Nigeria	0,3	4,0
Norway	1,9	2,0
Yugoslavia	2,6	0,9

Kenya

Until the recent break-up of the East African Community, Kenya, Tanzania and Uganda were all members of a single customs union, and a distinction was made between the trade which took place between the three countries themselves, which was known as inter-territorial trade, and that which involved countries which were outside of the East African Community, and which was referred to as overseas trade.

Overseas trade

Table 112 shows that in recent years Kenya had a very unfavourable balance of visible trade with overseas countries. This deficit is, however, partly offset by the fact that Kenya had a favourable balance with the other members of the East African Community, and also by invisible earnings from its flourishing tourist industry.

Table 112 Kenya's visible trade with overseas countries (values in K£ million)

Year	Imports	Exports	Balance
1967	106,6	59,6	−47,0
1968	114,8	62,9	−51,9
1969	117,0	68,5	−48,5
1970	142,0	77,4	−64,6
1971	184,1	78,4	−105,7
1972	177,6	95,5	−82,1
1973	205,8	129,9	−75,9
1974	353,0	170,1	−182,9

The overseas export trade of Kenya is largely composed of agricultural products. Because of the wide range of crops which can be successfully grown in Kenya, these exports are more varied than in many tropical countries, although coffee and tea together accounted for one-third of the overseas export earnings in 1974. Agricultural exports of lesser importance included sisal, hides and skins, meat, pyrethrum extract, canned pineapples, wattle bark and extract, and a wide variety of fresh fruits and vegetables.

At present mineral production in Kenya is on a very small scale, the only significant export being soda ash from Lake Magadi. A small quantity of fluospar is now also exported, since mining began in the Kerio valley.

Kenya has a more highly developed manufacturing sector than most other tropical African countries, and exports of manufactured goods are increasing in importance. Particularly important are refined petroleum products and cement. Although Kenya does not at present produce any petroleum, the refinery at Mombasa which imports crude oil from the Middle East, is capable of producing more refined products than Kenya needs, and there is a considerable surplus for sale to neighbouring countries.

The bulk of Kenya's import trade is made up of a wide range of manufactured goods. Of particular importance are machinery and transport equipment which in 1974 accounted for 22,1 per cent of the total. Also of considerable importance are iron and steel (7,6 per cent), paper and paperboard products (5,0 per cent), manufactured fertilisers (4,3 per cent), medicinal and pharmaceutical products (1,9 per cent), clothing, cotton fabrics, and fabrics of synthetic fibres. Imports of foodstuffs are relatively small, accounting for only 6,7 per cent of the overseas import trade in 1974. Important food imports include sugar, tea, rice and dried milk. With the opening of the new sugar factory at Mumias in 1974, Kenya is in future likely to import less sugar. Large quantities of crude petroleum are imported to supply the refinery at Mombasa, and this accounted for 19,0 per cent of Kenya's overseas import trade in 1974.

Table 113 Kenya's overseas export trade, 1974

Major export items (as % of total by value)			
Coffee	20,9	Pyrethrum extract	2,8
Petroleum products	18,8	Canned pineapples	2,1
Tea	13,6	Soda ash	1,4
Sisal	4,4	Beans, peas, etc.	1,1
Hides & skins	3,2	Wattle bark	
Meat & meat		and extract	1,1
preparations	3,0		

The United Kingdom is still Kenya's most important overseas trading partner. Other important European trading partners are West Germany, Sweden, Italy, the Netherlands, France and Belgium. All of these European countries are mainly interested in the purchase of Kenya's agricultural products, and in return supply manufactured goods of various types. The United Kingdom purchases a large part of Kenya's tea exports, while West Germany and Sweden are important purchasers of coffee. The United States purchases mainly coffee and tea, and supplies manufactured goods and some foodstuffs. Japan sells large quantities of manufactured goods to Kenya, but purchases relatively little in return. India and Hong Kong also supply manufactured goods. India is Kenya's leading customer for wattle bark and extract. Iran and to a lesser extent Saudi Arabia supply large quantities of petroleum. Of the African countries, Zambia is Kenya's leading overseas trading partner.

Inter-territorial trade

Because a customs union has been in existence for a long time, there is far more trade between the various countries of East Africa, than is the case in West Africa. In 1974 almost 11 per cent of Kenya's total international trade was with Tanzania and Uganda. Kenya produces a wider range of agricultural products and manufactured goods than either Tanzania or Uganda, and consequently it is able to sell far more to those countries than it needs to buy from them. In 1974 22 per cent of Kenya's total exports went to its East African neighbours, while they in return supplied less than 4 per cent of Kenya's total imports.

By far the most important of Kenya's exports to Uganda is refined petroleum products. Other important export items include dairy products, cereal preparations, chemicals and metal manufactures. Cotton textiles are the most important of the commodities imported from Uganda. Also of importance are unmanufactured tobacco, animal feeding stuffs, and vegetable oils. In the past Kenya has bought large quantities of sugar from Uganda. Uganda also supplies Kenya with electricity from the Owen Falls power station. Exports from Kenya to Tanzania include dairy products, chemicals and paper products. Imports from Tanzania include cotton textiles, unmanufactured tobacco, and fruits and vegetables.

Table 114 Kenya's main overseas trading partners, 1974

Country	Percentage of total value	
	Destination of exports	Origin of imports
United Kingdom	11,3	18,1
W. Germany	10,9	10,3
Japan	3,3	11,5
Iran	0,2	10,1
USA	4,9	5,9
Netherlands	7,0	4,1
Saudi Arabia	0,3	6,8
Italy	2,7	3,5
France	1,1	3,6
Belgium/Luxembourg	5,0	1,8
Sweden	2,7	1,9
Zambia	5,2	0,6
India	1,7	1,8

Table 115 Kenya's inter-territorial trade (K£ millions)

		1970	1971	1972	1973	1974
With Tanzania						
a)	Exports	14,7	14,7	16,3	16,9	19,0
b)	Imports	5,9	7,9	5,9	7,6	9,6
c)	Balance	+8,8	+6,8	+10,4	+9,3	+9,4
With Uganda						
a)	Exports	16,7	19,1	16,5	21,9	29,3
b)	Imports	10,0	8,0	7,6	4,7	3,8
c)	Balance	+6,7	+11,1	+8,9	+17,2	+25,5
With Tanzania and Uganda						
a)	Exports	31,4	33,8	32,8	38,8	48,3
b)	Imports	15,9	15,9	13,5	12,3	13,4
c)	Balance	+15,5	+17,9	+19,3	+26,5	+34,9

Venezuela

Venezuela is one of the relatively few tropical countries which regularly has a highly favourable balance of visible trade. In 1974 Venezuela earned 63 940 million Bolivars from exports, and only spent 16 281 million Bolivars on imports. This fortunate situation can largely be attributed to the fact that Venezuela is very rich in minerals. Venezuela is the world's fifth largest producer of petroleum, and is also an important producer of iron ore. During the early 1970s the world market price of petroleum rose dramatically, with beneficial effects for the major oil producing countries.

Venezuela's export trade is dominated by the petroleum industry, which usually accounts for at least nine-tenths of the country's export earnings. A large part of Venezuela's petroleum is still exported in crude form, although exports of refined products are now also of considerable importance, and seem likely to become even more important in the future. The second most important export is iron ore, which is mined in the Guayana Region, and shipped to the USA. Agricultural products are of relatively minor importance, the leading ones being coffee, cocoa and sugar. Other minor export items include aluminium, iron and steel, uncut diamonds and shellfish.

Table 116 Venezuela's export trade, 1974

Major export items (as percentage of total by value)	
Petroleum and products	96,2
Iron ore	1,9
Aluminium	0,1
Coffee	0,1
Cocoa	0,1

Venezuela's import trade is largely made up of a wide range of manufactured goods. In 1969 machinery and transport equipment together accounted for about 47 per cent of the total imports. Other types of manufactured goods imported in large quantities include chemicals (11 per cent), iron and steel (6 per cent), manufactures of metal (4 per cent), and paper and paperboard (2 per cent). Venezuela also imports substantial quantities of foodstuffs, and in 1972 these accounted for about 7 per cent of the total imports. The most important of the foodstuffs imported are cereal preparations, dairy produce, and fruits and vegetables.

In 1972 the United States was by far the most important of Venezuela's trading partners, supplying almost half of the country's imports, and purchasing more than one-third of its exports. Venezuela's exports to the United States consist mainly of mineral fuels and iron ore. In return the United States supplies manufactured goods. Venezuela sells large quantities of petroleum to the Netherlands Antilles, to supply the refineries on the islands of Aruba and Curacao, but they supply very little in return. A similar situation exists with relation to Trinidad and Tobago. Although Trinidad produces some petroleum, the local production is insufficient for the needs of the island's oil refineries, and large quantities have to be imported. Other important purchasers of mineral fuels from Venezuela are Canada, the United Kingdom, Puerto Rico, and Panama. Several European countries such as West Germany, Italy, France and the Netherlands, are mainly important as suppliers of manufactured goods. Japan also supplies large quantities of manufactured goods to Venezuela.

Table 117 Venezuela's main trading partners, 1972

Country	Destination of exports	Origin of imports
USA	39,7	45,0
Netherlands Antilles	19,2	0,1
Canada	12,9	3,4
W. Germany	1,2	10,7
United Kingdom	4,1	5,3
Japan	0,7	9,1
Italy	1,5	5,6
France	1,8	4,2
Spain	1,0	1,7
Netherlands	1,0	1,5
Brazil	1,3	1,0
Panama	1,6	0,1
Trinidad & Tobago	1,1	0,0

Singapore

In spite of the vast difference in the size of India and

Singapore (India's population was more than 260 times as large as that of Singapore), in 1974 the total value of Singapore's external trade was greater than that of India. Much of Singapore's trade, however, is entrepot trade. In addition to the goods needed for its own domestic consumption, Singapore imports a vast quantity of goods which it does not retain, but which it re-exports to other countries. A number of factors have contributed toward the growth of Singapore's entrepot trade, important among which are the fact that:

1 it has a fine natural harbour;
2 it has an extremely favourable geographical position.

Singapore is the focal point of the main trade routes from Europe to the Far East. Because of its position astride the Malacca Strait which is the main shipping entrance to the rich primary producing areas of Southeast Asia, Singapore is the natural collecting and distribution centre for on the one hand the region's raw materials destined for the industrialised nations of the west, and on the other hand for the western manufactured goods destined for markets in Southeast Asia.

In recent years the primary producing nations of Southeast Asia have tried to by-pass Singapore by developing their own ports, thus enabling them to export their products directly to the ultimate consumer. The relative importance of the entrepot trade to Singapore's economy has therefore tended to decline, and since the 1960s Singapore has increasingly turned its attention towards the development of manufacturing industry.

Singapore's entrepot trade consists of the importation and subsequent re-export of three main classes of goods:

1 petroleum and refined petroleum products;
2 other primary products from Southeast Asia on their way to the more industrialised countries;
3 manufactured goods from the highly industrialised countries destined for markets in Southeast Asia.

The outstanding commodity in the second category is rubber, although substantial quantities of oil palm products, coconut products and timber are also handled. In the past tin concentrates were also an important component, but the tin smelter has now closed down. The major sources of primary products are West Malaysia and Indonesia, but Sabah, Sarawak, Brunei, South Vietnam and Thailand are also important suppliers.

The manufactured goods which are re-exported from Singapore mainly originate in the countries of Western Europe, the USA and Japan, although Singapore now has its own well-developed manufacturing sector. Of particular importance are exports of textiles, machinery and transport equipment, and iron and steel.

Crude petroleum is imported from such countries as Indonesia, Kuwait and Iran, and after refining it is re-exported. In 1975 Singapore had seven oil refineries in operation, the Shell refinery which is located on a small island off Singapore ranking as the largest in Asia and the fourth largest in the world.

Table 118 Singapore's external trade, 1974

Commodity	Percentage of total value	
	Exports	Imports
Petroleum	0,0	19,2
Petroleum products	31,8	4,7
Chemicals	6,5	6,0
Rubber	14,5	5,6
Palm oil	1,9	1,4
Spices	1,1	0,7
Cereals and preparations	0,9	2,2
Animal feeding stuffs	0,9	0,5
Preserved fruit	0,5	0,4
Fish and preparations	0,4	0,6
Timber	1,5	0,9
Plywood and veneer	1,3	0,3
Textile yarns, fabrics, etc.	2,4	4,8
Textile fibres	0,4	0,6
Clothing	2,2	0,7
Iron and steel	1,3	6,1
Instruments, watches, clocks, etc.	1,3	2,7

Hong Kong

Hong Kong is unusual among the countries of the

tropical world, in that its export trade is composed almost entirely of various types of manufactured goods. The outstanding export item is clothing, which in 1974 accounted for 28 per cent of the total export earnings. Other particularly important export items include textiles, plastic toys and dolls, and electrical equipment of various types.

The goods which are manufactured in Hong Kong are exported to nearly every country in the world, but the major markets for these commodities are in the developed countries of the temperate lands. In 1974 the USA purchased 32 per cent of Hong Kong's domestic exports. Other outstanding customers were the United Kingdom (12 per cent), West Germany (11 per cent), Australia (6 per cent), Japan (5 per cent) and Canada (3 per cent).

Table 119 Hong Kong's domestic exports, 1974

Commodity	Percentage of total value
Clothing	28,3
Footwear	1,1
Wigs, etc.	0,2
Textile yarns, fabrics, etc.	12,2
Toys, sporting goods, etc.	6,2
Travel goods, handbags, etc.	1,5
Electrical machinery	12,6
Lighting equipment	1,1
Instruments, clocks, watches, etc.	5,0
Manufactures of metal	2,5
Metalliferous ores and scrap	0,9
Fish and preparations	0,8

Although domestic supplies of agricultural produce and fish are substantial, densely populated Hong Kong has to import large quantities of foodstuffs to supplement local production. In 1974 food and live animals accounted for about 18 per cent of the total value of Hong Kong's import trade. Of particular importance were imports of rice and other cereals, live animals, fish and fish preparations, meat and meat preparations, and dairy produce. China is the chief supplier of foodstuffs, in 1974 providing 52 per cent of all Hong Kong's food imports.

Other major imports consist of raw materials and semi-manufactured goods, which are needed by Hong Kong's industrial establishments. Of particular importance are textile fibres, yarns and fabrics; base metals; plastics moulding materials; and paper and paperboard products. Other important items include machinery and transport equipment and mineral fuels. Japan was Hong Kong's chief supplier in 1974, accounting for 21 per cent of its total import trade. A large part of Japan's trade with Hong Kong is made up of textile yarns and fabrics. Other leading suppliers of Hong Kong's imports in 1974 were China (18 per cent), USA (14 per cent), Singapore (6 per cent), United Kingdom (6 per cent), Taiwan (5 per cent) and West Germany (3 per cent).

As in the case of Singapore, Hong Kong has an important entrepot trade. In 1974 re-exports accounted for 24 per cent of the total value of Hong Kong's export trade. The principal commodities involved were diamonds, medicinal and pharmaceutical products, textile fabrics, watches and clocks, electrical equipment, fruits and vegetables, and coffee, tea and spices. The most important re-export market was Japan, followed by Singapore, India, the USA, Taiwan and Macao.

Exercises

1 a) Explain what is meant by the term 'balance of visible trade'.

b) With reference to actual examples, suggest reasons why some tropical countries have a favourable balance of visible trade, while others have an unfavourable one.

c) With reference to actual examples, explain how some tropical countries are able to offset an unfavourable balance of visible trade by means of invisible earnings.

2 a) Describe the international trading problems faced by the developing countries of the tropical world.

b) Suggest means by which these problems could be alleviated.

3 a) Explain what is meant by 'entrepot trade'.

b) Describe the main features of Singapore's entrepot trade.

c) What factors have contributed toward the growth of Singapore's entrepot trade?

4 Make a comparative study of the external trade of either Ghana and Nigeria or Kenya and Tanzania.
5 Write an explanatory account of the external trade of any one tropical country.

Suggested reading

B. W. HODDER: *Economic Development in the Tropics* — Chapter 13

A. M. O'CONNOR: *An Economic Geography of East Africa* — Chapter 14

A. M. O'CONNOR: *The Geography of Tropical African Development* — Chapter 9

H. P. WHITE AND M. B. GLEAVE: *An Economic Geography of West Africa* — Chapter 8

Sources of statistics

UNITED NATIONS — *Yearbook of International Trade Statistics*

The Statesman's Yearbook

Whitaker's Almanack

CHAPTER NINETEEN

Transport

In most parts of the tropical world, transport facilities are poor. In many countries there is an urgent need to improve and extend the existing facilities in order to make it possible to open up new lands for settlement, and to improve the marketing of agricultural and other types of produce.

In parts of the tropical world, particularly in South America, there are extensive areas of land which are suitable for settlement, but which are at present largely unoccupied. The opening up of these areas is made difficult by the fact that they are distant from markets and ports, and are not served by roads or railways. The valleys on the eastern side of the Andes in Peru and Bolivia, for example, are potentially fertile, and could in future be used to resettle some of the surplus population of the Sierra. At present, however, that part of South America has few roads, and so far settlement has been on a fairly small scale.

In many countries a fuller development of the agricultural potential is hampered by the inadequacy of transport facilities. In parts of the forest zone of West Africa, for example, farmers often find difficulty in transporting their surplus foodstuffs to market, particularly during the rains, when untarred roads may become impassable for days or even weeks at a time. The need to provide feeder roads to enable farmers to get out their produce is well recognised in countries such as Ghana. In some countries the development of mineral and forest resources is also hampered by their remoteness from ports.

Human porterage

In parts of the tropical world transport is still to a considerable extent provided by human beings, with

Collecting coconuts near Cape Coast, Ghana. In many parts of West Africa heavy loads are carried on the head.

men and sometimes women carrying heavy loads over considerable distances. Human porterage is an extremely slow form of transport, and is very much more costly than transport by motor vehicle or railway. It is, however, necessary in areas where railways do not exist, where rivers are not navigable, and where there are no roads suitable for motor vehicles.

The exact method by which loads are carried varies from one area to another. In West Africa, for

279

example, loads are commonly balanced on the head. In the highlands of Kenya, however, women frequently carry heavy loads on their backs, supported by a strap which passes round the forehead.

In recent years the bicycle has become an important means of transport in parts of the tropical world. The bicycle is particularly useful in areas where there are tracks which are cyclable, but which are not suitable for motor vehicles. In Malaysia, for example, there are now large numbers of bicycles, both in urban and rural areas. In the rural areas of Malaysia the bicycle is widely used in carrying bulky and heavy loads, both along main roads, and also along tracks and footpaths. In the urban areas of Southeast Asia, the 'trishaw' (a type of bicycle-drawn carriage with three wheels) is often used for transport of passengers.

Animal transport

In many parts of the tropical world animals are used for riding, as well as for carrying or pulling loads. Animal transport is appreciably cheaper than human porterage, but is more expensive than transport by lorry. The type of animal used for transport purposes varies from one area to another, and includes horses, donkeys, mules, camels, cattle, water buffalo, llamas and elephants.

In the savanna zone of West Africa, for example, the donkey is the most common beast of burden, while in the more arid areas further north the camel is used. In parts of Asia and Central America, carts drawn by cattle are still an important form of transport. In the highland areas of Bolivia and Peru the llama is an important beast of burden. The llama is capable of carrying loads of up to about 45 kg in weight, but must be driven very slowly. In Southeast Asia elephants are still sometimes used for hauling logs from the forest to the banks of the rivers.

Inland water transport

Transport by water is the cheapest of all the forms of transport. The importance of inland waterways as a means of transport varies considerably from one part of the tropical world to another. Some tropical rivers offer excellent opportunities for navigation, while the navigability of others is greatly reduced by the

Donkeys carrying sand to a building site in Lamu, Kenya

A ferry on the Ankobra river, Ghana. In many parts of the tropical world ferries are used to carry passengers and vehicles across rivers and lakes.

existence of one or more of the following impediments:

1 waterfalls or rapids which prevent the use of the river throughout its whole length. In some countries short railway lines have been constructed around waterfalls or rapids, in order to link up the navigable sections of the river.

2 sandbars at the mouth of the river. The shallowness of the water over these sandbars often makes it difficult for ocean-going vessels to enter the river itself.

3 seasonal fluctuations in water level. Many tropical rivers flood during and immediately after the rains, but during the latter part of the dry season the level of water is frequently too low to permit navigation. At Ciudad Bolivar on the Orinoco, for example, the difference between high and low water levels averages 12 metres, and in some years has been known to reach 18 metres.

4 masses of floating vegetation. In the nineteenth century the Bahr el Jebel (White Nile) in Sudan was frequently closed by blocks of floating vegetation, known in Arabic as sudd. In the period between 1899 and 1904 the Bahr el Jebel was cleared of floating vegetation, and since navigation

on the river became regular and frequent, blocks of sudd have only rarely been formed on the main stream. In recent years the appearance of water hyacinth has posed a threat to navigation on the Zaïre and its tributaries, and spraying with chemical weed killers has been needed to control it.

In some countries, lakes also provide an important means of transport. This is particularly the case in East Africa and Central Africa, where regular boat services are maintained on such lakes as Victoria, Tanganyika and Malaŵi. In some coastal areas, lagoons provide sheltered waterways which can be used by small craft.

The rivers of tropical America

In South America the Amazon river provides an excellent natural routeway. During the flood season the Amazon and its tributaries offer some 58 000 km of navigable waterways. On the main river, ocean-going vessels of up to 10 000 tonnes can reach Manaus, 1 600 km from the sea; while vessels of up to 4 000 tonnes can reach Iquitos in Peru, which is 3 700 km from the mouth. Smaller vessels can continue 780 km beyond Iquitos. Many of the tributaries of the Amazon are also navigable for

281

considerable distances, although the right bank tributaries in particular are interrupted in places by rapids. The whole of the Amazon Basin has only three short lengths of railway line and very few roads, and most of the settlements are therefore dependent upon water transport. Both Manaus and Iquitos are important collecting centres for the produce of the Amazon Basin. To these river ports are brought such products as Brazil nuts, timber and rubber. The total volume of traffic on the Amazon and its tributaries is, however, relatively small, as the hinterland is very sparsely populated and poorly developed.

The Magdalena in Colombia is interrupted by rapids in several places, and its lower course is susceptible to silting. In spite of these impediments to navigation, in the past the Magdalena provided the main link between the highland heartland of Colombia and the outside world. In recent years the importance of the Magdalena for the transport of passengers and freight has greatly declined, as a result of the development of internal air transport, and the opening in 1961 of a railway line which runs parallel to the river.

The Orinoco is subject to very marked seasonal fluctuations in water level. The lower part of the river has, however, become of considerable importance for the transport of iron ore, since the development of the mines of Cerro Bolivar, El Trueno and El Pao. The lower Orinoco has been dredged to a depth of 8 metres from Ciudad Guayana to the mouth, a distance of 360 km.

The inland waterways of tropical Africa
Of the rivers in tropical Africa, the Zaïre is of particular importance for navigation. The Zaïre receives tributaries from both sides of the equator, and has a much more even flow than most tropical rivers. Unfortunately its course is interrupted in several places by waterfalls and rapids. Of the main river's 4 350 km, some 2 700 are navigable. Several of its tributaries, particularly the Kasai, also have extensive navigable sections. Short railway lines have been constructed round the Zaïre's unnavigable sections, and also around those of several of its tributaries.

The lower Zaïre is navigable for ocean-going vessels as far as the port of Matadi, some 130 km from the sea. Between Matadi and Kinshasa naviga-

bility is interrupted by a series of waterfalls and rapids, and the two towns are linked by a railway line. Kinshasa is a very busy river port. The longest navigable section of the Zaïre is from Kinshasa to Kisangani, a distance of 1 750 km. The upper section of the river is navigable from Ubundi to Kindu, and again from Kongola to Bukama. These navigable sections are linked to each other by short railway lines. The Kasai tributary is navigable as far as Ilebo (formerly Port Francqui). From Ilebo a railway line runs to Bukama, and then on to the copper mining area of Shaba Province.

There are several sizeable rivers in West Africa, but most of them are of only limited use for navigation. Although the Niger is some 4 200 km in length, its importance as a means of transport is by no means as great as might be expected. The river is subject to marked seasonal fluctuations in water level, and is interrupted by rapids in several places. These rapids divide the river into four main navigable sections:

1 From Kouroussa in Guinea to Bamako in Mali. This section is navigable between July and October. It can only be used by boats of up to about 1 metre in draught, and carries very little traffic. The Milo tributary of the Niger is also navigable for part of the year as far upstream as Kankan.

2 From Koulikoro to Ansongo. This section is entirely within Mali, and is only navigable when in flood. Vessels can ply between Koulikoro and Ansongo when the river is in full flood, and between Mopti and Gao in lesser flood. This section of the Niger has been connected to the upper navigable section by the construction of the Sotuba Canal, which passes round the rapids between Bamako and Koulikoro.

3 From Niamey to Gaya. This section is entirely within Niger, and is navigable from October to March. It carries very little traffic.

4 From Jebba to the sea. This section is entirely within Nigeria, and is by far the busiest section. Many of the Maritime Delta mouths of the Niger are navigable throughout the year as far as Onitsha, and from June to March the river is navigable as far as Lokoja at the confluence of the Benue. Boats can reach Jebba between August and

February, but in fact seldom go beyond Baro, where a rail link gives more direct contact with the north of Nigeria. The navigability of the lower Niger has been improved by the construction of the Kainji dam and the formation of the Kainji lake. Locks have been built to allow boats to pass round the dam.

The Benue is also navigable for part of the year. It can be used by river vessels as far as Makurdi (240 km from Lokoja) between June and November; as far as Yola (840 km) between July and early October; and as far as Garoua in Cameroon in August and September. The Benue is at present probably more important to Cameroon than to Nigeria, but its importance is likely to decline when the Cameroon railway system is extended to the north of the country.

In the past the rapids at Kpong and at Kete Krachi reduced the navigability of the Volta river. The construction of the Akosombo dam, which resulted in the formation of Lake Volta has, however, created a fine waterway linking northern Ghana with the south of the country.

The Gambia is one of the most navigable rivers in tropical Africa. Ocean-going vessels of up to 6 metres in draught can reach Kuntaur (240 km upstream from Banjul) throughout the year. Kuntaur is an important collecting centre for groundnuts. Vessels of up to 2 metres in draught can reach Fatoto (464 km), which is the last wharf used by steamers. The government maintains a service of river steamers which carry passengers and freight up and down the Gambia, calling at 33 settlements. Unfortunately the usefulness of the Gambia river has been greatly reduced by the existence of the political division between Gambia and Senegal, which has resulted in the river being divorced from its natural hinterland. If it were not for the existence of this division, the Gambia would be the natural outlet for much of Senegal's groundnut growing zone. As it is, the river handles almost all of Gambia's groundnut traffic, and is also used to distribute those imports which are not consumed in Banjul.

The Senegal is a much less navigable river than the Gambia. Longshore drift, the Maritime Trade Winds and strong waves have combined to turn the mouth of the river southward, and resulted in the formation of a large sand spit known as La Langue de Barbarie. The variable end of this spit, and a sand bar across the mouth of the river, make the estuary of the Senegal dangerous to shipping. The river itself has a

Train ferry at Kisumu on Lake Victoria, Kenya

highly seasonal regime. The Senegal is navigable throughout the year for boats of up to 2½ metres in draught as far as Podor (285 km upstream from St. Louis). Between August and mid-October small boats can with difficulty reach Kayes in Mali (970 km). The amount of traffic from Kayes, however, has never been great.

Around Abidjan in the Ivory Coast, and also between the mouth of the Volta and the Niger Delta, the mainland is cut off from the open sea by sandbars. Between the sandbars and the mainland there are narrow lagoons, which provide an excellent sheltered waterway for small craft. By using these lagoons, canoes and small powered launches can travel from Porto Novo in Benin as far as Obopo in the Niger Delta, without having to enter the open sea.

There are few navigable rivers in East Africa. Most East African rivers are subject to marked seasonal fluctuations in water level, and are interrupted in places by rapids. The larger lakes, on the other hand, offer excellent opportunities for transport. Although many small-scale enterprises ferry foods and passengers from place to place around the lake shores, all large-scale inland water transport was until its recent

break-up undertaken by the East African Railways Corporation, which operated regular boat services on both Lake Victoria and Lake Tanganyika.

Because of its size, and the relatively dense population and high level of production around its shores, Lake Victoria has always had most passenger and freight traffic. Although in recent years many of the smaller ports on Lake Victoria have been closed down, water transport between the main centres such as the Kisumu, Mwanza, and Kampala-Jinja areas is still very important. Between 1966 and 1969 rail ferry terminals were brought into operation at Kisumu in Kenya, Jinja in Uganda, and Musoma and Mwanza in Tanzania. Railway waggons can be loaded on to ferry boats at one ferry terminal, shipped across the lake, and unloaded at another terminal. Important commodities carried across Lake Victoria are cotton and coffee.

Although the Lake Tanganyika services are very important to communities around its shores, the volume of traffic is much smaller than on Lake Victoria. The main movement of freight on Lake Tanganyika is between lake ports in Burundi and Zaïre, and the railhead at Kigoma in Tanzania. The distance by lake and rail from Kalemie in Zaïre to the

Metal punts loaded with sugar cane are towed along the canal to a sugar factory in Guyana.

port of Dar-es-Salaam in Tanzania is less than 1 600 km, compared with about 3 200 km from Kalemie to Matadi on the Atlantic coast of Zaire.

Ocean transport

Shipping

Because of their high degree of dependence upon overseas trade, most tropical countries make considerable use of ocean shipping. Most countries still depend upon the ships of other nations for the transport of their bulky exports and imports, but a few have their own fleets of merchant ships.

With the exception of Liberia and Panama, the tropical country with the largest merchant fleet is India. The Shipping Corporation of India, which was set up in 1961, had a fleet of 105 ships in 1974. Brazil also has a sizeable merchant fleet, and in addition is one of the few tropical countries which has developed its own ship-building industry. In 1974 the Black Star Line of Ghana had 16 ships, and the Nigerian National Shipping Line also had 16. The ships of both of these countries mainly operate between the ports of West Africa and Europe. In 1971 the Black Star Line carried about 35 per cent of Ghana's exports, and 25 per cent of its imports. Most of East Africa's overseas trade is still carried by ships of other nations, although the East African National Shipping Line was set up in 1966 by the governments of Kenya, Tanzania, Uganda and Zambia.

A large number of ocean-going ships are now registered in Liberia and in Panama. In 1976 Liberia had a greater registered tonnage of merchant vessels than any other country, accounting for almost 20 per cent of the world's total tonnage. Panama ranked seventh with 4 per cent of the world's total. Most of the ships which are registered in Liberia and Panama, however, are owned by non-nationals, who are using flags of convenience in order to avoid the higher taxation rates and the stricter labour laws of their own countries.

The seaports of West Africa

The coastline of West Africa has very few good natural harbours. Except for the section between the mouth of the Gambia river and the southern part of Sierra Leone, the coastline is smooth, and has few sheltered inlets. Off-shore the water is generally shallow, and the shore itself is pounded throughout the year by a heavy surf. The mouths of many of the rivers are obstructed by sand bars. Because of the shallowness of the water, ocean-going vessels are unable in most cases to cross these bars, and so cannot enter the rivers themselves.

Until very recently lighterage ports handled almost all of West Africa's overseas trade. At these ports ocean-going vessels had to anchor some distance from the shore, in the deeper water beyond the surf. They were loaded and unloaded by means of either surf boats or lighters. The surf boats were paddled through the surf, and landed on the beach. Where lighters were used, there were small wooden or metal jetties, built out from the shore. The lighters tied up against the jetties, when taking on or discharging cargo. Lighterage ports were slow and dangerous to work, and the cost of handling cargo was high.

In recent years several artificial deep-water ports have been created, and as a result the importance of lighterage ports has declined considerably, although a few still continue to operate. The development of artificial harbours in West Africa has usually involved the construction of large breakwaters, to

Table 120 Merchant shipping fleets of selected countries, 1975 (thousand gross registered tonnes)

World total: 372 000					
Liberia	73 479	Brazil	3 096	Mexico	594
Panama	15 631	Somalia	1 793	Venezuela	543
Singapore	5 482	Indonesia	1 046	Peru	525
India	5 094	Philippines	1 018	Cuba	404

provide an area of calm water, where ships can anchor in safety, or tie up alongside the quays. In most cases the depth of water inside these harbours has had to be increased by dredging. The more important of West Africa's ports are discussed below.

Before 1928 all of Ghana's overseas trade was handled by surf ports. The most important of these were Accra and Sekondi, while Half Assini, Axim, Cape Coast, Salt Pond, Winneba, Ada and Keta were of lesser importance. In 1928 Ghana's first modern port was opened at Takoradi. The harbour at Takoradi consists of two breakwaters, which enclose

a water area of some 90 hectares. On the inside of the lee breakwater there are berths for five ships, a coal wharf, and a wharf for loading manganese ore. On the seaward side of the lee breakwater there is a conveyor loading berth for bauxite, and an oil berth where tankers can discharge oil. The five berths on the inside of the lee breakwater are only used for handling general cargo. Between the two breakwaters there are eight moorings, where ships are loaded with cocoa and timber. The sacks of cocoa are carried from the storage sheds to the moorings in lighters. Sawn timber, and logs which are too heavy to float,

Fig. 19.1 Takoradi Harbour

286

are also carried to the moorings in lighters. Most of the logs, however, are towed out by launches. At the moorings, the ships' own lifting equipment is used in loading the cargo.

After the opening of Takoradi harbour several surf ports ceased to operate, but those at Cape Coast, Winneba and Accra continued to be used until they were finally closed down in 1962, when Ghana's second deep water port was opened at Tema. The port of Tema is located some 30 km to the east of Accra, and is linked to it by a short railway line. The harbour at Tema consists of two breakwaters, which enclose a water area of some 200 hectares. When it was opened the harbour at Tema had berths for 10 ships, but is capable of expansion to provide up to 20 berths. In addition to its functions as a general port, Tema has developed as an important centre for the fishing industry.

In 1972 Tema handled 54 per cent of all the cargo handled by seaports in Ghana, and Takoradi 46 per cent. The functions of the two ports are distinct. Takoradi is primarily an exporting port, handling all of Ghana's exports of timber, manganese ore and bauxite, as well as some of its cocoa. Although Tema also exports a lot of cocoa, it is primarily an importing port.

The most important general ports in Nigeria are Lagos and Port Harcourt. Lagos is situated on an island in the Lagos Lagoon. Up until 1914, a submerged bar at the entrance to this lagoon prevented ocean-going vessels from entering Lagos. Much of the cargo destined for Lagos was transhipped to coastal vessels at Forcados. In 1914 the harbour at Lagos, which previously had a depth of only $3\frac{1}{2}$

metres was dredged to 8 metres, and breakwaters were built out from the coast to protect the entrance from waves and sand deposits. The modern port of Lagos consists of the old Customs Quay on Lagos Island which is mainly used for incoming cargo, and Apapa Quay on the mainland. The port of Lagos at present suffers from severe congestion, involving shipping in long delays. There are now plans to build a new deep-water port near Lagos, to relieve this congestion.

Port Harcourt lies 66 km up the Bonny river. It was founded as a coal port in 1913, but as a result of the extension of the railway northward, it now serves a much wider hinterland. In 1958 Nigeria's first shipment of petroleum was made from Port Harcourt. The port had, however, a number of disadvantages as an oil terminal, of particular importance being the fact that the depth of water in the river restricted the size of the tankers which could be handled. In 1961 a new oil terminal was opened at Bonny, lower down the river. A number of other oil terminals have since been built to serve the Nigerian oil industry.

The ports of Burutu, Sapele, Warri and Koko are situated in the western part of the Niger Delta, and all are approached by the same entrance, namely the Escravos river. These western ports have suffered from the silting of the entrances to the Niger river. The Escravos Project, which was completed in 1964, was designed to keep the entrance of the Escravos river open, and to expand the trade of the western delta ports. This project involved the construction of an 8 km long breakwater, and the dredging of the estuary.

Table 121 Cargo handled by Ghanaian ports (1968–72)

Cargo unloaded	1968	1969	1970	1971	1972
Total (thousand tonnes)	2 361	2 945	4 231	3 276	2 481
Takoradi (% of total)	18,8	22,1	15,6	22,8	18,1
Tema (% of total)	81,2	81,9	84,4	77,2	81,9
Cargo loaded					
Total (thousand tonnes)	2 143	2 205	2 189	2 412	2 810
Takoradi (% of total)	68,5	63,0	68,2	67,0	69,9
Tema (% of total)	31,5	37,0	31,8	33,0	30,1

Fig. 19.2 West Africa – seaports and railways

The port of Calabar is situated to the east of the Niger Delta, some 77 km up the Cross river. Although an important port in the past, in recent times it has lost much of its trade to Port Harcourt. Unlike Port Harcourt, Calabar is not the terminus of a railway system, and has a much more restricted hinterland.

The Ivory Coast had no modern port facilities until 1950, when Abidjan was opened to ocean-going vessels. Before 1950, the Ivory Coast was only served by lighterage ports, of which the most important was Grand Bassam. Others included Sassandra and Tabou. Abidjan, which is on the north shore of the sheltered Ebrié Lagoon, could not be reached by ocean-going vessels because of the existence of a coastal bar. Between 1904 and 1907 several attempts were made to cut a canal through this bar, but all of them ended in failure, because the movement of sand by long-shore drift quickly caused the canal to silt up. In 1950, however, the Vridi Canal was opened, with the result that ocean-going vessels were able to

enter the Ebrié Lagoon for the first time. The whole economy of the Ivory Coast was greatly stimulated by the development of Abidjan as a deep water port. In the early 1970s a new deep-water port was constructed at San Pedro. At present this port mainly handles timber, but it is hoped that it will also facilitate the development of the agricultural and mineral resources of the western part of the Ivory Coast.

Before the Second World War, Liberia's port facilities were practically non-existent. Between 1945 and 1948, however, the country's first modern deep-water port was built at Monrovia, with American aid. The port of Monrovia has berthing for several general cargo vessels, as well as two mechanised ore loading piers. In 1974 Monrovia dealt with just over half of all the cargo handled by Liberian ports. Most of this was iron ore from the mines at Bomi Hills, Mano River and Bong Range. A second modern deep-water port has recently been built at Buchanan by the Liberian-American-Swedish Minerals Company (LAMCO). This port is mainly used for the export of iron ore from the mines at Mount Nimba, and in 1974 dealt with just under half of all the cargo handled by Liberian ports. The ports of Harper and Greenville are of very minor importance. At present the hinterland of these two ports is very little developed, and the ports only handle small quantities of logs, rubber, cocoa and palm kernels. There are extensive reserves of timber behind Harper and Greenville, and the importance of these ports may well increase in the future.

Sierra Leone has four ports, Freetown, Pepel, Point Sam and Bonthe. Freetown is the only importing port, and also exports agricultural produce. Freetown has one of the finest natural harbours in the world, but was only a lighterage port until 1953 when the Queen Elizabeth II deep-water quay was built. Pepel and Point Sam are both specialised mineral handling ports. Pepel is situated across the bay from Freetown, and is a private port belonging to the company which mined iron ore at Marampa. The annual tonnage of ore loaded at Pepel was several times greater than the total tonnage of cargo handled by Freetown. At Point Sam, lighters are loaded with bauxite which they carry down the shallow waters of the Bagru Creek, to ships lying at anchor in the deeper waters off Sherbro Island. Bonthe, on Sherbro Island was a very important port during the last century, but its importance has declined considerably during the present century, as a result of the silting up of the Sherbro estuary. It now handles small quantities of piassava fibre and coffee.

Dakar is the major port of Senegal, handling most of that country's overseas trade, as well as that of Mali. Dakar ranks as one of the great seaports of Africa. It is largely an artificial port, being enclosed by breakwaters, although Cap Vert does give it natural protection from the north and west. The port of Dakar has 216 hectares of protected water, and can accommodate about 40 ships. Unfortunately Dakar does not have a very rich hinterland. The main export items handled are groundnuts and groundnut products from Senegal and Mali, and phosphates from Senegal.

In Mauritania, the port of Nouadhibou now handles the bulk of the country's overseas trade. A specialised mineral handling port has been built at Point Central some 10 km to the south of the town, for the export of iron ore brought by rail from the mines in the Khedia d'Idjil Range. As a result of dredging operations carried out in 1966, ore-carriers of up to 100 000 tonnes can be accommodated at Point Central. A small pier for handling general cargo has been built at Nouakchott, the capital of Mauritania.

Both Benin and Togo now have modern deep-water ports. These were opened in 1965 at Cotonou and in 1967 at Lomé, and replaced the existing lighterage ports. A 1 000 metre long metal wharf has been built at Kpémé in Togo, to handle the country's export of phosphates. The main port of Guinea is Conakry, which is a fairly modern port with berths for handling general cargo, as well as specialised berths for handling iron ore and bananas. Banjul is the only significant seaport in Gambia. It has one deep-water quay. Banjul's export trade consists largely of groundnuts and groundnut products.

The seaports of East Africa

East Africa is served by five main seaports, namely Mombasa, Dar-es-Salaam, Tanga, Mtwara and Zanzibar. The first four were until its recent break-up administered by the East African Harbours Corpora-

Table 122 Cargo handled by the East African Harbours Corporation, 1973 (thousand tonnes)

	Cargo unloaded	*Cargo loaded*	*Total cargo handled*
Mombasa	4 165	2 589	6 754
Dar-es-Salaam	2 391	815	3 205
Tanga	139	131	270
Mtwara	92	25	117
Total	6 787	3 560	10 347

Fig. 19.3 East Africa — railways, lake steamer services and seaports, 1973

tion, and Table 122 shows the amount of cargo handled by them in 1973.

Mombasa is by far the best equipped and busiest

seaport in East Africa. In 1973 Mombasa dealt with about two-thirds of all the cargo handled by the East African seaports. The importance of Mombasa as a port is clearly related to the size and productiveness of its hinterland. It is the only significant seaport serving Kenya and Uganda, and also handles some of the overseas trade of Rwanda, Zaïre and northern Tanzania. In recent years it has also handled some of Zambia's overseas trade. Important export items shipped from Mombasa include coffee, cement, maize, cotton, tea, sisal, soda ash, refined petroleum products, copper and fluospar. In addition to general imports, large quantities of crude oil are discharged at Mombasa, to supply the refinery there.

The town of Mombasa is situated on an island, which is now linked to the mainland by causeways. Mombasa has in fact two harbours. Mombasa Harbour, sometimes known as Old Harbour, lies on the eastern side of the island; while the wider, deeper Kilindini Harbour lies on the south-western side. The silt carried down by the many streams which flow into Mombasa and Kilindini harbours has prevented the growth of coral across their entrances.

Mombasa Harbour, which was of considerable importance in the past, is today mainly used by dhows and other small vessels, while Kilindini has been developed as a modern deep-water port. Construction of the first deep-water berths did not begin until 1921, but by 1972 there were 13 deep-water berths in operation, and a further two under construction. In addition there is a special wharf for the bulk-loading of cement and fluospar, and an oil jetty for the discharge of petroleum.

Dar-es-Salaam is by far the most important of the Tanzanian ports, although ranking a long way behind Mombasa in tonnage of cargo handled. Although Dar-es-Salaam's hinterland is as extensive as that of Mombasa, it is much less productive. Important export items handled at Dar-es-Salaam include Zambian copper, sisal, cotton, oilseed cake, coffee, cement, maize and tea. As in the case of Mombasa, crude petroleum forms a very important import.

The harbour at Dar-es-Salaam is in some ways comparable to that at Kilindini, although it is smaller and more difficult to enter. Before 1956 Dar-es-Salaam had only lighterage facilities. The first deep-water quay to accommodate three vessels was opened in 1956, and this was followed by the opening of an oil jetty in 1966. Since Zimbabwe's Unilateral Declaration of Independence part of Zambia's export trade has been diverted through Dar-es-Salaam. In order to cope with the additional traffic, three new deep-water berths were opened in 1970. It is expected that now the Tanzania–Zambia railway is completed, an even greater volume of Zambia's overseas trade will pass through Dar-es-Salaam. At present two more deep-water berths are being constructed, as well as an off-shore oil tanker terminal.

Tanga is now a much less important port than Dar-es-Salaam. In 1973 the total tonnage of cargo handled at Tanga was less than one-tenth of that handled at Dar-es-Salaam. Because of the shallowness of the water close to the shore, Tanga has only been able to develop as a lighterage port. The railway line leading inland from Tanga is very much shorter than those terminating at Mombasa and Dar-es-Salaam, and consequently the port of Tanga has a very much more restricted hinterland than either of the other two ports. Furthermore, because of its better facilities for handling cargo, Mombasa is able to draw much of the traffic of northern Tanzania away from Tanga. At present Tanga mainly depends upon the export of sisal. It is likely to handle more cargo in future, following the opening of a large fertiliser factory and a sisal pulp mill in the area.

Mtwara is the least important of the mainland ports. It was planned as the sea-port for the ill-fated Groundnut Scheme, and two deep-water berths were opened there in 1954. Although its harbour is good, the importance of Mtwara as a port is limited by the fact that it has a small and relatively poor hinterland. Until recently Mtwara suffered competition from the older but poorer port of Lindi, but the latter has now been closed to sea traffic. The leading items shipped from Mtwara are cashew nuts and cassava.

The port of Zanzibar is situated on the western side of Zanzibar Island. Zanzibar remains a lighterage port. Its harbour consists of an area of water which is sheltered by a semi-circle of coral reefs. Small coasting vessels can be brought alongside the main quay, but larger vessels must anchor some distance from the shore, in deeper water. The port of Zanzibar serves the islands of Zanzibar and Pemba, and its main exports are cloves, copra and coir.

The ports of India

India has eight major seaports, namely Bombay, Calcutta, Visakhapatnam, Murmagao, Madras,

Small coastal craft tied up at the wharf in Zanzibar. The sacks on the wharf contain copra. Because of the shallowness of the water near to the shore, larger vessels must anchor off-shore, and are loaded and unloaded by means of lighters.

Cochin, Kandla and Paradip. Mangalore in Mysore and Tuticorin in Tamil Nadu are also being developed as major ports. In 1971–2 the cargo handled by India's major ports amounted to 59,19 million tonnes, of which 29,96 consisted of imports, and 29,23 million tonnes of exports. About 59 per cent of the cargo exported consisted of iron ore.

Bombay is India's most important port. It is of particular importance for the handling of imports. Important commodities imported through Bombay include metals, machinery, petroleum and food-stuffs. Bombay's exports originate from the penin-sular hinterland of the port and include cotton goods, oil seeds, manganese and raw cotton. A considerable

Table 123 The traffic of India's major ports, 1971–2

Port	No. of ships entered	Cargo handled (million tonnes)		
		Imports	Exports	Total
Bombay	2 493	12,57	3,57	16,14
Calcutta	1 244	4,75	2,54	7,29
Visakhapatnam	640	2,79	5,85	8,64
Murmagao	625	0,43	11,27	11,70
Madras	916	4,10	2,69	6,79
Cochin	1 036	3,52	1,18	4,70
Kandla	251	1,80	0,23	2,03
Paradip	77	—	1,90	1,90

Kandla 1.80
0.23
Bombay
2.54 Calcutta
4.75
12.57
Paradip
2.79 1.90
3.57
5.85 Visakhapatnam
0.43
11.27
Murmagao
4.10
Cochin
3.52 2.69 Madras
1.18

Exports

12.57 Cargo handled
(million tonnes)
Imports

0 300 600
km

Fig. 19.4 Major ports of India, 1971–2

proportion of Bombay's trade is entrepot trade. The bulk of this is with minor ports along the western coast of India between Dwarka and Cape Comorin. A number of factors have favoured Bombay's development as an important port:

1 It has a fine natural harbour which is protected from the full effects of the South-west Monsoon by Bombay Island.
2 It is roughly centrally situated on the western coast of India, facing the Suez Canal sea route.
3 The Thal and Bhor passes in the Western Ghats give easy access to the interior. The hinterland of Bombay extends roughly as far as Delhi, Jabalpur, Nagpur and Hyderabad.

The port of Calcutta is situated on the Hooghly river about 190 km from the sea. The Hooghly river tends to silt up, and in order to maintain a waterway, extensive dredging is necessary. Calcutta is the natural outlet for the vast Gangetic Plain. Its export trade is largely composed of tea, jute and jute manufactures. During the 1960s a deep-water out-port was constructed at Haldia, to handle some of the larger cargo vessels which have difficulty in reaching Calcutta itself.

The port of Madras is situated on a surf-beaten section of the east coast, and in the past ships had to anchor about 1½ km offshore, and were loaded and unloaded by surf boats. At the beginning of the twentieth century, however, breakwaters were built to provide a sheltered harbour, which was dredged to a depth of 10 metres. Exports from Madras include groundnuts, hides, leather, raw cotton and cotton goods. Like Bombay, Madras has a considerable entrepot trade.

The port of Cochin is situated on the south-west coast of India. It is an old port, which was formerly famous for its spice trade. During the 1920s a deep-water channel was dredged through the sand bar to the lagoon behind, and since that time its trade has increased considerably. Imports consist mainly of rice and petroleum, while exports include coconut products, tea, rubber and cashew nuts.

The port of Visakhapatnam has an artificial harbour, and is the chief port of Andra Pradesh. Its exports, which usually greatly exceed its imports, consist largely of manganese ore and groundnuts. The port of Murmagao (Goa) is largely concerned with the export of minerals. The port of Kandla is situated on a creek in the Gulf of Kutch. It was opened as a port in 1955, and was built to replace the port of Karachi, which is now in Pakistan. The port of Paradip is mainly concerned with the export of iron ore.

The port of Singapore

Singapore is one of the world's busiest seaports. In the mid-1970s the port was used by more than 200 major shipping lines, as well as by local coastal services. Table 124 shows the amount of traffic handled by the port of Singapore in the period 1964 to 1974.

A number of factors have favoured the development of Singapore as a major seaport, including:

1 the existence of a fine natural harbour on the southern side of Singapore Islands, which provides a safe anchorage for ships of all sizes;
2 the extremely favourable geographical position. Singapore is situated at the southern end of the Malacca Strait, which links the Indian Ocean with the South China Sea. Because of its position, Singapore is able to act as a transhipment port,

293

Table 124 Shipping using Singapore (vessels over 75 net registered tonnes)

Year	No. of ships cleared	Total freight handled (million freight tonnes)	No. of passenger arrivals
1964	10 296	18,8	34 933
1966	12 188	27,6	35 743
1968	15 524	36,8	31 145
1970	18 269	43,5	33 855
1972	18 628	57,1	58 679
1974	19 617	60,5	72 688

linking many of the smaller ports of Southeast Asia with the world's major shipping routes.

3 the policy of free trade which was established by Raffles in the early part of the nineteenth century, and which is still largely in force today. This has contributed greatly to the success of Singapore as a major entrepot.

In the early days of British settlement, trading was mainly carried out from anchorages around the mouth of the Singapore river. The modern deep-water port facilities, however, are located further to the west around Keppel Harbour. The port area is controlled and managed by the Port of Singapore Authority (PSA). The PSA wharves at Keppel extend for almost 5 km, and are capable of accommodating

26 ocean-going vessels and five coasters at any one time. The wharf area is served by both roads and railway. These are linked to the West Malaysian road and railway networks, by the causeway which connects Singapore Island to the mainland.

Many of the vessels using the port of Singapore, however, do not tie up at the wharves, but instead anchor out in the Roads. These comprise the Inner Roads which provide a 5 metre anchorage for small coastal vessels, and the Outer Roads which provide an open natural anchorage for ocean-going ships. The two Roads are separated from each other by a breakwater. The vessels which use the Roads are loaded and unloaded by means of lighters, which carry goods to and from the Telok Ayer Basin and the banks of the Singapore river.

Fig. 19.5 The position of Singapore

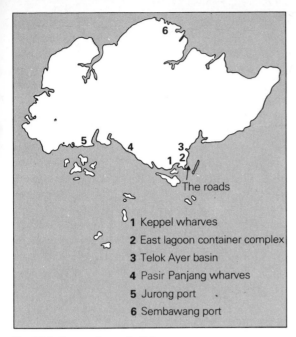

Fig. 19.6 Singapore's port facilities

In 1965 a new bulk-handling port was completed at Jurong, a few kilometres to the west of the main port. Jurong port is administered by the PSA, and serves the new Jurong Industrial Estate. It has berths for five ocean-going vessels, and handles such cargoes as cement clinker, potash, sugar, grains and fertilisers.

Another recent development has been the construction of the East Lagoon Container Complex, which was completed in 1971. This has facilities for the loading and unloading of container vessels, which are now tending to replace the conventional breakbulk cargo ships. Containers are weatherproof boxes, which are strengthened to withstand stacking and the motion of the sea. The cargo is packed into these containers, instead of being stored loose in the holds of the ship. The use of containers facilitates shipboard stowage. Containers can also easily be loaded onto land forms of transport.

At the northern end of Singapore Island, is the five berth Sembawang Port. This is mainly used for the handling of low-cost, high-volume cargo such as timber.

The Pasir Panjang Wharves were only opened in 1974. They can accommodate 21 lighters, eight coastal vessels and six LASH (lighter aboard ship)

barges at any one time. The LASH system involves the packaging of cargo into floating containers. These are stored on board the mother ship, and can be unloaded into the water by crane and towed ashore. This system can be used in ports where the water is too shallow for conventional container ships to operate.

The Panama Canal

In the past several attempts have been made to construct a canal across the narrow isthmus of Panama, and thus to connect the Pacific Ocean with the Caribbean Sea and the Atlantic Ocean. The French began constructing a canal during the 1880s, but disease decimated their work force, and the project had to be abandoned. The USA began work on the present canal in 1904, and completed it in 1914. A large part of the labour force employed in the construction of the Panama Canal was recruited from the islands of the British West Indies, and many of the descendants of these workers still live in the Panama Canal Zone.

Ships passing through locks in the Panama Canal

The Panama Canal is 82 km in length from deep water to deep water, and has a minimum depth of $12\frac{1}{2}$ metres. The canal runs from north-west to south-east, and is of the lock-and-lake type. Entering from the Caribbean Sea at Colón, ships first ascend the three flight Gatun locks, which lift them up to the Gatun Lake at a height of 26 metres above sea level. This lake has been formed by damming the Chaggres river. After passing through the Catun Lake, ships enter the Gaillard Cut (Culebra Cut), which is 13 km long and 61 metres deep. Leaving the Gaillard Cut, ships then descend the Pedro Miguel Locks and the Miraflores Locks, which lower them back to sea level. The terminal at the Pacific end of the Canal is Balbao. Two-way travel is possible in the Canal, and the average transit time is about eight hours.

According to the United States–Panama treaty of 1903, the United States had control over the canal and also over the Panama Canal Zone. The Canal Zone comprised a narrow strip of land, extending 8 km on each side of the canal, and divided the Republic of Panama into two parts. Many Panamanians resented the American occupation of what they considered to be the most important part of their national territory, and in 1978 succeeded in pressurising the Americans to relinquish the control of the Canal and the Canal Zone to Panama.

The opening of the Panama Canal reorientated the trade routes of the western hemisphere. In particular it greatly improved communications between the eastern and western coasts of the Americas, and also between Europe and the western seaboard of the Americas. The sea journey from New York to San Francisco is about 13 000 km shorter by way of the Canal than by way of Cape Horn. The journey from Liverpool to San Francisco is about 9 200 km shorter by the Canal route. The journey between the eastern seaboard of the USA and the eastern seaboard of Asia is also much shorter by way of the Canal, than by way of Cape Horn or the Cape of Good Hope.

In 1975 there were a total of 14 735 transits through the Canal, carrying a total of more than 140 million tonnes of cargo. Ships using the Canal have to pay toll charges, and in 1975 these amounted to US$ 143,4 million. About two-fifths of the tonnage of cargo passing through the Canal was travelling from the Pacific to the Atlantic, and three-fifths from the Atlantic to the Pacific. The most important items carried from the Pacific side to the Atlantic side were mineral ores, timber, petroleum, sugar, cereals, metals, canned foods, bananas and fish meal. In the other direction the most important items were petroleum, petroleum products, coal and coke.

In recent years there has been a considerable increase in the amount of traffic using the Canal, which is now approaching the limits of its capacity. When the Canal was first opened, it could accommodate the largest ships then afloat, but today a growing number of ships are too big to use the Canal. The lock chambers are 300 metres long and 34 metres wide, and this in effect means that fully laden ships of more than 80 000 tonnes are unable to pass through the Canal. In 1975 the world's largest ship, was a giant tanker of 484 000 tonnes. This tanker had a length of 379 metres, and a width of 62 metres.

In recent years there has been much discussion as to whether it would be better to improve the existing canal to enable it to handle the giant ships of the future, or whether it would be better to build an entirely new canal elsewhere in Central America. Several alternative sites for a new canal have been suggested. These include:

1 through the Isthmus of Tehuantepec in Mexico;
2 through Nicaragua, making use of Lake Nicaragua;
3 by way of the valley of the Atrato river in northern Colombia.

Road and rail transport

Most tropical countries still have a poor network of roads and railways. In many parts of the tropical world, the building and maintenance of roads and railways is difficult and expensive. The ruggedness of the terrain, for example, poses a serious problem to the road and railway builder in such areas as the Andean highlands of South America, in parts of Southeast Asia, and in some of the more mountainous islands of the West Indies. In many parts of the tropical world, the torrential nature of the rainfall also tends to create problems. Heavy rains sometimes wash away sections of roads and railways, and bridges may occasionally be swept away during floods. Roads which do not have a tarred surface frequently become impassable during the rainy season. In areas of rain forest, the denseness of the natural vegetation makes road and railway construction difficult.

In many parts of the tropical world, the roads have recently begun to capture a great deal of traffic from the railways. Although road traffic is generally more expensive than transport by rail, in many tropical countries it is very much faster. In Kenya, for example, the journey of about 480 km from Nairobi to Mombasa takes at least 12 hours by passenger train, but the same journey can be undertaken in less than half that time by car. Road transport is also much more flexible than rail transport. Small quantities of goods and small numbers of passengers can be moved between a large number of different points by road. For these reasons, roads are of particular importance for the transport of passengers, and for the short distance haulage of light freight. Railways, however, continue to be of considerable importance for the transport of heavy freight, particularly minerals.

The railways of West Africa
West Africa has a poor network of railways. Most of West Africa's railways run inland from the coast, but few of them penetrate far into the interior. In Ghana, for example, the inland terminus of the railway system is Kumasi, and the northern two-thirds of the country is not served by rail. At present three West African countries, namely Gambia, Guinea Bissau and Niger, have no railway system. In the case of Gambia, the lack of railways is no handicap, as the country is very small, and the Gambia river provides a good natural routeway linking the interior of the country with the sea. In the case of Niger, however, the lack of direct rail links with the coastal seaports undoubtedly hampers development.

Most of the railway lines in West Africa were built at the end of the nineteenth century or in the early part of the twentieth century. A number of new lines have, however, been built since the end of the Second World War. Most of these have been built primarily for the purpose of transporting minerals from the mines in the interior to the seaports.

Nigeria has some 4 300 km of railway. The Nigerian system consists of two main routes, which penetrate inland from the seaports of Lagos and Port Harcourt, and which merge at Kaduna. The line from Lagos to Ibadan was opened in 1901, and was extended as far as Kano in 1912. A branch line was built from Minna to the important river port of Baro on the Niger. In 1927 the main line was extended from Kano to Nguru, and a branch line was built in 1929 from Zaria to Kaura Namoda. These lines carry large quantities of groundnuts, groundnut oil and cotton from the main producing areas in the north of Nigeria, to ports in the south of the country. The railheads at Kano, Kaura Namoda and Nguru also handle some of the overseas trade of neighbouring Niger.

The line from Port Harcourt to Enugu was opened in 1916. This was built primarily for the purpose of transporting coal from the mines to Port Harcourt for shipment. The railway was extended from Enugu to Jos in 1927, and a branch line was built from Kafanchan to join the main Lagos–Kano line at Kaduna. In 1962–4 a line was built from Kuru near Jos, to Maiduguri in the extreme north-east of the country. This line may eventually be extended to N'Djamena (formerly Fort Lamy) in Chad.

The original impetus to railway construction in Ghana came from the gold mining companies. A line was opened in 1901 from the port of Sekondi to the gold mines at Tarkwa, and this was extended to the mines at Obuasi in 1902. The line was completed to Kumasi in 1903. Gold mining was also responsible for the construction of a branch line from Tarkwa to Prestea in 1912. In 1943–4 a branch line was constructed from Dunkwa to serve the bauxite mines at Awaso.

Although the exploitation of minerals was the main reason for the construction of railways in western Ghana, it was the development of cocoa farming which provided the main impetus to railway building in the east of the country. A line from Accra to Kumasi was built in easy stages between 1909 and 1923. In 1928 a branch line was built from Huni Valley to Kade, and in 1956 another line was built from Kotoku on the main Accra–Kumasi line to join it at Achiasi, thus providing a more direct rail link between Accra and Takoradi. In 1954 a short branch line was opened to link Accra and the new port of Tema.

A 1 144 km long railway runs northward from the

port of Abidjan in the Ivory Coast, to Ouagadougou the capital of Upper Volta. This line reached Bouaké in central Ivory Coast in 1912, and Bobo-Dioulasso in Upper Volta in 1934. It was extended to Ouagadougou in 1954. At some future date it may be extended a further 350 km, from Ouagadougou to Tambao in the north-east of Upper Volta. At Tambao there are deposits of manganese ore, which as yet have not been developed on account of their remoteness. The railway line from Ouagadougou to Abidjan carries much of Upper Volta's overseas trade. Upper Volta, however, is a very poor country, and the amount of freight handled by the Upper Volta section of the railway is relatively small.

In Sierra Leone the main railway line runs from Freetown to Pendembu, a distance of 500 km. It was opened in stages between 1899 and 1908, and was built mainly to serve the oil palm growing areas of Sierra Leone. A branch line to Makeni was opened between 1908 and 1911. In recent years these lines have lost much of their freight and passenger traffic to the roads, and because of this it has been decided to gradually close down the railways. The branch line to Makeni was closed in 1970, and services on the main line between Bo and Pendembu were discontinued in 1971. In addition to the public system, there is a 90 km long mineral line from Marampa to Pepel. This line was opened in 1933, to transport iron ore from the mines at Marampa to the coast for shipment.

The first railway in Senegal was built between Dakar and St. Louis, and was completed in 1885. The construction of this line made it possible to avoid navigating the difficult estuary of the Senegal river. With the river, the railway line provided a through route from Kayes in Mali to the port of Dakar. The construction of this line also greatly stimulated the commercial production of groundnuts in the area between Dakar and St. Louis. In 1904 a line was opened from Kayes to Bamako and Koulikoro, and in 1923 the line from Kayes to Thiès was opened, thus providing for the first time a direct rail connection between Bamako and Dakar. The railway from Bamako to Dakar carries much of Mali's overseas trade.

In Liberia all railway construction has taken place since 1950, and has been dependent upon the development of iron ore mining in the interior of the country. In 1951 a line was opened from Monrovia to the mines at Bomi Hills, and in 1962 this was extended to the mines at Mano river. In 1963 a line was built from the port of Buchanan, to the mines at Mount Nimba. Although this line was built by the mining company concerned, it is also open for public traffic. A line was built from Monrovia to the mines at Bong Range in 1965.

The only railway line in Mauritania runs from the mineral port at Point Central near Nouadhibou, to F'Derik in the interior of the country. It is 635 km long, and was opened as recently as 1963. It was owned by MIFERMA, and was built for the sole purpose of transporting iron ore from the Khedia d'Idjil range to the coast. A number of problems were encountered in the construction of this railway.

In Guinea the main railway runs from Conakry to Kankan on the navigable Milo tributary of the Niger. It is 604 km long, and was built in stages between 1900 and 1904. In 1958 a 140 km long branch line was constructed to the bauxite workings and alumina plant at Fria. There is now an 137 km long railway from the bauxite deposits at Sangaredi, to the new port of Kamsar. There is also the possibility of the building of new lines to open up the vast iron ore deposits in the Mount Nimba and Mount Simandou areas.

In Benin the most important railway line runs northward from Cotonou to Parakou. There is also a short line from Cotonou through Porto Novo to Pobe, which serves the rich oil palm growing belt. In Togo the main railway runs from Lomé to Blitta. Other short lines run from Lomé to Palimé, and from Lomé to Anécho. A mineral line has recently been built to transport phosphate rock from the mines at Hahotoe, to the treatment plant and wharf at Kpémé.

Road transport in West Africa

The amount of road traffic in West Africa has increased considerably in recent years. The number of passenger cars increased from about 100 000 in 1959, to almost 400 000 in 1972. During the same period the number of commercial vehicles increased from 90 000 to more than 250 000.

In contrast to the railways, the roads in West Africa are particularly important for the movement of people. In recent years road transport has also taken

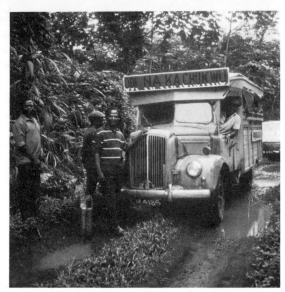

Road transport in Nigeria. Mammy wagons are widely used for short distance transport. They carry both goods and passengers.

Changing a wheel near Malindi in Kenya. Many roads in the tropical world do not have a tarred surface. The cost of maintaining vehicles which travel on untarred roads is high.

over a lot of short distance haulage of freight from the railways. The railways, however, continue to handle most of the region's heavy freight, including virtually all the minerals and some of the timber.

A very common conveyance on the roads of West Africa is the 'mammy waggon'. This vehicle usually consists of a locally made wooden body, mounted on a lorry chassis, and carries both passengers and goods. Mammy waggons are very much used by traders, when making short journeys to and from local markets.

The road network in most West African countries is still poor. The closest network of roads is usually found in areas close to the coast. Some of the major and most of the minor roads in West Africa still do not have a tarred surface. In Nigeria, for example, only about 17 per cent of the total road distance was tarred in 1974. During periods of heavy rainfall, the untarred roads frequently became impassable. Untarred roads are often badly corrugated, and the cost of maintaining vehicles which have to travel over such roads is high.

Except in a few areas such as the Fouta Djalon, the terrain does not pose a serious problem to road construction in West Africa. In the forest zone, however, the denseness of the vegetation often makes road construction difficult. There are also a great number of rivers and streams in the forest zone of West Africa, which must either be bridged or crossed by means of ferries. Ferries often cause considerable delays in the flow of traffic.

The Indian railways

India's transport pattern is dominated by its railways. In 1973–4 India had more than 60 000 km of railway, virtually all state-owned. The Indian railway network is the largest in Asia, and the fourth largest in the world, ranking after the railways of the USA, the USSR and Canada. In 1973–4 the Indian Government Railways ran an average of 10 800 trains a day. These trains carried a daily average of more than 7,3 million passengers, and about 0,55 million tonnes of freight.

The Indian railway system is a long-established one. The first line in India was opened in 1853, between Bombay and Thana. By the 1920s, a large part of the present system had been completed. Most of the line laid down during this early period was single track. Unfortunately three different gauges (the gauge is the distance between the inside of the lines) were used. In 1970–1 roughly 50 per cent of the total route distance was on broad gauge, 43 per cent was on metre gauge, and the remaining 7 per cent on narrow gauge. The existence of different gauges is a serious handicap to the cheap and rapid transportation of goods, as the rolling stock used on lines of one gauge cannot be used on lines of a different gauge. Consequently, it is often necessary to undertake either costly and time-consuming transhipment of goods from one set of railway waggons to another, or alternatively to send the goods by a much longer route in order to avoid break of gauge.

In 1973–4 the Indian Government Railways carried a total of 2 654 million passengers. The great majority of passengers on the Indian railways travel third class, which is extremely cheap. A great number of people travel daily to work in such cities as Bombay, Delhi, Madras, Calcutta, and Hyderabad, and more than 3 million of the 7,3 million passengers who used the railway in a day were in fact commuters.

The freight carried by the Indian railways amounted to a total of 185 million tonnes in 1973–4. The most important commodities carried by the railways are coal, iron ore, food grains, iron and steel, petroleum products and chemical fertilisers. The railways transport about 90 per cent of India's coal, and this commodity alone accounts for one-third of all the freight handled by the Indian

Table 125 Principal commodities carried on India's railways, 1973–4

Commodity	% of total value
Coal	33,6
Metallic ores	11,4
Food grains	7,9
Cement	5,4
Mineral oil	5,4
Iron and steel	5,0
Chemical manures	2,9
Salt	1,3
Sugar cane	1,0
Sugar	0,7
Manganese ore	0,6
Oil seeds	0,6
Paper and paper products	0,5
Raw jute	0,3
Raw cotton	0,2
Jute manufactures	0,2

railways. The iron and steel industry also depends very heavily on rail transport, for the carriage of both its bulky raw materials and its finished products.

The Indian railways were badly overworked during the Second World War, and since 1947 the government has been making a considerable effort to improve them. In the early years priority was given to the repair and replacement of locomotive and rolling stock, while more recently attempts have been made to modernise the system by doubling the track along important routes, and by the introduction of diesel and electric locomotives in place of steam ones. The manufacture of steam locomotives in India was discontinued in 1972. As late as 1970–1, however, steam locomotives made up 84,1 per cent of the total of 11 158 locomotives in service, while only 10,5 per cent were diesel and 5,4 per cent electric.

The railways of Brazil

In 1973 Brazil was served by some 32 100 km of railway. Most of Brazil's railways were built by British companies during the second half of the nineteenth and the first half of the twentieth centuries. They were mainly built for the purpose of transporting export commodities, such as coffee, from the producing areas to the ports. Most of these railways were isolated and independent systems, and were built on five different gauges.

Since the end of the Second World War most of the foreign-owned railways have been acquired by the state. The government has concentrated its efforts on the construction of linkage systems, to connect the various lateral east to west lines with each other. There has also been some electrification of the routes which serve the main industrial centres and areas of high population density. Most of the length of new track which has been laid, is that which extends the existing system to the new federal capital of Brasília.

The railways of Brazil are almost entirely confined to the eastern margins of the country, and a very large part of Brazil is not served by railway at all. There are only three areas in which some kind of network can be said to exist:

1 the coffee-growing and industrial areas of the south-east;
2 the southern states;

3 the cotton and sugar cane growing areas of the north-east.

Except for the line which runs from Belem to Bragança near the mouth of the Amazon, the whole of the vast Amazon Basin has only two short lengths of railway line. These are the Amapá and the Madeira-Mamoré railways. The Amapá railway was completed in 1956, and carries manganese ore from the mines at Serra do Navio to the new river port of Porto Santana near Macapá.

The Madeira-Mamoré railway is of much earlier origin. It runs for some 364 km between Porto Velho and Guajara-Mirim. The construction of this railway first began in 1872, but it was not completed until 1912. It was built to circumvent rapids on the Madeira and Mamoré rivers, and thus to make it possible to export the produce of the Oriente region of Bolivia by way of the Amazon river. The Madeira–Mamoré railway has never been extended to the Bolivian town of Riberalta on the Beni river as was originally intended.

Brazil has the following rail links with neighbouring countries:

1 A line from Santos and São Paulo extends westwards to the town of Corumbá on the Paraguay river, and then continues to Santa Cruz in Bolivia.
2 A line from the port of Porto Alegre runs through Santa María, to connect with the Argentinian system at Uruguaiana.
3 Another line runs southward from Santa María, to connect with the Uruguayan system at Livramento.

The Pan-American Highway

The Pan-American Highway was designed to link together all the countries of North America and South America by road. The decision to undertake the construction of such a highway system was reached in 1923, at the Fifth International Conference of American States, held at Santiago in Chile. Road construction began a few years later, and by 1970 there were only a few short sections still uncompleted. The Pan-American Highway was originally conceived as a single road, linking Alaska in the north with Argentina in the south. As the concept expanded, however, alternative routes were added, and today there is no one single road which can be identified as the Pan-American Highway. The Pan-American Highway system does in fact involve several routes in many countries through which it passes.

Each country is responsible for the construction and maintenance of its own sections of the Highway, although a number of countries have received some financial assistance from the USA. Wherever possible, the Highway has incorporated existing sections of road, but in most countries several entirely new sections have also had to be built. The standard of the road varies considerably from one country to another. In some countries it is a wide and well metalled highway. In the Andean state of Ecuador, on the other hand, the Highway runs through extremely difficult terrain, and for the most part is extremely narrow and winding.

The 4 800 km long section between the United States–Mexico border and Panama City is sometimes

Ore carriers being loaded with alumina at Port Esquivel, Jamaica. The alumina is transported by rail from the alumina plants in the interior of the island.

301

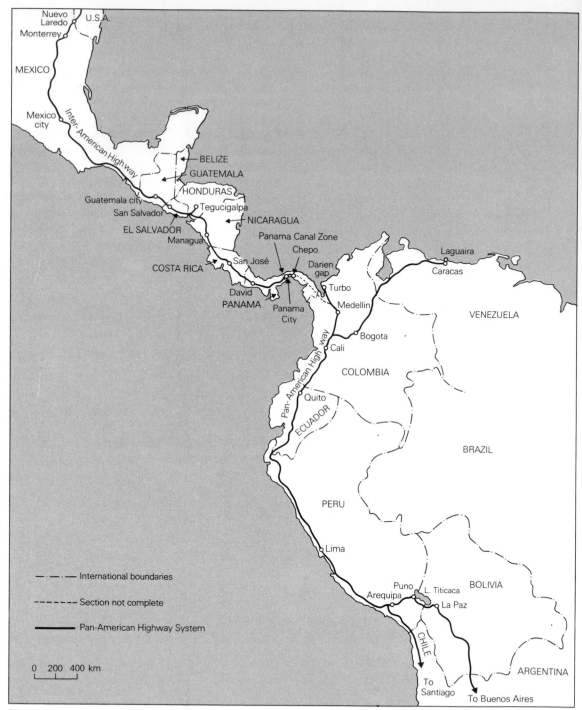

Fig. 19.7 The Pan-American Highway system

known as the Inter-American Highway. A metalled road planned as part of the Highway was opened from Larèdo in Texas to Mexico City in 1936, and was extended to the Guatemalan border in 1950. By the late 1960s all sections of the Inter-American Highway had been completed. From Mexico City the

Inter-American Highway passes through Guatemala City, San Salvador, Managua, and San José, before continuing through David to Panama City. By 1970 the Highway had been extended on the eastern side of the Panama Canal as far as Chepo. There remains, however, an uncompleted section between eastern Panama and northern Colombia, generally known as the Darién Gap. Road construction in the Darién Province of Panama is extremely difficult, because of the denseness of the rain forest and the swampy nature of the terrain.

In South America the Highway begins either at the Venezuelan port of La Guaira, or at the Colombian village of Turbo on the Gulf of Uraba, which is the terminus of a recently constructed road from Medellin. From La Guaira the Highway runs through Caracas to Bogota, and then on to Quito in Ecuador. From Quito it continues southward through rugged mountain country into Peru. Once in Peru the Highway follows the coast until it reaches the southern port of Camana, where it swings inland to Arequipa. Here it splits into two branches. One branch runs southward into Chile, while the other swings eastward to Puno on the shores of Lake Titicaca. From Puno the road continues to La Paz in Bolivia, and then on to Buenos Aires in Argentina. There are roads from Buenos Aires which run northward to link up with the highway systems of Uraguay, Paraguay and Brazil.

Even when the Pan-American Highway is finally completed, it is not likely to be greatly used for long-distance travel, except by the relatively few tourists who can afford to spend several weeks visiting the countries of Central and South America. The Highway does, however, provide a useful link between neighbouring Latin American countries.

Transport by pipeline

Although water has for a long time been moved by pipe, the use of pipelines for the transport of other commodities is relatively recent. In many parts of the world pipelines are used for the transport of petroleum from the oilfields to the refineries, and from the oilfields to the oil terminals on the coast where it can be loaded into ocean-going tankers. Other commodities which are commonly transported by

Fig. 19.8 Colombia – transport by pipeline

pipeline are refined petroleum products from the refineries to the market distribution terminals, and natural gas from the gasfields to the markets. In some countries finely ground coal, iron ore and copper ore in suspension have been moved through pipelines.

Colombia's pipeline network

Several tropical countries including Colombia, Venezuela, Mexico, and Nigeria, now have extensive networks of pipelines. Most of Colombia's oilfields and gasfields are remote from the coast, and their development has necessitated the laying of pipelines of considerable length. Because of the mountainous nature of much of Colombia, this has not been an easy task. Colombia's pipelines can be divided into three groups:

1 those which carry crude oil from the oilfields to the oil terminals at Mamonal, Covenas and Santa Marta for export;
2 those which carry natural gas from the gasfields to Baranquilla and Mamonal;
3 those which carry refined petroleum products from

303

the refinery at Barrancabermeja to cities such as Bogota, Medellin and Cali.

Air transport

In recent years there has been a considerable increase in the use of air travel in many parts of the tropical world. A large number of countries have established their own national airlines. Most of these are small, and only seek to provide limited internal services, but others also operate on international routes. Internal air services are particularly important in countries such as Colombia and Brazil, where the main centres of population tend to be far apart, and where other transport media are not very well developed.

Transport by air is by far the fastest of all the forms of transport. The flying time between Nairobi and Mombasa in Kenya, for example, is under one hour, while the same journey by rail takes more than 12 hours, and that by road about six hours. Air transport is, however, generally much more expensive than transport by road or rail, and for this reason it is only suitable for the long-distance transport of passengers, and for the carriage of such goods as mail and bullion which are of very high value in relation

to their weight. Air transport is also sometimes used for the carriage of highly perishable commodities, particularly if these commodities are produced at a considerable distance from their main markets. In Guyana, for example, meat from the Rupununi savannas in the interior of the country is transported by air to Georgetown on the coast. Some fresh fruit, vegetables and flowers are air freighted from Kenya to the United Kingdom and other countries in Europe, while meat is air freighted from Kenya to several neighbouring countries.

Air transport in East Africa

The role of air transport in the East African economy is still small, although it has expanded considerably in recent years. In particular there has been a large increase in the number of international flights to and from East Africa. This increase in international air traffic has been associated largely with the development of the East African tourist industry. There are international airports at Nairobi (Kenya), Entebbe (Uganda), and Dar-es-Salaam (Tanzania). In 1971 the Kilimanjaro International Airport between Arusha and Moshi in northern Tanzania was opened. The Tanzanians hope that the opening of this airport, which is conveniently located near to Tanzania's main tourist circuit, will encourage more tourists to

Air transport in Ghana. Passengers boarding a Ghana Airways plane at Accra, Ghana.

304

Fig. 19.9 East Africa – air transport in 1973

Recently, disagreement between the member states has resulted in the break-up of EAA. Each state has now established its own national airline.

Air transport is less used for internal movement in East Africa, than in some of the other countries of tropical Africa. This is largely because other transport media are relatively well developed in East Africa. In 1973 EAA operated scheduled passenger services calling at 18 airports in Tanzania, four in Kenya and one in Uganda. The fact that air transport plays a more important role in Tanzania than it does in Kenya or Uganda, is largely related to Tanzania's greater size, and also to the peripheral nature of its population distribution.

The busiest international airport in East Africa is Embakasi Airport just outside Nairobi, which handled 867 000 passengers in 1974. In addition to the regular scheduled flights operated by international airlines, Embakasi Airport now handles a large number of charter flights, mainly transporting tourists to and from the United Kingdom and other countries in Europe. In addition to Embakasi Airport, Nairobi also has Wilson Airport, which is used by light aircraft. The wealthier visitors to East Africa often charter light aircraft from Wilson Airport, to transport them to and from the more remote game lodges, most of which have their own landing strips. Also operating from Wilson Airport is the Flying Doctor Service, which transports seriously ill patients from remote areas for hospital treatment.

The transport problems of land-locked states

A number of tropical countries have no direct access to the sea, namely, Mali, Niger, Upper Volta, Chad, Central African Republic, Uganda, Rwanda, Burundi, Zambia, Zimbabwe, Malawi and Botswana in tropical Africa; Bolivia and Paraguay in tropical America; and Laos in tropical Asia. Many of these land-locked states experience serious transport problems.

In the first place, long overland hauls to the coastal seaports, and the fact that it is sometimes necessary to tranship goods between road, rail and river services, means that the cost of transporting goods to and from other countries tends to be unusually high. For example, by the time that goods

fly directly to Tanzania. In the past many of the overseas visitors to northern Tanzania have preferred to arrive in East Africa through Nairobi, which is much nearer to the Arusha–Moshi area than is Dar-es-Salaam.

East Africa is served by a number of airlines. The East African Airways Corporation (EAA) was established in 1946 to provide a domestic air service, but later operated on a number of international routes as well. In 1973 EAA operated regular air services between the three countries of East Africa and Lusaka (Zambia), Blantyre (Malawi), Tananarive (Madagascar), Mauritius, Kigali (Rwanda), Bujumbura (Burundi), Mogadishu (Somalia), Addis Ababa (Ethiopia), Aden, Karachi (Pakistan), Bombay (India), Athens (Greece), Rome (Italy), Frankfurt (West Germany), Zurich (Switzerland), Copenhagen (Denmark) and London (United Kingdom). The number of other international airlines serving East Africa increased from 10 in 1963 to 22 in 1972.

Three forms of transport in Jamaica. In the foreground cane carts are being loaded with sugar cane. Tractors will be used to haul the loaded carts to the factory. In the background a cruise ship and a jet aircraft bring tourists to the island.

imported from overseas reach the Central African Republic, they are frequently twice the price they were when they were unloaded at the Congolese seaport of Pointe Noire.

Secondly, the land-locked states are dependent upon the goodwill of their neighbours for access to coastal seaports. Political differences with these neighbours may result in the closure of vital routes to the sea. For example, when in early 1976 Uganda laid claim to a large area of Kenyan territory, the government of Kenya retaliated by imposing a boycott on all goods passing through the port of Mombasa on their way to or from Uganda.

The land-locked states of West Africa

In West Africa there are three land-locked states, namely Upper Volta, Mali and Niger. Upper Volta is fortunate in having a direct rail link with the coast, by way of the so-called Abidjan–Niger Railway, which runs from Ouagadougou to Abidjan. The bulk of Upper Volta's trade with countries outside of West

Africa is carried by this railway line. One of Upper Volta's outstanding export items, however, consists of live animals, and these are mainly driven on foot to neighbouring West African countries for sale.

Mali's most important link with the outside world is the railway which runs from Koulikoro and Bamako on the River Niger, to the port of Dakar in Senegal. In 1959 the two former French colonies of Senegal and French Soudan joined together to form the Federation of Mali. Less than a year later, however, political differences led to the breakup of this Federation, the former French Soudan continuing to be known as Mali. Transport links between Senegal and Mali were interrupted, and indeed a whole section of the railway track at Kidira on the border between the two countries was actually removed. Mali thus had to find an alternative route to the sea. A fleet of 400 lorries and road tankers was purchased, and these were used to haul goods to and from terminals on the Abidjan–Niger Railway in Upper Volta. This railway offered preferential rates for Mali's goods, and by the end of 1961 most of Mali's overseas trade was passing through the port of Abidjan in the Ivory Coast. Senegal and Mali resumed friendly relations in 1963, and once again much of Mali's overseas trade passes through the Senegalese port of Dakar, although some still continues to take the longer route through Upper Volta and the port of Abidjan.

Unlike Upper Volta and Mali, the third land-locked state in West Africa has no rail link with the coast, and Niger's overseas exports require lengthy hauls by road before reaching railheads in neighbouring countries. By far the most important of Niger's export items in terms of tonnage and value is groundnuts. These are mainly produced in the Maradi-Zinder area, just to the north of the Nigerian border. The shortest route from the Maradi-Zinder area to the coast involves road haulage to the railheads at Kaura Namoda or Kano in northern Nigeria, and then a long journey by rail to the Nigerian port of Apapa (Lagos). The distance from Zinder to Apapa is 1 387 km, of which 260 is by road to Kano, and the remaining 1 127 is by rail. An alternative route is by road to Parakou in central Benin (formerly Dahomey), and then by rail to the port of Cotonou. This is in fact the shortest route from Niamey to the coast, but from Zinder the Cotonou route (1 658 km) is longer than the Apapa route (1 387 km).

During the 1950s, an increase in the volume of Nigeria's internal traffic led to considerable congestion on the Nigerian railways, with subsequent delays in the handling of Niger's groundnut exports. A further problem arose with regard to the transfer of currency between Niger which was in the franc zone, and Nigeria which was in the sterling zone. During the 1950s the French authorities tried to divert as much of Niger's overseas trade as possible from the Apapa route to the Cotonou route. In 1959 the Organisation Commune Dahomey-Niger des Transports (OCDN) was set up with the express purpose of developing the route to the sea through Dahomey (now Benin). The road northwards from the railhead at Parakou to the Benin–Niger border was improved, and the River Niger was bridged between Malanville and Gaya. The transport of groundnuts by this route was subsidised. In 1963, however, political differences between Niger and Benin resulted in the port of Cotonou being temporarily closed to Niger's traffic, and Niger's overseas trade had to be sent through Apapa. Although friendly relations have since been resumed between Benin and Niger, a large proportion of Niger's groundnut exports still pass through Apapa.

Chad and the Central African Republic

In many respects Chad and the C.A.R. have even less satisfactory outlets to the sea than have the land-locked states of West Africa. During the colonial period the Route Fédérale was developed to provide an outlet to the sea for these land-locked countries. This route involves the use of the ocean port of Pointe Noire in the Congo, and the 515 km long Congo–Ocean Railway from Pointe Noire to the important river port of Brazzaville. At Brazzaville goods are transhipped into barges and carried 1 287 km by the Zaïre and Oubangui rivers, to the river port of Bangui in the C.A.R. N'Djamena (formerly Fort Lamy) more than 960 km beyond Bangui, can be reached by road during the dry season, and from Sarh (formerly Fort Archambault) by way of the Chari river during the rainy season.

After 1959, the Agence Trans-Equatoriale des Communications (ATEC) was set up to administer this route, and to maintain effective co-operation between the states using the port of Pointe Noire, namely Congo, Gabon, C.A.R., and Chad. Between 1959 and 1969 the port facilities at Pointe Noire were greatly expanded, the Congo–Ocean Railway was provided with more passing loops and sections of double track, the river ports of Bangui and Brazzaville were extended and re-equipped, and navigation of the Zaïre and Oubangui rivers was greatly improved by the removal of the worst rock obstacles, the provision of radar beacons, and by the addition of larger barges to the river fleet. Between 1960 and 1968 traffic over this route to Chad and the C.A.R. increased from 130 000 tonnes to 245 000 tonnes. Since 1969, however, the ATEC has effectively ceased to control the whole route, as first the Congo, and then the C.A.R. nationalised their own sections of the route.

Although a large part of Chad's traffic still uses the Route Fédérale several other routes are also of some importance. One of these alternative routes is by road to Maiduguri in Nigeria, and thence by rail to the

Fig. 19.10 Chad and Central African Republic – outlets to the sea

port of Apapa. The Nigerians extended their railway
system to Maiduguri in 1964, and its future extension to N'Djamena, a distance of 250 km, would
seem to be a possibility. Another route is by road to
Garoua in northern Cameroon, and thence by the
Benue and Niger rivers to the delta ports of Niger.
The main limiting factor on this route is the fact that
the upper Benue is only navigable for two months
each year. Another route which has been considered
as a possible outlet to the sea for Chad is by road
across the Sahara Desert to the port of Tripoli in
Libya.

The completion of the Trans-Cameroon Railway
could offer a possible solution to the transport

problems of Chad and C.A.R. The Cameroon railway
system originally extended from the port of Douala
to Yaounde, but in 1969 a 290 km long extension
from Yaounde to Belabo was completed. Work then
began on the 320 km extension from Belabo to
Ngaoundere, and this section was opened in 1974.
Ultimately this line could be extended to Bangui in
the C.A.R. The Trans-Cameroonian Railway will also
be of great benefit to the Cameroon itself. The
railway will greatly facilitate the development of the
agricultural, forestry and mineral resources of the
central and northern parts of Cameroon. The proposed Trans-African Highway, which is intended to
link Mombasa in Kenya with Lagos in Nigeria, could

also possibly help to alleviate the transport problems of the land-locked states of Chad and the C.A.R.

In view of the length and high cost of the overland haul to the coast, it is not surprising that the land-locked states of Chad and the CAR should place great emphasis on the development of air transport. Chad has a total of 43 airports. In 1970 the airport at N'Djamena handled more than 24 000 tonnes of freight. In particular, large quantities of frozen meat are air freighted from Chad to the coastal towns in Gabon, Congo and Zaïre.

Zambia's transport problems

There are several possible routes by which the exports of land-locked Zambia can reach the sea, although not all of them are at present in use:

1 The rail route through Zimbabwe to the ports of Beira or Maputo (formerly Lourenco Marques) in Mozambique or alternatively the longer rail route through Zimbabwe to ports in the Republic of South Africa. Because of the political differences between the governments of Zambia and

Fig. 19.11 Zambia – outlets to the sea

International boundary
River route
Road route
Oil pipeline
Railway
Possible routes to sea

1 Through Zimbabwe to Mozambique ports of Beira or Maputo, or Cape Town in South Africa – entirely rail route – no longer used because of political differences with Zimbabwe

2 Through Shaba province of Zaire to Angolan port of Lobito – entirely rail route.

3 Rail to Ilebo in Zaire – river to Kinshasa – rail to port of Matadi. Not much used at present

4 Road to Salima in Malawi – rail to port of Nacala in Mozambique.

5 The Tazara railway or road to the ports of Dar-es-Salaam in Tanzania or Mombasa in Kenya. Oil pipeline from Dar-es-Salaam to refinery at Ndola.

Zimbabwe, these routes are not at present used.

2 The rail route through the Shaba Province of Zaïre to the Angolan port of Lobito on the Atlantic Ocean. This route has one great advantage for Zambia, namely that Lobito is much nearer to markets in Europe and North America than are the ports on the Indian Ocean, particularly when the Suez Canal is closed. Unfortunately traffic movement along the railway to Lobito is slow, because of the steep gradients involved and the limited passing places available. Also the port of Lobito has suffered in recent years from congestion, with the result that Zambian cargo is subject to considerable delay. Nevertheless, in the early 1970s Lobito was handling about half of Zambia's exports. This route was closed for a short period during the Angolan Civil War.

3 The rail and river route through Zaïre. This involves transport by rail to the port of Ilebo on the Kasai river. Here the goods must be transshipped into barges and carried down the Kasai and Zaïre rivers to the ports of either Kinshasa or Brazzaville, and then taken by rail again to the ocean ports of either Matadi in Zaïre or Pointe Noire in the Congo. This route is not at present used by Zambia, as it is overloaded and slow. It could, however, become an important outlet for Zambia, if the railway is ever extended from Ilebo to the coast, thus providing a through rail route.

4 The road and rail route through Malaŵi to ports in Mozambique. This involves road haulage to the railhead at Salima in Malaŵi, and thence by rail to the ports of either Beira or Nacala in Mozambique. The rail link between Malaŵi and Nacala was only completed in 1970. Although in the past Nacala has handled very little traffic, it has one of the finest natural harbours in tropical Africa, and its importance is likely to increase in the future. The governments of both Zambia and Mozambique are anxious to establish a direct rail link between the two countries, and there is a proposal for a new line to be built from Lusaka to Beira via Zumbo.

5 The road or rail route to either Dar-es-Salaam in Tanzania, or Mombasa in Kenya.

Before the break-up of the Federation of Rhodesia and Nyasaland in 1963, Zambia (then Northern Rhodesia) was mainly dependent upon Portuguese ports for the handling of its overseas trade. Following Zimbabwe's Unilateral Declaration of Independence (UDI) in 1966, Zambia felt it necessary to seek new outlets to the sea, which would avoid passing through Zimbabwe and the then Portuguese colonies of Angola and Mozambique. In particular Zambia turned itself northwards to the Tanzanian port of Dar-es-Salaam.

The first route to be used was the so-called Great North Road, which runs from Kapiri Mposhi to Dar-es-Salaam. The Zambia–Tanzania Road Services Limited was formed to operate a fleet of road tankers between the Copperbelt and Dar-es-Salaam. These vehicles were specially designed to carry petrol from Dar-es-Salaam to the Copperbelt, and copper bars on the return journey. Although the Great North Road now has a tarred surface, until recently it was only a gravel road. Travel over this route was often difficult, and it earned for itself the name of the 'Hell Run'. During the dry season the road was badly corrugated and full of potholes, while during the rainy season parts of the road turned into quagmires in which vehicles frequently got stuck. During the late 1960s and early 1970s the port of Dar-es-Salaam tended to suffer from congestion, with the result that some of Zambia's copper exports continued northward by road to the Kenyan port of Mombasa.

In 1968 a 1 700 km pipeline was opened to carry petroleum products from the refinery at Dar-es-Salaam to Ndola in the Copperbelt. This pipeline is operated by Tazama Pipelines Ltd., in which the Zambian Government owns a 67 per cent share, and

Table 126 Zambia's trade routes in 1973 and 1974

	Percentage of trade (by volume)	
	1973	1974
Overseas trade		
(1) Through Lobito	51,2	49,7
(2) Through Dar-es-Salaam	28,9	31,9
(3) Through Mombasa	6,8	9,1
Other trade		
(4) With Malaŵi	9,0	7,1
(5) With other countries	4,1	2,2

the Tanzanian Government 33 per cent. Since the opening of the refinery at Ndola, the pipeline carries crude petroleum instead of refined products.

In 1967 China signed an agreement with the governments of Zambia and Tanzania, whereby it agreed to construct a railway line from the Copperbelt to Dar-es-Salaam. The line was opened in 1975. It seems likely that in future the Tazara railway will carry a great deal of Zambia's overseas trade. It is also hoped that the opening of the Tazara railway will stimulate economic development in southern Tanzania. This part of Tanzania has considerable potential for development and contains sizeable deposits of coal and iron ore, but in the past has suffered from remoteness.

Bolivia's outlet to the sea

The land-locked state of Bolivia has rail links with the sea to the west, east and south. There are three rail links with ports on the Pacific Ocean, and it is these lines which transport Bolivia's mineral exports to the coast, and carry the bulk of the country's import trade. Bolivia's outlets to the sea are as follows:

1 La Paz to the port of Arica in northern Chile. This is the shortest rail route to the sea. The distance involved is 447 km of which 241 km lie within Bolivia. Unfortunately the ascent from the coast by this route is extremely steep, the Chilean–Bolivian border being crossed at a height of more than

Fig. 19.12 Bolivia – outlets to the sea

4 000 metres. This railway makes use of a long section of rack and cog.

2 La Paz through Oruro and Uyuni to the Chilean port of Antofogasta. The distance involved is 1 173 km of which 729 km lie within Bolivia.

3 The combined rail-lake route from La Paz to the Peruvian ports of Mollendo and Matarani. From La Paz a railway line runs to Guaqui, where it connects with a steamer service which crosses Lake Titicaca to Puno in Peru. From Puno, a railway line runs to the coast.

4 The rail route from La Paz through Uyuni to the Argentinian border at La Quiaca, where it connects with the Argentinian railway system.

5 The rail route from Santa Cruz southward to Yacuiba, where it connects with the Argentinian system.

6 The rail route from Santa Cruz eastward, to Corumbá in Brazil, a distance of 652 km. At Corumbá it links up with the Brazilian railway system, thus giving Bolivia access to the Brazilian port of Santos.

Exercises

1 Discuss the importance of inland water transport in tropical Africa.

2 Write a comparative account of the importance of road and rail transport to the economic development of any one tropical country.

3 With the aid of a sketch map, examine and account for the railway pattern in West Africa.

4 Write an account of the major seaports of either West Africa or East Africa.

5 With the aid of a sketch map, discuss the extent to which the railway pattern of West Africa is related to the distribution of mining centres.

6 With reference to actual examples from the tropical world, discuss the transport problems of land-locked countries.

7 With the aid of a sketch map, describe and discuss the various possible routes by which Zambia's exports can reach the sea.

8 With reference to actual examples from the tropical world, discuss the advantages and disadvantages of air transport.

Suggested reading

JOHN I. CLARKE, Ed.: *An Advanced Geography of Africa* — Chapter 12

J. P. COLE: *Latin America — An Economic and Social Geography* — Chapter 6

KWAMINA B. DICKSON AND GEORGE BENNEH: *A New Geography of Ghana* — Chapter 12

CHARLES A. FISHER, Ed.: *Essays in Political Geography* — Chapter 14

WILLIAM A. HANCE: *The Geography of Modern Africa* — pp. 29–41; 175–92; 313–20; 381–6; 441–5

WILLIAM A. HANCE: *African Economic Development* — Chapter 5

R. J. HARRISON-CHURCH: *West Africa* — Chapter 9

B. W. HODDER: *Economic Development in the Tropics* — Chapter 12

B. S. HAYLE: *Seaports of East Africa*

B. S. HAYLE AND D. HILLING: *Seaports and Development in Tropical Africa*

ANDREW M. KAMARCK: *The Economics of African Development* — pp. 217–25

A. M. O'CONNOR: *An Economic Geography of East Africa* — pp. 181–90

A. M. O'CONNOR: *The Geography of Tropical African Development* — Chapter 7

N. C. POLLOCK: *Studies in Emerging Africa* — Chapters 5 and 6

J. M. PRITCHARD: *Africa — A Study Geography for Advanced Students* — Chapter 11

H. P. WHITE AND M. B. GLEAVE: *An Economic Geography of West Africa* — Chapter 9

Index